The social structure of accumulation (SSA) approach seeks to explain the long-term fortunes of capitalist economies in terms of the effect of political and economic institutions on growth rates. This book offers an ideal introduction to this powerful tool for understanding capitalist growth, analyzing the social and economic differences between countries and the reasons for the successes and failures of institutional reform. The contributors cover a wide range of topics, including the theoretical basis of the SSA approach, the postwar financial system, Marxian and Keynesian theories of economic crisis, labor–management relations, race and gender issues, and the history of institutional innovation. Comprising newly written essays and classic articles of the SSA school, the book examines the international economy and the economies of Japan, South Africa, and Puerto Rico, as well as the United States, and will be an essential guide to the subject for students and specialists.

Social structures of accumulation

Social structures of accumulation

THE POLITICAL ECONOMY OF
GROWTH AND CRISIS

EDITED BY
DAVID M. KOTZ
TERRENCE McDONOUGH
MICHAEL REICH

CAMBRIDGE
UNIVERSITY PRESS

Published by the Press Syndicate of the University of Cambridge
The Pitt Building, Trumpington Street, Cambridge CB2 1RP
40 West 20th Street, New York, NY 10011–4211, USA
10 Stamford Road, Oakleigh, Melbourne 3166, Australia

First published 1994

Printed in Great Britain by Bell and Bain Ltd., Glasgow

A catalogue record for this book is available from the British Library

Library of Congress cataloguing in publication data

Social structures of accumulation: the political economy of growth and crisis / edited by
David M. Kotz, Terrence McDonough, and Michael Reich.
p.   cm.
Includes bibliographical references.
ISBN 0 521 44250 8 (hardback)
ISBN 0 521 45904 4 (paperback)
1. Economic development – Social aspects.
2. Social structure.   3. Saving and investment.
I. Kotz, David M.   II. McDonough, Terrence.   III. Reich, Michael.
HD75.S63   1994
338.9 – dc20   93–15866   CIP

ISBN 0 521 44250 8 hardback
ISBN 0 521 45904 4 paperback

Contents

Contributors

RANDY ALBELDA
University of Massachusetts, Boston

RICHARD EDWARDS
University of Massachusetts, Amherst

DAVID FAIRRIS
University of California, Riverside

DAVID M. GORDON
New School for Social Research, New York

DAVID M. KOTZ
University of Massachusetts, Amherst

TERRENCE MCDONOUGH
Canisius College, Buffalo

EDWIN MELENDEZ
Massachusetts Institute of Technology

NICOLI NATTRASS
University of Cape Town

MICHAEL REICH
University of California, Berkeley

JIM SHOCH
Dartmouth College, Hanover

CHRIS TILLY
University of Massachusetts, Lowell

TSUYOSHI TSURU
Hitotsubashi University

THOMAS E. WEISSKOPF
University of Michigan, Ann Arbor

MARTIN H. WOLFSON
University of Notre Dame

Introduction

DAVID M. KOTZ, TERRENCE MCDONOUGH, AND MICHAEL REICH

The social structure of accumulation (SSA) approach provides a new way to analyze the structure and development of capitalist economies and societies. The term SSA refers to the complex of institutions which support the process of capital accumulation. The central idea of the SSA approach is that a long period of relatively rapid and stable economic expansion requires an effective SSA. While an SSA promotes growth and stability for a period of time, eventually the SSA decays. A period of stagnation and instability follows until a new SSA can be built.

The SSA includes political and cultural institutions as well as economic ones. The institutions comprising an SSA include both domestic and international arrangements. The domestic institutions may include the state of labor–management relations; the organization of the work process; the character of industrial organization; the role of money and banking and their relation to industry; the role of the state in the economy; the line-up of political parties; the state of race and gender relations; and the character of the dominant culture and ideology. The international institutions may concern the trade, investment, monetary–financial, and political environments.

The development of the SSA approach was motivated by at least three analytical concerns: historical, comparative, and programmatic. An *historical* concern suggests that individual capitalist economic systems, and the world system of which each is a part, go through periodic booms and periodic times of trouble. These alternating periods have been called "long swings." These long swings appear to be associated with the bunching of institutional changes, which take place in a discontinuous manner. Such patterns require an explanation.

The SSA approach is not directed only at the problem of uneven economic expansion and discontinuous institutional change over time. It is also concerned with differences between the economic systems of various capitalist nations. The *comparative* concern suggests that, contrary to the view of traditional neoclassical economics, institutions and social structure make a difference to the functioning of economic systems. While Japan, Germany, the United States, Sweden, and South Africa are all market-oriented capitalist economies, their structures and performances also differ considerably from one another. To explain these different outcomes, we need a theory that incorporates the institutional differences among the capitalist countries.

A *programmatic* policy concern asks how new institutions develop and are consolidated. Why do some attempts to reform and transform the economy and social structure meet considerable success, while others have only a limited impact, and still others fail completely? We need a theory that can help answer these questions.

The SSA approach frames our understanding of many contemporary debates. Does Europe suffer from a rigidity sometimes called "Eurosclerosis," which compares unfavorably to a "flexible" US capitalism? Has Japan developed a style of business management that is superior to that of other industrialized capitalist economies? Can a nation make a choice between a low-wage, low-skill development path and a high-wage, high-skill one? Did Thatcherism in Britain and Reaganomics in the US resolve the problems that had been plaguing the British and American economies, creating the basis for sustained and healthy economic growth – or, on the contrary, are Britain and America still awaiting the creation of an effective institutional framework for economic expansion?

Historical background of the SSA approach

In the late 1960s and early 1970s, severe economic problems returned both to the United States and to international capitalism, after nearly twenty-five years of rapid and stable postwar economic growth. High unemployment, rapid inflation, and international monetary instability undermined the complacent belief that capitalism had outgrown its crisis-ridden youth. As the 1970s wore on, the failure of Keynesian interventionist techniques to bring back prosperity grew increasingly obvious. The ground was prepared for the development of new theories seeking to explain the alternation of long periods of prosperity with long periods of stagnation and instability.

In 1978, a year of surging inflation and chaos in world currency markets, David Gordon (1978) introduced the idea of an SSA explanation of economic crisis. He argued that capital accumulation must be based upon certain institutional requirements. The SSA is the "full set of integrated institutions ... necessary for individual capitalist accumulation to continue" (p. 27). Expanding his argument two years later, Gordon (1980) criticized other theories of the rhythm of capital accumulation as attempting "to account for alternating periods of economic prosperity and stagnation without properly considering the connections between the structure and contradictions of the social relations conditioning capital accumulation and the 'purely' economic dynamics through which long cycles appear to manifest themselves" (p. 10). The key to these alternating periods is to be found in the successive creation, collapse, and construction anew of SSAs.

The SSA approach achieved its definitive form with Gordon, Edwards, and Reich's *Segmented Work, Divided Workers* (1982). This volume had several advantages over the earlier articles. It was more easily accessible to a broad readership. It applied the SSA framework to the analysis of a century and a half of the development of capital–labor relations in the US, demonstrating the utility and analytical power of the framework. It broadened the concern of the SSA approach beyond the initial focus on uneven economic growth to encompass the analysis of institutional innovation, consolidation, and decay.

In Gordon *et al.* (1982) the dynamics behind the successive periods of growth and stagnation are located squarely in the construction and breakdown of the SSA. In Gordon's earlier work, both traditional Marxian crisis tendencies and the echo effects of infrastructure investment booms (an idea found in Kondratieff [1935]) play a role in the termination of a period of prosperous expansion. Gordon *et al.* (1982) are still concerned with developing a largely endogenous theory of crisis. However, they do this, not by focusing exclusively on the economic factors that normally underlie endogenous crisis theories, but by expanding their analysis to encompass political and ideological institutions alongside the economic. Thus, the SSA framework brings politics, ideology, and culture into the heart of the theory of economic growth and crisis.

Several intellectual traditions have been influential in the development of the SSA approach. A number of the central concepts come from the Marxian tradition, particularly from the Marxian theories of historical materialism, exploitation and surplus, and economic crisis. These include the interdependence of the economic, political, and ideological aspects of a society; the idea that the development of a system tends over time to undermine that system; a stress on class conflict and the exercise of class power as key determinants of social and economic development; and the centrality of the capital accumulation process for the overall development of capitalist society. However, the SSA approach differs from much of the Marxian literature, in the former's emphasis on the importance of non-economic factors, the absence of any inevitable tendency for capitalism to be superseded by socialism, and the rejection of any single mechanistic cause of economic crises.

Keynesian thought also influenced the SSA approach. The basic conception of the relation between the SSA and the investment decision draws upon the Keynesian concept of the uncertainty attendant upon investment decisions in a capitalist economy. An SSA encourages investment by creating greater stability and predictability. However, the SSA approach rejects the traditional Keynesian focus on demand problems to the exclusion of supply problems. In fact, most analyses of the recent problems of capitalism utilizing the SSA approach emphasize problems of cost and supply rather than demand.

Another influence has been the institutionalist tradition in American economics, descended from the work of Thorstein Veblen and John R. Commons early in the twentieth century. As the name suggests, institutionalists emphasize careful study of institutions and their relation to economic behavior. Shunning *a priori* theorizing, institutionalists expect the specific features of an economy, and the character of typical economic behavior, to differ across time and place. They study the historical evolution of economic systems over time. All of these features of traditional institutionalism are found in the SSA approach. However, the SSA school differs from traditional institutionalism in its greater openness to broad generalizations about economic development.

The long-wave theories pioneered by Kondratieff (1935) and Schumpeter (1939) influenced the development of SSA theory, particularly in Gordon's early work. The concept of an SSA first emerged out of the effort to account for long swings in macroeconomic activity, and both Gordon, in his early work, and Gordon *et al.* felt it necessary to make a case for the existence of such long swings. However, over time the work of the SSA school has placed less stress on explaining the recurrence of relatively regular long-term macroeconomic fluctuations, and it has not accepted the economic and technological determinism associated with the long-wave theoretical tradition.

The unifying theme of the SSA approach is the importance of institutions in the economic process. Yet it must be emphasized that the precise form that institutions take in particular countries is not specified by the general SSA approach. While SSA theorists have written about the particular institutions that have made up the SSAs of the United States (for example, peaceful collective bargaining and a welfare state in the postwar era), it does not follow that the same institutions make up the SSAs of postwar Japan or South Africa. Any mechanical transfer of the SSA approach from the United States to another country and period is bound to be inadequate. A specific analytical and historical undertaking is required in order to theorize the particular institutions comprising the SSA of a specific country and period.

Related theories

There are several competing theories of institutional and historical change in the economy. North and Thomas (1973) and Williamson (1985) provide a neoclassical theory of economic change. This theory suggests that institutions change gradually in response to relative price changes and to changes in transaction costs, with the implication that institutions therefore tend to be efficient. Although simple and appealing to many economists, this theory does not explain the persistence of clearly inefficient institutions, or the bunched nature of institutional change.

Piore and Sabel (1984) have proposed a technologically based theory to explain the demise of traditional mass production and the rise of what they call flexible specialization. The theory suggests that in recent times new technologies have offered advantages to small and flexible producers over large and rigid ones. This theory goes too far in suggesting that technology is the all-determining factor in social development.

The monopoly capital school (Baran and Sweezy [1966] and the journal *Monthly Review*) proposes the concept of an aggregate surplus that tends to rise faster than the normal uses of that surplus. This theoretical apparatus is used to analyze long-run macroeconomic fluctuations, as well as such particular problems of modern capitalism as financial instability and the growth of government and private debt. However, their focus on the problem of inadequate demand has appeared one-sided to many social analysts.

The French regulation theory developed by Aglietta, Lipietz, Boyer, and others contains many similarities to SSA theory in its emphasis on the specific institutional framework of the accumulation process. However, it also has many points of difference. Both similarities and differences are discussed in one of the following chapters of this volume (ch. 5).

SSA theory has developed in a parallel fashion with a "new institutionalist" emphasis in mainstream economics. The concept of a policy regime – the underlying principles that determine actors' responses to particular policies and actions – in macroeconomics has similarities to the SSA approach. The policy regime idea has been applied to the analysis of the role of ideological commitment to the gold standard in the interwar period (Temin, 1991). The increased recognition of the role of historical factors in the economy (known as path-dependence in the work of David [1985]), and the role of governance mechanisms (Williamson, 1985), reciprocity and effort-based wages (Akerlof and Yellen, 1986) in the microeconomic process, also provides similarities to SSA themes. Comparative theorists (Aoki, 1988), looking at Japan, Germany, and the United States, focus on the differing labor-market institutions and the differing relations of financial institutions to productive organizations in each country. While this renewed recognition of institutions is welcome, SSA theory remains distinctive in emphasizing the relations among different institutions and in theorizing the dynamics of institutional development and crisis.

About this book

Since the SSA approach appeared at the end of the 1970s, it has inspired a great deal of analysis and writing. Conference papers, journal articles, books, and doctoral dissertations have appeared which analyze, criticize, apply, or seek to further develop the SSA approach. The bibliography at the end of this book gives some idea of the scope of this literature. Until now, no suitable single source has been available for someone seeking to learn about the SSA approach. It has been necessary to search among widely scattered sources for that purpose. This situation provided a major impetus for producing this book, which seeks to give the reader a wide-ranging introduction to, and overview of, the SSA approach.

We have tried to capture in this book the diversity of work that has been done within the SSA approach. The SSA approach has been applied within many fields, including labor history, the analysis of capital–labor relations, macroeconomics, financial relations, government regulation of business, international economics, and political party realignments, as well as general economic history. While much of the work in this school has focused on the United States, other countries have been studied as well. The techniques of analysis found in the SSA literature include the traditional historical approach, the case study method, mathematical modeling, and econometric hypothesis testing.

This volume begins with "Long swings and stages of capitalism" which is excerpted from chapter 2 of Gordon *et al.* (1982). This chapter presents the definitive explication of the SSA framework. Following this are three chapters discussing theoretical issues raised by Gordon *et al.* (1982) and the literature to which that book gave rise. Michael Reich ("How social structures of accumulation decline and are built") seeks to answer several questions raised by the original work. He argues that the fundamental institutional changes brought about by the American Civil War can be integrated into the SSA account of US history. He contends that there was indeed a crisis at the end of the nineteenth century. In the second part of the chapter, Reich turns to the question of how SSAs are built, arguing that there are specific events which set the framework of the institutions in one design which then governs the subsequent construction of the SSA.

In the following chapter, David Kotz ("Interpreting the social structure of accumulation theory") conducts a detailed analysis of the SSA approach, devoting special attention to situating the approach in relation to earlier analyses of the capital accumulation process. This chapter argues that the central role of an SSA is the regulation of class conflict and competition, which explains how an SSA promotes stable economic growth. Kotz concludes with the development of the concept of the "core" of an SSA, which is put forward to resolve problems with the original version of the SSA approach. The chapter by Terrence McDonough ("Social structures of accumulation, contingent history, and stages of capitalism") identifies several theoretical weaknesses in the SSA framework. He proposes to resolve them through the recognition of the role of historical contingency in the construction and disintegration of SSAs. McDonough argues that the SSA approach should be interpreted as a theory of stages of capitalism. Part I of the volume concludes with a chapter by Kotz ("The regulation theory and the social structure of accumulation approach") which considers the similarities and differences between the SSA framework and its close cousin, the French regulation school.

Part II examines a number of applications of the SSA approach. McDonough ("The construction of social structure of accumulation in US history") applies the SSA framework to the past century of capitalist history in the US. The chapter analyzes the construction of the monopoly SSA in the 1890s and the postwar SSA during and after World War II. Martin Wolfson ("The financial system and the social structure of accumulation") examines the history of one particular institution of the postwar SSA, tracing the rise and demise of the postwar financial system.

Thomas Weisskopf ("Alternative social structure of accumulation approaches to the analysis of capitalist booms and crises") compares neo-Marxian and neo-Keynesian models of the postwar boom and crisis in the US economy. This chapter exemplifies the use of mathematical modeling within the SSA framework, and Weisskopf draws on several of the major econometric analyses done by SSA adherents to support his conclusions in favor of the neo-Marxian model. Jim Shoch ("The politics of the US industrial policy debate, 1981–1984") applies the SSA approach to government policy toward business, analyzing the abortive attempt to promote industrial policy in the US in the early 1980s. This piece is especially timely in view of the renewed interest in an active government program in support of business competitiveness on the part of influential business groups and the Clinton administration in the United States.

Part III takes up questions of class, race, and gender. David Fairris ("Shopfloor relations in the postwar capital–labor accord") uses the SSA framework to chart the trajectory of struggles on the shopfloor in the US during the postwar period. Randy Albelda and Chris Tilly ("Towards a broader vision: race, gender, and labor market segmentation in the social structure of accumulation framework") argue that the SSA framework to date has laid insufficient stress on the role of race and gender in structuring labor relations crucial to the construction of SSAs. They examine how racial and gender dynamics modify and extend the SSA analysis.

Part IV extends the SSA framework to countries other than the United States and to the international economy. Edwin Melendez ("Accumulation and crisis in a small and open economy: the postwar social structure of accumulation in Puerto Rico") applies the macroeconomic model developed by Bowles, Gordon, and Weisskopf (1983) to the postwar economy of Puerto Rico. Nicoli Nattrass ("Apartheid and capitalism: social structure of accumulation or contradiction?") examines whether the SSA framework can be usefully applied to the postwar economy of apartheid in South Africa. She concludes that empirical investigation does not support the existence and disintegration of an SSA in postwar South Africa.

Tsuyoshi Tsuru ("The social structure of accumulation approach and the regulation approach: a US–Japan comparison of the reserve army effect") examines changes over time in the effect of unemployment on unit labor costs – the "reserve army effect" – in Japan and the United States. He utilizes propositions derived from the SSA approach and the regulation theory to analyze changes in the collective bargaining systems of the two countries. David Gordon ("The global economy: new edifice or crumbling foundations?") argues that recent changes in the international economy do not represent a new global capitalist order, but instead reflect the continuing breakdown of the postwar SSA. Gordon argues that the future shape of international economic institutions is more of an open question than many analysts currently believe.

In an Afterword, the editors discuss the nature of the international institutions which may condition a future SSA. We argue that a new period of vigorous expansion would require a new set of international institutions. These new institutions must be consistent with the developing domestic institutions in the major capitalist countries. We analyze two possible alternatives, a classically liberal free-market regime and a system of trade blocs, concluding that a new bloc system is the most likely one to emerge.

References

Akerlof, George, and Janet Yellen, 1986. *Efficiency Wage Models of the Labor Market*. Cambridge University Press.

Aoki, Masahiko, 1988. *Information, Incentives and Bargaining in the Japanese Economy*. Cambridge University Press.

Baran, P., and P. Sweezy, 1966. *Monopoly Capital*. New York: Monthly Review Press.

Bowles, Samuel, David Gordon, and Thomas Weisskopf, 1983. *Beyond the Wasteland: A Democratic Alternative to Economic Decline*. Garden City, N.J.: Anchor Press/Doubleday.

David, Paul, 1985. "Clio and the Economics of QWERTY," *American Economic Review*, 75(2): 332–7.

Gordon, David, 1978. "Up and Down the Long Roller Coaster," in *U.S. Capitalism in Crisis*, ed. Union for Radical Political Economics, pp. 22–35. New York: Union for Radical Political Economics.

1980. "Stages of Accumulation and Long Economic Cycles," in *Processes of the World System*, ed. T. Hopkins and I. Wallerstein, pp. 9–45. Beverly Hills, Calif.: Sage Publications.

Gordon, David, Richard Edwards, and Michael Reich, 1982. *Segmented Work, Divided Workers*. Cambridge University Press.

Kondratieff, Nicolai D., 1935. "The Long Waves in Economic Life," *Review of Economic Statistics*, 17(6): 105–15.

North, Douglass, and Robert Thomas, 1973. *The Rise of the Western World*. Cambridge University Press.

Piore, Michael, and Charles Sabel, 1984. *The Second Industrial Divide*. New York: Basic Books.

Schumpeter, Joseph, 1939. *Business Cycles: A Theoretical, Historical, and Statistical Analysis of the Capitalist Process*. New York: McGraw-Hill.

Temin, Peter, 1991. *Lessons from the Great Depression*. Cambridge, Mass.: MIT Press.

Williamson, Oliver, 1985. *The Economic Institutions of Capitalism*. New York: Academic Press.

I

THE THEORY OF SOCIAL STRUCTURES OF ACCUMULATION

I

Long swings and stages of capitalism

DAVID M. GORDON, RICHARD EDWARDS, AND MICHAEL REICH

Capitalism can be defined as a wage-labour system of commodity production for profit. The owners of the means of production (capitalists) employ immediate producers (workers). Employers pay workers wages, keeping the fruits of the labour process for vending on the market at a profit (or loss).

Given these defining characteristics, several conditions must be satisfied for the existence and reproduction of capitalist economies. The legal system must recognize and protect rights of private property. There must be a substantial supply of wage workers. Capitalists must be able to generate profits in production, requiring reliable and reproducible mechanisms of labor management. At least some basic decisions about production and distribution must be mediated by markets, requiring money as a medium of exchange and a measure of exchange value. Both the household and the state must serve some critical supportive functions, providing steady and continued access to wage labor, shaping the political space within which capitalists can enjoy and command whatever profits they achieve, and contributing to cultural and ideological perceptions that reinforce individualism.[1]

Even if these conditions are met, capitalist economies do not stand still. As the historical materialist perspective suggests, capitalist economies continually change and develop, driven constantly by the dual dynamic forces of intercapitalist competition and capital–labor conflict. The version of the historical materialist perspective that we use illuminates five principal tendencies that have dominated the trajectory of capitalist development.[2]

(1) Capitalist accumulation continually attempts to expand the boundaries of the capitalist system.

(2) Capitalist accumulation persistently increases the size of large corporations and concentrates the control and ownership of capital in proportionately fewer hands.

(3) The accumulation of capital spreads wage labor as the prevalent system of production, draws an increasing proportion of the population into wage-labor status, and replenishes the reserve pool of labor. The relative power of capitalists and workers is mediated by the rate at which this replenishment proceeds.[3]

(4) Capitalist accumulation continually changes the labor process, both through employers' introduction of improved technologies and new machines and through the imposition of increasingly intensive labor-management systems upon workers.

(5) In order to defend themselves against the effects of capitalist accumulation, workers have responded with their own activities and struggles.[4]

Each of these five tendencies has developed unevenly, and it would take us too far afield to recount the details for each case. These five dynamic tendencies, framed even within a relatively traditional Marxian analysis, account for a great deal of the concrete history of capitalist societies. However, several considerations have led us and many others to move beyond this perspective in order to correct some of its weaknesses and to add additional tools with which to understand the history of capitalist development.

First, many traditional Marxists have used this dynamic analysis to generate mechanical theories of historical inevitability in which the emergence of a class-conscious proletariat always lurks around the next corner. In recent decades many Marxists have corrected this mechanical determinism by adding to the traditional analysis a variety of complicating factors and insights. This recent literature has featured the role of intermediate strata and classes and the resulting variety of possible multiclass alliances, the relative autonomy of political and ideological forces, an emphasis on human agency rather than abstract laws in historical change, an emphasis on the influence of production relations upon the evolution of production forces, the importance of historical contingency in shaping the responses of different groups to capitalist development, and the diverse spatial and temporal paths of capitalist development. These additions permit a more creative approach to the study of historical change, moving beyond kismetic views of inevitable historical evolution (see, for example, Marglin [1974], Laclau [1977], Tabb and Sawers [1978], Wright [1981], Thompson [1979], Gintis [1980], and Plotke [1981]).

Second, the Marxian analysis of capitalist dynamics, no matter how subtly one pursues its modern reformulation, remains indeterminate when it is pursued only on this abstract level.

While the dynamic tendencies outlined above help shape the organization of capitalist production in general, the specific evolution of production relations also depends on the changing relative power of the opposing classes and their respective instruments of struggle. These depend most importantly, but not exclusively, on the character of the production relations. This interdependence between production organization and the shape of the capital–labor conflict means that a final specification of the character of production at any point and time cannot depend solely on analysis at an abstract level but must also focus on more concrete determinations.

Similar caution should inform analyses of the labor market. Here, employers and workers bargain over the effective wage rate, the hours of work, and other elements of the wage-labor contract. The outcome of this bargaining reflects an extra-ordinarily wide range of forces: the extent to which workers are united or divided, the intervention of the state, the ability of capitalists to develop new wage-laboring populations, the availability of new labor-saving technologies, the elements of race and ethnicity, the pace of accumulation and hence the strength of the macro-economy. Noting the extent of development of the five major dynamic tendencies of capitalist economies is not sufficient.

To overcome these limitations, many historians, following the lead of E. P. Thompson in Britain and Herbert Gutman in the United States, have placed virtually singular emphasis on concrete and specific analyses of the daily lives of workers and employers in particular periods and locations. Although extremely valuable, these studies are usually quite divorced, especially in the United States, from more abstract theoretical formulations; consequently, their broader meaning remains uncertain (for useful reviews, see *Radical History Review*, 1978-9, Brody [1979], Davis [1980], and Montgomery [1980]).

We propose that an intermediate level of analysis, focusing on the logic of long swings and stages of capitalism, is necessary for an understanding of capitalist development. This intermediate analysis is intended to complement both the traditional and abstract Marxian approach to capitalist development and the more recent concrete analyses of everyday life.

Long swings and stages of capitalism

Many scholars within the Marxian tradition have argued the importance of uneven development and stages of capitalism (see Mandel [1975], chs. 2 and 4, for some suggestions and review). These analyses have often led theorists to posit stages of "competitive" and "monopoly" capitalism, focusing on the transformation of the conditions of product market competition. In our view, writers in this theoretical tradition (including ourselves, in our early work) fail to capture the breadth and complexity of the process of capital accumulation. Our analysis of this process has led us to develop a concept of the social structure of accumulation for the purposes of historical analyses of capitalist development.[5]

Our development of this concept begins with a simple proposition: the accumulation of capital through capitalist production cannot take place either in a vacuum or in chaos. Capitalists cannot and will not invest in production unless they are able to make reasonably determinate calculations about their expected rates of return. Both the Marxian and mainstream traditions of economics have recognized this relation between investment and expectations.[6] Unfortunately, however, both traditions have tended either to elide the importance of the external environment in the formation of expectations about the rate of profit or to fail to provide a substantive account of that environment. Although many economists may recognize the importance of external factors, most have nonetheless left the investigation of those factors to sociologists and political scientists.

We argue, in sharp contrast, that macrodynamic analyses should begin with the political-economic environment affecting individual capitalists' possibilities for capital accumulation. Without a stable and favorable external environment, capitalist investment in production will not proceed. We refer to this external environment as the social structure of accumulation. Its elements derive from the specific set of requirements, neither unlimited nor indeterminate, that must be satisfied for capital accumulation to take place. We derive this finite set of requirements from the Marxian analysis of the process of capital accumulation.[7]

The process of capital accumulation contains three major steps. Capitalists, in business to make profits, begin by investing their funds (money capital) in the raw materials, labor power, machinery, buildings, and other commodities needed for production. Next, they organize the labor process, whereby the constituents of production are set in motion to produce useful products or services – the input commodities are transmitted through production into output commodities. Finally, by selling the products of labor, capitalists reconvert their property back to money capital. These funds then become the basis for the next round of capital accumulation.

The social structure of accumulation consists of all the institutions that impinge upon the accumulation process. Some institutions have a general impact; others relate primarily to one specific step in the process. We discuss each in turn.

As capitalists push their capital through each step of the accumulation process, they are touched by some general institutional features of their environment. Among the most important institutions are the system ensuring money and credit, the pattern of state involvement in the economy, and the structure of class struggle. Money and credit are essential at every step because money is required for exchange, or credit is needed until the exchange can take place. The pattern of state involvement in the economy likewise affects all the steps of capital accumulation because the state can enhance the profitability of investment (through subsidies, enforcement of regulations, greater commodity purchases, and so forth) or diminish it (through taxation, regulation, legitimizing unions, and so forth). Finally, the structure of class struggle, whether conducted through unions, in political parties, sporadically by spontaneous outburst, or through the electoral system, conditions the expectations of capitalists at every stage.

The first step in the capital accumulation process, the collection of the necessary inputs, relies more particularly on systems of natural resource supply, intermediate (produced goods) supply, and labor supply. The structure of natural supply will determine the extent to which capitalists can secure access to needed quantities of raw materials and energy at predictable prices. The supply of intermediate goods determines access to produced goods used in production. Labor supply, the most problematical of the three, involves both the structure of the labor market, determining the immediate supply of labor, and the social institutions (family, schools, etc.) that reproduce the labor force generationally.

The process of production, the second step in the capital accumulation process, takes place inside the capitalist enterprise itself, an institution under the capitalist's own control. The enterprise consists of two related parts: the top management structure and the organization of the actual labor process.

The final step in capital accumulation, the selling process, involves at least three institutional features. First, the capitalists' success in realizing their profits depends upon the structure of final demand, including consumer purchases, government expenditures, export markets, and so forth. Second, the pace of capital accumulation is conditioned by the structure of intercapitalist competition, namely, the degree to which elements of competition and monopoly are present and the various forms of that competition. Third, this step relies upon sales and marketing systems, including distribution networks and advertising.

The construct of the social structure of accumulation, comprising a specific set of institutions, has both an inner and outer boundary.[8] Its inner boundary demarcates the institutional environment for capital accumulation (that is, the "social structure") from the capital accumulation process itself. Its outer boundary distinguishes this social structure from other social structures in the rest of a society.

We understand the capital accumulation process to be the microeconomic activity of profit-making and reinvestment. This activity is carried on by individual capitalists (or firms) employing specific workforces and operating within a given institutional environment. We wish to separate that process from its environment.

The inner boundary of the social structure of accumulation, then, divides the capital accumulation process itself (the profit-making activities of individual capitalists) from the institutional (social, political, legal, cultural, and market) context within which it occurs.

In the other direction we specify the outer boundary so that the social structure of accumulation is not simply a shorthand for "the rest of a society." We do not deny that any aspect or relationship in society potentially and perhaps actually impinges to some degree upon the accumulation process; nonetheless, it is not unreasonable to distinguish between those institutions that directly and demonstrably condition capital accumulation and those that affect it only tangentially. Thus, for example, the financial system bears a direct relation whereas the character of sports activity does not.

In our judgment, the imprecise and hence inevitably arguable nature of this outer boundary does not reduce the usefulness of the concept of a social structure of accumulation. Moreover, we recognize that different social structures of accumulation may incorporate (or exclude) differing sets of social institutions. Ind ed, it would be possible to argue (although we have not done so below) that successive social structures of accumulation have incorporated increasing aspects of social life, thus making, for example, the post-1945 structure the most complex and societally far-reaching.

Based on this analysis of the process of capitalist accumulation, we further propose that a social structure of accumulation alternately stimulates and constrains the pace of capital accumulation. If the constituent institutions of the social structure of accumulation are stable, working smoothly and without challenge, capitalists are likely to feel secure about investing in the expansion of productive capacity. But if the social structure of accumulation begins to become shaky, if class conflict or past capital accumulation have pressed the institutions to their limits and they begin to lose their legitimacy, capitalists will be more disposed to put their money in financial rather than direct investments, earning a financial rate of return whose security compensates for its lower average expected levels.[9]

Because capital accumulation depends on disconnected investment decisions by individual firms, it appears that one can understand those decisions through models of individual behavior. Investment in capitalist economies is mediated fundamentally by social (or institutional) forces, however – that is, by factors external to individual capitalists that are determined by collective social activities. Macrodynamic analyses of growth and disequilibria must take the structure and contradictions of this conditioning environment into account. The social structure of accumulation, in short, is external to the decisions of individual capitalists, but it is internal to the macrodynamics of capitalist economies.

Long swings and social structures of accumulation

Both mainstream and Marxist economists have tended to agree that capitalist economies are likely to experience periodic short-term and self-correcting business cycles. Many economists within both traditions have also suggested that capitalist economies may be prone to disequilibria, leading at least potentially to crisis tendencies or stagnation from which the economy is incapable of recovering without external assistance. Our model of stages of capitalism goes beyond both traditions, suggesting not only that capitalist economies are prone to longer-term fluctuations in the pace of capital accumulation but also that these fluctuations are mediated by a determinate institutional structure, the social structure of accumulation, which cannot be analyzed separately from (and therefore is not exogenous to) the capitalist economy itself.

Our analysis builds upon a series of propositions about the connections between social structures of accumulation and long swings in world capitalist economic activity. The scholarly literature has long debated both the existence of long swings and their causes and significance (Mandel [1975, 1980], Rostow [1978, part 3], and Barr [1979] provide recent surveys). Our position is that long-swing arguments are plausible and warrant serious attention. We do not believe that the existence of long swings has been "proved," since the interpretation of the data involves judgment rather than the administration of a universally accepted existence test. More to the point, we find the notion of long swings extremely useful in helping to illuminate the institutional macrodynamics we are studying.

The most interesting issues concern the causes and significance of long swings. Economists have attributed long swings to the effects of uneven spurts in the rate of technical change, to long-term trends in population growth and movement, to the effects of financial institutions, and to changes in patterns of consumption, relative prices of raw materials, and international capital mobility, with differences in emphasis on the relative weight of each of these factors and on their causal interrelations. A related debate has focused on the endogeneity or exogeneity of the causes of long swings. If they are endogenous, the theory emphasizes automatically repeating long cycles. If the swings are prompted by exogenous forces, recoveries from stagnation and the periodicity of long swings result from a succession of unique historical factors or accidents.

In our view these debates suffer from two misperceptions. First, they tend toward single-factor theories of long swings; our emphasis on the importance of social structures of accumulation leads us to emphasize the multidimensional character of the capitalist accumulation process and the macrodynamics that it generates. Second, these debates tend to define the internal–external boundary with respect to the individual entrepreneur; our attention to social structures of accumulation leads us to shift that boundary and to refocus the question of internal and external elements.

We propose an alternative model that views long swings as in large part the product of the success or failure of successive social structures of accumulation in facilitating capital accumulation. Although we do not wish to deny the important consequences of largely exogenous events in producing long swings, we note that such forces as demographic trends and technological innovation are heavily influenced by endogenous economic conditions, particularly when we concentrate on the world (as opposed to national or regional) capitalist system. Our institutional analysis suggests that the conditions creating a period of prosperity contain endogenous contradictions that ultimately bring the prosperity to an end. But the manner in which the ensuing crisis is resolved is not fully endogenous, for the crisis exacerbates conflict over the structural reforms that are necessary for a recovery, and the resolution of this conflict involves unpredictable political elements. The periods of boom and stagnation alternate, then, partly in response to exogenous events but more importantly in response to endogenous changes in the institutional context (see Gordon [1980], and Weisskopf [1981], for related treatments).

We develop our model here by tracing the connections between the social structure of accumulation and the pace of accumulation through a single stage of capitalist development. We then consider some theoretical issues that arise in this model.

Our scenario begins at the onset of a period of expansion in a capitalist economy (such as the late 1840s, late 1890s, or early 1940s in the United States). We have already noted that rapid economic growth depends upon the existence of a favorable social structure of accumulation. We are therefore presupposing that a previous crisis has somehow been resolved through the construction of a new social structure of accumulation. In particular, given the importance of production for capital accumulation, we are specifically presupposing a stabilization of conditions of production and, therefore, a moderation of whatever class struggle has intensified during the previous period of crisis.

Once begun, the expansion is likely for several reasons to continue for many years. First, the previous crisis is likely to have restored many of the conditions of profitability in the economy, for example, through depreciation or abandonment of less productive capital or through the stimulation of new technological and managerial innovations. Second, the initial investments necessary to form the social structure of accumulation are likely to provide a large (multiplier/accelerator) stimulus at the beginning of this period of expansion. Most importantly, the boom period is long because favorable conditions for capital accumulation have become institutionalized. In other words, these conditions become established not just as the current policy of the current dominant political party; rather, they become embedded in the society's institutional structure.

It seems just as likely, however, that the expansion will not continue at a rapid pace indefinitely. (We discuss this problem more formally in the following section.) First, as we have already noted, the growth process in capitalist economies is prone to a variety of disequilibria that can choke the boom; the Great Depression of the 1930s was set off by such a development. Second, and more important for our purposes, the expansion itself is likely to set off forces that undermine the institutional basis of the expansion. At first, short-term business cycles appear and act as self-correcting economic adjustment mechanisms. Such corrections take place within the context of the established institutions, which are slow to change and remain relatively unaffected by the short-term cyclical fluctuations. But at some point barriers to accumulation begin to appear that persist through the short-term business cycle.

These barriers develop because successful capital accumulation ultimately either runs up against limits imposed by the existing institutional structure or begins to destabilize that structure. In the first case, the institutions themselves produce the constraints; in the second case, the disruption of the institutions produces the constraints. In either case, further rapid capital accumulation becomes more problematic within the existing set of institutions.

Although the development of these barriers in each of our three periods is discussed in detail in subsequent chapters, it will be useful to provide some illustrations here. The initial proletarianization and the homogenization periods provide examples of how the prevalent organization of work can begin to limit the profitability of production. In the late nineteenth century the artisans' control over the production process limited further advances in productivity in many industries. In the 1930s the homogenization of labor produced the conditions under which mass-production workers could successfully organize unions, thereby undermining the profitability of the homogenization system. The segmentation period provides an example of how a long boom period can upset its own institutional bases. The prosperity of the 1960s undermined the postwar capital–labor accord by giving labor and other noncapitalist groups greater economic and political power, thereby destabilizing one of the principal institutional arrangements that had made the long boom possible. In each case, prevailing institutions no longer worked favorably for rapid capital accumulation.

As the economy begins to stagnate, the institutions of the social structure of accumulation are further disrupted, complicating the process of recovery.

Institutional destabilization may occur either because the resources that are required for the maintenance of the institutions themselves are becoming scarcer or because those institutions presuppose a smoothly functioning economy. Class conflict may intensify during this phase, as it did in the 1870s or 1890s and again in the 1930s. Given the stagnation, there is less chance for a labor peace purchased out of the (reduced) growth dividend.

Individual capitalists are then unlikely to engage in productive investment until a new and reliable environment emerges. Consequently, the resolution of a period of economic instability will depend upon the reconstruction of a social structure of accumulation. Indeed, we can define an economic crisis as a period of economic instability that requires institutional reconstruction for renewed stability and growth. For capitalists seeking such reconstruction the process is difficult and unpredictable, because it requires some collective action and the creation of a political consensus. Individual capitalists acting in isolation cannot restore prosperity.

As economic crisis deepens and the social structure of accumulation begins to become unfavorable, capitalists are in ever greater need of collective strategies capable of restoring the rate of profit. At first they may not engage in self-conscious collective action, for the early phases of crisis are likely to generate virulent intercapitalist competition. In those instances reforms may be forced upon them by the state or by noncapitalist groups. Even if capitalists are able to overcome their differences, their collective actions are likely to coexist with efforts by other classes and groups that seek to protect their working and living conditions. As a result, the resolution of an economic crisis is likely to be shaped by the relative power and the respective objectives of capitalists, workers, and other economic groups.

This point is illustrated in the United States by the responses to the economic crises of the late nineteenth century and the 1930s. In each case, major structural changes were required to create the basis for a subsequent long swing of prosperity; but the character of the outcomes differed substantially in the two cases.

The economic crisis at the end of the nineteenth century was resolved by institutional changes in the form of intercapitalist competition, in the role of government, and in the organization of the labor process. The merger movement produced oligopolies in most major industries, but a split between small and large capitalists prevented the immediate consolidation of a new social structure. Only the war provided the context for building a political constituency that could stifle anti-business reform and establish a favorable regime. By the 1920s large capitalists were relatively united and labor had been defeated. Management had succeeded in capturing greater control over the organization of work and in reducing the effectiveness of labor resistance (see Edwards [1979]).

The crisis of the 1930s was also ultimately resolved on the basis of a greater role for the state, this time involving Keynesian demand management and changes in capital–labor relations. The state now regulated capital–labor relations directly, both at the workplace (through the machinery set up by the Wagner Act and its successors) and through the provision of a variety of social welfare programs.

Although employers were relatively divided during this period, workers were better organized, and they were able to influence the outcome on terms that were substantially more favorable than in the previous crisis period.

Both of these examples indicate that the onset of a stagnation phase marks the beginning of increasing pressure on all classes to maintain their positions. As stagnation tips into crisis, all classes must maneuver to restructure economic relations so as to protect and advance their own interests – some, of course, with more power and self-consciousness than others. Although there is no guarantee that a successful new social structure will emerge, if one does it will reflect the alignment of class forces (and other social influences) that produce it. Thus, the rise of a new social structure of accumulation depends upon the previous downswing and more specifically on the concrete historical conditions that the period of the downswing bequeaths to the major classes.

In this respect, "exogenous" forces may be very important. For example, the war devastation elsewhere in the world during World War II left the United States in an overwhelmingly powerful economic and political position, and the nuclear monopoly created an awesome military advantage, all of which may be considered at least partly exogenous. In this context, it was possible to create a new social structure of accumulation based in part on steadily rising real wages for American workers.

Regardless of the importance of exogenous forces, it is significant that the old institutions are not restored intact once the crisis has been resolved. This pattern results from systematic factors. Because collective actors are seeking solutions to their problems within a context of institutional instability, their struggles during crisis are likely to make problematic the re-establishment of the previous existing social structure of accumulation. For example, after US workers had organized industrial unions in the late 1930s, it was virtually inconceivable that a resolution of the economic crisis of the 1930s could build upon old labor process and labor market structures from the 1910s and 1920s. The restoration of favorable conditions for capital accumulation after an economic crisis usually requires the shaping of a new social structure of accumulation, whose character is formed in large part by the nature of capitalists' and workers' collective struggles during the previous period of economic crisis.

We thus have the likelihood of a succession of social structures of accumulation within the capitalist epoch. We refer to the periods featuring these respective social structures of accumulation as stages of capitalism.[10]

This scenario, focusing on the connections between long swings and social structures of accumulation, can be summarized in the following series of discrete propositions:

(1) A period of expansion is built upon the construction and stabilization of a favorable social structure of accumulation.

(2) The favorable institutional context for capital accumulation generates a boom of investment and rapid economic activity.

(3) The success of the capital accumulation process pushes investment to the limits that are possible within the social structure of accumulation. Continued rapid capital accumulation requires (among other changes) either a reproduction of the conditions existing at the beginning of the boom or a transition to a new organization of the labor process and labor markets. The initial conditions are difficult to reproduce, and needed reforms are not easily achieved.

(4) Accumulation slows and the period of stagnation is entered. Attempts to alter the institutional structure are met with opposition, especially in a stagnationary context.

(5) Economic stagnation promotes the further dissolution of the existing social structure of accumulation.

(6) The restoration of the possibility of rapid capital accumulation during an economic crisis depends on the construction of a new institutional structure.

(7) The internal context of this institutional structure is profoundly but not exclusively shaped by the character of the class struggle during the preceding period of economic crisis.

(8) The new social structure of accumulation is virtually certain to differ from its predecessor, thereby generating a succession of stages of capitalism.

(9) Each stage of capitalism is likely to feature a long period of expansion, then a subsequent long period of stagnation.

In presenting this theoretical approach to long swings and stages of capitalism, we do not mean to imply that this dynamic constitutes the only structural and conflictual force affecting social and economic change in capitalist societies. Structural conflicts arising from relations among races, genders, and nations, for example, are also likely to have their own relatively independent logic and dynamics. Such forces are not unimportant or even necessarily less important than those that we address in our analysis. We have simply concentrated on one important dimension of our social and economic history; these other critical dimensions are not our main focus in this work.

Problems in long-swing theory

We have proposed that capital accumulation takes place only within the context of a social structure of accumulation. If this proposition is correct, it is not logically possible to develop formal models of capitalist growth and instability without simultaneously developing models of social structure of accumulation. However much it may challenge several traditions of economic analysis, we are suggesting both that macrodynamic behavior depends upon the environmental conditions necessary for capital accumulation and that instability in that environment is likely. To develop a theory of long swings from these propositions, however, one must also account for the duration of the different moments of instability. In this section we discuss the duration issue more explicitly and attempt to clarify three important theoretical questions that a long-swing theory must address:

(1)   Why do the expansions that are stimulated by new social structures of
      accumulation last longer than short-term business cycle expansions?

(2)   Why are these longer periods of expansion limited in duration, and how does
      the concept of the social structure of accumulation contribute to our under-
      standing of the causes of the length of the expansion as well as the eventual
      stagnation?

(3)   Why is a slowdown of accumulation (conditioned by the social structure of
      accumulation) not self-correcting? Why is it likely to push the economy from
      stagnation and instability to crisis? And why is it likely to create a long period
      of contraction before recovery once again becomes possible?

These are difficult questions, to which we do not have complete answers. We
outline here the directions in which our analysis leans.

First, the expansion phase of a long swing spans several short-term business
cycles because the institutions composing the social structure of accumulation are
durable and remain favorable to capital accumulation. These advantages continue
to accrue even during short-term cyclical contractions, enhance the profitability of
individual investments, and help speed recovery.

For example, the postwar accord between capital and labor provided a stable and
cooperative collective bargaining system, permitting employers to institute produc-
tivity-enhancing innovations in technology and the organization of work. In return,
workers received regular increases in wages as well as expanding social welfare
benefits provided by the government. Employers could count on the stability of
this system for some time, and it worked quite well to generate an underlying
favorable context for capital accumulation.

The social structure of accumulation can be conceptualized as a durable investment that, once installed, pays off over a long period of time. It is durable because
much investment has gone into its institutionalization; and it is successful because
it results from the distillation of a long period of experimentation.[11]

Second, at the same time, the institutions of a social structure of accumulation
themselves are likely to limit the potential for indefinite expansion. The end of the
boom begins when successful capital accumulation creates obstacles that stand in
the way of continued accumulation. Such problems may appear in any of a variety
of the constituent institutions of the social structure of accumulation: output
markets may become saturated; important inputs (for example, labor or energy
supplies) may become exhausted as sources of continued growth; accumulation
may change the relative strengths of classes, weakening some and strengthening
others and disrupting the old patterns of class relations.

Thus the postwar capital–labor accord institutionalized expectations of continuing increases in real wages as well as rising benefits from social welfare
programs. Although these expectations fueled a rising rate of inflation by the 1970s,
they could not be dampened within existing institutions. The structure of the
capital–labor accord now blocked rapid capital accumulation. Or, to take another
example from the postwar period, US growth was built, among other factors, upon

the expansion of US corporations in European markets and upon the international economic relations established at Bretton Woods in 1944. Yet it was essentially inevitable that the growth of European firms would ultimately eliminate the initial advantages of US corporations and that the recovery of Europe (and Japan) would strain and break up the Bretton Woods system.

These examples suggest that the limits imposed on an expansion are specific to the particular institutions of the existing social structure of accumulation. This hypothesis is analogous to traditional economic hypotheses about eventually diminishing returns to scale within a fixed productive environment. If one keeps the same capital equipment, returns to labor are likely to diminish at some point as one reaches the capacity of labor or capital or both. Similarly, an economy that expands within the same social structure of accumulation is likely to encounter diminishing returns to continual expansion; as the "capacity" of that institutional structure is approached, its effectiveness in promoting accumulation is diminished.

Third, why does a capitalist economy retain the same social structure of accumulation once it has begun to display diminishing returns? The answer to this question arises from the relatively disconnected and unplanned character of the decisions of individual units of capital accumulation in a capitalist economy. Although individual capitalists depend upon their social environment, they retain relative autonomy in their individual enterprises. Individual capitalists are jealous of their individual prerogatives. Even if state planners begin to recognize some of the increasing friction or inefficiency of an existing social structure of accumulation, capitalists and others with perceived vested interests in the old order are unlikely to welcome changes in the environment. Thus, individuals in a class may block the reforms that would advance the general interest of the class (see Block [1977] for some related comments).

These remarks must be amplified in order to provide better support for our contention that the economy must plunge into crisis before individuals and groups will achieve the institutional adjustments necessary for renewed growth. Why is gradual change in the social structure of accumulation unlikely? Why is abrupt structural change such a recurring feature of the long-swing dynamic of capitalist economies?

A kind of negative answer is provided by those neoclassical economists who have recently extended optimization analysis to the study of macroinstitutional change. (We refer to a tradition initially simulated by Coase [1937] and best exemplified in recent years by North and Thomas [1973]; Davis and North [1973], and Higgs [1980] also apply some of these insights to issues related to this study.) Confronted with our argument thus far, this group of economists would probably argue that individuals can continuously calculate the costs and benefits of potential institutional change and build the least costly coalition necessary to change institutions in desired directions. These neoclassical economists would therefore argue that social structures of accumulation are likely to experience a continuing process of marginal institutional adjustment and that the costs of institutional frictions would rarely get out of line.

Our answer is substantially different. To begin with, it is extremely unlikely that many individuals will have perfect information or foresight about the benefits or costs of present or prospective institutional arrangements. Habits formed by ideology and the traditions of cultural practice during the boom are likely to impose blinders on individuals' perceptions and calculations, lending a conservative bias to their evaluation of the relative merits of prevailing and potential institutional structures. Consequently, the desirability of serious institutional change will be underestimated.

Moreover, the multidimensionality of social structures of accumulation makes coalition-building extremely complicated. Some interest groups, defined with respect to their interests in one set of institutions, may prefer movement in a particular direction of change, whereas some other interest groups, defined by their relationship to other institutions, may prefer potentially inconsistent directions of change. And since sharp group conflicts about the distribution of the relative costs and benefits of alternative paths of institutional change are likely to emerge, some resolution of these conflicts must be achieved. These considerations do not mean that successful coalition-building is impossible, but they do suggest that the process of constructing coalitions of sufficient scope and strength to forge new social structures of accumulation is likely to prove complex and time-consuming.

In short, social structures of accumulation will exhibit considerable inertia, and coalitions aiming to change those institutions will emerge only slowly. As a result, capital accumulation within a given social structure of accumulation is likely to encounter diminishing returns to continuing capital investment, and this deceleration is likely to intensify until substantial adjustments in the social structure of accumulation can be made. But these adjustments are not likely to occur for some time.

We thus provide an answer to the third question about the duration and persistence of contraction and crisis. The length of the stagnation phase of a long swing results from the long lag before individual actors can mobilize collectively and from the long lag before collective struggle reaches the point of compromise or clear-cut victory that permits construction of a new social structure of accumulation.

This consideration leads us to suggest that long-swing contractions cannot be self-correcting and that a recovery cannot begin unless and until individual actors are able to mobilize coherent and collective forces which – either through some kind of social "compromise" or, alternatively, through decisive class victory – effect the necessary structural adjustments in the social structure of accumulation. Until this happens, initial stagnation is likely progressively to erode the stability of the reigning social structure of accumulation, leading to deepening economic crisis. Within this context, it would be surprising if crises were resolved in anything shorter than a long period of complex political struggle and conflict among capitalists, workers, and other groups.

This brings us to another common question about long-swing analysis: why do each of the phases of a long swing regularly last for twenty-five years? Our institutional analysis does not suggest that the expansion and contraction phases of a long swing will last any specific number of years and certainly does not indicate that each long swing will have the same duration. On the contrary, we expect that the duration of each phase of a long swing is best understood within the specific context of each stage of capitalism.

Indeed, we suspect that much of the previous literature on long swings has exaggerated their symmetrical periodicity. We can take the United States during the past three long swings as an example. Even if one believed in the precision of a dating exercise, which we do not, one does not find regular periodicity. The five successive expansion and stagnation phases of the last two and a half long swings have lasted thirty-two, sixteen, twenty, twenty-four, and thirty-two years, respectively. This pattern hardly indicates perfectly symmetrical cycles.

Several additional considerations should guide the application of this framework of long swings and stages of capitalism. To begin with, it is important to emphasize that the analysis of stages of capitalism derives from propositions about the operation of the world capitalist system. Since capitalism operates on a world scale, one should analyze its contradictions and social structures of accumulation on a world scale. Hence, evidence of long swings should be organized, as much as possible, for the world capitalist economy as a whole. At the same time, the analysis must also focus on the structure and contradictions of the social structure of accumulation within specific nations. While international factors provide pressures on national institutions, the content of the social structure of accumulation may vary significantly from one country to another, and many institutions are determined primarily by domestic forces.

As a related issue, we suspect that the relative synchronization of long swings among individual national economies within the world capitalist economy as a whole depends upon the character of the respective stages of capitalist development. In both the 1840s-to-1890s stage and the post-World War II stage one group of national capitalists, first the British and then the Americans, dominated the world capitalist economy. In each case the hegemonic power was able to create a relatively stable international environment, and the rhythms of many countries closely followed the rhythm of the dominant power. In contrast, in the first four decades of the twentieth century, intercapitalist competition among nations generated a much more unstable international environment, and individual countries' growth rates were less influenced by a single national power. The expansion phases of the stages featuring British and American hegemony were relatively long – thirty-one and thirty years respectively, according to this particular dating scheme – whereas the expansion phase of the stage featuring a less stable international environment lasted only about twenty years. Although we do not want to make too much out of the specific dates involved, these differences among stages do illustrate the importance of analyzing the international contexts within which successive long swings unfold.

We have further suggested that the construction of a social structure of accumulation requires explicit and self-conscious actions by leading political actors. By emphasizing these conscious acts we do not intend to suggest a purely conspiratorial, behind-the-scenes process that is hidden from the public's view until it is unveiled as an accomplished fact. Instead, we see this process as occurring quite openly and as involving first the development and then the mobilization of a consensus supporting the new institutional structure.

It is also important to emphasize that the stages-of-capitalism analysis is fundamentally qualitative in nature, based on propositions about the social relations necessary for continued capital accumulation. The stages of capitalism that emerge historically cannot be characterized by a single dimension of institutional transformation. As we have already noted, the social structure of accumulation comprises a fairly long list of institutions. Each one is necessary if rapid capital accumulation is to proceed, and each may therefore require reconstruction during and after an economic crisis. Consequently, the institutional transformation from one stage to the next has a multidimensional character. Therefore, studies of and evidence about long swings should build as much as possible upon qualitative institutional analysis and should not be reduced exclusively to the study of a series of quantitative indices of economic variables.

Finally, we emphasize that our stages should not be distinguished by single-point dating schemes. Rather, they should be conceived of as overlapping institutional distributions, with the end of one stage coinciding through several years with the beginning of the next. The complexity of the process of construction and consolidation of a new social structure of accumulation precludes narrow dating. As we have argued, this process does not happen overnight. It is likely to take many years, beginning long before the end of a crisis and continuing substantially into the period of the new stage of capitalism. As a result, it is difficult to determine the precise moment when a given historical tendency becomes dominant; one can find events that support or fail to support a particular narrow dating scheme. For this reason, our historical analysis pays more attention to the differing developmental characteristics that distinguish one period from the next and less attention to issues of specific dating and time.

Publication note

This chapter is excerpted from chapter 2 of *Segmented Work, Divided Workers: The Historical Transformation of Labor in the United States*, Cambridge University Press, 1982.

Notes

1 For analytical development of the necessary conditions for the reproduction of capitalist economics, see, for example, Harris (1978) or Roemer (1981). The condition focusing on the household and the state was not normally stressed in earlier Marxian work but has received substantially greater emphasis in the recent Marxian tradition. See, for example, Gough (1979).

2 This list of five tendencies should be read as our distillation of the most illuminating components of the historical materialist framework. Other elements of the Marxian literature have proved less illuminating. As we note below, we believe that much of the traditional Marxian analysis requires, and has undergone, considerable reformulation; some of these reformulations remain controversial. However, this book is not the place to debate these issues.

3 Marglin (1984, ch. 3) has clarified the theoretical importance of this dynamic, arguing that the differential between the average rate of growth of capital, g, and the average rate of growth of the labor force, n, determines whether or not the capitalist economy tends continuously to extend its boundaries. If $(g - n)$ is greater than zero (in "steady state"), the relative power of workers inside the previous boundaries of the capitalist economy is likely to increase; this pressure forces capitalists to expand beyond those boundaries.

4 There has been relatively little formal theoretical Marxian work on this tendency toward collective working-class activity.

5 See Gordon (1980) for a related theoretical discussion of many of the arguments outlined in this section and for a brief critical review of earlier literature on stages of capitalism.

6 Marglin (1984) provides a careful review of neoclassical, neo-Marxian, and neo-Keynesian theories of growth and investment.

7 For further discussion of the dynamics of capital accumulation, see Harris (1978) or Roemer (1981).

8 Gordon (1980) reviews the set of institutions constituent to a social structure of accumulation and provides one formal listing of these institutional requirements.

9 This relation between the financial rate of return and the rate of profit on industrial capital has not been carefully analyzed within the Marxian tradition. For one recent effort, see Panico (1980).

10 Plotke (1980) and Mandel (1980) have both recently criticized an earlier formulation of this analysis of stages of capitalism (in Gordon [1980]) as "economistic." The analysis appears to them to elevate "economic" forces arising from the accumulation process to a position of undue primacy in analyses of historical change. We do not intend such an elevation. We recognize that our analysis of stages of capitalism must be combined with cultural and political analyses for a fuller understanding of history, and we have tried in this book to link our analysis with other determinants of working-class movements. Our analysis of long swings and stages of capitalism provides only a starting point, albeit an absolutely necessary one, for a full theoretical and historical account of the important forces that have shaped production and the working class in US capitalism.

11 Gordon (1980) hypothesizes that substantial infrastructural investment is concentrated at the beginning of a new stage of capitalism as a result of new productive structures and new systems of transportation and communication. Such bunching of infrastructural investment would impart a large stimulus to the economy at the beginning of a new social structure of accumulation.

References

Barr, Kenneth, 1979. "Long Waves: A Selective, Annotated Bibliography," *Review*, 2 (Spring): 675–718.

Block, Fred, 1977. "The Ruling Class Does Not Rule: Notes on the Marxist Theory of the State," *Socialist Revolution*, 7 (May–June): 6–28.

Brody, David, 1979. "The Old Labor History and the New: In Search of an American Working Class," *Labor History*, 20 (Winter): 111–26.

Coase, Ronald, 1937. "The Nature of the Firm," *Economica*, 4 (Nov.): 386–405.

Davis, Lance, and Douglass C. North, 1973. *Institutional Change and American Economic Growth.* Cambridge University Press.

Davis, Mike, 1980. "Why the U.S. Working Class is Different," *New Left Review*, 123 (Sept.–Oct.): 3–44.

Gintis, Herbert, 1980. "Communication and Politics: Marxism and the 'Problem' of Liberal Democracy," *Socialist Review*, 10 (May–June): 189–232.

Gordon, David M., 1980. "Stages of Accumulation and Long Economic Cycles," in *Processes of the World System*, ed. Terence Hopkins and Immanuel Wallerstein, pp. 9–45. Beverly Hills, Calif.: Sage Publications.

Gough, Ian, 1979. *The Political Economy of the Welfare State.* London: Macmillan.

Harris, Donald J., 1978. *Capital Accumulation and Income Distribution.* Stanford, Calif.: Stanford University Press.

Higgs, Robert, 1980. *Competition and Coercion: Blacks in the American Economy, 1865–1914.* Chicago: University of Chicago Press.

Laclau, Ernesto, 1977. *Politics and Ideology in Marxist Theory.* London: New Left Books.

Mandel, Ernest, 1975. *Late Capitalism.* London: New Left Books.

1980. *Long Waves of Capitalist Development.* Cambridge University Press.

Marglin, Stephen A., 1974. "What Do Bosses Do? The Origins and Functions of Hierarchy in Capitalist Production," *Review of Radical Political Economics*, 6 (Summer): 60–112.

1984. *Growth, Distribution, and Prices: Neoclassical, Neo-Marxian, and Neo-Keynesian Approaches.* Cambridge, Mass.: Harvard University Press.

Montgomery, David, 1980. "To Study the People: The American Working Class," *Labor History*, 21 (Fall): 485–512.

North, Douglass C., and Robert Paul Thomas, 1973. *The Rise of the Western World.* Cambridge University Press.

Panico, Carlo, 1980. "Marx's Analysis of the Relationship Between the Rate of Interest and the Rate of Profits," *Cambridge Journal of Economics*, 4 (Dec.): 363–78.

Plotke, David, 1980. "The United States in Transition: Toward a New Order?" *Socialist Review*, 10 (Nov.–Dec.): 71–123.

1981. "The Politics of Transition: The United States in Transition, II," *Socialist Review*, 11 (Jan.–Feb.): 21–72.

Radical History Review, 1978–9.

Roemer, John E., 1981. *Analytical Foundations of Marxian Economics.* Cambridge University Press.

Rostow, Walt W., 1978. *The World Economy: History and Prospect.* Austin: University of Texas Press.

Tabb, William, and Larry Sawers (eds.), 1978. *Marxism and the Metropolis.* Oxford University Press.

Thompson, E. P., 1979. *The Poverty of Theory and Other Essays.* New York: Monthly Review Press.

Weisskopf, Thomas E., 1981. "The Current Economic Crisis in Historical Perspective," *Socialist Review*, 57: 9–53.

Wright, Erik Olin, 1978. *Class, Crisis, and the State.* London: New Left Books.

2

How social structures of accumulation decline and are built

MICHAEL REICH

The social structure of accumulation (SSA) approach offers a theoretical and historical account of the long-run dynamics of institutional change and economic growth in US capitalism. As initially formulated, the SSA comprises the economic, social, and political institutions that constitute the environment within which the capital accumulations process operates (Gordon *et al.*, 1982). The institutions that make up an SSA undergo a life-cycle that is related to long swings in economic activity. An old, and relatively rigid, SSA prolongs a long stagnation period, while a new, and still evolving, SSA promotes a long boom period.

The SSA approach proposes that the institutions of a new SSA must be in place before the next long boom period can begin. In a declining SSA, although stagnation undermines an institution's resource base, it is not easily reformed, because of vested interests, old political coalitions, fixed bargains and expectations, and ideology. The historical account (Gordon *et al.*, 1982) illustrates this process for each of the three SSAs in US history. By emphasizing the obstacles that constrain institutional adjustment to changing conditions, the SSA approach suggests that institutional rigidities can bring a long boom to an end or can perpetuate stagnation over a long period. On the other hand, the construction of a new SSA must begin before the next long boom period can take hold. But can an old SSA be revived by exogenous institutional changes? How does a new SSA get built?

In this chapter I clarify and elaborate these life-cycle aspects of the SSA approach. In the first part, I focus on SSA decline. I first review the evidence for the SSA life-cycle in the second half of the nineteenth century. I show that even though the Civil War brought about fundamental institutional changes, the SSA analysis of institutional rigidity and economic stagnation still holds.[1] I also demonstrate, in response to recent controversy, that a slowdown in economic growth did occur at the end of the nineteenth century.

In the second part of the chapter I turn to the question of how SSAs get built. I argue that there are very definite *turning points* in the construction of social structures of accumulation, specific events that set the foundations of the institutions in one design rather than another. But once the main foundation has been set, the institutions are not built (nor destroyed) overnight. Indeed, their construction

29

may be ongoing throughout most of the boom period. To illustrate this process I consider examples from the construction of the second and third SSAs.

For the second SSA, I regard the election of 1896 as the key turning point. I discuss the evolution of labor–management relations and domestic financial regulation in succeeding decades, showing how these institutions were constructed gradually, but in an already set pattern. For the third, or postwar, SSA I see the Second World War as the key turning point. I discuss the gradual construction of the three central institutions for the postwar SSA: Keynesian demand management, the liberal international economic order, and the limited capital–labor accord. The discussion again indicates how the pattern for these institutions was set earlier, at the key turning point.

An SSA in decline

Some critics of the SSA approach have suggested that the period 1865 to 1900 does not support the SSA account of institutional change and long swings. The institutional impact of the Civil War does not fit our periodization and the rapid growth of the postbellum years belies our contention of a growth slowdown at the end of the nineteenth century. The discussion in this section addresses these issues.

The Civil War and industrialization

Gordon et al. (1982) does not contain a sustained discussion of the conflict over slavery and the impact of the Civil War because its attention is focused on the wage-labor sector of the economy. For similar reasons little attention is paid to agrarian conditions and the growth of agrarian protest in the last decades of the nineteenth century. Yet these are important developments that must be connected to the SSA framework.

According to the Beard–Hacker thesis, the Northern triumph in the Civil War constituted a capitalist revolution and industrialization was consequently given a big spurt. In this view, the era from the Civil War to the Great Depression represents a single period. Each decade of the period is characterized by rapid technological change, high rates of growth and the rapid development of an industrial labor force and economy. The old days of an artisan-based, small-scale manufacturing age gave rise to the big trusts, the mass production worker, and the growth of highly capitalized industry. According to this conception, labor struggles surged upward from the onset of the postbellum era, repeatedly but always temporarily defeated by a hostile business class until the great watershed of the 1930s.

My view of this period is more differentiated and it generates an alternative periodization of US history. The US economy did grow rapidly after the Civil War, assisted by the institutional transformations that had been previously blocked by the antebellum slavery–capitalism conflict. But the Northern victory in the Civil War did not, contrary to the Beards and Hacker, usher in industrial capitalism, which was already well in place. It did, however, permit the final step in the consolidation of the existing social structure of accumulation.

The new elements and their impact are well known. Most important, of course, the North gained control over national government. During and after the war Northern industrialists were able to implement a long-stalled agenda that consolidated the national economy and promoted rapid industrial growth. Higher tariffs on industrial goods, encouragement of land development for Western agriculture, subsidies for railroad expansion, the development of a national banking system, the encouragement of immigration, and support for education all had the effect of integrating national markets, expanding the labor supply, and promoting rapid capital accumulation.[2]

These consolidations of the capitalist order did permit dramatic growth for a time, consistent with the Beard–Hacker thesis. Table 2.1 indeed shows that GNP, productivity, and industrial production were growing quite rapidly in the early 1870s, evidence of the vitality of the consolidated social structure of accumulation in this period. This growth was nonetheless unstable and unsustainable: the first social structure of accumulation was in deep crisis by the time of the Great Depression of 1893–96. As I document further below, it is misleading to see a single period of US capitalism or of labor history stretching from the Civil War to the Great Depression of 1929.

The late nineteenth-century slowdown

The period from 1873 to 1896 is marked by increasing cyclical economic instability and progressively slower trend growth rates. Economic growth did not stop altogether, as the term stagnation might imply, for growth occurred in every decade, and particularly in the 1880s. But a slowdown in growth did occur from 1873 to 1896, marked by a profit squeeze, productivity bottlenecks and the increasing frequency of stock market panics and serious business cycle downturns. Instability in the seventies and eighties gave way to crisis in the nineties. The resolution of the crisis involved the defeat of insurgent farmers and workers and the construction of a new set of institutions for accumulation. Only then could rapid capital accumulation resume.

The evidence for the slowdown in growth is reviewed in some detail by Gordon et al. (1982). Nonetheless, the argument is contested by labor historian David Brody (1984) and labor economist Frank Wilkinson (1983). Brody and Wilkinson each cite extensive data to deny the existence of a slowdown. Both seem to prefer the alternate Beard–Hacker periodization. As a response to these points, I present here additional evidence for the slowdown. In order to avoid repetition, the quantitative evidence I present here is restricted to sources that we did not use in our earlier review (Gordon et al., 1982).

In determining whether a slowdown in the trend rate of growth occurred in a certain period, it is crucial to separate cyclical and trend movements. This separation is usually accomplished by dating the starting and ending points of the

Table 2.1. *Output and productivity growth rates, 1869–1908*[a]

	GNP (1860 prices)	GNP per worker	Industrial production[b]
1869/78–1874/83	5.58	2.66	2.47
1874/83–1879/88	4.76	2.11	3.30
1879/88–1884/93	3.68	0.40	2.52
1884/93–1889/98	2.55	0.19	1.11
1889/98–1894/03	3.39	1.61	2.37
1894/03–1899/08	4.31	1.94	3.00

Notes: [a] Figures are annual compound percentage growth rates and are based on the Gallman–Kuznets GNP series, the Lebergott labor force series, and the Lewis industrial production series.
[b] Manufacturing, mining, and construction.
Sources: GNP and GNP per worker from Williamson (1974, table 4.2B, p. 70). Industrial production calculated by the author from Lewis (1978, table A7, p. 273).

period in years that fall in similar phases of the short-run business cycle, or by smoothing cyclical variations through the use of moving averages of annual data. Although both Brody and Wilkinson use the same output series that we draw upon, they fail to separate carefully trend from cycle. We do so in our book, and additional research is also consistent with our argument.

Critical of previous estimates, economic historian W. Arthur Lewis (1978) has developed his own industrial production indices for this period. Lewis finds that a slowdown did occur after 1873 in all the core industrial countries (UK, US, France, and Germany). His calculations indicate that the slowdown was smaller in the United States than in the other core countries. Nonetheless, the overall growth rate is significantly less than in the preceding or following periods. Using Lewis' series, my own calculations of the trend growth rate show a consistent slowdown in industrial growth from the seventies to the nineties (see Table 2.1). Throughout the period, and even in the boom eighties, Lewis finds (p. 102) a falling profit rate.

From the early 1870s on, the US economy grew at a slower rate than in the preceding long upswing. Williamson (1974) shows that the trend rates of growth of both output and productivity slowed further with each successive short-term cycle. As Table 2.1 indicates, real GNP was growing at 5.58 percent per year in the 1870s, 4.76 percent in the early 1880s, 3.68 percent in the late 1880s, and 2.55 percent in the early 1890s. Productivity growth in the same period slowed down from 2.66 percent per year in the 1870s to 0.19 percent in the early 1890s. These downward trends were reversed after the recovery from the Great Depression of 1893–96, when the next long upswing began.

The hypothesis that instability in the eighties was giving way to crisis by the nineties also receives confirmation from the recent work of Gordon *et al.* (1983) on long swings and nonreproductive business cycles. These authors suggest that "normal" short-term business cycles in US economic history are reproductive of the profit rate. In a reproductive business cycle, the downturn acts to recreate the conditions of profitable accumulation that had been eroded during the short-term upturn; the profit rate is higher at the end of the downturn than at its beginning. But in a nonreproductive cycle the conditions of profitable accumulation are not re-created; the profit rate does not consistently recover in the downturn. Gordon *et al.* show that the major depressions of the 1890s, the 1930s and the 1970s were each preceded by nonreproductive downturns, signaling that the current social structure of accumulation was no longer working, and that major institutional restructuring was needed to re-create profitable conditions for rapid capital accumulation.

Considering each of these findings together with the data presented by Gordon *et al.* (1982), I submit that, despite the skeptics, the growth retardation thesis rests on a persuasive evidential basis. A relative stagnation did occur, culminating in the economic crisis of the late nineteenth century. The years from 1865 to 1929 should be divided into two periods, with a major turning point occurring near the end of the century. Of course, demonstrating the existence of relative stagnation does not amount to explaining the cause of the economic crisis of the late nineteenth century. Our analysis (Gordon *et al.*, 1982) suggested a specific account: a profit squeeze caused by increasing intercapitalist competition in a labor–management regime that sustained considerable worker power. In this period, we suggested, prices were falling and workers were able to increase their real wages while employers were inhibited from further advancing labor productivity. In order to support this argument beyond the tentative suggestions offered in our book, I have drawn together several pieces of the relevant quantitative materials. I present and discuss this evidence in the appendix to this chapter.

How SSAs are built

Building the second SSA

Our account of long swings and institutional change claims that an economic boom began in the late 1890s because a new social structure of accumulation was put into place at that time. But labor unrest and labor revolts, by many accounts, including ours, continued their upward rise through the record-breaking strike wave of 1919. For example, both Brody (1980, ch. 1) and Gordon *et al.* (1982, p. 122) cite the rapid growth in union membership, from 447,000 in 1897 to over 2 million in 1904. And David Montgomery (1987) has drawn attention to the militancy of the "new unionism" of 1909–22. It thus seems that one of the central institutions comprising the social structure of accumulation was not in place until 1920. Where does this leave our theory?

In answer, I would supplement the extensive discussion of exactly this issue in Gordon *et al.* (1982) by again suggesting the importance of the discontinuity of the 1890s. A brief review of the political crisis of the 1890s and the manner in which it was resolved will help in periodizing the labor struggles of the subsequent two decades. I suggest that capital's resolution of the political crisis of the 1890s did in fact constitute a decisive victory over labor, and that labor struggles in subsequent years were fought in an altered structural context.

The political crisis of the 1890s represented a major challenge for capital. The dimensions of the crisis were apparent in the growth of agrarian protest, labor unrest and business bankruptcies in what was then the worst time of economic troubles the country had ever experienced. Already in 1892 the Populist Party had mounted a serious political challenge and was reaching out to urban workers to construct a potentially formidable farmer–labor alliance. Workers themselves were engaged in new forms of struggle after the disastrous defeats of the 1892 strike wave. Industrial unionism grew rapidly among railway workers and miners and political action also exploded; one indicator is provided by Coxey's Army, another by the support the American Federation of Labor (AFL) gave to a socialist platform in 1894 and its efforts that same year on behalf of Populist candidates. Capitalists were painfully aware that something had to be done, and quickly, and they focused their efforts on dividing industrial workers from agrarian Populists.

Promising workers a tariff and stable currencies, capital mobilized on a tremendous scale to defeat the widespread popular revolt. In the 1896 election, business contributions to the Republicans doubled over the 1892 level and the Republicans spent five times what the Democrats could muster (Jones, 1964). The political challenge was defeated, and the potential farmer–labor coalition divided (Goodwyn, 1976; Pollack, 1987). A critical realignment of the political party system toward the Republicans was thus effected; the "System of '96," as it was called, registered the political dominance of big business (Burnham, 1970, 1981; Sundquist, 1983).

The swing to the Republicans was further solidified by the removal of blacks and poor whites from Southern electoral politics. During this period such Supreme Court decisions as *Plessy* vs. *Ferguson* in 1896 and *Williams* vs. *Mississippi* in 1898 as well as a series of state disfranchising conventions made interracial class alliances opposed to business close to impossible in the South.[3]

Having achieved political dominance, business turned to the difficult task of building a new social structure of accumulation. From 1897 to 1903, a frenzied and unprecedented merger wave reduced the level of intercapitalist competition and promoted corporate capitalism. At the same time, business promoted overseas expansion to re-stimulate economic growth, and then, beginning especially with the employer offensive of 1903, it turned its attention to the continuing labor unrest that had been the unintended consequence of homogenizing tendencies.

The consolidation of the period of homogenization involved a lengthy and arduous process. During the Progressive period big business faced opposition from small business, urban reformers and other quarters. This was also a period of growing AFL strength, syndicalist upsurges, and socialist insurgencies. Much has been made of the fact that many of these conflicts were not resolved until the First World War. However, the length and number of struggles should not obscure the central tendency of this period: because of the groundwork laid down in 1896, these contests were being fought on terrain that was basically favorable to big business.

The heightened labor struggles of this period illustrate this point. After 1903 business was able to decisively defeat the labor challenges. The defeat of labor in this period is registered in a variety of indicators, including in quantitative strike data. While the frequency of strikes stayed at high levels between 1900 and 1920, the percentage of strikes won by workers declined sharply after 1900. By 1921 it stood at half the rate of the early 1880s.[4] Brody (1980, ch. 1) rightly characterizes the Progressive era as a period of retreat for the labor movement.

The SSA approach explains these defeats and the associated economic boom. But the identification of a key turning point, the election of 1896, strengthens and clarifies the SSA account. Although the institutions surrounding labor continued to evolve and undergo consolidation during this period, their basic framework had been constructed earlier. The key turning point had been reached with the defeat of the potential farmer–worker alliance in 1896. After that point, a broad oppositional coalition with an alternative vision was not an immediate possibility.

As we lay out in detail, except in the cases of coal-mining and apparel, business policies to reinforce the drive system overwhelmed labor. The labor movement and its allies, whether socialist or syndicalist, or whatever, were forced into more particularistic and defensive positions, and could not regain the offensive until after the collapse of the second social structure of accumulation in 1929. The further defeat of the labor Left during and after World War I represented a continuation of the trends of this period, rather than an accident of the war.

The reorganization of the financial system

Another example of how SSA institutions are built comes from the reorganization of the banking system in the period from the 1890s to the 1920s. The Panic of 1893 and much of the economic turmoil of the 1890s are often attributed to fears raised by the fundamental political challenges of the Populists to the gold standard and the structure of the financial system. Once again, the election of 1896 constituted an important turning point. After that realignment election the commitment of the United States to the gold standard was no longer in doubt.

Although the fundamental challenge from the Populists had been defeated, the complete rebuilding of the financial institutions took many years. While the Gold Standard Act was passed in 1900, firmly committing the United States to gold, many of the elements of a reconstructed financial system were not yet in place. The credit system, as many contemporary bankers were well aware, was too decentralized and inelastic to respond adequately to changing credit needs. Already in the late 1890s, as Faulkner (1951, p. 47) documents, bankers' commissions had identified these defects of the banking system and urged reform.

Conflicts among bankers concerning the details of reform dominated the restructuring process. Although many bankers favored reform, powerful bankers with vested interests, mainly in New York, were opposed. Such conservative Senators as Nelson Aldrich stalled the reform process until prodded by the Panic of 1907. Soon thereafter, they relented, resulting in the passage of the Aldrich–Vreeland Act in 1908.

The process of institution-building proceeded nonetheless, in part through the voluminous studies and debates generated by the newly created National Monetary Commission (set up by the Aldrich–Vreeland Act). In 1912 the Commission issued its lengthy report. After further political infighting, mainly involving the distribution of power between the New York bankers and bankers elsewhere, conflicts were finally resolved by setting up a regional system with New York as a super-region. The Federal Reserve Act of 1913 then created the modern system of Federal Reserve banks (Faulkner, 1951). Needless to say, the Federal Reserve system was more attuned to capital's vision of a financial system than to the alternative vision (the so-called sub-Treasury plan) put forward by the Populist–labor alliance in its heyday (Goodwyn, 1976).

Once again, a key turning point in the construction of an SSA institution can be identified. In this case, the 1896 election affirmed US adherence to the gold standard and to reorganizing the financial system along lines favorable to business. After this turning point, the basic commitment to a particular kind of institution was firmly established. And once again, the complete building of the institution – in this case the Federal Reserve system – occurred gradually and over time.

The construction of the postwar SSA

A similar pattern of SSA-building appears when we examine the construction of the three key institutions of the postwar SSA: the commitment to demand-stimulus, the liberal international order, and the capital–labor accord. In each case, a key turning point is identified, and is followed by a long period of gradual institution-building.

The commitment to demand-stimulus

The story of the coming of Keynesian policy and theory to the United States has been told many times (for example, Galbraith [1987]). Nonetheless, the SSA approach provides a new framework for understanding and interpreting the main points of this history. The most important consideration is that the Keynesian element of the postwar SSA is best understood as the adoption of demand-management in its broadest meaning and the abandonment of the principles of "sound finance" that had previously dominated policy-formation. During the course of the 1930s, a consensus did develop that the government could and should avoid the recurrence of major depressions by intervening in the economy using a wide variety of stimulative instruments.

This broader consensus for demand-stimulus, I emphasize, differs substantially from the later, and narrower, Keynesian theory of counter-cyclical economic policy. Keynes' own theory arrived after the abandonment of *laissez-faire* ideology; still later, the IS–LM models of Hicks and Hansen were applied to approach full employment and counter-cyclical fine-tuning via very specific fiscal and monetary instruments. This narrower meaning and the associated consensus for it developed only in the 1960s and had a short lifetime. The broader meaning and associated consensus shaped the foundations of the major postwar SSA institution of demand-stimulus. Later postwar debates and policy turns centered on the specific means to complete the building of the institution.

The stimulating effects of public works, government deficits and the economy of high wages were already understood, and proposed, even if not well formalized in economic theory, at the beginning of the Great Depression. The theory behind the National Recovery Act suggested that limiting price and wage flexibility provided a means of maintaining the level of economic activity. Similarly, the Preamble to the National Labor Relations Act of 1935 (the Wagner Act) stated the desirability of maintaining mass purchasing power to support the level of economic activity. Underconsumptionism was a popular explanation of the causes of the Depression as well of its longevity. The recession of 1937, moreover, shattered the illusions of many who believed that the restoration of prosperity would occur through a self-regulating process. After this point, public opinion shifted, enhancing popular support for the government to engage in demand-stimulus.

The willingness of business to permit large-scale government spending of a magnitude that would be stimulative, nonetheless, did not come until the outbreak of war. Once business opposition was removed, and wartime experience illustrated the benefits of government intervention, the commitment to demand-stimulus became a national consensus. The magnitude of the shift that occurred became apparent after the war. The common fear that another major depression would occur with demobilization at the end of the war was assuaged by the new counteracting role of government. It therefore seems appropriate to designate the war as the turning point.

In the postwar period, the commitment to Keynesianism in the Eisenhower years remained quite limited. Although Military Keynesianism played a long-term stimulative role, fiscal and monetary policy remained contractionary during much of both Eisenhower administrations. Keynesianism as US mainstream economists usually identify it – in the narrower version – only became policy in the Kennedy–Johnson years. Still, demand-stimulus was practiced throughout this period through the military budget, through the so-called automatic stabilizers, through Federal housing and veterans' programs that stimulated the purchases of consumer durables, and through an evident consensus for massive government intervention should there be another 1930s-type depression (Stein, 1969; Epstein and Schor, 1990).[5] The Kennedy–Johnson Keynesianism of the 1960s and macroeconomic policy afterwards thus constituted the evolution of a process that began earlier and was already underway.

The liberal international order

A second example of institution-building is provided by the process of creation of the liberal postwar international order. Temin (1989) has argued that the key step was the abandonment of the gold standard in 1933, but that only marks the end of the old order. I would identify the turning point as the Bretton Woods conference of 1944.[6] Again, the system was not really constructed in the space of a few days at a resort hotel in New Hampshire. However, the outlines of, and commitment to, such a system certainly were. Bretton Woods not only established a system with a defined relationship between Britain and the United States (the resolution of the controversies over the Keynes plan and Harry Dexter White's plan), established pegged exchange rates and solidified the role of the US dollar as the reserve currency. It also established a commitment to liberalism and the repudiation of protectionism, and it thereby set the direction of the evolution of the international order.[7]

Although international trade constituted a very small fraction of economic activity for most of the major developed capitalist economies in the early postwar period, trade was important as a handmaiden of growth in this period (Glyn et al., 1990). The reduction of tariffs, the creation of the Common Market and the convertibility of currencies all occurred gradually, and again not until the late 1950s or into the 1960s (Dam, 1982). Nonetheless, it is clear that the design of these institutions was established much earlier. Occasional currency devaluations simply reset pegged exchange rates, and did not degenerate into a flexible rate system.

Finally, it should be noted that US military and economic hegemony was established by the end of the war. The subsequent development of liberal international economic relationships among the major capitalist countries proceeded within this central reality.

The limited capital–labor accord

I turn next to the postwar limited capital–labor accord, in which I include the provision of various income maintenance programs. The key political and economic turning point, I suggest, occurred in 1946 to 1948. Containment began in the industrial arena, with the General Motors–United Automobile Workers faceoff in 1946, and the subsequent expulsion of Communists from the Congress of Industrial Organizations unions. The key political steps were the passage of the Taft–Hartley Act in 1947 and the defeat of the Progressive ticket in 1948. These defeats signalled a political commitment by business to call a halt to further liberal reform.

Although a turning point had been reached, the policies that regulated the capital–labor accord continued to evolve. Important labor legislation has proceeded in every decade. In the 1950s, for example, the Walter–McCarran Act was passed in 1952 and Landrum–Griffin in 1957. Similarly, the development of multi-year collective bargaining agreements occurred gradually and spread relatively slowly through manufacturing. And the development of cost-of-living escalators, which was supposed to play such an important role in undermining the accord, was not even a part of it until well into the 1960s (some would say, with good reason, not until the 1970s).

Income maintenance programs evolved in a similar pattern. Although set into place in the late 1930s and 1940s, they remained relatively unimportant for most of the first part of the postwar period. Changes made in the 1960s, not policies of the 1940s, played a prominent role in subsequent years. Still, these social programs were put into place, in broad outline, at the beginning of the period.

Conclusion

This examination of how social structures of accumulation decline and are built has yielded interesting findings for both the nineteenth and twentieth centuries. In the nineteenth century, the incorporation of the institutional changes wrought by the Civil War elaborates the SSA approach and does not require any fundamental modification. A re-examination of the evidence for a late nineteenth-century slowdown and general crisis for capital supports the SSA interpretation.

In the early twentieth century, or more precisely after the watershed of the 1890s, the construction of the second SSA proceeded. The building of the SSA institutions concerning labor and finance occurred gradually, but along foundation lines laid down in the critical realignment years. A similar analysis could be conducted, I would suggest, for such other key institutions of the second SSA as oligopolistic industrial organization and expansionist international economic policy.

With respect to the postwar social structure of accumulation, each of the three main institutions of the postwar SSA were set in place by the late 1940s. The governmental commitment to demand-stimulus (and later to macroeconomic management), the liberal international order, and the capital–labor accord could all be seen in rough outline by that time.[8] Still, each of these institutions continued to be built, and their further evolution at first (but not later) favored the process of capitalist accumulation.

Acknowledgment

I am grateful to the Institute of Industrial Relations, University of California at Berkeley, for research support.

Appendix: Causes of the late nineteenth-century slowdown

The US economy experienced rapid economic growth as a result of the industrializing spurt generated by the Civil War and its aftermath. Yet, in the last three decades of the nineteenth century, the United States' economy experienced a long economic slowdown. Although concern over the future of the gold standard and bank failures provided symptoms of the crises of this period, the root causes lay in the growing challenges to capitalist power from both domestic sources, epitomized in an insurgent farmer–worker coalition, and international sources, epitomized by the advance of international competition.

The crises came to a head in the Presidential election campaign of 1896, which resulted in a decisive rout of the domestic farmer–worker coalition challenging business. I suggest that 1896 thus constituted one of several significant turning points in the history of long swings in the US economy. After 1896, capital regained its power and used that power to restructure decayed economic institutions to its advantage. As a result, profitability was restored, and investment and economic growth resumed.

Although the existence of the slowdown is well documented in Table 2.1, the quantitative evidence connecting this retardation to class power and profitability is not. Gordon *et al.* (1982) provide suggestive anecdotal and circumstantial evidence that the slowdown was caused by the conjunction of growing international competition and growing domestic challenges to capitalist power, which squeezed profit rates and slowed investment. But systematic evidence for such a profit-squeeze hypothesis is not presented, and alternative explanations of the slowdown are not ruled out by their account.

The purpose of this appendix is to review a number of alternative possible causes of the slowdown, and to present new quantitative evidence that supports the profit-squeeze hypothesis.

Alternative explanations

The literature on the Great Depression of the nineties is notably more descriptive and less analytical than the literature on the 1930s. With the exception of Williamson (1974), historical economists have not engaged in the systematic hypothesis-testing and debate that is exemplified by Peter Temin's (1976) *Did Monetary Forces Cause the Great Depression?* Still, a number of explanations have been offered, corresponding to the usual list of suspects. Two such lists can be composed, one consisting of long-swing type analyses and explanations, and another consisting of short-run business cycle analyses and explanations.

Long-swing writers have stressed slowdowns in technological change and the closing of the frontier (Schumpeter, 1939; Hansen, 1941; Baran and Sweezy, 1966); downswings in the growth of the money supply (Friedman and Schwartz, 1982); upswings in the relative price of primary products (Rostow, 1978; Lewis, 1978); and changes in the movement of population (Thomas, 1954; Kuznets, 1961). Neoclassical economists, such as Williamson (1974) and Temin (1971), attribute the long slowdown to a decline in investment, but through a supply-side rather than a demand-side mechanism.

The short-run business cycle literature also consists of the usual suspects: monetarist, Keynesian (Hansen, 1941; Hoffmann, 1956, 1970), and traditional Marxist (by which I mean the rising organic composition of capital theory).

In this appendix I consider alternative explanations of the slowdown. My primary concern is with the long-swing theories. However, I also advance an interpretation that attempts to integrate short-run business cycles with long-swing patterns. I consider in turn the technological explanation (exemplified by the Schumpeterian approach), the neoclassical explanation (exemplified in Williamson's causal emphasis on the capacity-creating effects of investment), the Keynesian explanation exemplified in Hoffmann's and Hansen's emphasis on the demand-determining effects of investment), the traditional Marxian explanation (exemplified in Shaikh's causal emphasis on the rising capital–output ratio), and an alternative neo-Marxian profit-squeeze mechanism (exemplified in increasing price competition and capital–labor conflict).[9]

Technological change

The technological change explanation of the downswing can be described as the exhaustion of growth based on the construction of the railways and telegraphs. The succeeding long

Table 2.2. *Investment growth rates, 1869–1906*

1869/73–1872/76	3.4
1872/76–1877/81	3.9
1877/81–1882/86	4.7
1882/86–1887/91	6.2
1887/91–1892/96	7.0
1892/96–1897/01	1.0
1897/01–1902/06	7.3

Note: Figures are annual compound percentage growth rates of real gross domestic private fixed nonresidential investment and were calculated by the author from Kuznets (1961).

upswing was then based on urbanization, including street-cars, electrification, telephones, and automobiles. The evaluation of the technological change explanation is hampered by three principal problems.

First, technological change played a small role in nineteenth-century growth, so a slowdown in technological change cannot explain very much of a decline in growth. Indeed, Williamson found that the decline in technological change, measured by the residual from multifactor productivity growth, was a negligible factor in explaining the slowdown.

A second problem for the technological change argument concerns the difficult issue of causal interpretation. New products and new processes are more likely to emerge during an upturn because that is when they are more profitably developed. The diffusion of technological change may occur in spurts as an effect of other factors, instead of as an exogenous force.

Third, technological change is often embodied in new investment, in replacement investment as well as net investment. Consequently, the evidence for the role of technological change may be inseparable from the evidence for the role of investment. For this reason, it may be preferable to combine the two explanations and examine patterns of gross rather than net investment.

Investment

Williamson (1974, p. 111) has argued that the crisis of the nineties was due to a decline in the rate of capital accumulation, itself caused by the exhaustion of profitable investment opportunities. Williamson suggests that a temporarily large set of profitable opportunities arose immediately after the Civil War, but this argument can also be cast in terms of later diminishing opportunities, such as the closing of the frontier and the completion of the national railroad net. In this explanation, the decline in investment caused the decline in productivity and output growth noted in Table 2.1. Using the Kuznets capital stock series, Williamson (1974, p. 72) presents decadal data (based on five-year moving averages) on the rate of growth of the capital stock that seems to bear out this decline. He also points out that the decline in the rate of investment occurred despite a substantial increase in the rate of savings.

Williamson is correct to identify a fall in the rate of profit and in the rate of growth in the late nineteenth century. But he is wrong to attribute the economic retardation primarily to a decline in the rate of capital accumulation. My own calculations, using the Kuznets investment series, but drawing upon quinquennial rather than decadal differences, provide a rather different picture.

Table 2.3. *Capital–output and capital–labor ratios, 1869–1909^a*

	Capital–output ratio	Capital–labor ratio
1869–78	131.8	88.3
1879–88	100.0	100.0
1889	113.1	103.4
1894	130.8	136.3
1899	115.0	132.9
1904	115.9	139.2
1909	106.5	141.4

Note: ^{a}Private domestic nonfarm economy. Indices exclude trade, construction, finance, forestry, fisheries, and personal services. 1879–88 = 100.
Source: Kendrick (1961).

In order to show greater chronological detail and to incorporate possible embodied technological change effects, I have calculated real investment rates, using quinquennial rather than decadal differences, and gross rather than net investment. Real investment, as Table 2.2 shows, was increasing in each five-year period from 1869 to 1896, not decreasing. Moreover, investment was increasing at an accelerating rate. This finding of a speed-up of investment is consistent with the indication, in Table 2.3, that the capital–labor ratio was increasing during this period. It seems unlikely that a *decline* in investment could have been the primary culprit in the growth slowdown.

Marxian and neo-Marxian explanations

Traditional Marxian economics suggest that the increase in investment might have been the cause of the growth slowdown. Drawing upon the arguments made by Weisskopf (1979), I consider the capital–output ratio as the appropriate proxy in the price system for the organic composition of capital in the labor theory of value system. As shown in Table 2.3, the capital–output ratio fell between the 1870s and 1880s, and then rose until the mid-1890s, as the traditional Marxian account predicts. This declining effectiveness of increased investment might explain the growth slowdown, for the growth rate can be expressed as the ratio of the propensity to save (and invest), which was rising slowly, to the capital–output ratio, which was rising much faster. These considerations support the traditional Marxian explanation.

A rising capital–output ratio is also consistent with a profit-squeeze theory of the crisis. The rising capital–output ratio need not have resulted from diminishing returns, in the technological sense of the term. A productivity slowdown associated with increased capital–labor conflict could also diminish the output-enhancing effects of investment and raise the capital–output ratio. Then the profit rate would be squeezed by a different mechanism.

The traditional Marxian (rising capital–output ratios) and neo-Marxian (profit squeeze) theories seem difficult to distinguish empirically. Some insights can be obtained by examining the causes of the decline in the rate of productivity growth. Labor productivity, or output per worker, can be expressed as the product of the output–capital ratio and the capital–labor ratio.[10] The fall in the output–capital ratio (the inverse of the capital–output ratio) thus might be consistent with the slowdown of productivity growth. However, the rising capital–labor ratio would have exerted a counteracting force. But productivity growth fell faster, not slower, than the output–capital ratio, casting doubt on the efficacy of the capital–output mechanism of the traditional Marxian explanation.

Table 2.4. *Employment, wages, output, and labor's share, 1870–1908*

	Industrial employment (L)	Wage (1914$)	Output (1899 = 100)	Labor's share
1870	5.85	375	25	87.75
1871	6.00	386	26	89.08
1872	6.40	416	31	85.88
1873	6.44	407	30	87.37
1874	6.46	403	29	89.77
1875	6.46	403	28	92.98
1876	6.53	393	28	91.65
1877	6.77	388	30	87.56
1878	7.03	397	32	87.22
1879	7.43	391	36	80.70
1880	7.93	395	42	74.58
1881	8.84	415	46	71.40
1882	8.84	431	49	77.76
1883	9.18	459	50	84.27
1884	9.27	478	47	94.28
1885	9.54	492	47	99.87
1886	10.48	499	57	91.75
1887	11.00	509	60	93.32
1888	11.47	505	62	93.43
1889	12.07	510	66	93.27
1890	12.76	519	71	93.27
1891	12.92	525	73	92.92
1892	13.29	527	79	88.66
1893	12.86	505	70	92.78
1894	12.77	484	68	90.89
1895	13.62	520	81	87.44
1896	13.26	521	74	93.36
1897	13.70	529	80	90.59
1898	14.37	527	91	83.22
1899	14.89	563	100	83.83
1900	14.52	573	100	83.20
1901	15.97	582	111	83.73
1902	17.20	612	127	82.89
1903	17.64	607	126	84.98
1904	17.10	606	121	85.64
1905	18.47	621	140	81.93
1906	20.86	627	152	86.05
1907	21.12	631	156	85.43
1908	18.06	631	127	89.73

Sources: Industrial employment: Calculated from data of Williamson (1974, tables C2, C4).
Wage: Lebergott (1964, table A19). Real annual earnings of employed workers.
Output: US Department of Commerce (1975, series P-17). Frickey industrial production index.

An examination of the movement of real wages in relation to productivity may provide some clues here. Lebergott's series on real wages (reproduced in Table 2.4) indicates that annual earnings of nonfarm employees fell from 1872 to 1876, were stagnant from 1876 to 1880, rose substantially from 1880 to 1882, fell from 1892 to 1894, and rose steadily in the subsequent decade. Note that the growth in real wages during 1880 to 1892 occurred at a time of slowed productivity growth, as the profit-squeeze hypothesis would suggest.

Two additional calculations further support the profit-squeeze hypothesis. First, drawing

MICHAEL REICH

Table 2.5. *Manufacturing profitability in selected industries, 1869–1919*

	Value added	Wages	Surplus (1) – (2)	Capital	Surplus/capital
	\$'000				percent
	(1)	(2)	(3)	(4)	(5)
A. Iron and steel (blast furnaces)					
1869	24,142	12,475	11,667	56,145	20.78
1879	30,696	12,655	18,041	89,531	20.15
1889	35,544	14,614	20,930	129,547	16.16
1899	52,100	18,484	33,616	143,159	23.48
1904	52,881	18,935	33,946	236,146	14.38
1909	70,791	24,607	46,184	487,581	9.47
1914	53,074	22,781	30,293	462,282	6.55
1919	173,181	73,769	99,412	802,417	12.39

Sources: Frickey (1947, p. 205, table 24); US Department of Commerce (1917, p. 640; 1923, p. 659).

B. Boots and shoes, excluding rubber boots and shoes					
1879	63,608	43,001	20,607	42,994	47.93
1889	101,863	60,667	41,196	95,282	43.24
1899	90,337	58,441	31,896	99,819	31.95
1904	122,744	69,060	53,684	122,526	43.81
1909	165,163	92,359	72,804	197,090	36.94
1914	191,403	105,695	85,708	254,591	33.66

Source: US Department of Commerce (1923, p. 591).

C. Iron and steel (steel works and rolling mills)					
1869	47,540	27,040	20,500	65,627	31.24
1879	74,591	42,796	31,795	120,374	26.41
1889	115,870	74,659	41,211	276,224	14.92
1899	206,317	102,336	103,981	430,232	24.17
1904	232,761	122,492	110,269	700,182	15.75
1909	328,222	163,201	165,021	1,004,735	16.42
1914	327,839	188,142	139,697	1,258,371	11.10
1919	1,148,326	637,637	510,689	2,656,518	19.22

Source: US Department of Commerce (1923, p. 658).

D. Woolen and worsted goods					
1869	66,755	31,246	35,509	108,910	32.60
1879	71,298	31,519	39,779	116,470	34.15
1889	79,796	41,084	38,712	199,075	19.45
1899	90,658	44,850	45,808	256,554	17.86
1904	110,453	55,097	55,356	302,767	18.28
1909	146,305	69,727	76,578	415,378	18.44
1914	132,987	75,953	57,034	389,653	14.64
1919	399,839	168,109	231,730	831,695	27.86

Source: US Department of Commerce (1923, p. 592).

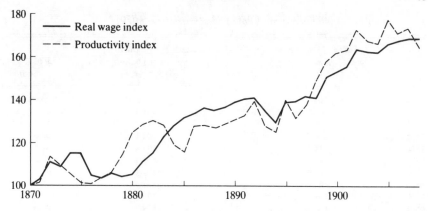

Fig. 2.1. Real wages and output per worker in industry, 1870–1908. (*Source*: See Table 2.6.)

from the periodic manufacturing censuses, I have calculated trends in the wage share of net output (value-added) for a sample of four industries over this period (see Table 2.5). For each industry, I find declining profit rates (rising labor shares) from the 1880s until the 1890s, and increasing profit rates subsequently.

Second, using Frickey's index of annual production and annual data on industry employment generated by Williamson, I have calculated an *annual* output per worker series for 1870 to 1908 (see Table 2.4 and Figure 2.1). The result of these calculations shows that productivity growth in industry was rapid between 1876 to 1908. Moreover, as Table 2.6 and Figure 2.1 show, productivity grew faster than real wages from 1876 to 1882, whereas wages grew faster than productivity from 1882 to 1896; after 1896, productivity growth again outpaced real wage growth.

Table 2.6 and Figure 2.1 thus demonstrate that the depression of the 1870s slowed wage growth below the level of productivity growth, thereby restoring profitability until 1883. This restoration of the profit rate through a recession comprises what Gordon *et al.* (1983) call a reproductive business cycle.

The recession of the mid-1880s, however, did *not* slow wage growth. With profits already squeezed, the depression of 1894 reduced productivity growth *more* than wage growth, leading to a further profit squeeze. Here we have indications of a non-reproductive business cycle, one that does not restore the profit rate. After 1896, productivity rises faster than wages, restoring profitability and signaling a new long upswing with reproductive business cycles.

Conclusion

The above evidence is consistent with two hypotheses. First, profits were squeezed in the period up to 1896 but grew thereafter. Second, growing capital–labor conflict at the workplace, or increasing national and international competition, or a combination of these two factors, provided the initial source of the profit squeeze and crisis. If this hypothesis is correct, the investment decline that did take place in the 1890s resulted from these sources of a squeeze on profits rather than causing it in the first place. However, these bits of evidence are only suggestive and must be supplemented by further research.[11]

Table 2.6. *Real wages and productivity, 1870–1908*

	Index of real wages w (1870 = 100)	Q/L	Index of productivity $q = Q/L$ (1870 = 100)	q/w (1870 = 100)
1870	100.0	4.27	100.0	100.0
1871	102.9	4.33	101.4	98.5
1872	110.9	4.84	113.3	102.2
1873	108.5	4.66	109.1	100.6
1874	114.7	4.49	105.2	91.7
1875	114.7	4.33	101.4	88.4
1876	104.8	4.29	100.5	95.9
1877	103.5	4.43	103.7	100.2
1878	105.9	4.55	106.6	100.7
1879	104.3	4.85	113.6	108.9
1880	105.3	5.30	124.1	117.9
1881	110.7	5.46	127.9	115.5
1882	114.9	5.54	129.7	112.9
1883	122.4	5.45	127.6	104.2
1884	127.5	5.07	118.7	93.1
1885	131.2	4.93	115.5	88.0
1886	133.1	5.44	127.4	95.7
1887	135.7	5.45	127.6	94.0
1888	134.7	5.41	127.7	94.1
1889	136.0	5.47	128.1	94.2
1890	138.4	5.56	130.2	91.1
1891	140.0	5.65	132.3	94.5
1892	140.5	5.94	139.1	99.0
1893	134.7	5.44	127.4	94.6
1894	129.1	5.32	124.6	96.5
1895	138.7	5.95	139.3	100.4
1896	138.9	5.58	130.7	94.1
1897	141.1	5.84	136.8	97.0
1898	140.5	6.33	148.2	105.5
1899	150.1	6.72	157.4	104.9
1900	152.8	6.89	161.4	105.6
1901	155.2	6.95	162.8	104.9
1902	163.2	7.38	172.8	105.9
1903	161.9	7.14	167.2	103.2
1904	161.6	7.08	165.8	102.6
1905	165.6	7.58	177.5	107.2
1906	167.2	7.29	170.7	102.1
1907	168.3	7.39	173.1	102.9
1908	168.3	7.03	164.6	97.8

Source: Calculated from data in Table 2.4.

Notes

1 See Reich (1989) for a revised summary historical account of SSAs in US history.
2 The outcome for the South was very different, of course. Barrington Moore (1967, ch. 4) argues that the Civil War constituted an incomplete capitalist revolution. Sharecropping, not wage labor or family farming, became the dominant mode, and the ex-slaveholders retained

their primacy through their extensive land holdings. This process has been elucidated by Montgomery (1967), Wiener (1978), Billings (1979), and Foner (1988). I present an extended synthesis of class and race developments in the postbellum South in Reich (1981, ch. 6).

3 *Plessy* legitimated racial segregation and *Williams* endorsed disfranchisement of black voters.

4 Nolan and Edwards (1984, table 2). See also Gordon *et al.* (1982, pp. 155–7) for a more detailed discussion of strike trends.

5 As Martin Feldstein has put it: "officials in the United States feared a postwar relapse into depression and avoided policies which would encourage saving." (Council of Economic Advisers, 1983, p. 81).

6 Although I differ with some of his interpretations, the writings of Fred Block (1977, 1987) provide invaluable accounts of this period.

7 In Sargent's (1983) and Temin's (1989) terminology, the Bretton Woods system established a new policy regime.

8 See Wolfson (1986) for a similar analysis of the evolution of domestic financial institutions.

9 Since both the short-run and long-run monetarist explanations have been amply debated and critiqued elsewhere (e.g. Cooper [1982]), I do not pursue these approaches here.

10 I ignore here capacity utilization variations because I am considering smoothed data that eliminate short-run business cycle variations.

11 The results presented here are not sensitive to recent revisions of prewar GNP estimates by Balke and Gordon (1988).

References

Balke, Nathan S., and Robert J. Gordon, 1988. "The Estimation of Prewar GNP: Methodology and New Evidence," working paper, National Bureau of Economic Research, Inc., Cambridge, Mass.

Baran, P., and P. Sweezy, 1966. *Monopoly Capital*. New York: Monthly Review Press.

Beard, Charles A. and Mary R., 1927. *The Rise of American Civilization*, 2 vols. New York: Macmillan.

Billings, Dwight B., 1979. *Planters and the Making of a "New South": Class, Politics, and Development in North Carolina, 1865–1900*. Chapel Hill: University of North Carolina Press.

Block, Fred, 1977. *The Origins of International Economic Disorder*. Berkeley: University of California Press.

1987. *Revising State Theory: Essays in Politics and Postindustrialism*. Philadelphia: Temple University Press.

Brody, David, 1980. *Workers in Industrial America*. Oxford University Press.

1984. Review of "Segmented Work, Divided Workers," *Journal of Interdisciplinary History*, 14 (Winter): 701–5.

Burnham, Walter Dean, 1970. *Critical Election and the Mainsprings of American Politics*. New York: W. W. Norton.

1981. "The 'System of Ninety-Six': An Analysis," in *The Evolution of American Electoral Systems*, ed. Paul Kleppner *et al.*, pp. 147–202. Westport, Conn.: Greenwood Press.

Cooper, Richard N., 1982. "The Gold Standard: Historical Facts and Future," *Brookings Papers on Economic Activity*, no. 1: 1–56.

Council of Economic Advisers, 1983. *Economic Report of the President 1983*. Washington, D.C.: US Government Printing Office.

Dam, Kenneth W., 1982. *The Rules of the Game: Reform and Evolution in the International Monetary System*. University of Chicago Press.

Epstein, Gerald A., and Juliet B. Schor, 1990. "Macropolicy in the Rise and Fall of the Golden Age," in Marglin and Schor, pp. 126–52.

Faulkner, Harold U., 1951. *The Decline of Laissez-Faire.* New York: Holt, Rinehart, and Winston.

Foner, Eric, 1988. *Reconstruction: An Unfinished Revolution, 1863–77.* New York: Harper and Row.

Frickey, Edwin, 1947. *Production in the United States, 1860–1914.* Cambridge, Mass.: Harvard University Press.

Friedman, Milton, and Anna J. Schwartz, 1982. *Monetary Trends in the United States and the United Kingdom.* University of Chicago Press.

Galbraith, John K., 1987. *Economics in Perspective.* Boston: Houghton Mifflin.

Glyn, Andrew, Alan Hughes, Alain Lipietz, and Ajit Singh, 1990. "The Rise and Fall of the Golden Age," in Marglin and Schor, pp. 39–125.

Goodwyn, Lawrence, 1976. *Democratic Promise: The Populist Movement in America.* Oxford University Press.

Gordon, David M., Richard Edwards, and Michael Reich, 1982. *Segmented Work, Divided Workers: The Historical Transformation of Labor in the United States.* Cambridge University Press.

Gordon, David M., Thomas E. Weisskopf, and Samuel S. Bowles, 1983. "Long Swings and the Nonreproductive Cycle," *American Economic Review*, 73 (May): 152–7.

Hacker, Louis M., 1965. *The Triumph of American Capitalism.* New York: McGraw-Hill.

Hansen, Alvin, 1941. *Fiscal Policy and Business Cycles.* New York: W. W. Norton.

Hoffman, Charles, 1956. "The Depression of the Nineties," *Journal of Economic History*, 16 (December): 137–64.

    1970. *The Depression in the Nineties: An Economic History.* Westport, Conn.: Greenwood Press.

Jones, Stanley L., 1964. *The Presidential Election of 1896.* Madison: University of Wisconsin Press.

Kendrick, John, 1961. *Productivity Trends in the American Economy.* Baltimore: Johns Hopkins University Press.

Kuznets, Simon, 1961. *Capital in the American Economy: Its Formation and Financing.* Princeton University Press.

Lebergott, Stanley, 1964. *Manpower in Economic Growth: The U.S. Experience.* New York: McGraw-Hill.

    1984. *The Americans: An Economic Record.* New York: W. W. Norton.

Lewis, W. Arthur, 1978. *Growth and Fluctuations 1870–1913.* London: George Allen and Unwin.

Marglin, Stephen A., and Juliet B. Schor (eds.), 1990. *The Golden Age of Capitalism.* Oxford: Clarendon Press.

Montgomery, David, 1967. *Beyond Equality: Labor and the Radical Republicans.* New York: Knopf.

    1987. *The Fall of the House of Labor.* Cambridge University Press.

Moore, Barrington, Jr., 1967. *Social Origins of Dictatorship and Democracy.* Boston: Beacon Press.

Nolan, Peter, and P. K. Edwards, 1984. "Homogenize, Divide and Rule: An Essay on 'Segmented Work, Divided Workers,'" *Cambridge Journal of Economics*, 8 (June): 197–215.

Pollack, Norman, 1987. *The Just Polity: Populism, Law and Human Welfare.* Urbana: University of Illinois Press.

Reich, Michael, 1981. *Racial Inequality: A Political-Economic Analysis.* Princeton University Press.

    1989. "Capitalist Development, Class Relations and Labor History," in *Perspectives on American Labor History*, ed. Carroll Moody and Alice Kessler-Harris, pp. 30–54. De Kalb, Ill.: Northern Illinois University Press.

Rostow, Walt W., 1978. *The World Economy: History and Prospect.* Austin: University of Texas Press.

Sargent, Thomas J., 1983. "The Ends of Four Big Inflations," in *Inflation: Its Causes and Effects*, ed. Robert E. Hall, pp. 41–97. University of Chicago Press.

Schumpeter, Joseph A., 1939. *Business Cycles*. New York: McGraw-Hill.

Shaikh, Anwar, 1978. "An Introduction to the History of Crisis Theories," in *U.S. Capitalism in Crisis*, pp. 23–9. New York: Union for Radical Political Economics.

Sklar, Martin J., 1988. *The Corporate Reconstruction of American Capitalism, 1890–1916*. Cambridge University Press.

Stein, Herbert, 1969. *The Fiscal Revolution in America*. University of Chicago Press.

Sundquist, James L., 1983. *Dynamics of the Party System: Alignment and Realignment of Political Parties in the United States*, revised edn. Washington, D.C.: Brookings Institution.

Temin, Peter, 1971. *Did Monetary Forces Cause the Great Depression?* New York: W. W. Norton.
1989. *Lessons from the Great Depression*. Cambridge, Mass.: MIT Press.

Thomas Brinley, 1954. *Migration and Economic Growth*. Cambridge University Press.

US Department of Commerce, Bureau of the Census, 1917. *Abstract of the Census of Manufactures, 1914*. Washington, D.C.: US Government Printing Office.
1923. *Abstract of the Census of Manufactures, 1919*. Washington, D.C.: US Government Printing Office.
1975. *Historical Statistics of the United States: From Colonial Times to 1970*. Washington, D.C.: US Government Printing Office.

Weisskopf, Thomas E., 1979. "Marxian Crisis Theory and the Rate of Profit in the Postwar U.S. Economy," *Cambridge Journal of Economics*, 3 (September): 341–78.

White, Gerald T., 1982. *The United States and the Problem of Recovery after 1893*. Montgomery: University of Alabama Press.

Wiener, Jonathan, 1978. *Social Origins of Dictatorship and Democracy, Alabama 1860–1885*. Baton Rouge: Louisiana State University Press.

Wilkinson, S. F., 1983. Review of "Segmented Work, Divided Workers," *Contributions to Political Economy*, 2 (March): 92–8.

Williamson, Jeffrey G., 1974. *Late Nineteenth-Century American Development: A General Equilibrium History*. Cambridge University Press.

Wolfson, Martin H., 1986. *Financial Crises: Understanding the U.S. Experience*. Armonk, N.Y.: M. E. Sharpe.

— 3 —

Interpreting the social structure of accumulation theory

DAVID M. KOTZ

Introduction

The social structure of accumulation theory first appeared in the late 1970s and early 1980s in a series of articles and books: Gordon (1978, 1980); Weisskopf (1981); Gordon *et al.* (1982); and Bowles *et al.* (1983). The fundamental claim of this theory is that the alternation between long periods of rapid economic expansion and long periods of stagnation in capitalist history can be explained by the successive creation and then collapse of sets of growth-promoting institutions. Such a set of growth-promoting institutions is referred to as a social structure of accumulation.

This chapter offers a clarification, critique, and reinterpretation of the social structure of accumulation theory. It is organized as follows: after this introductory section a historical context for the social structure of accumulation approach is provided by reviewing some earlier theories of long-run macro-instability. The following section explains the social structure of accumulation approach and offers evaluations and clarifications. This is followed by a critique, in which both conceptual problems and historical applicability are considered. The final section offers a modified version of the social structure of accumulation approach which overcomes some of the difficulties in the current version.

Antecedents

The first formulations of the social structure of accumulation theory, particularly Gordon's (1980), adopted the concept of "long waves," which refers to regular, fifty-year-long cycles in economic growth associated with the work of Kondratieff (1935) and Schumpeter (1939). It was long waves in economic growth that the new theory sought to explain. Over time the advocates of the social structure of accumulation theory moved away from any belief in the regular pattern of long waves in economic growth, and shifted to the term "long swings." This was meant to convey the idea of alternating long periods of rapid growth and stagnation, but without the cyclical regularity suggested by the term "long waves." Table 3.1 gives several dating schemes for long swings in economic growth.

Table 3.1. *The dating of long swings for the world economy*

Turning point	Kondratieff[a]	Mandel[b]	Gordon, Edwards, and Reich[c]	van Duijn[d]
trough	late 1780s–early 1790s	end 18th c.	1790s	—
peak	1810–17	1823	1820	—
trough	1844–51	1847	mid-1840s	1845
peak	1870–75	1873	1873	1872
trough	1890–96	1893	late 1890s	1892
peak	1914–20	1913	World War I	1929
trough	—	1939	World War II	1948
peak	—	1966	early 1970s	1973

Sources: [a]Kondratieff (1935, p. 111).
[b]Mandel (1975, p. 122).
[c]Gordon, *et al.* (1982, table 1.1, p. 9).
[d]van Duijn (1983, table 9.11, p. 163)

The claim that capitalist economic growth exhibits long waves of roughly half-century duration has always been regarded with skepticism by neoclassical economics, which views the economy as strongly stable, particularly in the long run. Thus, it is not surprising that long-wave theory has been the province of unorthodox investigators. The leading early proponents of long waves, Kondratieff (1935) and Schumpeter (1939), worked at fringes of the neoclassical tradition.

Kondratieff's (1935) long-wave theory is based on a capital goods replacement cycle for very long-lived capital goods, which interacts with a cyclical pattern in the mechanism for financing long-run investment. Schumpeter's (1939) theory is also based on the bunching of long-run investments, but the bunching is due to the clustering of major innovations, rather than the periodically favorable credit market conditions and the eventual need to replace old capital goods of Kondratieff's theory.

Despite the differences, the two theories have in common a view of the long wave as an automatic, internally generated phenomenon of the capitalist economy. It is economic factors – capital investment, credit markets, innovations – which are operating, in a predictable and regular way, to cause the long wave. Non-economic developments which might seem to be important causal factors, such as wars, revolutions, and gold discoveries, are viewed either as consequences (rather than causes) or as causal factors of secondary importance.

Neither Kondratieff's nor Schumpeter's theory of the long-wave mechanism has won a wide following, and part of the reason is that most economists have found the theories unconvincing. Comprehensive critiques have been offered by Garvey (1943) for Kondratieff and by Rosenberg and Frischtak (1984) for Schumpeter. The basic problem is the lack of a convincing explanation for why major investments should be bunched over a roughly fifty-year cycle, rather than taking place more evenly over time. Some of the resistance to these long-wave theories springs from the neoclassical belief in the long-run stability of capitalist growth.

But it is by no means limited to that source. Most business cycle theorists, who readily accept the premise that capitalism is inherently unstable on the macro level, have found the above long-wave theories interesting but ultimately unconvincing (e.g. R. A. Gordon, 1961). Probably the most widely held view is the one expressed by Kondratieff's early critics: that the pace of capital accumulation over the long run is indeed uneven but not with any regular, systematic pattern, and that the cause of such unevenness is the occurrence of accidental historical events such as wars, new territorial discoveries, and major technological developments.[1]

Two of the leading Marxist economists of the postwar period, Paul Sweezy and Ernest Mandel, offer theoretical frameworks through which alternating periods of accelerated and depressed growth can be explained. In Sweezy's view the basic laws of motion of capitalism in its monopoly state produce a tendency toward stagnation, because aggregate surplus tends to rise faster than the normal outlets for the absorption of surplus (Baran and Sweezy, 1966). Long periods of vigorous expansion are explained by the presence of external stimuli, such as epoch-making innovations and wars, that temporarily override the basic stagnation tendency. Such stimulus eventually wears out, and the underlying stagnant nature of monopoly capitalism reasserts itself. While Sweezy is critical of the long-wave concept, his theory can explain a pattern of alternating periods of prosperity and stagnation. Prosperous periods come from accidental, external events; depressed periods expose the normal working of the system.

Unlike Sweezy, Ernest Mandel (1980) has embraced the concept of long waves and has sought to ground the concept in Marxian analysis. For Mandel the fundamental law guiding the long-run movement of capital accumulation is Marx's law of the tendency of the rate of profit to fall, resulting from a rising organic composition of capital. A long-wave expansion occurs when several factors tending to counteract the falling rate of profit operate "in a strong and synchronized way" (Mandel, 1980, p. 15). A long period of a rising profit rate follows, which brings vigorous accumulation. Eventually the counteracting factors peter out or are undermined by the growth process, and the law of the falling profit rate reasserts itself. A long-wave depressive phase follows.

For Mandel the transition from long-wave expansion to long-wave contraction is a necessary one which follows from the "internal logic of capitalist laws of motion" (1980, p. 21), that is, from the rise of the organic composition of capital. However, the initiation of a new long-wave expansion is *not* viewed that way: "This upturn cannot be deduced from the laws of motion of the capitalist mode of production by themselves" (1980, p. 21). The upturn is accidental and results from "noneconomic factors" (such as gold discoveries, major innovations, or capitalist victories over the working class), which activate the counteracting tendencies to the falling rate of profit.

It becomes apparent that, despite important differences between Mandel's and Sweezy's theoretical outlooks, significant commonalities are found in their analyses of the long-run course of capital accumulation. For both, the basic laws of motion of capitalism produce stagnation, which is due to internal, automatic, economic factors. The two theorists point to different laws of motion (rising surplus versus rising organic composition), but the end result is the same. Similarly, long expansionary periods are explained by the operation of historically specific factors which counteract the basic law of motion of capitalism. Mandel and Sweezy frequently cite the same historical development to explain a long expansionary period, although the precise impact of any such historical development is viewed differently: e.g. the railroad may be viewed as stimulating investment (Sweezy) or as increasing capital turnover (Mandel). In both views, the historical factors which set off long expansions are seen as accidental, external, and in some instances, non-economic.

The social structure of accumulation approach

In the social structure of accumulation approach, a large array of social factors is incorporated into the explanation of both the expansion and stagnation phases of what are called long swings in economic growth. The causal elements include non-economic as well as economic factors. The crucial innovation offered by the social structure of accumulation approach is that the wide range of causal factors are not viewed as accidental or external. Rather, it is assumed that a large array of social factors, including some in the political and ideological spheres, can be viewed as governed by laws of motion. More precisely, the interaction between the accumulation process and a large set of social factors is assumed to follow a significantly regular and predictable course. This violates an unspoken assumption in previous long-run growth analyses, both Marxian and non-Marxian, that only a small set of narrowly economic factors can produce regular, law-governed behavior. To both Schumpeter and Kondratieff, both expansion and stagnation are caused by a narrow set of economic factors and both phases are regular and predictable. To Mandel and Sweezy, one phase is caused by such a narrow set of economic factors, while the other phase is not; the former phase is law-governed while the latter is accidental.

The primary assertion of the social structure of accumulation approach is that a period of vigorous capital accumulation, or long-swing expansion, requires the existence of a broad set of social institutions which support or facilitate the accumulation process. This set of institutions, which includes political and ideological structures as well as economic ones, is referred to as a social structure of accumulation. The creation of a viable social structure of accumulation ushers in a long period of expansion. However, the long expansion contains the seeds of its own destruction, and ultimately both the social structure of accumulation and accumulation itself collapse, ushering in a long period of stagnation. Eventually a new social structure of accumulation is constructed and the process begins again.

Such is the skeleton of this theory. To flesh it out a bit, four questions must be answered: (1) How does a social structure of accumulation support accumulation? (2) Why does the long-swing expansion phase come to an end? (3) Why does the long-swing stagnation phase come to an end? (4) Why are both phases of long duration, producing an entire swing of roughly fifty years length?

How does a social structure of accumulation support accumulation?

The pursuit of profits is what drives the accumulation process. But profits come only at the end of that process, so capitalists must be able "to make reasonably determinate calculations of their expected rate of return" (Gordon, 1980, p. 12) if they are to undertake accumulation. The social structure of accumulation somehow creates the social stability required to permit the formation of such "reasonably determinate calculations." Without such stability, capitalists put their surplus value, or a large share of it, into financial or speculative investments rather than real accumulation.[2]

To explain how a social structure of accumulation achieves such stability, a laundry list of requirements of the accumulation process is produced, organized around the three major steps in the circulation of capital: the purchase of means of production and labor power (M–C), the production process (C–C'), and the realization process (C'–M'). Gordon's (1980) article offers thirteen institutional requirements for accumulation, and the later book of Gordon et al. (1982) reduces the number to an even dozen. They include such requirements as the following: the availability of raw materials at stable prices (relevant to M–C), effective organization and control of the labor process (relevant to C–C'), an appropriate structure of final demand (relevant to C'–M'), an appropriate system of money and credit (relevant to all three steps in accumulation). The social structure of accumulation, then, is all the social institutions which significantly contribute to fulfilling the requirements of the accumulation process.[3] The institutions making up a particular social structure of accumulation range from the narrowly economic (e.g. large, monopolistic business enterprises which attenuate rivalry and hence aid realization of surplus value) to the political (labor laws which reduce class conflict at the workplace) to the ideological (racist and sexist ideas which divide and weaken the working class and hence stabilize capitalist control of the labor process). The appendix to this chapter offers a list of institutions making up the three social structures of accumulation which have existed in the US.

The laundry list approach is somewhat unsatisfying theoretically, despite efforts to organize the list into subcategories. Why, one wonders, does accumulation have a list of "requirements"? Is it due to the nature of economic growth itself? Or to the specific nature of capitalist expansion? One would expect a Marxian approach to adopt the latter view.

Viewed as a purely technical process, economic growth has certain requirements: appropriate quantities and qualities of inputs, technological advance, and so forth. But *capitalist* economic growth is not simply economic growth in the abstract. A critical feature of the specifically capitalist accumulation process is that it takes place in an environment of conflict. This is not accidental; capitalist relations of production and exchange generate conflict. Such conflict takes two forms: class conflict and competition.

There are various forms of class conflict under capitalism.[4] The fundamental class relation of capitalism, that between capital and labor, entails class conflict over the creation of surplus value and over the conditions attendant upon that process. As the capitalist processes of production and exchange evolve historically, other kinds of class conflict develop, as this historical evolution creates a changing internal structure of the capitalist class. Thus, in contemporary capitalism there is conflict between industrial and financial capital and between monopoly and competitive capital. Such conflicts between sections of the capitalist class are usually viewed as conflicts over the distribution of surplus value, but they may involve other related issues such as control over the production process or influence over the state. If we take account of the existence of nation-states and the international scope of economic relations in the capitalist era, then another type of class conflict becomes apparent: conflicts between capitalists in the country under consideration and various classes in other countries (capitalists, workers, peasants).

In addition to class conflict, the capital accumulation process generates a second source of conflict: competition among capitals. Competition has been modified in various ways as capitalism has evolved; for example, price warfare is normally avoided by large enterprises. But, though the forms have changed, competition for shares of surplus value remains, as it must as long as capital takes the organizational form of more than one enterprise. Since competition is a relation between similar individual units of capital, it cannot be considered a *class* relation or a type of class conflict.

This brings us back to the starting point of the social structure of accumulation approach: the assertion that a long period of vigorous accumulation requires "social stability." The underlying reason *why* a social structure of accumulation must be present for a long-swing expansion to take place is that capitalism is ridden with class conflict and competition. The role of the social structure of accumulation is to regulate class conflict and competition to create sufficient stability and predictability to permit rapid accumulation. An examination of the dozen "requirements of accumulation" listed by Gordon *et al.* (1982) shows that each can be interpreted as arising from the need to contain class conflict and/or competition.[5]

The institutions making up a social structure of accumulation cannot eliminate class conflict, since that is a necessary outgrowth of capitalist relations of production and exchange. What the social structure of accumulation does is to stabilize class conflict and channel it in directions that are not unduly disruptive of accumulation. Class conflict can be stabilized in two ways that represent polar opposites: one class can be crushed, so that its ability to fight for its interests is severely limited; or a compromise can be struck so that the contending groups share, to some degree, the fruits of the accumulation process. Actual social structures of accumulation have reflected a combination of these two modes of operation. For example, the post World War II social structure of accumulation in the US included a "capital–labor accord" which had two sides: the militance and radicalism of organized labor were crushed through Red Purges and repressive labor laws, while labor's cooperation with capital was secured through the legitimation of collective bargaining and big capital's willingness to grant regular pay increases to labor. The capital–labor accord helped meet three of Gordon *et al.*'s requirements for accumulation: it stabilized the labor market, it assured effective capitalist control of the labor process, and it helped create a growing demand for final products.

A social structure of accumulation must also regulate the process of competition so that it does not take forms destructive to accumulation. It does this by creating structures and rules of behavior that prevent intra-industry rivalry from undermining the realization of surplus value. For example, several of the institutions of the early twentieth-century social structure of accumulation in the US dealt with this problem: the monopolization of the industrial sector, the rise of finance capital, direct government regulation of certain industries, and the emergence of a more cooperative "corporate liberal" ideology to replace *laissez faire* individualism.

The role of a social structure of accumulation in relation to the accumulation process can be seen more clearly if we contrast the Marxian view to the neoclassical view of economic growth. In the neoclassical view, capitalism is based on free individuals continually choosing among alternatives. No exploitation is possible, since no coercion is possible. Hence, class conflict plays no essential economic role. Long-run economic growth flows automatically from the assumptions that individuals have unlimited wants and that technology keeps improving. One can still speak of the requirements for rapid economic growth, such as a high savings rate, a culture that validates individual acquisitiveness, and political willingness to rely on free markets. But once the basic political and cultural prerequisites are established, long-run growth is unproblematic.

The Marxian view agrees that capitalism has a powerful tendency to produce economic growth. But the very relationships that create a growth tendency also generate sharp conflicts. Simply having the basic institutions of capitalism in place is seen, by advocates of the social structure of accumulation approach, as insufficient to yield vigorous growth.[6] The latter requires an additional set of social institutions, the social structure of accumulation, to stabilize the conflicts of capitalism. Only then is rapid growth possible.

The existence of a social structure of accumulation has been viewed as permitting capitalists to make reasonably secure estimates of the profit rate. This view is not based on the conventional theory of risk aversion. Rather, the point is that, without a social structure of accumulation, productive investments may be avoided, not because the risk is too high relative to the expected return, but because capitalists cannot form any reasonably secure estimate of the expected return.

This view of the relation between the social structure of accumulation and profitability is too narrow. A social structure of accumulation would also be expected to increase the actual rate of profit as well as permitting secure predictions. Disruptive class conflict reduces the pool of surplus value that is created, and excessive competition reduces the portion of surplus value that is realized. When a social structure of accumulation is established, and class conflict and competition become more stable, profit rates should rise as well as becoming more predictable. This addendum to the social structure of accumulation approach places it more in line with conventional Marxian notions of the determinants of the accumulation process.

Why the expansion phase ends

The social structure of accumulation literature asserts that a long-swing expansion based on a social structure of accumulation cannot go on forever. No simple reason is given for the belief that the long expansion must inevitably give way to stagnation. The crucial event is the weakening and then collapse of the social structure of accumulation. The question is, why must this occur? The reasons found in the literature fall into three categories.

First, the accumulation process contains crisis tendencies (underconsumption, rising organic composition, etc.) which eventually break out in the form of a serious accumulation crisis. This, in turn, undermines the social structure of accumulation, because the latter requires resources for its maintenance, which dry up as the economy stagnates, and because an accumulation crisis creates social pressures and conflicts which undermine the social structure of accumulation (Gordon, 1980, p. 19).

Second, like the accumulation process, the social structure of accumulation is presumed to contain contradictions which may lead to its collapse (Gordon, 1980, pp. 19–20). If, as has been suggested in this chapter, we conceive of a social structure of accumulation as stabilizing, yet not eliminating, class conflicts and competition, then we can think of the continuing, although stabilized, class conflicts and competition as being the root of internal contradictions in the social structure of accumulation. Continuing class conflict and competition ultimately cause institutions in the social structure of accumulation to collapse. For example, Bowles et al. (1983) argue that in the late 1960s the capital–labor accord broke down, causing a productivity growth slowdown and ultimately contributing to the accumulation crisis of the 1970s.

A third cause of breakdown is found in the relationship between accumulation and its supporting social structure of accumulation. Here there are two subcases. First, the accumulation process undermines the social structure of accumulation (Gordon et al. 1982, pp. 29, 34). For example, the rapid world accumulation in the post World War II period led to recovery and rapid progress in war-ravaged Europe and Japan, which ended the total US economic domination of world markets and hence undermined a key institution of the postwar social structure of accumulation, the Bretton Woods monetary system, which had been based on US economic dominance. In the second subcase, the very same social structure of accumulation shifts from being a support of accumulation to being a hindrance. An example involves the institution of "technical control," which refers to the adoption of technical production systems which have, built into them, effective modes of control over the labor process (Edwards, 1979, ch. 7). The assembly line is viewed as an instance of technical control. Growing use of technical control is viewed as one of the institutions of the early twentieth-century social structure of accumulation. While this institution initially was effective, in that it forced individual workers to perform at the desired intensity of labor, eventually workers learned to use that institution to their advantage: a strike by a part of a plant's workers could quickly shut down an entire plant complex. Thus, technical control was transformed from an aid to accumulation into an obstacle.

The common root in all of these cases of breakdown is the presence of contradictions within the totality, *accumulation process–social structure of accumulation*. Eventually such contradictions cause the social structure of accumulation to collapse and accumulation to be arrested. The relevant contradictions are found in the accumulation process, in the social structure of accumulation, and in the relationship between the two.

Why the stagnation phase ends

In the usual Marxian view of the short-run business cycle, the recession phase is seen as having a restorative effect, resolving the problems which led to the recession and creating the conditions for a new business cycle expansion. The social structure of accumulation approach emphasizes that, while this is true of business cycle recessions, there is no automatic mechanism which causes a long period of stagnation (sometimes called a long-swing crisis) to pass over into another long-swing expansion. Resolving a long-swing crisis is believed to require the construction of a new social structure of accumulation, which can only emerge from a complex economic, political, and ideological process that has no inevitability about it. A long-swing crisis may end in a socialist transformation, if the working class has sufficient strength and consciousness and the capitalist class is sufficiently weak and demoralized. Barring that possibility, in principle a long-swing crisis might go on for an indefinite period of time, if contending groups and classes were unable to construct a new, viable social structure of accumulation. Thus, the social structure of accumulation approach may appear to be similar to the Mandel and Sweezy theories, with the turn from expansion to stagnation automatic and the turn from stagnation to expansion dependent on purely accidental events.

However, drawing that conclusion would involve a misreading of the social structure of accumulation approach. While the construction of a new social structure of accumulation may not be inevitable, there are powerful forces that push in that direction. A long period of stagnation sets off sharp struggles among various groups and classes. Initially each tries to protect its narrow interests and its real income in the face of economic decline. As the crisis continues, it puts pressure on every group to come up with institutional reform proposals that would get the economy growing again. This pressure will intensify until a workable social structure of accumulation emerges from the fray.

But exactly how a new social structure of accumulation emerges is unclear. Does it result from a coherent coalition of classes and groups creating a program which it then puts into effect? Or does a social structure of accumulation emerge out of parts of various non-allied groups' programs? The former route would explain how a cohesive, integrated social structure of accumulation could be created, but one wonders how close to the reality of history that is. The latter route corresponds more closely to the actual history of institutional reform, but one wonders how a unified, integrated social structure of accumulation could emerge out of such a process. We shall return to this problem in the next section.

The social structure of accumulation literature asserts that the social structure of accumulation underlying each new long-swing expansion is unique; a previous social structure of accumulation cannot be resurrected to do the job. Thus, each long expansion represents a new stage of capitalism, not merely a repetition of a past cycle of expansion and decline.

None of the literature gives a clear reason for the uniqueness of each social structure of accumulation. Gordon (1980, p. 21 and n. 41) suggests that the reason is the integrated nature of a social structure of accumulation. Gordon et al. (1982, pp. 31–2) suggest it results from the change in concrete historical conditions over time. If, as suggested in this chapter, one views the role of a social structure of accumulation as the stabilization of class conflicts, then the fact that classes and class relations change over time implies that a set of institutions which had effectively stabilized class relations in the past would no longer do so at a later date. For example, the ideology of rugged individualism was an effective one in the mid nineteenth-century United States, an era of small capitalists and significant upward mobility among workers. Such an ideology would not serve to stabilize class relations in the 1980s or 1990s, with the dominance of giant enterprises closely intertwined with the state, and limited upward mobility from the working class. A new set of institutions is required to handle each new stage in the evolution of classes and class relations.[7] However, this does not preclude the continuation of some institutions from one social structure of accumulation to another, perhaps with some modifications.

Why are long swings long?

Why should the successive expansion and stagnation periods that are based on the rise and fall of a social structure of accumulation be so long? Why the roughly fifty years claimed by Kondratieff? Why not ten or twenty years? Gordon's (1980) answer is that the construction of a new social structure of accumulation necessitates very-long-run investments to create the infrastructural underpinnings of the social structure of accumulation, which include new transportation systems, communications systems, systems of raw materials supply, etc. The length of the long-swing expansion results from the long-lasting impetus from such an infrastructural investment boom.

This neo-Kondratieffian view was relegated to a footnote in Gordon et al. (1982). There the length of the long-swing expansion was explained by the durability of the social institutions that make up a social structure of accumulation. The length of the stagnation phase is due to the protracted process of struggle and compromise required to create a new social structure of accumulation. This explanation does not seem completely satisfactory. What determines how durable institutions are, and how long it takes to build new ones? The social structure of accumulation literature admits that this is an imprecise business, and hence one cannot predict, nor should one expect, a uniform length for successive phases. We shall argue in the next main section that the durability of institutions making up the social structure of accumulation has been exaggerated, which would seem to undermine the usual explanation for why long-swing expansions are so long.

The promise of the social structure of accumulation approach

The social structure of accumulation approach is a step forward in the effort to explain alternating periods of accelerated and retarded growth in capitalist history. Earlier theories based on the innovation process or capital replacement cycles were not very plausible, and despite some problems with the social structure of accumulation approach, it offers a more coherent, believable explanation. Within the Marxian tradition, it offers an alternative to theories such as Mandel's and Sweezy's which view stagnation as the normal state of capitalism. The latter type of theory may be compared with the mainstream view that the normal state of capitalism is healthy growth. Capitalism has been around for a long time, and both conditions keep recurring for significant time periods. There seems no good reason to suppose that either pole of capitalist performance is more "normal" than the other. The social structure of accumulation approach recognizes this and treats both types of performance as normal.

The social structure of accumulation approach broadens the range of social phenomena that are considered to work in systematic ways. It breaks with the view that only narrowly economic phenomena can influence the accumulation process in a significant and systematic way. In so doing, a wide body of historical developments can be linked together and analyzed. The social structure of accumulation approach offers a new way to understand institutional change under capitalism. It helps explain why in certain periods all institutions seem to be susceptible to major transformation (short of transforming the mode of production), whereas in other periods institutions seem relatively immune to assault.

The social structure of accumulation approach also contributes to the theory of the transition from capitalism to socialism. Earlier Marxian theorists suggested ever more severe crises would lead to the transition, or that a complete breakdown would one day force the transition. The social structure of accumulation approach suggests the transition comes in a long-swing stagnation in which the balance of class forces is sufficiently favorable for the working class and its allies.

This provides a new context for understanding the role of reform struggles. For a century Marxists have debated the relation between the fight for reforms within capitalism and the effort to abolish capitalism. One pole in this debate has argued that successful reform struggles strengthen the socialist movement, weaken capital, and thus help pave the way toward socialism. The other pole has asserted that successful reform struggles lead to cooptation of the working class, a stabilization of capitalism, and hence a postponement of socialism.

According to the social structure of accumulation approach, a long-swing crisis period is inevitably a period of institutional change. Furthermore, the precise nature of the institutional changes that will emerge is not foreordained. It will arise out of the complex class struggles of the period. Even if socialism is not yet on the agenda, the working class and the socialist movement can still influence the character of the next social structure of accumulation. And one possible social structure of accumulation may be more favorable than another for the working class and for the development of the socialist movement during the next long-swing expansion. This in turn will influence the possibilities for socialist transformation in the next long-swing stagnation.

Problems in the social structure of accumulation approach

In its present stage of development, the social structure of accumulation approach is still insufficiently worked out and leaves a number of important questions unanswered. One is whether there are rules governing the structure of the social structure of accumulation. That is, beyond saying that a social structure of accumulation aids accumulation and does so by stabilizing class conflicts and competition, can anything further be said about how a social structure of accumulation works? What sort of institutions are possible constituents of a social structure of accumulation and what sort are not? Are there any trends in the successive social structures of accumulation (such as increasing centralization of power and decision-making)? Or are we left with the conclusion that every social structure of accumulation is unique?

Is there a common pattern to the breakdown of a social structure of accumulation that leads to stagnation? Or is each breakdown historically unique, within the broad framework described above of contradictions within the totality, accumulation process–social structure of accumulation, setting off the crisis?[8] Once the crisis arrives, can we say anything specific about the manner in which a new social structure of accumulation emerges from the cauldron of class conflict? Does the creation of a new social structure of accumulation require the assembling of a class coalition with the power to make the necessary institutional changes? Or does the social structure of accumulation emerge more haphazardly out of the small victories of many different groups? If the latter is the case, what makes the social structure of accumulation an integrated, workable whole?

The problems with the social structure of accumulation approach are not limited to its incompleteness. There is a set of interconnected problems that are of a mixed conceptual and historical nature. That is, the problems involve weaknesses in the conceptual apparatus that are closely linked to the historical applicability of the approach. These interconnected problems are three: the timing of the creation of a social structure of accumulation in relation to the associated long-swing expansion; the stability and durability of the institutions which make up the social structure of accumulation; and the conception of the social structure of accumulation as a unified, integrated whole.

The social structure of accumulation literature asserts that the construction of a new social structure of accumulation is the necessary prerequisite for the initiation of a long-swing expansion.[9] Yet historical investigation shows that some constituent institutions of past social structures of accumulation did not develop until long after the associated long-swing expansion had begun. I will give two examples.

The US experienced a long-swing expansion from the late 1890s through the 1920s.[10] In the social structure of accumulation literature one learns that an important institution in the social structure of accumulation associated with that expansion was state regulation of business (Bowles *et al.*, 1983, pp. 248–9; Weiss-kopf, 1981, p. 14). This refers to new government initiatives in such as areas as antitrust, regulation of natural monopolies, regulation of banking and finance, and consumer protection regulation (e.g. meat inspection and drug regulation). The basic argument is that such state interventions had the effect of stabilizing the new system of giant corporations.

However, a careful reading of the historical record reveals a different picture. Significant extension of the Federal government's regulatory role began shortly after the turn of the century, under Theodore Roosevelt's administration. These initiatives sprang from several sources, of which two were most important. One source was opposition to the new giant corporations and powerful financial groups that had emerged from the turn-of-the-century merger movement. This opposition came primarily from smaller capitalists, farmers, and sections of the professional class.[11] From these groups there developed an anti-monopoly movement which had significant power during the so-called Progressive Era (1900–16). The second source of regulatory initiatives was the new monopolists themselves who, seeing the gathering storm, sought to channel reform in directions that would not only avoid harm to their interests but actually advance them.[12]

The anti-monopoly movement had sufficient power, until about 1916, to press the state into undertaking a series of actions which, far from stabilizing big business, created serious instability and uncertainty for them. The most dramatic example is the major antitrust suits filed against almost all of the biggest corporations during this period.[13] Two of them, Standard Oil and American Tobacco, were actually broken up, and several others had their operations significantly affected by the suits. These antitrust actions were a major part of the new government relation to business in this period, and it would strain credulity to interpret these as a factor which helped stabilize the environment in which capitalists operated.[14]

It is true that the monopolists tried to bend the reforms to their purposes, and in some cases they succeeded. Nevertheless, the anti-monopoly movement was at least equal in power to the monopolists in those years, and the latter suffered as many defeats as victories. A notable defeat was the big-business-based National Civic Federation's failure to secure passage of the Hepburn Act in 1908, due to opposition from smaller business to the proposed Act's weakening of antitrust enforcement.[15]

It was only during the war and postwar years of 1917–20 that the anti-monopoly movement collapsed and the monopoly capitalists were able to establish a securely dominant position with regard to the state in general and state regulatory policy in particular. By that point the new state regulatory role was operating so as to stabilize big business.[16] But the long-swing expansion was already about twenty-five years old! In fact, it had only one more decade to go before the great crash.

Another example of the tardy development of an institutional component of a social structure of accumulation involves the Bretton Woods system, widely viewed as a central part of the post World War II social structure of accumulation. The Bretton Woods system was a set of international monetary, trade, and investment relations which included a gold-backed US dollar, freely convertible currencies at fixed exchange rates, and an open world economy. The IMF was the key agency created to oversee the system.

The famous conference was held at Bretton Woods, New Hampshire, in 1944. But the Bretton Woods system itself did not begin functioning right away. The US dollar began to operate as the major world trading currency right away, and the IMF set up shop by 1946. But two of the key elements of the system, an open world economy and freely convertible currencies, fell into place much later. Political opposition to an open economy remained strong enough in much of Western Europe to ensure the retention of significant controls through the early 1950s. And the major European currencies did not become freely convertible until December 1958. Until the late 1950s US–European trade limped along based on a series of expedients, such as the Marshall Plan and the economic effects of US rearmament (Block, 1977). The Bretton Woods system is supposed to have aided accumulation by creating a stable system of fixed exchange rates and open economies which stimulated international trade and investment and made more secure any long-run investment having international exchange implications. But the Bretton Woods system was not fully enough established to play such a role effectively until the mid to late 1950s, a decade or more into the expansion. Until then it was not certain that Bretton Woods would ever work as designed. And, ironically, the very year in which Bretton Woods was completed, 1958, was also the first year that the US experienced a sizeable gold drain – the phenomenon that would, over the next fifteen years, bring the Bretton Woods system crashing down.

Thus, it appears that some institutions believed to be part of a social structure of accumulation actually arose long after the start of the long-swing expansion. One could resolve this problem most simply by revising the list of institutions in each social structure of accumulation to exclude the late developers. But that solution would raise another problem: the two late-developing institutions cited, once they had developed, did indeed operate as significant aids to accumulation. Given the definition of a social structure of accumulation found in the literature – "all the institutions that impinge on the accumulation process," excluding "those that touch it [accumulation] only tangentially" (Gordon et al., 1982, pp. 23, 25) – it seems inescapable that government regulation of business and the Bretton Woods system were indeed part of their respective social structure of accumulation, at least for the latter part of the long-swing expansion. The alternative solution to this problem is to reject the assumption that the entire social structure of accumulation must be present for the long-swing expansion to begin. Such a rejection leads to a modified view of the relation between accumulation and the social structure of accumulation, which will be discussed in the next section of this chapter.

The view of institutions making up the social structure of accumulation as stable and durable plays an essential role in the social structure of accumulation analysis. Institutions support accumulation by stabilizing conflicts and creating an atmosphere of predictability; this effect would seem to depend on the institution being stable and durable. And, as mentioned above, the length of the long-swing expansion is explained as a result of the durability of institutions.

Yet a careful examination of the institutions that make up social structures of accumulation suggests that some, rather than being stable and durable over the course of the long-swing expansion, have instead undergone significant change and development over that phase. For example, Keynesian demand management is viewed as an element of the postwar social structure of accumulation in the US. In the late 1940s and early 1950s such a policy was applied, in a halting and inconsistent manner, mainly aimed at keeping unemployment down. During the Eisenhower Presidency, Keynesian demand management was used even more haltingly and was mainly aimed at preventing low unemployment from leading to inflation. In the 1960s Keynesian policy was finally openly proclaimed and applied in a relatively consistent manner toward economic stimulation, at least through the end of the long-swing expansion. Another example is US government regulation of business in the early twentieth century, discussed above. No sooner had it been set right, during World War I, then it began to fade away, as *laissez faire* came to reign in the Roaring Twenties.

If the institutions of the social structure of accumulation are not stable and durable, how do they support accumulation? And why is the expansion long? This too will be addressed in the following section.

A social structure of accumulation is viewed not just as a collection of accumulation-supporting institutions but rather as an integrated whole. This explains why, when one or more institutions begin to break down, the entire social structure of accumulation will cease to function and a crisis will ensue. Not just one or two institutions but a broad range of them must be reformed, which explains the length of the long-swing crisis.

If some institutions in the social structure of accumulation arise late, and if others change and develop over the course of the expansion, then the social structure of accumulation no longer appears as a unified, integrated whole. It seems to be able to function despite the temporary absence of some institutional components and the continual change of others. We thus have another problem in need of resolution.

A modified social structure of accumulation approach

The observations in the previous section suggest a somewhat modified picture of the relation between a social structure of accumulation and the capital accumulation process. First, the initiation of a new long-swing expansion may require, not the presence of a complete social structure of accumulation, but rather a core of a social structure of accumulation. That is, a small set of new institutions may be sufficient to set off the long-swing expansion. This core of institutions must be sufficient to significantly stabilize class conflicts and competition, and to assure long-term markets. For the early twentieth-century expansion in the US, the following institutions might have made up the core: monopoly/finance capital, repression of trade unions, and an aggressively imperialist policy. The core institutions of the post World War II expansion in the US might have been peaceful collective bargaining, militarization of the economy, and US ascent to a dominant position in the world. In each case, the institutions cited were in place right at the beginning of the expansion. Each institution cited displayed significant stability and durability over the expansion period. And each institution was an important force in stabilizing class conflicts and/or competition and/or creating markets.

The new core of a social structure of accumulation must be compatible with any holdovers from the past social structures of accumulation. Thus, the peaceful collective bargaining of the postwar social structure of accumulation fitted in with the monopolized economy; it would not have been conceivable in a small business economy. The possibility of creating the core of a social structure of accumulation out of the chaotic class struggle of a crisis period is more believable than the simultaneous creation of a whole range of new institutions. One can even imagine such a core emerging out of one coalition's program.

The next step is that, as the accumulation process gathers momentum and the core institutions gain strength and acceptance, the remaining institutions of the social structure of accumulation are gradually created. Through this process the remaining institutions are constrained to fit in with the core. Seen in this light, the development of a relatively unified, integrated social structure of accumulation appears plausible.

However, neither core nor peripheral institutions of the social structure of accumulation are entirely stable, and both undergo evolution under the impact of continuing class conflict and competition. Contradictions within the social structure of accumulation appear early in its life, as do contradictions between the social structure of accumulation and the accumulation process. But the expansion rolls on, stimulated by the continuing extension of the social structure of accumulation through the creation of new institutions and through the stimulating effect of long-run investments made at the early stage of the long-wave expansion (the Kondratieff–Gordon effect).

The crisis occurs when the contradictions within the totality, accumulation process–social structure of accumulation, grow sharp enough that the core institutions begin to break down. This leads the social structure of accumulation as a whole to collapse. Without a viable core of institutions, the process of institution creation and development that had proceeded relatively smoothly is now stymied and rudderless. Only a lengthy period of debate, experimentation, and coalition-building can create a new viable core of institutions and usher in another long-swing expansion. Here history plays an important role, in that the particular contradictions that were most important in causing the breakdown may influence the kind of core that is ultimately created at the end of the crisis. Groups and classes will try to understand the reasons for the crisis, and this understanding will affect the reform programs that emerge. For example, the perceived importance of underconsumption (resulting from highly unequal income distribution) as a cause of the Great Depression had an impact on the kind of core institutions that were created in the following period.

The core model of the social structure of accumulation theory has two advantages over the previously accepted view. It seems to fit the historical evidence better. And it offers a more plausible scenario for the creation of a social structure of accumulation. A brief, and tentative, example of how the core model can be used to explain a long swing might be helpful here.[17]

It was mentioned above that for the postwar social structure of accumulation the core institutions might have been the following three: US dominance in the world, peaceful collective bargaining, and militarization of the economy.[18] Each of these institutions was present at the beginning of the long-swing expansion in the 1940s. US dominance was evident by 1945. Peaceful collective bargaining emerged from the defeat of the 1946 strike wave, the passage of Taft–Hartley in 1947, and the purge of left-wing unions and unionists, beginning in 1946. Militarization of the economy was achieved during the war; military spending declined in 1946–47, but to a rate nearly double the prewar level (relative to GNP), and in 1948 it began to grow again.

These three institutions can plausibly be viewed as emerging from a coherent political program: the Cold War liberalism espoused by a particular coalition of politicians and corporate officials in the 1940s. The three institutions were stable for a long period, remaining in place throughout the long-swing expansion. They were very favorable for accumulation. US dominance in the world assured access to cheap raw materials and foreign markets. Peaceful collective bargaining maintained a stable, predictable labor process and wage relation. A militarized economy assured growing demand in ways that were particularly profitable for industrial capital and did not harmfully impinge on private profit-making activity.

These three institutions were also important bases for the development of other institutions of the postwar social structure of accumulation. US dominance in the world made it possible finally to impose the full Bretton Woods system on reluctant allies, and it facilitated the promotion of a Cold War atmosphere that was favorable for accumulation in a variety of ways. Peaceful collective bargaining provided a framework for the introduction of bureaucratic control of labor. Militarization of the economy provided a means of operating a policy of demand management, and it created a large base of support for the Cold War.

The demise of two of these institutions in the 1960s coincided with the onset of crisis. US dominance was eroded in the late 1960s, as the US armed forces became increasingly mired in Vietnam, and as European and Japanese capitalists rose to a position of parity with US capital. Collective bargaining turned from peaceful to conflictual during the 1960s, as prolonged low unemployment strengthened labor and as capital sought to clamp down through speedups and increased supervision. Military spending relative to GNP finally began to decline significantly somewhat later, in the early 1970s. The earlier collapse of the other two key institutions may have been enough to undermine the social structure of accumulation as a whole, and the accumulation process it had supported. As US dominance weakened, the Bretton Woods system became unworkable, collapsing during 1967–73, and OPEC was able to reverse the cheap raw materials policy in 1973. The collapse of peaceful collective bargaining and the resulting intensification of class conflict at the workplace led to slower productivity growth and reduced profits.

The core version of the social structure of accumulation approach has a number of ambiguities and potential problems of its own. How can one determine which institutions, from among those present at the start of a long-swing expansion, make up the core of the new and developing social structure of accumulation? Are there limitations on the type of institution that can be in the core of a social structure of accumulation? What is the role of institutions which assure long-term adequacy of markets for the products of capitalist production (such as militarization of the economy)? How do such institutions fit into the picture of the social structure of accumulation as essentially stabilizing class conflicts and competition?

These ambiguities and problems need resolution. Refining the core model, and making a judgment between it and the traditional version, will require more than theoretical inquiry. The next step will be to apply the core model in a program of historical investigation of capital accumulation and the social structures of accumulation of various countries. It will be through confrontation between theoretical analysis and historical investigation that further progress will be made in answering these questions.

Acknowledgment

This chapter is a revised version of "Long Waves and Social Structures of Accumulation: A Critique and Reinterpretation," *Review of Radical Political Economics*, 19(4): 16–38, published in 1987.

Appendix: Social structures of accumulation in the US

Nowhere in the social structure of accumulation literature does one find an attempt to provide a definitive list of the institutions comprising the successive social structures of accumulation of a country. The following list of institutions of the three social structures of accumulation which are presumed to have existed in the US is offered as a reference point for the discussion of social structures of accumulation in this chapter. The institutions listed below have been culled from the various writings in the literature, both published and unpublished, including Gordon *et al.* (1982), Bowles *et al.* (1983), Edwards (1979), and Weisskopf (1981). No attempt has been made to create a comprehensive, consistent listing, since the historical research necessary for that task has not yet been done.

(A) Mid nineteenth-century social structure of accumulation: 1840s–1870s

(1) Competitive industrial structure
(2) Labor process based on craft skill
(3) Simple control of labor (one-person management; see Edwards [1979])
(4) Open immigration
(5) Free land at Frontier
(6) State aid for creation of transportion system
(7) Philosophy of individualism
(8) Work ethic

Breakdown of mid nineteenth-century social structure of accumulation: *1870s–1890s.*

(B) Early twentieth-century social structure of accumulation: 1890s–1910s

(1) Concentrated industrial structure
(2) Finance capital (close financial–industrial links, with coordinating role for major banks)
(3) Homogeneous, semi-skilled labor
(4) Technical control of labor (machine-pacing; see Edwards [1979])
(5) Corporate welfare plans
(6) State repression of trade unions
(7) Imperialist expansionism beyond continental US
(8) New state regulation of business (see Kolko [1963] and Weinstein [1968])
(9) Corporate liberal philosophy (see Weinstein [1968])

Note: Gordon *et al.* (1982) use the term "the drive system" to encompass aspects of numbers (3) and (4) above together with increased reliance on foremen and supervisors to control the labor process.

Breakdown of early twentieth-century social structure of accumulation: *1920s–1940s (1930s–1940s in some accounts).*

(C) Mid twentieth-century social structure of accumulation: 1940s–1960s

(1) Bretton Woods system
(2) US military, political, and economic dominance in world
(3) Multinational corporation
(4) Cheap raw materials policy
(5) Cold War ideology
(6) Militarization of economy
(7) Peaceful collective bargaining
(8) Segmentation of labor
(9) Bureaucratic control of labor (see Edwards [1979])
(10) Racism and sexism
(11) Keynesian demand management

(12) Modest welfare state
(13) Microstabilization programs for key sectors (agriculture, oil)
(14) State promotion of growth (education, highways, R&D)
(15) State regulation of financial sector
(16) New Deal Democratic coalition

Note: In Bowles *et al.* (1983), numbers (1)–(6) are grouped under "Pax Americana," numbers (7)–(10) are a "capital–labor accord," and (11)–(14) are a "capitalist–citizen accord."

Breakdown of mid twentieth-century social structure of accumulation: *1960s–present.*

Notes

1 See Day (1976, p. 71).
2 Financial and speculative investments do not actually use up the resources invested. However, by indirect processes, the decision of capitalists to make such investments, rather than productive investments, does slow the accumulation process.
3 Nearly every social institution has some effect, direct or indirect, on the accumulation process. But a social structure of accumulation includes only those institutions whose effect on accumulation is positive and is judged to be significant.
4 The term "class conflict" is used here to include not only conflict between two different classes (e.g. capital and labor) but also between two sections of the same class (e.g. financial and industrial capital). Some writers reserve the term "class conflict" for the former type of conflict, using a term such as "intra-class conflict" for the latter type.
5 Unfortunately, Gordon *et al.* (1982) separate out the regulation of class conflict and competition as two of their twelve requirements for accumulation. In my view, the regulation of class conflict and/or competition lies behind their remaining ten requirements for accumulation. They also list as one of the twelve requirements for accumulation an appropriate pattern of state involvement in the economy. This can be more usefully viewed as an aspect of all the other requirements of accumulation, which the state will influence in one way or another.
6 The basic institutions of capitalism are generalized commodity production, ownership and/or control of the means of production by a distinct class of capitalists, and the wage labor relationship.
7 Another possible explanation for the uniqueness of each social structure of accumulation might be the development of the forces of production over time, which would require new institutions to underpin accumulation in a later time period.
8 In Gordon *et al.* (1982), there does not seem to be a common pattern to long-swing contractions. By their account, the early twentieth-century social structure of accumulation in the US ultimately collapsed because of the success of its key element, the drive system of labor control. This system of labor control held down wages while promoting rapid productivity growth, causing an underconsumption problem that ushered in the Great Depression of the 1930s. By contrast, the mid twentieth-century social structure of accumulation collapsed in the 1960s and 1970s when the previously effective capital–labor accord was eroded, bringing heightened class conflict and slower productivity growth. Gordon *et al.*'s (1982) analysis of social structure of accumulation breakdowns is found on pp. 94–9, 162–4, and 215–27.
9 Gordon (1980) states: "the social composite of these individual structures [the social structure

of accumulation] must exist and function reliably in order for capital accumulation to proceed smoothly." (p. 17).

10 Most analysts date the end of that worldwide expansion around the time of World War I. However, vigorous expansion continued in the US for most of the 1920s, and some analysts regard this expansion as lasting until 1929, at least in the case of the US (Bowles *et al.* 1983, p. 243; van Duijn, 1983, ch. 9).

11 See Weinstein (1968) for a useful analysis of this process.

12 This aspect of the Progressive Era reforms is discussed, to the exclusion of other aspects, by Kolko (1963).

13 Targets of such suits included Standard Oil, American Tobacco, US Steel, International Harvester, Armour, Swift, American Sugar Refining, Aluminum Company of America, and Dupont Chemical.

14 Kolko (1963) interprets the Progressive Era reforms as essentially pro-big business. When faced with the active trust-busting that took place under President Taft, he refers to the latter as "an enigma." (p. 165).

15 The Hepburn Act was an early version of what was later passed into law as The Federal Trade Commission Act. The former was much more favorable to big business than was the latter. See Weinstein (1968, pp. 79–82).

16 After World War I antitrust policy was never again used for a general assault on big business. Instead, it became an institution for smoothing over the relations between big and small capital and within big capital.

17 To keep this example brief, it will of necessity be oversimplified.

18 Bowles *et al.* (1983) describe the post World War II social structure of accumulation in the United States as based on three "institutional structures": "Pax Americana," "The Limited Capital–Labor Accord," and "The Capitalist–Citizen Accord" (pp. 65–79). This differs from the core version of the social structure of accumulation model being proposed here, in that Bowles *et al.*'s three institutional structures are simply categories for grouping the entire set of institutions that make up that social structure of accumulation. By contrast, the core of a social structure of accumulation, as conceptualized here, is a subset of the institutions of that social structure of accumulation.

References

Baran, P., and P. Sweezy, 1966. *Monopoly Capital*. New York: Monthly Review Press.

Block, Fred, 1977. *The Origins of International Economic Disorder*. Berkeley: University of California Press.

Bowles, S., D. Gordon and T. Weisskopf, 1983. *Beyond the Wasteland: A Democratic Alternative to Economic Decline*. Garden City, N.J.: Anchor Press/Doubleday.

Day, R., 1976. "The Theory of the Long Cycle: Kondratieff, Trotsky, Mandel," *New Left Review*, no. 99: 67–82.

Edwards, Richard C., 1979. *Contested Terrain*. New York: Basic Books.

Garvy, George, 1943. "Kondratieff's Theory of Long Cycles," *Review of Economic Statistics*, 25(4): 203–20.

Gordon, David, 1978. "Up and Down the Long Roller Coaster," in *U.S. Capitalism in Crisis* ed. Union for Radical Political Economics, pp. 22–35. New York: Union for Radical Political Economics.

    1980. "Stages of Accumulation and Long Economic Cycles," in *Processes of the World System*, ed. T. Hopkins and I. Wallerstein, pp. 9–45. Beverley Hills, Calif.: Sage Publications.

Gordon, D., R. Edwards, and M. Reich, 1982. *Segmented Work, Divided Workers*. Cambridge University Press.

Gordon, R. A., 1961. *Business Fluctuations*, 2nd edn. New York: Harper and Row.

Kolko, Gabriel, 1963. *The Triumph of Conservatism*. New York: Macmillan.

Kondratieff, N. D., 1935. "The Long Waves in Economic Life," *Review of Economic Statistics*, 17(6): 105–15.

Mandel, Ernest, 1975. *Late Capitalism*, rev. edn., London: New Left Books.

1980. *Long Waves of Capitalist Development*. Cambridge University Press.

Rosenberg, N., and C. Frischtak, 1984. "Technological Innovation and Long Waves," *Cambridge Journal of Economics*, 8: 7–24.

Schumpeter, Joseph, 1939. *Business Cycles: A Theoretical, Historical, and Statistical Analysis of the Capitalist Process*. New York: McGraw-Hill.

van Duijn, J. J., 1983. *The Long Wave in Economic Life*. London: George Allen and Unwin.

Weinstein, James, 1968. *The Corporate Ideal in the Liberal State, 1900–1918*. Boston: Beacon Press.

Weisskopf, Thomas, 1981. "The Current Economic Crisis in Historical Perspective," *Socialist Review*, 11(3): 9–53.

— 4 —

Social structures of accumulation, contingent history, and stages of capitalism

TERRENCE MCDONOUGH

The current economic and social crisis has brought Marxian theories of crisis to the forefront of Marxian debate. Traditionally, Marxian crisis theories have sought the origin of capitalist crises within the abstract economic laws of motion of capitalism. These theories were developed and refined in the context of the capitalist crises of the late nineteenth century and the 1930s, which appeared to portend the end of capitalism and to demand the transition to socialism as their only solution. The subsequent capitalist recoveries at the turn of the century and after World War II have informed current discussions of Marxian crisis theory. It is more widely recognized today that theories of capitalist development over time must account for recurrent periods of relatively healthy growth as well as periods of chronic stagnation. This realization revived interest within the Marxist tradition in the Kondratieff long cycle.

It is the purpose of this chapter to discuss the current state of this revival of Marxian long cycle theory. I will examine in detail one strand of this tradition, the Gordon, Edwards, and Reich social structure of accumulation (SSA) approach. I will identify several theoretical problems within the SSA approach. I will then analyze the implications of these problems for the future of the SSA approach as a theory of long waves, concluding that the SSA framework is more adequate as a theory of stages of capitalism than of specifically long waves. Finally, I conclude the chapter with a brief observation concerning the role of this kind of stages theory in integrating the current concern with the political and ideological aspects of society with the more traditional Marxian concern with the history of accumulation.

The Marxian long cycle

Kondratieff (1935) wrote in the twenties in the Soviet Union, hypothesizing a long cycle of growth and stagnation of approximately fifty years duration. While not the first writer to consider the existence of such long cycles within capitalist economies, Kondratieff's work marks the starting point of a tradition of investigation and theorizing about the long cycle which has led a tenuous but persistent existence in the eddies and backwaters of economic thought. One current of long-cycle theorizing has remained within the neoclassical framework where it has received an uneasy welcome. The mainstream of the discipline has been unreceptive to the possibility of long-term instability in capitalist economies implied by the existence of fifty-year cycles. Thus the long cycle within the non-Marxist tradition of economics has been left to institutionalists and others outside the neoclassical tradition (Forrester, 1977; Rostow, 1978; Schumpeter, 1939; van Duijn, 1983). The long cycle has also been taken up within the Marxist tradition, though until recently its welcome in this camp has been even less enthusiastic. The existence of long cycles implicitly denied the existence of the "final crisis of capitalism."

While explaining the lengthy periods of stagnation which long-cycle theory predicts has been perhaps the greatest challenge facing neoclassical theorists of Kondratieff cycles, Marxian theorists have been equally bedevilled by capitalist resurgence and subsequent extended periods of expansion. Most Marxian theorists have traditionally operated within a framework which predicts capitalist stagnation, resulting from a secularly falling rate of profit, chronic underconsumption, class conflict, or some combination of these factors. The challenge to Marxian theorists of alternating periods of capitalist expansion and collapse has been to explain the relatively lengthy periods of apparently unproblematic capital accumulation. Since virtually all brands of Marxian economics predict the breakdown of the capitalist economic institutions of society, Marxists have been forced to look outside of the strictly economic institutions to explain capitalist expansion. For this reason, all the major Marxist writers on Kondratieff phenomena have focused their theories on the accumulation of sets of extra-economic factors which raise the profit rate and encourage reinvestment. These extra-economic factors prominently include political and ideological institutions.

Several recent treatments of Marxian crisis theory operate within this general framework. While retaining the falling rate of profit as the explanation for periods of crisis, Ernest Mandel (1980) ascribes the periods of subsequent recovery to the effect of non-economic factors on the rate of profit. Operating within the Althusserian structuralist tradition, Michel Aglietta (1979) develops a "theory of capitalist regulation" which examines the institutional conditions of existence for various modes of extracting surplus labor. Aglietta explains crisis as the result of the disruptions of these institutions which reproduce historical regimes of capitalist accumulation. Eric Olin Wright (1979), also writing within the Althusserian tradition, argues that several of the competing Marxian crisis theories are true, though each holds for a specific crisis in capitalist history. These crises are resolved through economic, political, and ideological changes which resolve the contradictions which exist at the economic level.

The SSA approach

Perhaps the most explicit integration of political and ideological institutions into Marxian crisis theory is the social structure of accumulation (SSA) approach offered by David Gordon, Richard Edwards, and Michael Reich (1982) in the opening chapters of their book, *Segmented Work, Divided Workers*. They argue that capitalists will not invest in production unless they are able to make reasonably certain calculations concerning expected rates of return. The external environment, that is the socio-politico-economic institutions which influence the accumulation process, is the most important determinant of these expectations. Without a stable and favorable external environment, capitalist investment in production will not proceed. This external environment is the SSA. More specifically, this SSA is defined as all of the institutions that impinge significantly on the accumulation process. The construction, durability, and disintegration of successive SSAs can be used to explain long swings of growth and stagnation in a capitalist economy.

Unresolved theoretical problems

This Marxian focus on the institutional environment of economic growth, especially the variant summarized in Gordon, Edwards, and Reich's social structure of accumulation approach, is the most promising attempt to explain long swings of capitalist growth and stagnation. Using the SSA framework to analyze long waves of capitalist development is, however, a relatively new enterprise. The approach contains three major theoretical problems which are as yet unresolved.[1]

The first major problem concerns a lack of specificity about the exact character of SSAs themselves. Just what constitutes an SSA has not been clear. Most of the existing literature on the SSA approach implicitly treats SSAs as a list of differing institutions, each of which separately impacts upon the profit rate or the capitalist accumulation process. Ernest Mandel (1980) in his treatment of long swings argues that there is not a unified structure which goes beyond a temporary conjunction of several social factors which temporarily raise the profit rate. Gordon et al. devote more energy to locating the specific points in the accumulation process where differing kinds of institutions intervene, but do not ultimately go beyond characterizing the SSA as a list of institutions. Aglietta devotes more attention to identifying the unifying factor in his regimes of accumulation, arguing that the institutions are organized around the extraction of either absolute or relative surplus value. This argument, however, leaves Aglietta unable to account for differing regimes based on the same method of surplus extraction.

This oversight in the theory is serious. Without a theory of the SSA as a whole, the SSA is unable to play the role assigned to it in the explanation of long waves. A long period of stagnation is initiated when the SSA breaks down. An SSA as a whole can only experience breakdown if it contains some internal unity which is in turn susceptible to disintegration. Were the SSA merely a list of autonomous institutions, one or another, or some subset of the institutions might undergo breakdown at any one time. This would not, however, necessarily threaten the reproduction of the SSA as a whole or consequently the capitalist accumulation process. It would only make the list of institutions supporting the profit rate longer or shorter at a given time. If the breakdown of the SSA is to be used to explain the initiation of a long period of stagnation, we must have a concept of the SSA as a unified whole.

The second weakness in the theory concerns the initial construction of the SSA. Explaining the construction of the SSA is essential because this construction marks the beginning of the period of expansion and hence marks the concluding boundary of the long period of stagnation. The timing of the construction of the SSA is crucial in determining the length of the stagnation period. If we are to argue that the period of stagnation is necessarily long we must locate the principles upon which the SSA is constructed. What is it which delays the construction of a new SSA until a long period of time has passed? What explains the construction of the SSA at a particular point in time? The existing SSA literature tends to treat this question in a somewhat perfunctory manner. Mandel goes so far as to argue that the coming together of the institutions which raise the profit rate, and hence initiate the long expansion, is the result of a chance confluence of events. Gordon *et al.*, on the contrary, emphasize conscious intervention and political programs in the genesis of the SSA. Given the political crisis which is often precipitated by an economic crisis, this explanation has an *a priori* plausibility. Indeed, SSAs have usually included the construction of a political coalition which organizes state intervention in the economy and society so as to support, or at least not undermine, the impact of the SSA on the accumulation process. The key issue, however, is whether such political factors are always the motivating force in the construction of the SSA. I don't believe this can be historically supported. We must look elsewhere for the organizing principles in SSA construction. This question is treated below.

SSA theorists have had little trouble explaining why SSAs are ultimately prone to breakdown.[2] The third weakness of the theory of SSAs involves the lack of an explanation as to why the SSA, once constructed, would necessarily endure for a relatively long period of time, especially given the tendencies toward breakdown. This is crucial if the construction of an SSA is to explain the long wave of expansion.

Mandel argues that a rise in the profit rate and a boost from previously unused technical innovations explains the durability of the long wave. Conversely, the inevitable fall in the rate of profit, as the organic composition of capital rises, explains the onset of stagnation. While the utilization of new opportunities for investment may be an important factor in initially fueling a long-wave upturn, a rejection of the inevitability of the falling rate of profit would leave Mandel without a convincing theory of the downturn.[3]

Gordon *et al.* argue that SSAs last for comparatively long periods of time because the institutions which compose them are durable. This explanation of why SSAs endure, however, is unsatisfying. Without a more specific explanation of the longevity of the institutions which compose the SSA, their argument becomes circular; the durability of a set of institutions is explained by the durability of the institutions which compose the set. The theory as it stands has no trouble explaining the disintegration of the SSA, but has difficulty explaining why each SSA should necessarily underpin a specifically long wave of expansion.

In sum, the theory lacks a definition of an SSA which goes beyond a simple list of institutions and describes how these institutions cohere into a single structure which can be considered as a unit. It has no satisfactory account of how such a coherent structure is built in the first place and, while the Marxian long-wave theorists have had no trouble explaining how the deterioration of various SSAs has actually taken place, they have not explained why such deterioration must necessarily be delayed until a long cycle of growth has been produced. These problems have already led Marxian theorists of the Kondratieff phenomenon away from explaining it as the manifestation of a cycle in the strict sense, where expansion follows decline and vice versa with a regular periodicity. Instead these theorists more often speak of long "swings" or "waves" of capitalist development.

The notion of a long swing still, however, lays some claim to being able to identify at least the relative length of the alternating periods of growth and crisis. That is, these periods are "long" rather than short. Vague as this claim is, our identification of the theoretical weaknesses within Marxian long-wave theory calls this contention into question. All new theories contain unanswered questions and areas of vagueness. The existence of these problems in the Marxist theory of long swings does not fundamentally challenge the validity of the theory. It merely defines an agenda of theoretical investigation for the partisans of the theory. Whether the Marxist institutional theories of the long wave, exemplified by the SSA approach, survive will depend on how these questions are answered. In the remainder of this chapter I would like to propose a set of answers to these questions which preserves the SSA approach as an explanation for periods of alternating growth and stagnation in capitalist history, but which challenges its ability to predict that these periods will be necessarily long rather than short.

Possible resolutions

The first theoretical problem we identified is that the theory is without a description of how the SSA constitutes an integrated whole which goes beyond a listing of its component institutions. What is it which integrates an SSA into a coherent whole? I believe the most promising direction in which to look for the answer to this question was proposed by Gordon in one of the earliest expositions of the SSA framework. In this early article, Gordon (1980) proposes that "the interdependencies among the individual institutions create a combined social structure with a *unified* internal structure of its own – a composite whole, in effect, whose intrinsic structure amounts to more than the sum of the individual institutional relationships" (p. 17). For Gordon this unified internal structure is the reason that "changes in any one constituent institution are very likely to reverberate throughout the entire structure, creating instability in all of the other constituent institutions" (p. 17). Thus, postulating this unified integral structure for the SSA is crucial in explaining how the breakdown of the SSA proceeds and eventually produces a crisis of accumulation. This integral structure is thus at the heart of the SSA framework. Gordon solves our first problem by contending that the unifying factor in an SSA arises from the interrelationships between the SSA's constituent institutions. Since each SSA is composed of different institutions, it is likely the relationships between these institutions must be unique to each SSA and hence historically contingent.[4]

If the unity which constitutes an SSA out of a list of separate institutions operating at different levels of society is necessarily specific to each particular SSA, one is led to suspect that the process through which each SSA is constructed must be different as well. However, this is not necessarily the case. Both of the major explanations of how SSAs are put into place, Mandel's fortuitous juxtaposition of relatively autonomously developing institutions and Gordon *et al.*'s political process, are flexible enough to allow the creation of very different types of SSAs. Whether the different historical SSAs were constructed by a similar process can only be determined by looking at actual historical case studies. I take up this task elsewhere in this volume and will only quickly summarize the results below.[5]

In the case of US history, Gordon *et al.* identify two periods when the construction of an SSA took place within a capitalist environment. These are the transition from competitive to monopoly capital at the turn of the twentieth century and the transition to the post-World War II social order which took place in the few years before, during, and after that war.[6] My examination of the construction of SSAs in American history has discovered an organizing principle of sorts in each of the SSAs considered. It is, however, a different principle in each case. The new monopoly capitalist SSA, built at the turn of the twentieth century, was organized around the construction of one powerful central institution – the monopolistic market structure. All of the other core institutions of the SSA developed either in support of this changed market structure or were made possible by it. By contrast, the post-World War II SSA contained a number of powerful institutions, each consistent with the others, but none obviously dominant. In this case, the mobilization around World War II provided the organizing principle. These results are inconsistent with Mandel's notion of a chance confluence of events. Nor are they examples of the political construction of SSAs hypothesized by Gordon *et al.* Most significantly, I have been unable to locate a unified principle of SSA construction. Each of the two American examples of SSA construction appears to have a unique and hence historically contingent principle of SSA construction. If the construction of the SSA is contingent, it is reasonable to assume that its timing will be as well. As the construction of a new SSA marks the end of the stagnation period, there appears to be no basis on which to predict the duration of the stagnation period.[7]

The third problem we noted earlier is that the SSA theory does not have an explanation for the duration of the SSA once it is constructed which accounts for its survival for a long period of time. Gordon *et al.* ultimately argue that "the limits imposed on an expansion are specific to the particular institutions of the existing social structure of accumulation." Thus Gordon *et al.* conclude that the factors which lead to the termination of the accumulation phase of the SSA are historically contingent. This is symmetrical with our conclusion concerning the historically contingent character of the organization of the construction of SSAs and has similar implications for the SSA approach as a theory of long waves. The disintegration of the SSA marks the termination of the expansion phase of the long wave. If the causes of this disintegration are historically contingent, it is reasonable to postulate that its timing must be historically contingent as well. There is thus no *a priori* theoretical reason why any particular SSA should endure for a relatively long or relatively short period of time. Thus the SSA framework is without a convincing explanation of why the period of expansion inaugurated by the construction of an SSA must necessarily be long.

Coupling this observation concerning the historically contingent character of the disintegration of the SSA with our conclusion about the historically contingent character of the construction of the SSA leaves the SSA framework vague on both the length of the expansion period and the length of the crisis.

The role of historical contingency

Thus, resolving the major weaknesses in the SSA framework leads to characterizing the construction of each SSA as historically contingent, its internal unity as historically contingent and its disintegration as historically contingent. Each SSA appears to have its own organizing principle, its own particular history of construction, and disintegrates under the pressure of class struggle and capitalist competition for its own individual reasons at its own particular time. These observations seriously challenge the potential of the SSA framework to account for long swings, long cycles, or long waves of capitalist development. The framework is unable to make statements concerning the timing of the transition from one phase of the wave to the next, from expansion to stagnation and from stagnation to expansion.

These arguments do not, however, challenge the power of the SSA framework to account for periods of relative capitalist prosperity and capitalist crisis in the past and the alternating character of periods of accumulation and stagnation. These observations also do not challenge the necessity of the construction of an SSA to mark the transition from a period of stagnation to a period of expansion. Thus while the SSA framework cannot predict the timing of the emergence of the capitalist economy from crisis, it does predict that the crisis will not be resolved in the absence of the construction of an SSA. While it cannot predict the timing of the breakdown of the SSA, it can predict that such a breakdown is necessary for and marks the inauguration of a capitalist crisis. Thus while the SSA framework has serious problems as a theory of long waves, it is still essential for an understanding of capitalist crisis and recovery. This challenge to the ability of the SSA framework to account for *long* waves is by no means a fatal blow to the usefulness of the theory.

While the SSA approach was developed within the tradition of long-cycle theorizing, there is no reason why the theory must necessarily remain within this tradition. The historical evidence that periods of relative capitalist prosperity and crisis persist over "long" stretches of time is not so compelling as to demand an explanation. The number of observations is necessarily limited by the relatively recent advent of capitalism. The examples we do have are somewhat ambiguous.

Gordon *et al.* observe that their dating of the long-swing phases of expansion and contraction produce phases which vary from sixteen to thirty-two years in length.

Gordon *et al.*'s data presume worldwide capitalist long swings of growth and stagnation. Thus, their dating tends to smooth out differences in the national timing of crisis and recovery. Since political and ideological institutions are an important part of any SSA, and politics and ideology are often specific to particular regions or even nations, it seems appropriate to consider SSAs as national or regional phenomena rather than as ones encompassing the whole of the capitalist world. The interrelatedness of the economies of the various capitalist nations in an age of imperialism will, of course, work to synchronize periods of crisis and recovery. Thus, at least occasionally, periods of worldwide stagnation and accumulation will be produced, without necessarily involving a single worldwide SSA. If the crisis and recovery of the various national SSAs were to be dated, we might expect that the range of the durations of the contraction and expansion phases of the SSAs would be even greater than Gordon *et al.*'s figures of sixteen to thirty-two years.

It could very easily be the case that the relatively long swings in capitalist development in the past are merely the phenomena of those particular SSAs and the subsequent crisis periods resulting from their breakdown. If this is the case, the task which faces the economic historian is the explanation, not of long swings, but of alternating periods of general growth and stagnation. This task the SSA framework does quite satisfactorily.

Stages of capitalism

While the SSA framework may not be usefully characterized as a theory of long waves or long swings, it may provide the starting point for a theoretical solution to two equally long-standing problems in Marxian theory. The first is a clarification of the Marxian concept of stages of capitalism and the second is the relationship between Marxian theories of accumulation and politics and ideology.

Gordon *et al.* provide us with an alternative to characterizing the SSA as the expansion phase of a long swing. They occasionally refer to the successive SSAs as stages of capitalism. In his earlier article introducing the concept of the SSA, Gordon (1980) even defines his project as one of providing a "rigorous theoretical foundation for a theory of stages of accumulation," criticizing Lenin, Hilferding, Baran, Sweezy, and Uno for an *ad hoc* use of the term without a serious attempt to define what is meant by a stage of capitalism (p. 11). Gordon then uses the SSA *as a concept rigorously defining a stage of accumulation* as the basis for defining a "political-economic theory of long cycles." Given the problems we have identified in using the SSA framework as a theory of long cycles or long waves, it is our contention that perhaps Gordon should have contented himself with his characterization of the SSA as a stage in the accumulation of capital and then used it to explain historical periods of alternating growth and stagnation.

Gordon's attempt to use the SSA as a theory of long cycles proved both too ambitious and not ambitious enough. The SSA framework does not contain the mechanisms necessary to control the timing of recovery and crisis and is hence unable to predict long cycles. Despite this problem, in Gordon's subsequent work with Edwards and Reich the aspect of the SSA as a theory of long swings has been accentuated and the characterization of the SSA as a theory of stages of capitalism has receded into the background. Gordon's case that the Marxian notion of stages of capital accumulation is conceptually fuzzy at best is a strong one. Yet the suggestion that capitalism proceeds through various stages has nonetheless been very evocative. Despite its conceptual indeterminacy, it has led a somewhat charmed existence in Marxian economic history, appearing frequently from Lenin's imperialism as the highest stage of capitalism to the characterization of the current period as the era of monopoly capitalism or state monopoly capitalism.

The Marxian notion of stages of capitalism is thus frequently used, but not well defined. The SSA framework holds the promise of resolving this problem in Marxian theory. A stage of capitalism can be conceived as the ensemble of economic, political, and ideological institutions which serve to reproduce capitalist relations of production and accumulation. This is the definition of the SSA. Capitalism proceeds from one stage to the next when the SSA undergoes disintegration, producing crisis. The crisis can only be resolved through the construction of a new SSA, inaugurating a new stage of capitalism. The successive stages of capitalism are thus the successive SSAs in capitalist history.

It is not surprising that the SSA framework should be the resolution of the problem posed to Marxian theory by Lenin's description of imperialism as the highest stage of capitalism. Lenin's *Imperialism: The Highest Stage of Capitalism* (1939 [1916]) was written in the context of an ongoing debate within the international socialist movement which began with Bernstein's *Evolutionary Socialism* (1961 [1899]). Bernstein's volume was an attempt to come to terms with the resurgence of capital accumulation at the turn of the century in Europe. The European depression of the late nineteenth century was widely regarded by socialists as the final crisis of capitalism predicted by Marx. This crisis presaged the final victory of the working–class movement. When the capitalist economy appeared to arise phoenix-like from the dead, the European socialist movement was thrown into a political and theoretical crisis.[8]

Marxists have responded to crises in Marxist theory in one of three ways.[9] The first is to deny the existence of the crisis and assert the complete adequacy of Marxist orthodoxy. This was Karl Kautsky's original position in the ensuing debate. The second method of attempting to deal with the crisis is to introduce into Marxist discourse concepts from other systems of thought. This was Bernstein's strategy. This method of dealing with problems in Marxist theory was eventually criticized by Lenin as revisionism. Lenin's major theoretical contributions, *State and Revolution* (1972 [1917]) and *Imperialism* were both attempts to intervene in this debate over the crisis in Marxist theory generated by the resurgence in capitalist accumulation. Lenin proposed to resolve the problems in Marxist theory by working within the Marxist theoretical framework.

In *Imperialism*, Lenin attempts to give a Marxist account of capitalism's recovery. Within the SSA framework, the rekindling of accumulation in Europe in the late nineteenth century can be accounted for through the construction of a new SSA resolving the preceding crisis. While he contended that the imperialism he described was the final stage of capitalism, Lenin's multidimensional approach to the subject resembles the multi-institutional character of an SSA. Lenin identifies imperialism as not only the international investment of capital and the partition of the globe into colonies controlled by the major capitalist powers. He closely connects imperialism with the new monopoly structure of markets and corporate organization. He argues strongly that the new corporate organization involves the newly achieved supremacy of finance over industrial capital. He contends that monopoly also involves an alteration in the traditional relationship between capital and labor. Significant sectors of the labor movement would become more accommodating toward capital, both economically and politically. He states that the only reason he does not more extensively discuss the political implications of his analysis is to avoid Czarist censorship. Thus, in proposing a Marxist solution to the problem of capitalist resurgence, Lenin not only presents the notion of stages of capitalism, but presages the SSA framework as a more rigorously developed theory of such stages.

By developing a theory of stages of capitalism which includes the full range of institutional conditions of the reproduction of capitalist relations, the SSA framework also points the way toward the resolution of another problem in Marxist theory. The historical failure of economic contradictions to precipitate socialist revolution in the West has generated a great deal of interest in developing a Marxist theory of dynamics in the political and ideological levels of society. This quest was auspiciously initiated by Gramsci's discussion of civil society and coercion and consent. It was continued with less fortunate results by the Frankfurt School's efforts to deal with the triumph of fascism in prewar Europe and the New Left's attempts to explain the absence of a revolutionary working class. This discussion was to regain some of its bearings in the Althusserian structuralist school of Marxism, only to lose them again in post-structuralism.

Interest in these questions has been especially strong lately because of the vitality of the movements collectively labeled the "new social movements." These movements include the black liberation struggle and other national minority movements, the women's movement, the gay movement, the peace movement and the environmental movement. The attempt to understand the sources and implications of this progressive activity from a revolutionary scientific perspective has revived interest in Marxist theories of politics, culture, and ideology. A good deal of important work has been done in these fields. Little has been done, however, to explore how at a conceptual level to integrate advancing understandings of political and ideological dynamics with more traditional concerns with the economic dynamics of the capitalist mode of production.

This lack of integration has impoverished Marxist economic theory and has, to a certain extent, marginalized political and cultural theoretical work within the

Marxist paradigm. The SSA framework solves this problem neatly by bringing political and ideological factors into the center of Marxist analysis of the capital accumulation process. Our formulation of the construction, organizational principles, and disintegration of SSAs as historically contingent strengthens this aspect of the SSA framework. If the unifying organizational principle of an SSA once constructed depends upon the relationships established among its component institutions, then the political and ideological elements within the SSA play the same role in supplying the SSA with an integrative principle as the economic institutions.

If the construction of SSAs is organized in ways which are specific to each SSA, this opens the possibility that political and ideological as well as economic factors can play the key role in the construction of an SSA. Indeed our identification of the prosecution of World War II as the key factor in the construction of the postwar SSA gives prominence to a quintessentially political event. Further examples can be gleaned from the construction of SSAs in other countries.

Recognizing that the factors which lead to the disintegration of an SSA are unique to that SSA opens theoretical space for considering the importance of political and ideological institutions. Class struggle and capitalist competition as the dynamic factors in capitalist social formations have the potential to erode and change the political and ideological, as well as the economic, institutions. Because of the integrated character of the SSA, erosion of any of its important institutions has the potential to precipitate the disintegration of the SSA and hence capitalist crisis. Thus political and ideological institutions play essential roles not only in the composition of the SSA but in its dynamics of construction, reproduction, and disintegration. Because capital accumulation rests on these dynamics within the SSA, the history of capital accumulation also rests on the history of political and ideological institutions alongside the economic factors.

In summary, I have argued that the historically contingent unity of each SSA and the historically contingent construction and disintegration of each SSA weakens the SSA framework as a theory of long waves. I argued, however, that this finding does not significantly diminish the usefulness of the SSA framework, as *long* waves may not really exist and hence not demand an explanation. The SSA may be more usefully and, in some ways, more excitingly designated as a rigorous reformulation of the Marxian notion of stages of capitalism. I also argued that the SSA framework is a way to bring political and ideological institutions into the center of Marxist political economic discourse, not in an *ad hoc* manner, but in a way consistent with the further development of Marxist science.

Notes

1 In addition to the three major problems treated below, it is also important to clarify the relationship between the SSA approach and the basic concepts of historical materialism. See Kotz (this volume, ch. 3) and McDonough (1990).

2 Eric Olin Wright (1979) treats this question while addressing the periodization of capitalist history in the crisis section of his book *Class, Crisis, and the State*. Wright attempts to build a

general structural model of how potential impediments to capital accumulation develop into crises. Basically, Wright argues that class struggle and capitalist competition are the dynamic factors which eventually push the economic level of society out of sync with its broader social environment. Aglietta extends this argument, contending that class struggle can potentially erode any of the institutional conditions of accumulation, be they economic, political, or ideological. This argument is stronger in Aglietta's version, but does not explain why a social structure of accumulation should disintegrate later rather than sooner. Gordon *et al.* contend that SSAs disintegrate because accumulation itself creates obstacles to further successful accumulation and may directly weaken institutions within the SSA. This observation, when taken together with Wright's and Aglietta's emphases on the dynamic character of class conflict within a social structure, holds promise as an explanation as to why SSAs ultimately come unglued.

3 For a review of both sides of the inevitably falling rate of profit controversy, which ultimately comes down in the camp doubting the necessity of the falling rate of profit, see van Parijs (1980).

4 While it is possible for different sets of institutions to have the same set of relations among them, this is unlikely and becomes more unlikely the more institutions are involved.

5 See McDonough (this volume, ch. 6).

6 There are three SSAs in American economic history. The first extends from roughly the end of the Civil War to the turn of the century, the second from the turn of the century to World War II, and the last from World War II to the present. The initiation of the post-Civil War SSA can be considered to be an example of primitive accumulation. There are obviously analogies between the assembling of the economic, political, and ideological conditions for the initiation of capitalist relations of production and the assembling of the conditions for the rekindling of the capitalist accumulation process. Primitive accumulation, however, takes place within a social environment not dominated by capitalist relations of production. Primitive accumulation must be seen as a problem involved in the transition from one mode of production to another. Therefore the construction of the first SSA in each capitalist country takes place under special circumstances which could not be repeated. For this reason, I will not include the construction of the first SSA in US economic history in this discussion.

7 Even if there were a single organizing principle this would not necessarily allow us to make predictive statements as to the timing of the construction of the SSA. Both of the factors identified in our survey of the American construction of SSAs, a change in the industrial market structure and war, do not take place at regular intervals.

8 For a more extensive treatment of these issues see Colletti (1972) and McDonough and Drago (1990).

9 See Althusser (1978).

References

Aglietta, Michel, 1979. *A Theory of Capitalist Development*. London: New Left Books.

Althusser, Louis, 1978. "The Crisis of Marxism," *Theoretical Review*, no. 7 (Sept.–Oct.).

Bernstein, Edward, 1961 [1899]. *Evolutionary Socialism*. New York: Schocken.

Colletti, Lucio, 1972. *From Rousseau to Lenin*. New York: Monthly Review Press.

Forrester, Jay, 1977. "Growth Cycles," *de Economist*, 125(4): 525–43.

Gordon, David M., 1980. "Stages of Accumulation and Long Economic Cycles," in *Processes of the World System*, ed., Terrence Hopkins and Immanuel Wallerstein, pp. 9–45. Beverly Hills, Calif.: Sage Publications.

Gordon, David M., Richard Edwards, and Michael Reich, 1982. *Segmented Work, Divided Workers: The Historical Transformation of Labor in the United States.* Cambridge University Press.

Kondratieff, N. D., 1935. "The Long Waves in Economic Life," *Review of Economic Statistics*, 17 (6): 105–15.

Lenin, V. I., 1939 [1916]. *Imperialism: The Highest Stage of Capitalism.* New York: International Publishers.

1972 [1917]. *The State and Revolution.* Moscow: Progress Publishers.

McDonough, Terrence, 1990. "The Resolution of Crises in American Economic History," *Research in Political Economy*, 13: 129–83.

McDonough, Terrence, and Robert Drago, 1990. "Crises of Capitalism and the First Crisis of Marxism," *Review of Radical Political Economics*, 21 (3): 27–32.

Mandel, Ernest, 1980. *Long Waves of Capitalist Development.* Cambridge University Press.

Rostow, Walter, 1978. *The World Economy.* Austin: University of Texas Press.

Schumpeter, J., 1939. *Business Cycles*, 2 vols. New York: McGraw-Hill.

van Duijn, J. J., 1983. *The Long Wave in Economic Life.* London: George Allen and Unwin.

van Parijs, P., 1980. "The Falling-Rate-of-Profit Theory of Crisis: A Rational Reconstruction by Way of Obituary," *Review of Radical Political Economics*, 12 (1): 1–16.

Wright, Eric Olin, 1979. *Class, Crisis, and the State.* London: Verso.

— 5 —

The regulation theory and the social structure of accumulation approach

DAVID M. KOTZ

Introduction

The regulation theory arose in France at about the same time that the social structure of accumulation theory, which is the subject of this volume, was developing in the United States. The regulation school first appeared in print with the publication of Aglietta's *Theory of Capitalist Regulation* (1979, first published in French in 1976). The first published work of the social structure of accumulation school, Gordon (1978, 1980), appeared soon after the French edition of Aglietta's book.

The regulation theory holds that capitalism has experienced a sequence of "regimes of accumulation," each associated with a particular "mode of regulation" that governs the accumulation process. The regulation school is perhaps best known for its concept of "Fordism," the name given to the post World War II regime of accumulation. Fordism is a regime of accumulation based on assembly line production methods and mass consumption by the working class.

Both the regulation theory and the social structure of accumulation theory offer new theoretical frameworks for analyzing the long-run course of capital accumulation. Both approaches use Marxian categories and concepts for that purpose, yet both go beyond traditional Marxian formulations on that subject. These two theories have differences as well as similarities, and a consideration of both the similarities and the differences helps to understand both theories better. This chapter offers a comparative analysis of these two approaches. The analysis will consider the conceptual and theoretical structures of the two approaches, as well as some of the specific historical analyses produced by the two schools.

As with any school of thought, the writings of both the regulation school and the social structure of accumulation school display some diversity, with differences of emphasis and approach among writers within each school. I have selected a few writings of each school which I regard as formative and representative for that school. For the regulation theory, my interpretations rely most heavily on Aglietta (1979), Lipietz (1986, 1987), and Boyer (1984, 1987). For the social structure of accumulation theory, I rely mainly on Gordon (1980); Gordon *et al.* (1982); and Bowles *et al.* (1983).

This chapter is organized as follows. The first section considers the common elements in the theoretical apparatus of the regulation theory and social structure of accumulation theory; the subsequent section looks into the theoretical differences. Then, there is a criticism of the two schools' characterization of the labor process in nineteenth-century capitalism. The following section compares the two schools' analyses of the economic evolution of post World War II capitalism. A final section offers concluding comments.

Theoretical common ground

Like the social structure of accumulation theory, the regulation theory seeks to explain long-run patterns of capital accumulation by analyzing the relation between the capital accumulation process and a set of social institutions which affect that process. The central idea of both is that crucial features of the trajectory of the capital accumulation process, over a long time period, are the product of the supporting role played by a set of social institutions.

The social structure of accumulation theory uses the term "social structure of accumulation" to refer to a set of institutions, existing in a particular time and place, which encourage accumulation. The terminology used in the regulation literature to describe the relation between institutions and accumulation is complex and not fully standardized among authors. Various "regimes of accumulation" are possible. By that term Aglietta (1979) appears to mean a particular form of the accumulation process, as governed by a particular set of social norms. This suggests that a regime of accumulation is a concept that includes both the accumulation process and what the social structure of accumulation school calls a social structure of accumulation.

Lipietz (1987) offers a somewhat different usage of the key terms. In his work a regime of accumulation is essentially a reproduction scheme – a "long term stabilization of the allocation of social production between consumption and accumulation" (p. 14). The rules or norms of behavior affecting accumulation are referred to as a "mode of regulation." Lipietz' usage renders the concepts more similar to those of the social structure of accumulation theory, with a regime of accumulation analogous to the accumulation process and a mode of regulation analogous to the social structure of accumulation.[1] Boyer's (1987) usage is similar to that of Lipietz.

Like the social structure of accumulation school, the regulation school views capitalism as moving through a series of stages, each characterized by a specific form of the accumulation process embedded in a particular set of institutions. For example, Boyer (1987, pp. 19–21) sees three successive stages in the institutions governing accumulation in France: the "old regulation" of the eighteenth century, the "competitive regulation" lasting until World War II, and the postwar "mono-polist regulation." Different regimes of accumulation are associated with the different modes of regulation. This is similar to the social structure of accumulation school's conception of a series of distinct social structures of accumulation characterizing a capitalist country's history.[2]

Also similar to the social structure of accumulation theory is the regulation theory's use of the Marxian concept of an economic crisis as the prelude to transition between stages of the accumulation/institution relation. In the conventional Marxian view, the transition between dominant modes of production is marked by social crisis and, finally, social revolution. In both the regulation and social structure of accumulation approaches, the accumulation/institution relation undergoes a birth–growth–decay–transformation cycle, as does a mode of production. The social crisis that precedes the revolutionary transformation of the dominant mode of production is replaced, in the regulation theory as well as in the social structure of accumulation theory, by an economic crisis.

Both the regulation school and the social structure of accumulation school distinguish two meanings of "economic crisis." Imbalances in the accumulation process cause periodic crises which are automatically corrected within the existing form of institutions. In fact, such short-term crises are the means by which imbalances in accumulation are corrected (Lipietz, 1987, p. 34; Gordon et al., 1982, p. 26). A long-term, or structural, crisis involves a significant reduction in the rate of accumulation over a prolonged period of time. Such a long-term crisis occurs when serious problems develop in the accumulation/institution relation, as eventually they must. Thus, both schools interpret the Great Depression of the 1930s, and the contemporary crisis of capitalism, as the outcome of problems in the accumulation/institution relation.

The resolution of a long-term crisis requires a transformation of the accumulation/institution relation. We are not speaking here of a revolutionary transformation, however. The basic institutions of capitalism remain, while their specific form changes. Thus, although many of the adherents of these two schools look forward to the replacement of capitalism by socialism, the theories which they have produced are theories of how the process of social reform takes place within capitalism.

Another common feature of these two theories is that both present capital accumulation as a process that is not simply an economic one. Capital accumulation is related to a wide range of institutions, that includes not only economic institutions but political and ideological ones as well.

Both the regulation theory and the social structure of accumulation theory offer an intermediate level of analysis, more general and abstract than a detailed historical account of capitalist development would be, but more specific and concrete than the usual abstract theory of capitalism-in-general. This level of theory is more readily tested against empirical evidence than is more abstract theory, and much of the theory seems to be inferred from historical study. Indeed, the adherents of both schools have done a substantial amount of empirical work.

Theoretical differences

The two approaches do have differences on the theoretical level. Differences exist on the following issues (1) the kind of variations in the accumulation process that are considered (2) how institutions support capital accumulation (3) why each particular form of the accumulation/institution relation must eventually go into crisis (4) how the crisis is resolved.

Variations in the accumulation process

The social structure of accumulation theory was originally proposed as a solution to the problem of long waves in economic growth. The aim was to explain quantitative variations in the rate of capital accumulation over long periods of time. Thus, the impact of institutions on accumulation was considered in a particular way: how do institutions affect the *rate* of accumulation?

The regulation theory presents a different view of the possible variations in the accumulation process. While variations in the rate of accumulation are of interest to the regulation school, there is a broader focus on possible qualitative differences in accumulation. This lies at the basis of the concept of a regime of accumulation, a concept which has no precise counterpart in the social structure of accumulation theory.

According to Lipietz (1987) and Boyer (1987), a regime of accumulation can be extensive, which means that accumulation occurs without any major change in the labor process. Extensive accumulation occurs basically through increase in the work-week and expansion of the supply of wage laborers. Alternatively, a regime of accumulation can be intensive, which means that the labor process is transformed over time and labor productivity can continually rise.

Furthermore, an intensive regime of accumulation can be accompanied by the absence, or presence, of mass consumption by the working class. Steady growth in consumption by the average worker affects the structure of realization of the increases in value created through accumulation. With labor productivity growing under an intensive regime of accumulation, a stagnant consumption level by workers requires that a rising proportion of new value created by accumulation must be realized through growing purchases of means of production and/or growing consumption by nonproductive classes. This poses a potential problem of underconsumption.

This typology yields three kinds of regime of accumulation: an extensive regime of accumulation, an intensive regime of accumulation without mass consumption, and an intensive regime of accumulation with mass consumption. The three are seen as forming a historical sequence, with an extensive regime of accumulation characterizing nineteenth-century capitalism, an intensive regime of accumulation without mass consumption prevailing in the early twentieth century, followed by an intensive regime of accumulation with mass consumption since World War II. Each type of regime of accumulation operates within the framework of a particular mode of regulation.[3]

How institutions support accumulation

The two schools agree that the institutional setting has a major effect on the course of capital accumulation. But they differ on the exact nature of this relationship.

Given the social structure of accumulation school's focus on long waves, the question of how institutions are related to accumulation is posed in the following manner: how do institutions create the basis for a long period of relatively rapid accumulation? The social structure of accumulation theory answers that the institutions of the social structure of accumulation create the stability and predictability that are prerequisites for rapid and smooth accumulation. By assuring that the "requirements of the accumulation process" are fulfilled, the social structure of accumulation creates stability and predictability, which leads the capitalists to invest heavily, producing rapid accumulation.[4]

The regulation theory is more concerned with explaining the particular character of accumulation in a period, and less concerned with the issue of whether accumulation was relatively rapid or relatively slow. The regulation theory approaches this issue by emphasizing the effects of the conjuncture of a particular regime of accumulation and a particular mode of regulation on the traditional Marxian crisis tendencies: the rising organic composition of capital, underconsumption, and so forth.

Consider the example of the interwar period. According to Boyer (1987), this period was characterized by an intensive regime of accumulation without mass consumption and a competitive mode of regulation. The latter enforced a competitive form of wage determination that made wages sensitive to the size of the reserve army and precluded any significant rise in real wages over time, thus preventing mass consumption. But the intensive regime of accumulation raised labor productivity rapidly, creating a contradictory and unstable pattern of accumulation due to the underconsumption problem.

For the regulation theory the key to the accumulation/institution relation is the effect of that relation on the rate of profit and the realization of value, while for the social structure of accumulation theory the key is the effect of that relation on the degree of stability and predictability. The regulation theory view embodies a more traditionally Marxist conception of accumulation, whereas the social structure of accumulation theory view appears more Keynesian, given its emphasis on the capitalist's investment decision in an environment of uncertainty about the future.[5]

The onset of economic crisis

The regulation school and social structure of accumulation school agree that each accumulation/institution pairing eventually produces a crisis. The analyses of the genesis of such crises offered by the two schools have some similarities but also important differences.

Given that the social structure of accumulation school views rapid expansion as the result of the support provided to accumulation by a social structure of accumulation, an economic crisis is viewed as resulting from the collapse of the social structure of accumulation. Key institutions in the social structure of accumulation weaken and can no longer function effectively. Since the institutions of the social structure of accumulation are viewed as an integrated whole, the collapse of a few key institutions ends the supportive role of the social structure of accumulation, and accumulation slows or stops. This gives us the crisis.

Why does a social structure of accumulation eventually collapse? Given the social structure of accumulation theory's ambition to provide an explanation for long waves, one would expect a single mechanism for the collapse, which would repeat at fairly regular time intervals. But instead the literature offers a variety of mechanisms, unified only by the fact that each mechanism is an example of a contradiction that emerges in the accumulation/institution relationship.

The regulation school does not view the collapse of institutions as the basis of economic crisis. Similarly to the social structure of accumulation theory, the regulation theory holds that the intensifying contradictions in the accumulation/institution relation set off the crisis, but the crisis is entirely due to the effects on accumulation of the accumulation/institution contradictions, not a result of institutions collapsing.

Lipietz (1987) argues that a crisis indicates that "the mode of regulation is not adequate to the regime of accumulation,"[6] because either "the emergence of a new regime is being held back by outdated forms of regulation" or because "the potential of the regime of accumulation has been exhausted given the prevailing mode of regulation" (p. 34). An example of the former is the crisis of the 1930s, set off by an outdated competitive mode of regulation preventing the emergence of an intensive regime of accumulation with mass consumption. As we shall see in the later section analysing the postwar period, the present crisis is viewed as an example of the latter: the exhaustion of the potential of Fordism.

Once again the regulation theory shows a greater influence by traditional Marxist conceptions. Lipietz' formulation is suggestive of the historical materialist view that contradictions between the mode of production and the political and ideological superstructure produce a social crisis: the emergence of a new mode of production is being held back by an outdated superstructure, or the potential of the old mode of production has been exhausted.

This difference between the two schools illustrates the more materialist outlook of the regulation theory. For the social structure of accumulation theory, rapid accumulation is fully dependent on an appropriate social structure of accumulation. The crisis can occur if, and only if, the social structure of accumulation collapses. The regulation theory has a more materialist conception of this relation. The regime of accumulation itself can exhaust its potential, despite the continuing presence of the mode of regulation, leading to a crisis. Or, the mode of regulation, while still adequate to the old regime of accumulation, is holding back the new stage in the regime of accumulation. Either way, the development of the regime of accumulation plays a more active role in the process of development of a crisis than is the case in the social structure of accumulation theory.

The resolution of economic crisis

The two schools agree that the resolution of an economic crisis entails structural change. A new set of institutions is required to move beyond the crisis. But the process by which such a new set of institutions emerges is different in the two theories.

In the social structure of accumulation theory political innovations carried out by various classes and groups lead to the creation of a new social structure of accumulation. The conditions of an economic crisis set off sharp struggles between capitalists and workers, between sections of various classes, and among a variety of class and non-class groups in society. Each group is pressured to propose institutional reforms that will promote accumulation. Out of this process a new social structure of accumulation eventually emerges. The literature emphasizes that there is nothing automatic about this process and that the kind of social structure of accumulation that emerges is not preordained.

For the regulation theory the resolution of the crisis does not simply require a set of institutions that will be favorable for accumulation. It requires the establishment of a new regime of accumulation/mode of regulation pair. The new regime of accumulation develops as the capitalists find new ways of organizing the labor process, with the class struggle influencing the evolution. The creation of a new mode of regulation is presented, to some extent, as an outcome of the evolution of the regime of accumulation.

For example, Aglietta presents an elaborate structural argument concerning the creation of the postwar mode of regulation in the United States. As the Fordist regime of accumulation develops, the new mechanized labor process brings an increase in the intensity of labor. The workers must recuperate, and the most effective way to recuperate is to engage in consumption of individual commodities in one place, the home. This leads to the standardized home and the automobile to move the worker between job and home; the purchase of such commodities by workers requires mass consumption. But for workers to buy such expensive commodities requires a new structure of finance to provide the necessary long-term credit. Finally, to ensure that the workers can maintain their consumption, and keep paying back their loans, it was necessary to transform the wage formation process and provide social insurance for workers (Aglietta, 1979, pp. 158–9). While this is not all Aglietta has to say about the creation of the postwar mode of regulation, such a deterministic, structuralist account of the rise of new institutions never appears in the social structure of accumulation literature.

This suggests another difference between the two schools. Although the social structure of accumulation literature frequently insists that a social structure of accumulation is not simply a list of institutions but rather is an integrated whole, it is difficult to find the principle of integration of the various institutions, except that they are all good for accumulation in some way, and each tends to reinforce the others. But each institution in a social structure of accumulation appears to be an independently developed entity. By contrast, in the regulation literature, there seems to be a hierarchy of importance among the various facets of the accumulation/institution relation. Aglietta states this view most clearly, in his frequent assertion of the traditional Marxist position that production relations are central to capitalist development. The account cited above of a Fordist organization of production requiring a whole series of institutional innovations illustrates this view. Once again the regulation theory is found to be more materialist than the social structure of accumulation theory.

The labor process in nineteenth-century capitalism

The literatures of the regulation and social structure of accumulation schools offer similar and unconventional analyses of the technological development of nineteenth-century capitalism. Both schools argue that the labor process was relatively stagnant in that phase of capitalism. Lipietz (1986, p. 16) argues that in both the United States and France, "The 1848–1914 period is mainly characterized ... by a simple extension of productive capacity without dramatic change in the organic composition of capital or in productivity." Similarly, Boyer (1987, pp. 21–3) views the period 1895–1920 in France as one of "quasi-stagnating productivity," with growth due to increased labor input rather than technical progress. That is, pre World War I capitalism is viewed as based on an "extensive" regime of accumulation.[7] An intensive regime of accumulation does not replace the extensive regime of accumulation until some time early in the twentieth century.

The social structure of accumulation literature takes a similar position about nineteenth-century capitalist development. Gordon *et al.* (1982) characterize the first social structure of accumulation in the United States as based on "proletarianized but untransformed labor" (pp. 79–94). They argue that "the principal source of output expansion lay in extensive rather than in intensive growth, in the simple expansion of employment rather than in rising productivity per worker" during the 1840s–70s (p. 81). In their analysis, this extensive growth process began to change after 1870, but not until the 1890s, with the consolidation of a new social structure of accumulation based on "homogenization of labor," did intensive growth replace extensive growth.

If the claim being made were simply that technological change and productivity growth accelerated some time around the turn of the last century, then this would not be very controversial. But the assertion that there was little or no productivity growth – that absolute surplus value was the rule – in that period is indeed controversial, and it has been criticized by various authors. For example, Brenner and Glick (1991, pp. 67–8) cite data going back to 1840 compiled for the US economy by leading economic historians, which show significant productivity growth in the pre World War I period. The leading manufacturing industries in the US over that period – beginning with textiles in the mid nineteenth century, followed by steel in the late nineteenth century – do not fit the picture of stagnant technology.[8] Those industries which were just emerging from the artisan form of organization in that period may briefly fit this picture, but most historians have found that once the capitalist form of organization seized control of an industry during the nineteenth century, changes in the labor process leading to growing productivity became the norm.

It may be that a desire to fit capitalist development into a neat series of very distinct stages led both the regulation school and the social structure of accumulation school to propose this picture of nineteenth-century development. A transition from slow to fast productivity growth in the early twentieth century does not appear so dramatic as a shift from extensive to intensive growth, but it is more believable, and more consistent with what we know about the dynamic of capitalism.

Analysis of the postwar period

The similarities and differences between the two schools have effects on their analyses of postwar economic development. The similarities are striking. The two schools agree that a particular set of institutions produced unusually rapid and stable accumulation in the industrialized capitalist countries from the mid-1940s through the 1960s. The two cite many of the same institutions as responsible for this performance: peaceful collective bargaining, a welfare state, Keynesian macropolicy, and United States hegemony. While many non-Marxist economists date the beginning of a worsening in economic performance to the early 1970s, the regulation school and the social structure of accumulation school agree that the mid-1960s marks the beginning of the crisis. They also agree that the fundamental reason for the beginning of the crisis lay in growing strains within the accumulation/institution relationship that had underpinned the vigorous accumulation. There are also similarities in the claim that the solution to the crisis will entail, among other things, a further expansion in the state role in the economy.

However, the analyses of both expansion and crisis differ in a number of ways. The regulation school views the Fordist regime of accumulation as the centerpiece of the postwar expansion in the United States. Fordist organization of the labor process brought rapid increases in productivity, while collective bargaining and New Deal social programs generated mass consumption which helped realize the growing value of output. Keynesian policies also helped prevent realization problems, and the military content of state expansion generated new technologies that fed back into the rise in labor productivity. The oligopolistic pattern of price setting contributed to the stability of the regime, while imparting an inflationary tendency to it. The transformed system of money and credit of the postwar period both created the expanding credit and means of exchange necessary for rapid accumulation and also contributed to the inflationary bias of the regime. United States hegemony created a stable background for accumulation.

The regulation school emphasizes the effect of institutions on the crisis tendencies inherent in capital accumulation. Lipietz (1986, 1987) argues that the above institutional configuration counteracted the rising organic composition of capital, as productivity rose at the same rate as fixed capital per person in producer goods industries; while it also counteracted any tendency for the rate of surplus value to fall, as wages rose at the same rate as labor productivity in wage goods industries. The constant composition of capital and rate of surplus value kept the profit rate from falling, while rising workers' consumption helped solve the realization problem.

The greater emphasis of the social structure of accumulation school on class conflict, political innovation, and the need for social stability gives a different cast to the interpretation of the postwar boom, despite the overlap in institutions. Bowles *et al.* (1983) group the institutions of the postwar social structure of accumulation under three headings: the capital–labor accord, United States hegemony, and a capitalist–citizen accord. The first operated essentially to stabilize capital–labor relations. The second assured a cheap and reliable supply of raw materials and stable and growing world markets for goods and capital, by stabilizing relations between the United States ruling class and various classes and groups in other countries. The third consisted of Keynesian stabilization through military spending, government subsidization of key industries, and the maintenance of a welfare state; these policies were interventions in the market which created greater economic and social stability. The major theme is not maintaining the rate of profit but stabilizing all of the key internal and external social relationships of the system. The outcome was unusually rapid and stable accumulation.

The differences are even greater in the explanations of the crisis. The regulation literature focuses on the regime of accumulation reaching the limits of its ability to serve as the basis for further expansion. The labor process of Fordism reaches the limit of its ability to advance the forces of production. Aglietta (1979) refers to "the exhaustion of the possibilities for increased productivity in assembly line work" (p. 163). Elaborating on this idea, Lipietz (1986) suggests that the Fordist organization of production "at first generates more gains in productivity than increases in fixed capital, but then ends up becoming much too 'costly'" (p. 26). Boyer (1987) offers the conjecture that "Fordism is fairly efficient as regards labour and capital productivity when it replaces older systems, but it becomes harder and harder to get the same results when the issue is to deepen – and no more to extend – the same organizational methods" (pp. 30–1). The exhaustion of Fordist production organization causes a slowdown in productivity growth, which shows up in most industrial capitalist countries in the mid-1960s.

The Fordist regime of accumulation is not simply a form of organization of the labor process. It is also a norm of working-class consumption, involving mass consumption of commodities. This aspect of Fordism also goes into crisis. As noted earlier, a regime of accumulation based on mass consumption by workers requires social programs, providing collective consumption that maintains and stabilizes total consumption by the working class. But the Fordist mode of organization of the labor process is not adapted to producing collective consumption goods, which are mainly state provided. As a result, the costs of providing such goods (health care, retirement pensions, etc.) tend to grow rapidly "until they eventually cancel the general tendency toward a rise in the rate of surplus-value" (Aglietta, 1979, p. 166).

While other factors leading to crisis are mentioned in the regulation literature, the above developments play a central role, and they illustrate the idea that the regime of accumulation becomes unable to bring further advances in the forces of production. The problem arising in the 1960s was not any slowdown in the appearance of new technologies which could be adapted to industry, but a problem of the regime of accumulation in conjunction with its particular mode of regulation (Boyer, 1987).

The social structure of accumulation literature presents a different explanation of the onset of crisis, despite superficial similarities. The three sets of "accords" that underlay the postwar expansion – the capital–labor accord, United States hegemony, and the capitalist–citizen accord – were essentially institutional embodiments of United States capitalist domination of other classes and groups. What ultimately undermined these accords was the rising resistance of the dominated groups. The growing militancy of younger workers challenged the capital–labor accord. Popular movements succeeded in improving social programs, creating a true social wage, which increased the ability of the working class to press its demands for better wages and working conditions. People's movements also challenged the right of capitalists to destroy the environment, create unsafe workplaces, and foist a dangerous nuclear power industry on the country. And internationally, rising challenges from industrialized capitalist competitors undermined the economic arrangements of United States hegemony, while Third World challenges undermined United States military dominance and United States corporate control of raw material pricing (Bowles et al., 1983, ch. 3).

The social structure of accumulation school agrees that the productivity slowdown marked the start of the current crisis. But for the social structure of accumulation school, this slowdown is explained fundamentally as a result of successful popular challenges to United States capitalist domination (Bowles et al., 1983, ch. 6). The regulation school acknowledges that intensifying social conflict marked the crisis period. Aglietta (1979) notes that the crisis of Fordism "is expressed above all in the intensification of class struggles at the point of production" (p. 162). But such conflict is seen more as a consequence, or expression, of the crisis than as the fundamental cause. The latter is found in the exhaustion of the Fordist regime of accumulation, within the existing mode of regulation.

Thus, the regulation school offers a largely structural explanation of the current crisis of capitalism, while the social structure of accumulation school explains the crisis as basically a result of rising class struggle. For the former, sharpening class struggle arose mainly as an outgrowth of structural contradictions, while for the latter, structures failed largely due to sharpening class struggles.

Concluding comments

Since its inception as a social theory, Marxism has contained a tension between its structural and its class struggle dimensions. One caricature of Marxism sees it as a dogmatically structural theory, in which human action is fully determined by the outcome of impersonal structural forces. The opposite caricature sees Marxism as a fundamentally voluntarist theory of class struggle, in which the actions of classes, and their organizations and leaders, fully determine the course of structural development. While neither school under consideration here fits either caricature, the regulation theory leans more in the direction of the first, while the social structure of accumulation theory leans more in the direction of the second.

Neither pole is the "correct" one; history is the outcome of the interplay of both sets of forces. Over the very long run, structural forces are more important, and class struggles tend to reflect such structural forces. In the short run, the actions that classes take can be decisive. As theories of the intermediate run, the regulation theory and the social structure of accumulation theory deal with a time frame in which both structural forces and class conflicts play an important role. The regulation theory pays insufficient attention to the independent effects of class and other conflicts on the accumulation process, while the social structure of accumulation theory fails to give sufficient weight to structural forces. As analyses of the intermediate term, one is too structuralist and the other is too voluntarist. If greater interchange between the two schools moves each toward the position of the other, that should be good for both of them.

Notes

1 The analogy is not perfect. See the section on theoretical differences below.

2 See Kotz (this volume, ch. 3).

3 The definition of extensive and intensive regimes of accumulation given by Lipietz and Boyer differs from the one originally proposed by Aglietta (1979). Aglietta defines an extensive regime of accumulation as one in which "relative surplus value is obtained by transforming the organization of labor," but "the traditional way of life" of the working class is not transformed (p. 71). By contrast, an intensive regime of accumulation not only transforms the labor process but also "creates a new way of life for the wage earning class," establishing a "social consumption norm" (p. 71). That is, capitalism integrates working-class consumption into the accumulation process. Aglietta's intensive regime of accumulation is Lipietz' and Boyer's intensive regime of accumulation with mass consumption; Aglietta's extensive regime of accumulation is Lipietz' and Boyer's intensive regime of accumulation without mass consumption. We will use the Lipietz/Boyer definitions in this chapter.

4 For an elaboration of this point, see Kotz (this volume, ch. 3).

5 Some of the later work by social structure of accumulation advocates does give significant emphasis to the effect of institutions on the rate of profit. Examples are Weisskopf et al. (1985) and Bowles et al. (1986).

6 The English translation of that passage actually reads: "the mode of regulation is not adequate to the regime of regulation" (emphasis added). Given the context, and the absence of the phrase "regime of regulation" elsewhere in the text, that phrase evidently was in error, and should have read "regime of accumulation." See Lipietz (1987, p. 34).

7 Brenner and Glick (1991) mistakenly attribute this view to Aglietta as well as Lipietz and other regulation school writers. Brenner and Glick are misled by Aglietta's different definition of an extensive regime of accumulation from that used by later regulation school writers. As was noted above, Aglietta defines an extensive regime of accumulation, not as a regime of accumulation with little or no technical change, but rather as one without mass consumption by the working class. Aglietta does describe nineteenth-century US capitalism as based on an

extensive regime of accumulation, but by that he means a regime of accumulation without mass consumption. When Lipietz and Boyer assert that that same period was characterized by an extensive regime of accumulation, it has an entirely different meaning from Aglietta's characterization using the same term. This shows the mischief that can result from unrecognized changes in definitions of key terms.

8 Gordon *et al.* (1982, pp. 81–5) present data which, it is claimed, show that the bulk of economic growth in US manufacturing during 1840–70 came from labor force growth. But this seems to be the wrong piece of information. With population growth rapid in those years, it is not surprising that a large proportion of output growth was due to growth of labor inputs. The relevant question is whether productivity grew at a significant pace. Their own data show an increase in output per worker in manufacturing of 1.6 percent per year during 1840–70, which, while not a rapid growth rate, does indicate continuing significant productivity growth.

References

Aglietta, Michel, 1979. *A Theory of Capitalist Regulation: The U.S. Experience*. London: Verso (1987 edition used). (First published as *Régulation et Crises du Capitalisme*, Calmann-Lévy, 1976.)

Bowles, Samuel, David M. Gordon, and Thomas E. Weisskopf, 1983. *Beyond the Wasteland: A Democratic Alternative to Economic Decline*. Garden City, N.J.: Anchor Press/Doubleday.

1986. "Power and Profits: The Social Structure of Accumulation and the Profitability of the Postwar U.S. Economy," *Review of Radical Political Economics*, 18 (1/2): 132–67.

Boyer, Robert, 1984. "Analysis de la Crise Americaine: A Propos d'un Ouvrage Recent," no. 8501, CEPREMAP, Paris.

1987. "Technical Change and the Theory of 'Regulation,'" no. 8707, CEPREMAP, Paris (March).

Brenner, Robert, and Mark Glick, 1991. "The Regulation Approach: Theory and History," *New Left Review*, no. 188: 45–119.

Gordon, David M., 1978. "Up and Down the Long Roller Coaster," in *U.S. Capitalism in Crisis*, ed. Union for Radical Political Economics, pp. 22–35. New York: Union for Radical Political Economics.

1980. "Stages of Accumulation and Long Economic Cycles," in *Processes of the World System*, ed. T. Hopkins and I. Wallerstein, pp. 9–45. Beverly Hills: Sage Publications.

Gordon, David M., Richard C. Edwards, and Michael Reich. 1982. *Segmented Work, Divided Workers*. Cambridge University Press.

Lipietz, Alain, 1986. "Behind the Crisis: The Exhaustion of a Regime of Accumulation. A 'Regulation School' Perspective on Some French Empirical Works," *Review of Radical Political Economics*, 18 (1/2): 13–32.

1987. *Mirages and Miracles: The Crises of Global Fordism*. London: Verso.

Weisskopf, Thomas E., Samuel Bowles, and David M. Gordon, 1985. "Two Views of Capitalist Stagnation: Underconsumption and Challenges to Capitalist Control," *Science and Society*, 49(3): 259–86.

II

HISTORY, INSTITUTIONS, AND MACROECONOMIC ANALYSIS

6

The construction of social structures of accumulation in US history

TERRENCE MCDONOUGH

Introduction

The social structure of accumulation (SSA) framework is based in a tradition of theorizing which attempts to explain long movements in capitalist history. As such the historical test of the theory's accuracy and usefulness must ultimately be found in the explanation of long movements over time. Nevertheless, much of the historical work done within the SSA framework examines recent history, seeking to explain the demise of the postwar SSA in the 1970s and after.[1] This chapter seeks to expand the historical literature of the SSA framework by examining the construction of SSAs over the course of American history. This study also has the advantage of addressing the more theoretical question of how highly integrated SSAs are constructed in a period of economic crisis and heightened social conflict.

The lack of a convincing account of SSA construction is one of the main theoretical weaknesses remaining in the SSA framework. Ernest Mandel (1980), on the one hand, and Gordon, Edwards, and Reich (1982), on the other, take sharply differing positions on this question. Ernest Mandel, perhaps the best-known Marxist theorist of long waves, seeks to explain these waves through examining fluctuations in the average rate of profit. Mandel argues that the rate of profit tends to decline over time, owing to the tendency of the organic composition of capital to rise.[2] This tendency can be counteracted through an increase in the rate of surplus value, a sharp slowdown in the rate of increase of the organic composition of capital, a sudden quickening in the turnover of capital, or by a flow of capital into countries and sectors where the average organic composition of capital is lower than that in the basic industry of the industrialized capitalist countries. Long-wave expansions are initiated during periods in which the forces counteracting the tendency of the average rate of profit to decline operate in a "strong and synchronized" way. In explaining these upsurges in the profit rate, extra-economic factors play key roles. Mandel argues these upsurges can be understood only if "all the concrete forms of capitalist development in a given environment" are brought into play (1980, p. 21). As examples of "these radical changes in the overall social and geographic environment in which the capitalist mode of production operates," he mentions wars of conquest, extensions and contractions of the area of capitalist operation, intercapitalist competition, class struggle, and revolutions and counter-revolutions (p. 21).

Mandel's account of the upturn as due to changes in the social and geographic environment of the profit rate is an important insight. Mandel argues strongly throughout his volume, however, that these changes take place in each institution according to an independent dynamic, which is "relatively autonomous" with respect to what is happening with other institutions and with the capital accumulation process as a whole. In effect, the consolidation of the changes which lead to an upsurge in the profit rate and investment is seen to be the result of a largely chance confluence of events.

In contradiction to Mandel's vision of relatively autonomous, randomly developing institutions, Gordon, Edwards and Reich, in discussing the genesis of SSAs, lay considerable emphasis upon an open political process as the source of the drive to construct the new set of institutions. They speak of a process of forming coalitions which then "forge" the new SSA. They also seem to imply a kind of battle between worked out class programs concerning the restructuring. These battles result in victory for one plan or another or compromises on a new plan which is then implemented (Gordon *et al.*, 1982, p. 36). I do not think this scenario can be supported historically. Periods of crisis can and do generate open political debate over the method of resolving the crisis and this debate often generates class programs which address the rekindling of accumulation. I would argue, however, that these plans play a more limited role in the struggle over the restructuring than Gordon, Edwards, and Reich contend. These plans are just one factor among many. They are seldom comprehensive and often not completely coherent. Even in the case of a coherent and comprehensive plan for restructuring, there is no one agency in society which could adopt and attempt to implement the plan as a whole. Portions of the plan would be resisted, blocked, and transformed willy-nilly by opposing classes, class fractions, and other groups. Other plans being pursued by other classes might meet with partial success. Meanwhile, struggles over other issues throw up institutions which are not part of any coherent plan for restructuring, and yet have a profound effect on the accumulation process. For these reasons, the authors' emphasis on coalition-building around coherent planning seems misplaced.

Borrowing from Mandel, we must recognize that institutions can be created which are independent of any planned restructuring. Intentional restructuring plans are only one factor among many in determining the ultimate form of the SSA. Borrowing from Gordon, Edwards, and Reich, we observe that struggle during the downturn does begin to center around the accumulation process. Thus, while an institution's genesis often has little to do with any class's planned restructuring, its ultimate viability and longevity depends at least in part on the possibility of its incorporation in its original form, or transformed through struggle, into an SSA. This creation, transformation, and integration of institutions takes place with each institution's history autonomous from that of the others, but only relatively so. As the institutions develop, so too does the matrix of relationships between them. This matrix determines the possibilities for future development of each individual institution. The SSA which emerges from this process may only distantly resemble any planned in advance, but neither will it be the result of a chance confluence of events. Its shape will be determined by the course of the class struggle during the crisis period, and the objective conditions within which the struggle was carried out.

Nevertheless, if the SSA framework is to lay claim to being a theory of specifically long waves, we must be able to locate more specific points of commonality which reassert themselves in the course of the construction of each SSA. We must ask if there is some common organizing principle which underlies the construction of SSAs. If the construction of each SSA is a unique and unrepeated process, it would be difficult to predict the timing of such construction in advance. If this were the case, the end of the stagnation period, marked by the construction of the SSA, would take place after no particular interval. The depressive phase of the wave predicted by the SSA framework could then be either long or short. Whether such points of commonality can be found in SSA construction can only be determined in the examination of the actual historical process of SSA building. It is the purpose of this chapter to carry out this examination in the context of the SSAs constructed in the course of American capitalist history. I will argue that these SSAs are each built according to a unifying principle. These principles, however, differ in each case. This indicates that the organizing principles of SSA construction may, indeed, be historically contingent and unique to each SSA.

There are three SSAs in American economic history. The first extends from roughly the end of the Civil War to the turn of the century, the second from the turn of the century to World War II, and the last from World War II to the present. The initiation of the post-Civil War SSA can be considered to be an example of primitive accumulation.[3] Since the construction of the first SSA in each capitalist country takes place under special circumstances which could not be repeated, I will not include the construction of the first SSA in US economic history in this discussion. US history provides us with two later examples of the construction of SSAs. The first marks the transition from the post-Civil War SSA to the monopoly capitalist SSA at the turn of the century. The second construction took place during the transition from the monopoly capitalist SSA to the post-World War II social structure.

The construction of the monopoly SSA

Introduction

In this section of the chapter I will discuss the consolidation of the institutions of the monopoly SSA. I will argue that the new SSA was consolidated relatively rapidly. At least the core institutions had established their basic shapes in the six-year period between 1898 and 1904. I will also contend that neither Mandel's hypothesis of a relatively random confluence of events nor Gordon *et al.*'s scenario of the development and implementation of a political program of restructuring is adequate to explain the transition to the monopoly capitalist SSA. I will argue instead that the organizing principle of the SSA put into place at the turn of the century can be found in the oligopolistic market structure established in the merger wave of 1898 to 1902. Each of the other institutions was constructed around the emergence of the new monopoly structure of capital. This monopoly market structure can be regarded as the lynchpin of the SSA.

The monopoly SSA

In examining the construction of the monopoly SSA, our first task is to determine which institutions were involved. The definition of a social structure of accumulation includes all those institutions which directly or indirectly condition the accumulation process. It thus offers little guidance in narrowing the institutions we need to consider, as a large proportion of the institutions within a capitalist society have an important impact on the cultural, political, and/or economic conditions of accumulation. Our consideration of the construction of the SSA, or, in other words, the change in the institutional structure from one period to another, allows us to focus only on those institutions which change from the period of stagnation to the period of growth. Thus, we will not discuss the continuity of many institutions from one period to another, even though many of these institutions were very important in assuring accumulation. Further, this omission is not meant to deny that struggles over the preservation of institutions may be just as important to the successful integration of a new SSA as those parts of the SSA whose history appears to have a more dynamic character. Relationships between relatively static institutions and newly developing ones can be potentially very important in determining the ultimate character of the new institutional arrangement. Similarly, a matrix of new institutions can radically alter the function and significance of even an institution which has survived relatively unchanged.

While all of the institutions of the SSA acting in concert guarantee the continued success of accumulation during the period of expansion, nevertheless, it is the newly developing institutions which cause the transition from stagnation to growth. Thus, considering the construction of the newly developing institutions in the SSA will go a long way toward explaining the inauguration of the succeeding period of expansion.

The number of institutions can be further limited by confining our attention to only those institutions which constitute, in David Kotz' word, the "core" of the SSA needed to rekindle the accumulation process. Kotz argues that, while a large number of institutions constitute the total SSA, many of these institutions are established only after the long period of expansion has begun. For example, he observes that, while stable exchange rates are undoubtedly an important part of the post-World War II SSA, they were only fully implemented in 1958, well into the long-wave expansion. Kotz concludes that only a subset of the institutions which will ultimately constitute the SSA are needed to start the accumulation process associated with the long period of expansion (Kotz, 1987 and this volume, ch. 3).

In his article, Kotz lays out the following criteria for identifying the specific institutions which make up the core of a given SSA. The institutions must be in place at the beginning of the long period of expansion. Each institution must exhibit significant stability and durability over the expansion period. A core institution must also be an important force in stablilizing class conflict and/or capitalist competition and hence in supporting the accumulation process (Kotz, 1987 and this volume, ch. 3).

The criteria discussed above limit the number of institutions within the SSA which I will consider in connection with the construction of the SSA. I believe, however, that an exposition of the development of these institutions, and the relationships among them, will illuminate an important part of the story of the construction of the new SSA.

Six core institutions underpinned the monopoly SSA. The first was the new, more concentrated structure of industry. Prior to the turn of the century most American industries were still basically competitive in structure. Following the merger movement, the American industrial structure would be oligopolistic in nature. Second, the new SSA included a new balance in capital–labor relations favoring capital. Capital gained control of the work process on the shop floor through the introduction of the assembly line, machine-pacing and Taylorism. Business was also able to forestall the growth of unionism. Third, a new collaborative relationship between business and the state was established. Trusts were to be subjected to a mild regime of regulation, rather than declared illegal and broken up. Fourth, a new electoral system founded on Republican hegemony in national politics and decreased popular participation in the state would provide support for this new relationship between the economy and the state. Fifth, a new corporatist ideology, extolling the virtues of concentration, cooperation, and expertise would provide a rationale and justification for the new order. Sixth, inauguration of imperial expansion abroad by US business defined a new relationship between the United States and the international economy.[4]

The monopoly market structure

The core institutions of the twentieth-century monopoly capitalist SSA were all more or less in place, if not fully consolidated, soon after the turn of the century. The great merger wave began in 1898 and ended in 1902. Pressures pushing for consolidation had been building in the American economy at least since the Civil War. At the same time there existed significant barriers to further consolidation. One of the most significant was the lack of a securities market in industrial stock, making it difficult to raise the capital needed to finance large-scale consolidations. Incorporation laws were written in such a way as to forbid corporations from holding stock in other corporations. This outlawed the holding company, which was later to become the main vehicle of corporate consolidation. The implications of the Sherman Anti-trust Act, passed in 1890, were unclear and provoked a certain amount of caution. The generally bad times in the early 1890s discouraged the undertaking of new ventures and restricted the amount of ready capital the architect of a merger could draw on (Edwards, 1979, pp. 42–3).

By the end of the century the barriers to corporate consolidation had begun to wear down. A market in industrial securities had slowly taken shape. In 1900, Dow Jones began quoting their famous industrial averages (Navin and Sears, 1955, pp. 105–38). In 1889, the state of New Jersey revised its corporation laws, legalizing the holding company as a method of merging previously independent firms (Kirkland, 1967, pp. 204–5). Court interpretations of the Sherman act outlawed informal pools and cartels, but seemed to allow the creation of monopoly by merger.

By the end of the nineteenth century, most of the financial and legal impediments to corporate consolidation had been eliminated. The pent-up momentum toward consolidation awaited only the cyclical recovery from the 1890s downturn to launch the great wave of consolidations at the turn of the century. The beginning of the merger wave in 1898 corresponded quite closely to the cyclical upturn occurring in that same year.[5] Thus we can look to the underlying pressures toward consolidation to explain the merger wave's existence, the creation of its financial and legal preconditions to explain its general timing, and the underlying cyclical business conditions to explain the precise time of its occurrence.[6]

Once unleashed, the merger wave quickly reached impressive proportions. There were 3,653 recorded mergers between 1898 and 1902, twenty-five times the number in the succeeding five years (Gordon et al., 1982, p. 107). Edwards has calculated that between one-quarter and one-third of the entire US manufacturing capital stock underwent consolidation during this period (Edwards, 1979, p. 44). Using John Moody's estimates of market control, Nelson estimates that a minimum of one-half of firm disappearances and seven-tenths of merger capitalizations were accounted for by mergers that gained a leading position in their market. As these are minimum figures, he conjectures that the actual proportion of firm disappearances into market-leading consolidations may have been as high as two-thirds, involving as much as three-fourths or four-fifths of all merger capitalizations (Nelson, 1959, p. 102). The structure of American industry was radically altered in the years surrounding 1900. The era of a relatively competitive market structure in America's basic industries was over with the end of the merger wave in 1902. Henceforth, most industries would be organized along oligopolistic lines.

The electoral realignment

The traditional dating of the electoral realignment precedes the merger wave by two years. A significant school within the political science profession has identified McKinley's victory in 1896 as marking a transition to "the system of 1896" (Burnham, 1970, p. 71). Prior to this transition, politics was dominated by what Paul Kleppner refers to as "the third electoral system" (Kleppner, 1979). Following the Civil War, the Republican Party became the party of Union and the North, while the Democratic Party organized a virtual one-party regime in much of the old Confederacy (Sundquist, 1983, p. 101). Feeling unwelcome in the moralist Protestant atmosphere of the Republican Party, the increasing number of urban immigrants built a Democratic Party base in some Northern cities (Kleppner, 1979, pp. 198–237).

Each party was supported by its own block of capital with the predominant faction investing in the continuation of Republican dominance. Nevertheless, a significant sector of capital supported the Democrats. These were capitalists who for one reason or another opposed the Republican tariff policies. They included merchants, railroads, and bankers with close ties to Southern commerce, as well as manufacturers (like Cyrus McCormick) who dominated the world markets for their products (Ferguson, 1983, p. 47). These factors added up to a highly competitive system of national politics with neither party overwhelmingly dominant. Partisan identification was high as was voter participation (Kleppner et al., 1981, p. 130).

By contrast the electoral system following the 1896 elections was marked by a solid Republican hegemony which would not end until the New Deal. This hegemony was built of unusually strong capitalist solidarity and the integration of the urban working class into the Republican Party. Growing concentration of capital and the developing unity of finance and industrial capital increasingly united business around Republican policies of protectionism (Ferguson, 1983, pp. 53–4). Previously Democratic, the urban workers did not respond to Bryan's narrow program of currency inflation. For workers, inflation meant a shrinking paycheck and they threw their lot in with the industrial forces. In addition to organizing solid majority support for the Republican Party at the Presidential level, the "system of 1896" included a significant decrease in popular access to the electoral system. This decline in voter participation was much heavier among the lower classes (Burnham, 1981, p. 195). The new electoral alignment had arrived with the critical election of 1896 and was quickly consolidated in the subsequent years.

From trust-busting to regulation

While the new corporations were economically untried and a little shaky, political failure was a much more serious threat. Traditionally supportive of larger capital, the small-business and professional class felt threatened by the merger movement and formed the backbone of a renewed anti-monopoly movement. Coupled with the electoral backing of the small farmers of the West, and holding growing labor organizations in reserve, these middle-class reformers offered the distinct possibility of the merger movement snatching political defeat from the jaws of its economic success (Hofstadter, 1955, passim).

Within a few years of each other, Congress passed two laws which were to establish competing traditions in dealing with the "trust problem" at the national level. The first, passed in 1887, was the Interstate Commerce Act, which established the Interstate Commerce Commission to oversee and regulate the railroads (Kirkland, 1967, p. 126). The hope was that large corporations like the railroads could be saved if the abuses which often resulted from the concomitant domination of the market could be prevented through government oversight. This view that trusts were to be regulated, rather than busted, was to be legislatively challenged in 1890 by the passage of the Sherman Anti-trust Act. The Act appeared to outlaw outright any attempt to restrain or monopolize trade (Thorelli, 1954, p. 610). Henceforth, struggle over the question of monopolies would turn on the question of the interpretation and enforcement of the Sherman Act.

In 1902, the Roosevelt administration filed four antitrust suits including the case against J. P. Morgan's Northern Securities railroad combination. The Supreme Court handed down its decision on the Northern Securities case in 1904, ruling in favor of the government. The decision, however, was to have an ambiguous impact on the future of antitrust activity. The court held that J. P. Morgan's consolidation of the Great Northern and Northern Pacific railroads was illegal under the Sherman Act. At the same time, the judicial opinions accompanying the ruling evidenced that, for the first time, a majority of the court held the position that the Sherman Act did not outlaw all attempts at monopoly and restraints on trade. It only outlawed unreasonable restraints on trade (Thorelli, 1954, pp. 470–5, 562).

This tendency on the part of the court to apply standards of "reason" to the question of the legality of trusts and monopolies dovetailed neatly with developments in the legislative and executive branches of government. A regulatory Bureau of Corporations was created in 1903 by Congress (Thorelli, 1954, p. 561). Thorelli observes that "underlying this legislation was the theory that the light of publicity would check the abuse of concentrated economic power and vitalize the forces of potential competition" (Thorelli, 1954, p. 561). The Roosevelt administration favored the regulatory approach, despite the President's notoriety as a trust-buster. Roosevelt declared, "The line of demarcation we draw must always be on conduct, not on wealth. Our objection to any corporation must be, not that it is big, but that it behaves badly" (Kolko, 1963, p. 69). The administration much preferred *détente* to prosecution and used the Bureau of Corporations to conclude ineffective regulatory agreements with individual large corporations (Kolko, 1963, pp. 74, 79–81). This basic approach was to be continued in succeeding administrations (Kolko, 1963, pp. 166, 209).

By far the most important issue with which the new concentrated industrial structure had to contend in its relationship to the state was whether the state was going to allow the new giant firms to continue to exist. As early as 1904, the judicial, legislative, and executive branches had opted for trust regulation rather than trust-busting.

The rise of corporatism

This legal victory for the new more concentrated corporate order also marked the definitive entry of the new corporatist ideology on the American scene. In the latter half of the nineteenth century, the doctrine of Social Darwinism was the dominant intellectual justification of the rule of the Robber Barons over the economy. Social Darwinism simply applied Darwin's conception of evolution arising from the survival of the fittest to the actors in the economy. The Protestant religious establishment was quick to give this scientistic and apparently secular doctrine religious overtones. "The laws of natural selection are merely God's regular methods of expressing his choice and approval. The naturally selected are the Chosen of God" (Hofstadter, 1965, p. 151).

James Weinstein has argued persuasively that the economic and social changes at the turn of the century were accompanied by the introduction of a new and different vision of the proper functioning of the body political–economic. He sums up this new vision in the title of his book as the "corporate ideal in the liberal state" (Weinstein, 1969). Competition as an organizing principle was to be replaced with an ideology of cooperation. At the macro-societal level, this was to take the form of cooperation between capital, labor, and "the public." These various groups were to be represented by responsible leadership, willing to look beyond immediate and narrow self-interest to the larger good. This vision of high-level cooperation would be facilitated by consolidation; of business, of labor, and of other constituencies as well (Weinstein, 1969, *passim*). Any disagreement would be arbitrated by an impartial state set above politics and itself run by experts (Weinstein, 1969, p. 31).[7]

We can safely say that corporatism had at least emerged as an ideological force with the founding in 1900 of the National Civic Federation (NCF). The Federation was a nationwide business-dominated organization of businessmen, politicians, and labor leaders, dedicated to the promotion of corporatist principles. Weinstein argues that the ascendancy of corporate ideology within monopoly corporate circles dates from the Civic Federations' founding. It is more difficult to determine when a new ideology becomes firmly established as a material force in the society at large. One criterion that might be applied is to determine when its principles begin to actively guide the policies pursued by government and other important agencies in society. Prominent political leaders like Grover Cleveland and William H. Taft sat on the NCF's executive board. The government's policy of regulating rather than busting trusts was consistent with the corporatist view of the world. I have argued above that much of this policy was in place by 1904.[8]

Capital–labor relations

The new SSA also contained a change in capital–labor relations. This change was accomplished primarily in two arenas. The first involved the reorganization of the work process on the shopfloor. The second important element in the establishment of the new balance in capital–labor relations was a concerted attack on the organization of labor.

In the nineteenth century, employers found it expedient to leave the old methods of work and production untransformed as they concentrated more and more labor in their firms. By and large the employees of a concern retained control of much of the labor process, rather than the employer (Gordon et al., 1982, pp. 79–80). While industrialization had always been accompanied by workers' resistance, working-class activity seemed to be growing both more militant and more effective in the last decades of the nineteenth century.[9] Real wages were rising from the mid-1870s to the early 1890s (Gordon et al., 1982, pp. 96–9).

These rising real wages were an important part of the squeeze on profits that precipitated the crisis at the end of the nineteenth century. The reorganization which was to resolve the crisis necessarily involved a restructuring of labor relations. Gordon et al. (1982, p. 100) argue that this restructuring can be characterized as the "homogenization" of labor, which they describe as the reduction of jobs to a common semi-skilled denominator. This was to be accomplished primarily through the mechanization of work and the breakdown of work assignments into narrower and narrower tasks.[10] This strategy was adopted to counter the control of the labor process exercised by workers, due to their exclusive knowledge and control over particular skills (Gordon et al., 1982, pp. 128–9).[11] Gordon et al. (1982, pp. 111, 145) date the beginning of the consolidation of this strategy to 1900.

On the other hand, the increasing commonality of position and work experience, and the potential solidarity this engendered, opened up the possibility of effective resistance to the new corporate domination of life on the shopfloor. In order to effectively consolidate the new regime, corporations found it necessary to counteract this source of working-class solidarity.

A diverse set of strategies was adopted to achieve this end, such as centralized personnel offices, multiple job titles, job ladders, plants designed to physically isolate workers, piecework, and job segregation by race and ethnicity (Gordon et al., 1982, pp. 136–45). Gordon et al. (1982, p. 136) also date the beginning of these strategies to 1900.[12]

Labor responded to capital's consolidation movement with aggressive organizing. Nevertheless, employers were able to stall the growth of the union movement after 1904, counterattacking with an open-shop drive using a variety of tactics (Foner, 1964, p. 420). The number of unionized workers essentially stalled at its 1904 level until the beginning of World War I. After 1904, strikes declined markedly in frequency and success. The open-shop drive successfully eliminated unions in all the trustified industries except railroads, and it appeared unionism only had a future in the building trades and other small, highly skilled trades. (Foner, 1964, pp. 59–60). The new balance of power between capital and labor was established by 1904.

American imperialism

The especially severe economic slump in the 1890s brought the issue of overseas economic expansion to prominence in the debate over US foreign policy. It was widely believed that the cause of the depression was a lack of markets for American produce and manufacture. Expansion into foreign markets was the evident solution (Williams, 1962, p. 22).

While some early initiatives were taken during the Cleveland administration, most importantly in connection with Hawaii, an expansionist foreign policy was dramatically and definitively established with America's entry into the Spanish–American War and the annexation of Hawaii in 1898. This war resulted in the declaration of Cuba as an American protectorate and the annexation of the Philippines, Puerto Rico, and Guam. It demonstrated that the Monroe Doctrine had teeth, and the US meant to be supreme in the Western hemisphere. The months of war with Spain were also to result in the creation of a stepping-stone path of ports across the "American ocean" of the Pacific. Hawaii was annexed that summer. Wake Island was taken, in addition to Guam and the Philippines.

These successes on the world stage intensified the debate at home concerning the manner of conducting the incipient empire. One group, led by Theodore Roosevelt, advocated the acquisition of formal colonies. They were opposed by a group known as the anti-imperialists, led by Carl Schurz and William Jennings Bryan. Yet the imperialists were not adamant in their position and were somewhat mollified by the annexation of Hawaii and Puerto Rico. The anti-imperialists, for their part, were more anti-colonial than anti-imperialist. The middle ground, and increasingly the common ground, was occupied by those who opposed traditional colonialism and advocated, instead, the promotion of American trade through an "Open Door" to all the underdeveloped areas of the world. Those who held this position were confident that an "Open Door," combined with America's predominant economic strength, would result in American dominance of international trade (Williams, 1962, pp. 37–9).

It was this position which prevailed. Its victory was evident in the policy adopted by the McKinley administration toward China, long considered to be the most important potential market for American penetration. This policy was embodied in the Open Door Notes, authored by Secretary of State John Hay. The first note, of September 6, 1899, asserted that American entrepreneurs "shall enjoy perfect equality of treatment for their commerce and navigation" within all of China. The second note opposed the extension of the formal colonial system to China. A third note extended the open door principle to loans as well as trade (Williams, 1962, pp. 41–4).

Thus the United States had firmly embarked on a program of international economic expansion by the turn of the century. America was definitively committed to the imperial sweepstakes with the annexation of Hawaii and the Spanish–American War in 1898, and the promulgation of the Open Door Notes established the specific character of American participation, beginning in 1899.

The organizing principle of the monopoly SSA

The core institutions of the monopoly SSA were all consolidated within four years on each side of the turn of the century, from 1896 to 1904. This relatively brief period of consolidation would seem to indicate the implausibility of Mandel's hypothesis of a chance confluence of events, all working in the direction of raising the profit rate. Nor does the consolidation of this SSA appear to be the result of the victory of a political program. The political decision to regulate rather than bust trusts and the promulgation of the new corporatist ideology were certainly part of a single political program, advocated by the emerging monopoly capitalist class acting through the now relatively unchallenged Republican Party. Nevertheless, the other institutions do not fit so neatly into such a political framework. Capital's attack on labor ran directly counter to the stated logic of a program of corporatist regulation. While imperialism is always of necessity a partly political phenomenon, the entry of America onto the world economic stage was more directly a result of pressures toward economic expansion, the end of westward expansion on the American continent, and international competition for trade and territory. The merger wave certainly would not have gotten very far as part of an explicit political program. Rather, the merger wave expressed pent-up pressure for consolidation in the face of overcapacity and ruinous price-cutting and was undertaken more or less independently by the capitalist class under the leadership of finance capital.

Despite the fact that the core institutions consolidated in the monopoly capitalist SSA do not appear to have been established as part of a political program, their relatively rapid consolidation within a single short period of time leads one to look for some other organizing principle. This organizing principle can be found by viewing the growing concentration of industry, and the subsequent consolidation of the oligopolistic market structure, as the lynchpin of the new SSA. Each of the other institutions was in one way or another constructed around the emergence of the new monopolistic structure of capital.

The new electoral system was closely connected to the increasing concentration of industry. As industry consolidated and manufacturing became more concentrated, finance capital became more intimately invested in industry. As more and more American capital was tied to industry, there was less and less of a base for the traditional Democratic Party policy of free trade. As the party of the tariff, the Republican Party garnered an ever increasing amount of capitalist support. Capitalist flight from the Democratic Party was intensified by that party's embrace of the free silver movement with the nomination of William Jennings Bryan, and the absorption of Populist forces. Increasingly, capital was united behind the tariff, the gold standard and, not incidentally, imperial competition with European capital (Ferguson, 1983, pp. 49–57). These developing forces in the Democratic and Republican Parties collided head on the election of 1896. US business was informally taxed by Mark Hanna, McKinley's campaign manager, and poured millions into the victorious Republican presidential bid. It was the beginning of a Republican electoral hegemony which would not end until the New Deal.

The replacement of the anti-monopoly tradition in the legal approach to corporate consolidation was necessary if the new market structure of capital was to survive. Consolidation's defenders were forced to take up a political struggle to transform the relation of the state to the economy. The establishment of a new tradition of moderate regulation, generally in the service of the existing corporate order, represents the success of this struggle. The monopoly corporate order supported this new attitude of the state through support for the Republican Party. Monopoly corporations, also operating directly through the National Civic Federation, devoted much time and energy to promoting this approach to state intervention in the economy. Corporate representatives participated actively in government bureaucracies and helped to draft legislation for congressional action (Kolko, 1963, *passim*). Capital's newly achieved upper-hand in its relationships with labor also contributed to the maintenance of the new regulatory policy. While capital's aggressively anti-union stance undoubtedly undermined support for corporatism in many quarters, the unions' weakened condition led many moderate labor leaders into a strategy of appeasement and cooptation (Radosh, 1970, pp. 125–52). The new relation between the economy and the state was intimately bound up with the new more concentrated market structure.

The ascendancy of the new corporate giants in the previously competitive marketplace posed problems for Social Darwinism as the legitimating principle of the capitalist economic order. Older notions of free and unfettered competition had to be, if not replaced, at least supplemented if monopoly capitalism was to be seen as legitimate. The need for legitimation on the part of monopoly capital produced a struggle on the ideological level, spearheaded by the National Civic Federation, to gain widespread acceptance of the alternative corporatist conception of the just and efficient social order. This new ideology drew heavily from emerging concepts of social engineering and social efficiency which had grown up alongside industrial engineering and industrial efficiency. These new ideas about social organization found their most enthusiastic base, naturally enough, in the swelling ranks of professionals and managers employed within the growing bureaucracies necessary to coordinate the far-flung activities of the new industrial combinations (Weinstein, 1969, p. 252).

Changes in the legal structure and ideology were motivated by the peculiar incompatibility of monopoly capital with the character of the legal and ideological institutions inherited from the previous social formation. The relationship between the new market structure and change in labor relations is not so direct. The new capital–labor order was achieved because the monopolistic reorganization of capital decisively changed the balance of class forces. The elimination of excess capacity which followed the consolidation reduced the demand for labor. The ending of vigorous price-cutting through co-respective pricing behavior meant that workers were less likely to capture the benefits of increasing labor productivity through declines in the cost of living.[13] Gordon *et al.* find that mechanization (as a strategy of labor control) proceeded more rapidly in concentrated industries (1982, p. 129). Large corporations were also in a better position to pursue various strategies designed to undermine working-class solidarity. In addition, a more unified capital was in a much better position to resist unionization, transfer work between plants, and weather strikes. Gordon *et al.* summarize: "until the merger movement of 1898–1902, few corporations had either the margin to develop such strategies or the resources with which to implement costly innovations" (1982, p. 144).

Just as monopoly was not incompatible *per se* with the pattern of labor relations inherited from competitive capitalism, so it was not incompatible *per se* with the geographical boundaries inherited from the previous SSA. While there had long been an expansionist dynamic in American economic and political life, the advent of the monopoly corporation greatly accelerated this tendency. The large corporation naturally demanded a larger market and a more extensive and secure supply of raw materials. Most importantly the new larger corporations had the material and financial means to expand into the capitalist world market. The consolidation of monopoly capital everywhere in the capitalist world at the end of the nineteenth century brought a renewed scramble for foreign markets (Magdoff, 1969, pp. 31–40).[14] The United States was not to be left behind.

Each of the core institutions of the monopoly SSA was constructed around the new monopoly structure. Can looking for such an institution provide guidance in understanding the construction of other SSAs in other times and places? To answer this question we will now turn our attention to the construction of the post-World War II SSA in the United States.

The construction of the postwar SSA

Introduction

In the last section, I argued that the organizing principle of the SSA constructed at the turn of the century could be found in the dominance of one of the institutions over the others. In this section, I will argue that this observation of a single powerful institution serving as the centerpiece of the SSA cannot be generalized. SSAs have been constructed within which a single dominant institution cannot be located. Our second case of SSA construction in US economic history – that of the post-World War II SSA – provides us with such an example.

The postwar SSA

There are at least five institutions of the postwar SSA which meet Kotz' criteria for consideration as core institutions of the SSA. The first is the conservative Keynesian state. Following World War II, the state took substantial responsibility for the level of economic activity through the use of fiscal and monetary policy. This intervention was designed to minimize government influence over the allocation of resources through concentrating on the use of tax cuts, military, and infrastructural spending. US international dominance was a second core part of the postwar SSA. Third, labor relations after the war were dominated by bureaucratic bread-and-butter industrial unionism. Industrial unionism was firmly established in basic industry, but labor organization was largely excluded from the secondary sector of the economy creating a dual labor market. Unions tended to respect management prerogatives, bargaining within bureaucratic norms. Political action was limited to participation in the Democratic Party. A fourth institution was the Democratic coalition, which organized state support for the other institutions of the SSA.

Fifth, Cold War ideology helped to unite the country behind the postwar social order. All five institutions will be shown to have been consolidated early in the life of the postwar SSA.[15]

Cold War ideology does appear to have been subordinated historically to the development of US international dominance and to some extent to the other institutions in the SSA. A case can be made as well that the Democratic coalition was dependent on the other four institutions in the SSA, as they constituted the political program and a good part of the source of support for the coalition. It does not seem possible, however, to make a compelling case that the other three core institutions can be ordered in a strict hierarchy. While US international dominance facilitated both the Keynesian state and postwar labor relations, it was not the prime mover in their institutionalization, nor did it demand them for its own reproduction. Similarly the Keynesian state facilitated US international dominance and bureaucratic unionism, but was not a precondition for their existence, nor were they a precondition for the existence of the Keynesian state. Lastly, the conservative character of postwar labor relations facilitated both US international dominance and the Keynesian state, but was not the driving force of their existence, nor were these other institutions necessary for the change in postwar unionism.[16]

In the course of examining the construction of the core institutions which marked the transition to the postwar SSA, I will argue that each of them was in fact consolidated during and immediately after World War II. The war years mark the turning point in the transition from stagnation to growth. It is the argument of this section that it is the social influence of the war itself which constituted the organizing factor in the construction of the new SSA.[17]

The conservative Keynesian state

The Keynesian state was consolidated shortly after World War II. The changing of the guard in 1932 from Republican to Democrat seemed at first to mark little change in economic policy. Although Roosevelt made no serious immediate attempt to balance the budget, and various spending programs were undertaken for the purposes of relief, the first five years of the New Deal were "Keynesian only occasionally by coincidence" (Lekachman, 1966, p. 123). As the economy picked up through 1937, Roosevelt began to think seriously of balancing the budget, raising revenues and holding down expenditures (Stein, 1969, pp. 100–2). Roosevelt's fiscal prudence was rewarded with renewed recession.

The President was subsequently convinced to propose a program of increased expenditure, some of which was designed as "definite additions to the purchasing power of the nation" (Collins, 1981, p. 44; Stein, 1969, pp. 111–12). Congress passed the appropriation in June, 1938 and the recession obliged by bottoming out in the same month. The economy rose thereafter through World War II. While other factors surely contributed to the timing of the "Roosevelt recession," many observed the coincidence of the downturn with the attempt to balance the budget and the upturn with the renewal of government spending. (Stein, 1969, pp. 114–15).

The upturn of 1938 notwithstanding, the victory of the Keynesian policy prescription was by no means secure. The President himself continued publicly to regret the existence of the deficits, to hold the balanced budget as an ultimate goal, and to promise the eventual return of fiscal orthodoxy (Lekachman, 1966, p. 125). Business, generally opposed to the New Deal after an initial honeymoon, was not enthusiastic about deficit spending as a permanent government policy option.

In 1939, Roosevelt submitted a bill to the new Congress proposing that the Reconstruction Finance Corporation be authorized to borrow 3.86 billion dollars which it would then spend or lend. The bill met defeat at the hands of conservative legislators (Patterson, 1967, pp. 318–22; Stein, 1969, pp. 120–3). One Republican described the defeat of the Spend–Lend Bill as "the first definite clear-cut repudiation by Congress of the theory that we can spend ourselves into prosperity" (cited by Patterson [1967, pp. 321–2]).

By the start of World War II, Keynesian fiscal policy had achieved some application and success, particularly in connection with moderating the Roosevelt recession in 1938. It was not, however, widely accepted as a regular tool of government. Keynesianism certainly had not yet been tried on the scale necessary to achieve exemplary success. The experience of World War II altered the political fortunes of Keynesian state policy.

The massive mobilization of war production across the capitalist world and the equally massive destruction of that production propelled the world out of depression.[18] The war was a graphic lesson in the effectiveness of the Keynesian prescription for renewed prosperity. It was apparent that the Keynesian solution did not demand that the government spending projects be useful, as Roosevelt would have preferred. Neither did it necessarily involve the utilization of the public sector to achieve far-reaching reform.[19] It did not include the progressive socialization of ever greater sectors of the private economy as Keynesianism's business opponents feared. It involved waste, pure and simple.[20] And the more wasteful the expenditure, the easier it was to organize.

In addition to demonstrating the efficacy of the Keynesian prescription in practice, the war also had a number of other influences on the establishment of the postwar Keynesian state. Among the most important of these was the political effect of the full employment experienced during the war years. This experience moved the goal of full employment much higher on the political agenda (Stein, 1969, pp. 170–1).[21] The war years were also important in bringing many convinced Keynesians into government service (Lekachman, 1966, pp. 152–3; Collins, 1981, p. 13). The war provided Keynesian economists with the opportunity to refine the application of their theories to actual government fiscal problems (Lekachman, 1966, pp. 152–3; Stein, 1969, p. 191; Collins, 1981, p. 12).

In addition, the war period saw the establishment of a number of institutional changes in the state which facilitated the implementation of Keynesian fiscal policy. The Federal budget had to reach a certain size in order to be able to sufficiently influence the country's level of production by adjusting spending. The war achieved this. These higher expenditures would extend beyond the end of the war.

Supporting the new military establishment, paying benefits to veterans, and assisting in the world recovery after the war would all ensure larger Federal expenditures even in the absence of depression (Stein, 1969, p. 182). Financing the war raised government revenues to the point where tax cuts big enough to have a significant impact on the economy were possible. Accompanying this development was the spread of the income tax to ever greater segments of the population and its collection on a withholding basis (Stein, 1969, pp. 181–3; Collins, 1981, p. 146).

The new approach was embodied in the passage of the Employment Act of 1946. The debate over the bill made clear that a new policy consensus had emerged.[22] Congress accepted responsibility for the rate of unemployment, though what policies would be adopted to achieve high employment were left vague and undefined. Even the opponents of the more radical initial bill had felt constrained to offer constructive alternatives which implicitly accepted the goal of government responsibility for the maintenance of high employment (Lekachman, 1966, p. 175).

While the broadest parameters of a Keynesian policy of government responsibility for the level of economic performance had been sketched out, the specific content of that policy had yet to be determined. Keynesian demand management could be accomplished through any of a wide spectrum of policies. The postwar content of Keynesian policy was ultimately chosen to minimize government intervention in the market economy. Tax cuts would be frequently employed in preference to increased government spending. Truman's plans for expanding the public provision of housing and medical care in the postwar period were quickly defeated by the real estate lobby and the American Medical Association. Efforts to prop up demand would concentrate on military expenditure and the promotion of overseas demand. The acceptance of Keynesian demand management was achieved with the evaluation of the experience of the economic recovery during the war and the passage of the Employment Act of 1946. The direction of the content of Keynesian spending was set with the inauguration of the Marshall Plan in 1947 (see below) and the US entry into the Korean War in 1950 and the consequent jump in the military budget.

US international dominance and Cold War ideology

The US emerged from World War II the most powerful country on earth, both militarily and economically. The end of the war saw the productive capacities of France, the Netherlands, Germany, Italy, and Japan reduced by about 50 percent of their immediate prewar levels. By contrast, the United States emerged from the war with a 72 percent increase in its Gross National Product over 1939 (Kuznets, 1964, pp. 91–3). US industry entered the postwar era greatly strengthened.

The war contributed to the dissolution of the European colonial empires and consequently American dominance of the Third World (Cohen, 1973, p. 85). At the same time, the conduct of the war projected the US onto the world stage in a way it had not been before the war. The projection of American power onto the world scene ended the political influence of isolationist sentiment, eliminating domestic opposition to the United States' new international role.

One of the first and most far-reaching exercises of America's new-found influence was in the establishment of an open world trading order. This involved the prevention of the implementation of nationalist economic policies and meant the creation of a worldwide capitalist economy open to American investment and export. Marshall Plan aid was an important factor in encouraging European cooperation in creating a multilateral world order. Under the plan, US aid financed 25 percent of Western Europe's total imports and two-thirds of merchandise imports from the dollar area between 1947 and 1950 (Block, 1977, p. 240, n. 41).

World War II was fought in large part over the question of international capitalist hegemony (as well as the survival of the Soviet Union). The outcome of the war decisively answered this question. US dominance of the international capitalist economy had already been ordained by the end of the war and may be dated to the Bretton Woods agreements in 1944. The inauguration of the Marshall Plan in 1947 marks the success of the American effort to create an open capitalist economy.[23]

The military outcome of the war similarly moved the Soviet Union to the forefront of world affairs (Bagguley, 1967). The growing competition between the two superpowers (even if often primarily defensively motivated on the Soviet side) provided fertile ground for the nurture of the Cold War world-view. The war had also demonstrated the effectiveness of a common enemy in mobilizing consensus. The Cold War developed very rapidly in the context of American worldwide expansion and can be said to have been fully recognized in the promulgation of the Truman Doctrine of containment in 1947. This world-view argued that there was an intimate connection between the alleged totalitarian character of Soviet domestic policy and a logic of international expansionism. This view achieved its most consistent formulation in NSC-68, a secret policy document prepared by a joint committee of the Department of State and Defense in 1949 (Wolfe, 1979, pp. 12–14).[24]

Capital–labor relations[25]

Postwar capital–labor relations emerged as the outcome of a complex struggle whose terrain shifted repeatedly from the shopfloor to the state and back again. Building labor militancy was reflected in the famous Section 7(a) of the National Industrial Recovery Act (NIRA). A burst of labor-organizing followed in 1933 and 1934.[26] One outcome of this period of labor activity was the passage of the Wagner Act, which threw the force of law behind collective bargaining (Millis and Brown, 1950, pp. 27–8; Bernstein, 1970, pp. 322–49).[27]

The Committee for Industrial Organization was formed under the leadership of John L. Lewis in 1935 in frustration at the ultimate failure of the 1933–34 organizing drives and AFL intransigence in the defense of craft union prerogatives.

The Committee also acted both in response to and in hopes of preserving the favorable situation created by the passage of the Wagner Act (Brody, 1981, p. 140). The founding of the CIO coincided with another rank-and-file upsurge in 1936 and 1937. This upsurge, combined with competition between the new Congress of Industrial Organizations (CIO) and the American Federation of Labor (AFL), resulted in rapid growth in union membership. Both the AFL and the CIO increased their memberships to over 3 million by the summer of 1937 (Bernstein, 1970, pp. 684–7).

The momentum of the organizing drive was, however, decisively broken by the failure of the Little Steel strike in 1937 (Bernstein, 1970, pp. 478–9; Piven and Cloward, 1979, p. 144). The "Roosevelt recession" in 1938 hit the unions very hard (Lichenstein, 1982, pp. 13–14).[28] Joshua Freeman summarizes the state of CIO organizing before the war:

> As late as 1939–40, in each basic industry there was at least one important component that did not nationally recognize any union (Ford, Goodyear, Westinghouse, Little Steel, Southern Textiles, etc.). In some industries, such as meatpacking, the major producers did not sign their first contracts with the CIO until 1940. Even where unions had been recognized as bargaining agents, locals were often only beginning to develop as coherent and stable organizations. By June 1941, among the major industrial unions, only the UMW, the ACWA, and the UAW at Ford had union shops (Freeman, 1978, p. 576).

This impasse was resolved by the advent of World War II and the most extensive government intervention in the relationship between capital and labor to that date. In return for the no strike pledge, the War Labor Board granted unions recognition along with maintenance of membership and the dues checkoff.[29] The war ended with unions firmly established in America's basic industries. At the same time, the union leadership's reliance on the War Labor Board's enforcement of the membership and dues checkoff provisions separated the leadership from direct responsibility to the rank-and-file. Indeed, widespread wildcat strike activity often pitted the rank-and-file against a leadership pledged to enforce the no–strike pledge. This period undermined union democracy and established the bureaucratic tradition which was to plague American unionism in the postwar period (Lichenstein, 1982, passim).

When the war ended, the extent of union penetration of management prerogative was still open to dispute (Brody, 1981, p. 179). This issue was dramatically and decisively fought out in the 1945 GM strike. The UAW demanded a wage increase without a corresponding price increase. The union further demanded that General Motors "open the books" in order to demonstrate that the company had the financial resources to meet the demand. The ensuing strike lasted 113 days. The union successfully defended its wartime gains, but completely failed to expand its rights. This rough equilibrium on the question of management prerogative set the pattern for postwar contract settlements. Automatic cost-of-living and productivity-linked wage increases were quickly negotiated in subsequent contracts (Harris, 1982, pp. 131–51).

The passage of the Taft–Hartley Act in 1947 over Truman's veto marked a decisive change in labor's postwar political fortunes. This complex piece of legislation legalized state right-to-work laws and outlawed the secondary boycott and the sympathy strike, thus eliminating some of the most potent weapons of labor solidarity. In addition, those unwilling to sign an affidavit denying Communist affiliation were banned from union leadership posts.[30] This legislative setback tied the labor leadership even more closely to the fortunes of the Democratic Party in hopes of preventing further setbacks (Brody, 1981, pp. 215–34). Henry Wallace's decisive defeat in the 1948 elections sealed the fate of third-party impulses within the labor movement (Brody, 1981, pp. 223–7). The Communist Party's support of Wallace was also the last straw which led to the Red Purges in the CIO (Brody, 1981, p. 226; Lichtenstein, 1982, pp. 236–7).

The Red Purges, along with the passage of the Taft–Hartley Act, put a stop to the expansion of the union movement. The unorganized sectors were disproportionately female and minority. This abrupt halt in the spread of unionization set the stage for the hardening of the US market into a two-tier system. Several recent treatments by labor economists have identified this system as a dual labor market with white male workers in good union jobs and minorities and women unrepresented and in less favored positions.[31] Collective bargaining in the postwar period also saw the addition of bureaucratic methods of control to management's arsenal of shopfloor strategies.[32]

The early years of the postwar period saw the consolidation of a complex set of institutions, which were to channel capital–labor contention in the coming years. Labor had achieved stable unions organized along industrial lines in basic industry by the end of the war. After the immediate postwar strike wave, these unions often functioned in a bureaucratic manner, relying on "peaceful collective bargaining" agreements with cooperative management, rather than on the mobilization of a militant rank-and-file. Postwar unions generally confined themselves to bargaining within the pattern established by early settlements following the war, trading increases in wages for management control of the production process and other aspects of corporate decision-making. Many workers, disproportionately female and minority, were left unorganized in the secondary labor market.

The Democratic coalition

The critical elections literature marks the late twenties and early thirties as the start of broad and durable electoral realignment (Burnham, 1970; Key, 1955; Ferguson, 1983, 1984; Sundquist, 1983; Jensen, 1981; Andersen, 1979). The realignment of the thirties is most dramatically manifested in the end of Republican electoral hegemony, and the accession of the Democratic Party as the new majority party in American politics. The newly ascendant Democratic coalition consisted of a majority electoral coalition and a specific set of policies which this coalition espoused and implemented. The history of the construction of the Democratic coalition is the history of the assembling of this electoral majority and the adoption of Cold War liberalism as the guiding program of the coalition.

The new Democratic electoral majority was marked by both continuities and conversions (Ladd and Hadley, 1975, p. 41). The most conspicuous continuity was that of solid support for the Democratic Party in the white South. Along with this element of continuity, the new Democratic majority had its origins in two shifts in political allegiance. The first was a shift of a segment of the capitalist class toward a more internationalist, less anti-union stance. The second was the massive shift of the Northern urban vote away from the Republican Party and toward the Democrats. This shift was multidimensional, being rooted in the increasing political mobilization of the working class and poor Americans. This class cleavage revealed itself in the shift of union, black, Catholic, Jewish and lower-class Protestant votes into the Democratic column.

In his treatment of the transition "from normalcy to New Deal", Ferguson (1984) emphasizes the growth of a multinational liberal bloc within capital. Ferguson defines this bloc as made up of firms and industries which were capital-intensive rather than labor-intensive, and which became leaders in their fields, both nationally and internationally. As the economy grew during the expansion accompanying World War I and the Roaring Twenties, more and more American firms and industries underwent the technical change necessary to reduce their dependency on labor. Increasing numbers of firms moved into international leadership positions within their industries. These firms allied themselves with important international financiers who had always had relatively low labor costs. These sectors of capital stood to benefit from a more internationally oriented policy of free trade. This led them to break with the more nationally oriented protectionist bloc which dominated the Republican Party under the "system of '96." Their relative lack of exposure in the labor market made them more amenable to cementing an electoral alliance with organized sectors of labor, creating a powerful one-two punch of financial resources and votes (Ferguson, 1984).

One cannot ignore the various sources of popular mobilization seeking political solutions to the miseries of the Great Depression.[33] Perhaps the most important element in this political upsurge from below was the electoral mobilization of the new CIO unions behind the Roosevelt coalition. The AFL felt constrained to follow the CIO into the Democratic coalition and contend with it for influence over the administration's labor policy. If influence in the state was important to labor, labor's electoral mobilization was essential to the success of the New Deal coalition (Milton, 1982, pp. 90–3).

The New Deal coalition consisted of the yoking together of a mobilized lower-class vote and a sector of capital, distinguished by its internationalism and high capital–labor ratios and limiting its opposition to unionism. Important elements of this alliance were clearly in place by 1936. Labor's Non-Partisan League was an important part of Roosevelt's re-election victory in that year (Milton, 1982, pp. 90–3). Ferguson (1984) also dates the integration of the internationalist sector of capital into the New Deal coalition to this year, when this sector remained in the Democratic Party while other business interests bailed out. The war years, however, were important in consolidating this alliance.

It was Roosevelt's conservative conduct of the war mobilization effort which finally reassured American business of the nonrevolutionary character of the New Deal (Brody, 1975, p. 300 and *passim*). The production planning agencies in the Federal government were careful to interfere with business control of the economy to the minimum extent possible. Many key positions on the War Production Board (WPB) were filled with "dollar-a-year men" essentially donated by their previous employers in private industry. Davis describes this phenomena as a process in which "the previous estrangement of the dominant fractions of corporate capital from the New Deal was superseded by intimate collaboration, as the flower of Wall Street became the economic warlords of Washington" (Davis, 1986, p. 75).

Mike Davis argues that labor's participation in the New Deal was also consolidated during the war years. Both labor and the Roosevelt administration had reason to increase their reliance on one another. In the 1942 Congressional elections, the Democrats had lost much of the Midwest to the Republicans. The urban political machines were declining in effectiveness at a time when the urban vote was becoming ever more crucial. Labor could potentially mobilize these votes. On labor's side, Congress had just passed the repressive Smith–Connally Act, authorizing Federal intervention in strikes and banning direct union political contributions. Labor sought to counter this defeat, and the prospect of future defeats, by mobilizing its membership behind the Democratic Party (Davis, 1986, pp. 83–4).

The assembly of a majority coalition was only half of the project of creating the Democratic coalition. The other half involved giving political direction to this coalition in the form of a program. Fundamentally, the program of the Democratic coalition was to come to consist of support for the other institutions of the SSA. To oversimplify somewhat, this program consisted of liberal Keynesian policies at home and support for US dominance abroad. Labor would provide one of the main supports for these planks and would in return receive limited support from the state. The story of the development and acceptance of these institutions is told elsewhere in this chapter. I argue that the war and its effects were essential to the consolidation of Keynesian state policy, US international dominance, and the postwar pattern of capital–labor relations. Thus the development of the political program of the Democratic coalition would await the war years.

The consolidation of the SSA

Each of the core institutions in the SSA was consolidated within five years of the end of the war. The government had committed itself to Keynesian policy with the Employment Act of 1946. The content of much of this spending was determined with the Marshall Plan and the rearmament which accompanied entry into the Korean War. US international dominance was sealed by the end of the war. Much of the postwar pattern of capital–labor relations was in place following the securing of union recognition during the war, the postwar labor settlements and the passage of Taft–Hartley in 1947. While much of the Democratic coalition was in place by 1936, the war years further cemented the alliance, and the coalition would have to wait until the consolidation of the other institutions of the SSA after the war to give content to its program.

As with the consolidation of the monopoly capitalist SSA at the turn of the century, the relatively brief period of time in which the SSA was consolidated suggests that we should look beyond the coincidental confluence of autonomous institutions suggested by Mandel. Nor do these institutions seem to originate as part of a political program as suggested by Gordon *et al.* All of these core institutions were to be integrated into a political coalition and program aptly entitled Cold War liberalism. Cold War liberalism united the centrist labor leadership with sections of capital as the chief proponents of a conservative Keynesian growth strategy at home coupled with an aggressive defense of empire aboard. But this political unification of the principal institutions of the postwar SSA appears to have developed along with the institutions of the SSA and not as their prime mover.

The organizing principle of the SSA

Is it possible to identify a single institution within the core institutions of the SSA as providing the unifying principle around which the other institutions were constructed? In this postwar SSA it does not appear that one institution dominated the others to the extent that the oligopolization of industry dominated the mono-poly capital SSA. Cases for the centrality of conservative Keynesianism, American imperialism, and the postwar capital–labor order could all be made with equal plausibility. In the case of this particular SSA, it is World War II which provides the unifying principle in the construction of the SSA. In examining the develop-ment of each of the core institutions of the SSA, it can be seen that the World War II years were crucial in its consolidation.

The massive reorganization of society, the tremendous mobilization of the populace, the conscious and deliberate intervention of the state, and the monumental changes wrought by the conduct and consequences of the war itself, all served to create a hothouse environment for social change. New institutions and ways of doing things were brought about simultaneously in many areas of society during the war. The war demonstrated the effectiveness of Keynesian spending. US international dominance was a major consequence of the war. The no-strike pledge and War Labor Board recognition determined the character of postwar labor relations. The conduct of the war mobilization would also have an effect on the Democratic coalition. The immediate postwar years were destined to be a period of shakedown and adjustment, a period of bringing the new institutions into harmony with one another. This integration of the newly created institutions was accomplished quickly in the first few years after the war.

Contingent history and the long cycle

This chapter set out to determine whether or not it was possible to discover the organizing principles behind the construction of the SSAs which have conditioned long periods of expansion in US economic history. In this we have been successful. Each of the SSAs under consideration was not the result of a chance confluence of independent events as Mandel contended. The core institutions of each SSA were organized around a singular change in the society. In the case of the monopoly capitalist SSA constructed at the turn of the century, that change was the inauguration of one of the constituent institutions of the SSA, the transition from competitive to monopoly market structures. The emergence of this institution was in one way or another the catalyst for the changes which took place in the rest of society. The monopoly capitalist structure of industry demanded changes in some parts of the social formation if it was to be reproduced, and facilitated change in other institutions. The shorthand reference to the SSA constructed at the beginning of the twentieth century as the monopoly capitalist SSA appears to be justified. The monopolization of industry is the lynchpin in the construction of the entire social structure. By contrast, the post-World War II SSA contained a number of powerful institutions, each consistent with the others, but none obviously dominant. In this case, the social mobilization and transformations wrought by World War II proved to be the key to construction of the postwar SSA.

While SSA construction appears to have an organizing principle at its center, this organizing principle does not appear to be centered necessarily around the piecing together of a political coalition and program as Gordon *et al.* have contended. In each of the American cases, Gordon *et al*'s thesis has not been borne out. In the first instance the SSA was organized around a single powerful institution; in the second case around a war.

In sum we have found an organizing principle in each of the SSAs constructed, but this organizing principle has been different in each case. In fact it is difficult to imagine two more disparate principles.

This finding has several serious implications for the future development of the SSA school of Marxian crisis theory. The discovery of an organizing principle in each of the SSAs examined solves one of the major unanswered questions in the theory of social structures of accumulation. Previously, the theory was unable to account for the construction of a complex, highly integrated social structure including not only economic institutions but political, ideological, and cultural institutions as well. The discovery of the principles of SSA construction in each of the situations in US history within which the theory contends an SSA was constructed strengthens the theory considerably. The SSA theory has been bolstered as an explanation of alternating periods of stagnation and growth in the American past. We can now convincingly account within the SSA framework for the ending of the period of stagnation and the inauguration of the subsequent period of relatively healthy accumulation.

This strengthening of the SSA as an explanation of stagnation and growth in the past poses serious problems for the SSA theory as a predictor of future events. If each of the principles of SSA construction is different from the others, we have failed to find a general principle of the construction of SSAs. There are two possible explanations for this. The first is that one or both of the American cases we have examined is somehow anomalous, but that there is nevertheless a general principle of SSA construction which generally manifests itself. This general principle for exceptional reasons failed to manifest itself in the construction of either or both the monopoly capitalist and postwar SSAs in the US. The other possibility is that the construction of SSAs is in each case historically contingent.

It is beyond the scope of this chapter to definitively demonstrate which of these two possible explanations is the correct one. Such a demonstration would of necessity involve the close examination of the construction of SSAs in Europe as well as in some non-Western countries including at least the Japanese case. A superficial examination of the European case, however, seems to bear out the contention that the integrative factor in SSA construction is specific to each SSA. The end of the European depression in the late nineteenth century was marked by the transition to monopoly capitalism. It would be reasonable to hypothesize, by analogy to the American case, that this transition was organized around the institution of the monopoly market structure itself. Europe experienced two different resolutions of the worldwide Great Depression of the thirties. The first was the institution of fascism before the war, tried most successfully in National Socialist Germany. In this case, the Gordon *et al.* scenario of the mobilization of a powerful class alliance aimed at capturing state power seems to constitute the organizing principle of the fascist attempt to resolve the capitalist crisis of the thirties. The ruthless exercise of state power was essential to the restructuring of the other institutions in the society. The fascist experiment was aborted by its military defeat at the end of World War II. The radical scouring of the bedrock of European society by the scourge of war, coupled with a reconstruction under American auspices, aimed chiefly at forestalling a socialist victory in Europe, may go a long way toward explaining the construction of the Western European pattern of social democracy. This pattern constitutes the second post-Depression European SSA. A similar process appears to have resulted in the creation of a quite different structure of accumulation in Japan.

This short examination of the European case bears out the contention that the principles of SSA construction are historically contingent. In the first instance, one major institutional change, the change in market structure, appears to be the organizing principle. In the second case, the capture of the state in order to implement a far-reaching reorganization of the social structure seems to be the key. In the last case, the institutional leveling effects of war and subsequent reconstruction provide the integrating factor of the postwar SSA. Each of these organizing principles for the SSA is different from the others. Pending the introduction of further evidence and argumentation, we are forced to conclude that there is yet no definite identification of an overarching principle of SSA construction.

If the organizing principle of each SSA is unique to it, it is difficult to predict the character of that principle in advance. Certainly we cannot make any such predictions in the abstract concerning SSAs in general. If we cannot predict the character of the organizing principle of future SSAs, we are certainly unable to predict their timing.[34] This inability is not a problem if our mission is to explain alternating periods of growth and stagnation in the past. However, a theory of long cycles or long waves must predict that both periods of stagnation and periods of healthy accumulation must endure for relatively long periods of time. While long-wave theories abandon the strict periodicity of long-cycle theories, they must still be held responsible for explaining the relative duration of the different phases of the wave. If each SSA is constructed in a historically contingent manner, each period of stagnation ends in a historically contingent manner. Hence we have no basis upon which to predict confidently that such a stagnation period will be long or short. One might expect that it would generally take a substantial amount of time to encounter the historically contingent factor around which the next SSA will be constructed. Such an observation falls far short, however, of a theory which not only explains but predicts long periods of stagnation (alternating with long periods of relatively rapid accumulation).

Our examination of the principles underlying the construction of SSAs has explained the concrete historical genesis of the SSA in the American cases. In the process we have called into question the adequacy of the theory as an explanation for specifically long waves of capital accumulation. We have, however, fortified the theory as one of alternating periods of expansion and stagnation. We have introduced a greater element of historical contingency into the SSA theory at least as regards the SSAs' construction. At the same time, the recognition of this historical contingency strengthens the theory in its ability to analyze the actual movements of historical accumulation.[35]

Notes

1 See Weisskopf (this volume ch. 8).

2 The inevitable tendency of the organic composition of capital to rise is a point of contention within Marxian economics. For a review of both sides of this controversy which ultimately joins the camp doubting the existence of this inevitable tendency, see van Parijs (1980).

3 There are obviously analogies between the assembling of the economic, political, and ideological conditions for the initiation of capitalist relations of production and the assembling of conditions for the rekindling of the capitalist accumulation process. Primitive accumulation, however, takes place within a social environment not dominated by capitalist relations of production. Primitive accumulation must be seen as a problem involved in the transition from one mode of production to another.

4 Many important institutions within the SSA are not included in this short list. Among them is the set of institutions which regulates the money supply. The struggle over the maintenance of the gold standard was obviously important to the future of the accumulation process. It has been left off the list because it was a struggle about preserving an institution, rather than changing one. The establishment of the Federal Reserve system in 1914 was also an important

event, but it took place too late to constitute part of the core of the SSA. The family is also not discussed. An extremely important part of the accumulation process, the family has undergone a number of important changes in its internal structure. It is not clear, however, that these changes follow the periodization of the changes in the SSA which is the concern of this chapter.

5 Nelson (1959, pp. 106–26) has found that merger activity is in general closely correlated with the business cycle.

6 This general outline of the timing of the merger movement can be found in Edwards (1979, pp. 42–3).

7 This arrangement was reflected in microcosm in attempts to implement Taylorism on the shopfloor. The organization of the labor process was to be removed from the conflictual relationship between labor and capital and subjected to organization by the experts.

8 It is also not difficult to argue that the policy of much of the non-socialist labor leadership was guided by the principles propounded by the National Civic Federation. Samuel Gompers was the original First Vice-President of the Federation and retained that position until his death in 1924. John Mitchell of the United Mine Workers was an active member. The heads of the railroad brotherhoods and many AFL international unions were also on the executive committee (Weinstein, 1969, p. 8).

Ironically, it seemed that businessmen were the most prominent among the groups who were unwilling to put the corporate ideology into action. Montgomery (1981, pp. 48–90) and Foner (1964, pp. 61–110) argue forcefully that, despite the efforts of some in the NCF to promote collective bargaining with "responsible" union leaders, businessmen consistently preferred a union-free environment. Even Weinstein (1969, p. 18) admits that by 1904, in the face of an anti-union drive participated in by some of the NCF's most prominent corporate supporters, the NCF had to abandon the promotion of union recognition in favor of various corporate welfare schemes for workers. Nonetheless, the effectiveness of the ideology depended on its being practiced, not by big business, but by government, small business, and labor.

9 The organization of the Knights of Labor, the American Federation of Labor (AFL), and the strike waves of 1877, 1886, and 1894 were only the high points of this activity (Brecher, 1972). Three times as many workers were involved in strikes at the end of the 1880s as at the beginning (Gordon et al., 1982, pp. 96–9).

10 Gordon et al. (1982, p. 129) find that this mechanization proceeded more rapidly in consolidated industries.

11 Clawson (1980) sees the implementation of Taylorism as a crucial turning point in the struggle between labor and capital on the shopfloor. The essential character of Taylorism for Clawson is that it is the first capitalist strategy on the shopfloor to challenge seriously the worker's control of the labor process itself. Clawson argues that an understanding of Taylorism is central to the history of labor control strategies. Emphasizing specific features of Taylor's system, Edwards (1979) sees Taylorism as a failed experiment from which much was learned. Edwards emphasizes instead the introduction of technical control at the turn of the century and the development of bureaucratic control in the postwar era. Clawson for his part recognizes the importance of technology in labor control strategies, while placing less emphasis on it, and argues that Edwards' bureaucratic control is a version of Taylorism. Taylorism and technical control are not incompatible and potentially reinforce one another. The debate can be seen as one over the relative importance of Taylorism and technical control strategies in the new monopoly corporations. Clawson dates the dominance of Taylor's views in the management movement from the early 1900s.

12 The foregoing account of the development of capital–labor relations is drawn from Gordon et al. (1982, pp. 100–64).

13 Dan Clawson has suggested to me that an additional advantage for a stable price level is that corporations are not tempted to initiate wage cuts in response to falling prices. Wage cuts tend to provoke strikes and other labor strife, as people are frequently more militant in defending their current wage than in fighting for new benefits.

14 The literature on the relationship between monopoly and imperialism goes back to Hobson (1965 [1862]) and Lenin (1939 [1916]).

15 These are not the only important institutions in the postwar SSA. Institutions not dealt with include those organizing money and credit. Monetary policy is important, but during the period in question is generally subordinated to the conduct of fiscal policy. The family is not dealt with to any significant extent. The reproduction of the family structure was the object of intense struggle during the immediate postwar years, after the challenge posed by the entry of women into the wartime industrial workforce. This conflict was an important event for both gender relations and the construction of the SSA. It is not dealt with in the body of the chapter as I have ruled out discussion of struggles over the reproduction of existing institutions. Race and gender relations are discussed in relation to the development of the dual labor market. This does not exhaust the importance of race and gender in the postwar social order.

16 The change in the character of state policy is most often recognized as the feature of the institutional landscape which separates the pre-World War II situation from that of the postwar world. While the change in the character and range of acceptable state activity is important and striking, the change in this institution is no more radical than that in the international arena or in the nature of capital–labor relations. The Keynesian state is more often acknowledged than change in the other social institutions perhaps precisely because it is a state intervention in the economy and thus may be subsumed under the general category of reform.

17 In the previous section, I considered the consolidation of the monopoly SSA and then developed the argument about its organizing principle. The following section adopts a more chronological mode of presentation, suited to its argument about the crucial role of the war years.

18 The production of products which are then promptly destroyed is reminiscent of Keynes' parable about the possibility of fiscal stimulation through burying money in a mineshaft and then digging it up again.

19 This was the hope of the more radical disciples of Hansen's stagnation thesis.

20 I do not mean to suggest here that the defeat of fascism in World War II was not a worthy social goal. I am pointing out that the expenditure did not have as its purpose the increase of consumption or productive capacity.

21 The Republican presidential candidate in 1944, Thomas E. Dewey, accepted the goal of full employment and the role of government in bringing it about. In accepting the Republican nomination, he declared that "We Republicans are agreed that full employment shall be a first objective of national policy" (cited by Stein [1969, p. 173]). Later in the campaign he stated, "If at any time there are not sufficient jobs in private employment to go around, then government can and must create additional job opportunities because there must be jobs for all in this country of ours." The acceptance of government-sponsored full employment by the opposition party was an important step in the consolidation of Keynesian state policy.

22 The substitute version of the bill which ultimately passed was written by Mississippi Democrat Bill Whittington from material submitted to him by the US Chamber of Commerce (Collins, 1981, pp. 105–6). This represented a radical departure in the attitude and strategy of business leadership, which had previously held a position of purely negative opposition.

23 American expansion in the postwar period was, of course, not limited to Western Europe. The

penetration of the Third World was crucial to the establishment of the postwar international economic order.

24 Interestingly, the document also justified the increased military effort it recommended in Keynesian terms, arguing that the resultant spending would be good for the economy (Wolfe, 1979, pp. 76–7). NSC-68 turned the tide in the Truman administration in favor of drastically increased military spending (Block, 1977, pp. 104–8).

25 The description of the postwar order in capital–labor relations which follows is descended from the concept of the capital–labor accord developed by Bowles and Gintis (1982, pp. 51–93) and the union–capital truce described by Michelle Naples. Naples prefers "truce" to "accord," emphasizing that conflict is not ended with the establishment of stable institutions of capital–labor relations (Naples, 1982, pp. 24–74). David Montgomery makes similar observations concerning labor relations in the postwar era, labeling his set of institutions "the New Deal formula" (Montgomery, 1981, pp. 152–80). The description below also relies heavily on David Brody's (1981) emphasis on the role of class struggle at the level of the state. The argument concerning the influence of the war years on postwar labor relations relies heavily on Nelson Lichtenstein (1982).

26 Section 7(a) guaranteed labor the right to organize in industries covered by National Recovery Administration (NRA) codes. The Act contained little in the way of enforcement mechanism. The Act's effectiveness in encouraging labor organization proceeded from the politicization of the process of setting wages, hours, and working conditions inherent in negotiating the industry NRA codes under state auspices. This relative deprivatization of the labor contract was one price industry paid for public sanction to engage in planning and collusive practices. If labor was to have any influence on the conditions of its work in the emerging New Deal state, it was going to have to make its influence felt beyond the shopfloor and working-class neighborhood at the level of the industry and the nation. To do this, labor had to be organized.

27 The Wagner Act further politicized capital–labor relations in mandating government-supervised elections to determine representation and compulsory recognition of elected unions. The Act was only one aspect of a greatly altered balance of influence within the state (Brody, 1981, pp. 100–5).

28 Labor also suffered political reverses. FDR was seeking to distance himself from the CIO. Conservative victories in the 1938 Congressional elections severely undermined labor's legislative power. In the South and West, a variety of new anti-labor laws were passed. Labor suffered a number of state and local electoral defeats (Lichtenstein, 1982, p. 19). This political setback for labor, at the same time as it was experiencing reversals in organizing within industry, is indicative of the close relationship that had been developing between industrial and political action since the NRA period.

29 Maintenance of membership required that employees who were members of the union must remain members in good standing for the life of the agreement. While the unions would have preferred the union shop or the closed shop, maintenance of membership relieved the union of fear of losing its membership. The dues checkoff required the company to deduct the member's dues from his or her paycheck and pay this amount directly to the union. This provision put union finances on a solid basis. Both of these provisions were necessary to union survival during the war. However, they removed the membership's strongest means of disciplining the leadership, withdrawal from the union and the withholding of dues.

30 For a full account of Taft–Hartley's provisions, see Millis and Brown (1950, pp. 395–665).

31 See, especially, Edwards (1979).

32 Bureaucratic control approaches control of the labor process through elaborating a set of rules and procedures which specifies as closely as possible methods of supervision and evaluation.

Many of the concerns of bureaucratic control are the same as those of collective bargaining. The bureaucratic structure of the postwar capitalist firms came to embody the results of labor–management struggle over control of the workforce. Negotiating shopfloor issues within a framework of respect for bureaucratic norms would be institutionalized in the postwar period (Edwards, 1979, pp. 131–2; Gordon et al., 1982, pp. 189–90).

33 While Ferguson (1983) argues that electoral realignments are in general conditioned by realignments within the dominant blocs of capital, he makes a partial exception to this rule in the case of the New Deal realignment, allowing that working people were able to organize a significant degree of electoral mobilization in their own interests.

34 Even if there was a single organizing principle, this would not necessarily allow us to make predictive statements as to the timing of the construction of the SSA. Both of the factors identified in our survey of the American construction of SSAs, a change in the industrial structure and war, do not take place at regular intervals.

35 For a development of this argument, see McDonough (this volume, ch. 4).

References

Andersen, Kristen, 1979. *The Creation of a Democratic Majority, 1928–1936*. University of Chicago Press.

Bagguley, John, 1967. "The World War and the Cold War,"in *Containment and Revolution*, ed. David Horowitz, pp. 76–124. Boston: Beacon Press.

Bernstein, Irving, 1970. *Turbulent Years*. Boston: Houghton Mifflin.

Block, Fred L., 1977. *The Origins of International Economic Disorder*. Berkeley: University of California Press.

Bowles, Samuel, and Herbert Gintis, 1982. "The Crisis of Liberal Democratic Capitalism: The Case of the United States," *Politics and Society*, 11(1): 51–93.

Brecher, Jeremy, 1972. *Strike*. Boston: South End Press.

Brody, David, 1975. "The New Deal and World War II," in *The New Deal: The National Level*, ed. John Braeman, Robert H. Bremner, and David Brody, pp. 267–309. Columbus: Ohio State University Press.

1981. *Workers in Industrial America*. Oxford University Press.

Burnham, James, 1970. *Critical Elections and the Mainsprings of American Politics*. New York: W. W. Norton.

1981. "The 'System of Ninety-Six': An Analysis," in *The Evolution of American Electoral Systems*, ed. Paul Kleppner et al., pp. 147–202. Westport, Conn.: Greenwood Press.

Clawson, Dan, 1980. *Bureaucracy and the Labor Process*. New York: Monthly Review Press.

Clayton, James L., 1970. *The Economic Impact of the Cold War*. New York: Harcourt, Brace and World.

Cohen, Benjamin J., 1973. *The Question of Imperialism: The Political Economy of Dominance and Dependence*. New York: Basic Books.

Collins, Robert M., 1981. *The Business Response to Keynes, 1929–1964*. New York: Columbia University Press.

Davis, Mike, 1986. *Prisoners of the American Dream*. London: Verso.

Economic Report of the President, 1985. Washington D.C.: Government Printing Office.

Edwards, Richard, 1979. *Contested Terrain*. New York: Basic Books.

Ferguson, Thomas, 1983. "Party Realignment and American Industrial Structure," in *Research in Political Economy*, vol. VI, pp. 1–82. Greenwich, Conn.: JAI Press.

1984. "From Normalcy to New Deal: Industrial Structure, Party Competition, and American Public Policy in the Great Depression," *International Organization*, 38(1): 41–94.

Foner, Philip S., 1964. *History of the Labor Movement in the United States*, vol. III. New York: International Publishers.

Freeman, Joshua, 1978. "Delivering the Goods: Industrial Unionism during World War II," *Labor History*, 19 (Fall): 574–91.

Gordon, David M., Richard Edwards, and Michael Reich, 1982. *Segmented Work, Divided Workers: The Historical Transformation of Labor in the United States*. Cambridge University Press.

Harris, Howell John, 1982. *The Right to Manage*. Madison: University of Wisconsin Press.

Hobson, John Atkinson, 1965 [1862]. *Imperialism, a Study*. Ann Arbor: University of Michigan Press.

Hofstadter, Richard, 1955. *The Age of Reform*. New York: Knopf.

1965. *Social Darwinism in American Thought*, revised edn. Boston: Beacon Press.

Jensen, Richard, 1981. "The Last Party System: Decay of Consensus, 1932–1980," in *The Evolution of American Electoral Systems*, ed. Paul Kleppner *et al.*, pp. 203–42, Westport, Conn.: Greenwood Press.

Key, V. O., Jr., 1955. "A Theory of Critical Elections," *Journal of Politics*, 17(1): 3–18.

Kirkland, Edward C., 1967. *Industry Comes of Age: Business, Labor, and Public Policy, 1860–1897*. Chicago: Quadrangle Books.

Kleppner, Paul, 1979. *The Third Electoral System*. Chapel Hill: University of North Carolina Press.

Kleppner, Paul, *et al.*, 1981. *The Evolution of American Electoral Systems*. Westport, Conn.: Greenwood Press.

Kolko, Gabriel, 1963. *The Triumph of Conservatism*. New York: Macmillan.

Kotz, David, 1987. "Long Waves and Social Structures of Accumulation: A Critique and Reformulation," *Review of Radical Political Economics*, 19(4): 16–38.

Kuznets, Simon, 1964. *Postwar Economic Growth*. Cambridge, Mass.: Belknap.

Ladd, Everett C., Jr. and Charles Hadley, 1975. *Transformations of the American Party System*. New York: W. W. Norton.

Lekachman, Robert, 1966. *The Age of Keynes*. New York: Random House.

Lenin, V. I., 1939 [1916]. *Imperialism: The Highest Stage of Capitalism*. New York: International Publishers.

Lichtenstein, Nelson, 1982. *Labor's War at Home*. Cambridge University Press.

Magdoff, Harry, 1969. *The Age of Imperialism*. New York: Monthly Review Press.

Mandel, Ernest, 1980. *Long Waves of Capitalist Development*. Cambridge University Press.

Millis, Harry A., and Emily Clark Brown, 1950. *From the Wagner Act to Taft–Hartley*. University of Chicago Press.

Milton, David, 1982. *The Politics of US Labor: From the Great Depression to the New Deal*. New York: Monthly Review Press.

Montgomery, David, 1981. *Workers Control in America*. Cambridge University Press.

Naples, Michelle I., 1982. "Erosion of the Postwar Truce: Worker Militance and Labor Productivity," unpublished Ph.D. dissertation, University of Massachusetts, Amherst.

Navin, Thomas, and Marion Sears, 1955. "The Rise of a Market for Securities," *Business History Review*, 29 (June): 105–38.

Nelson, Ralph L., 1959. *Merger Movements in American Industry, 1895–1956*. Princeton University Press.

Patterson, James, 1967. *Congressional Conservatism and the New Deal*. Lexington: University of Kentucky Press.

Phillips, Joseph D., 1969. "Economic Effects of the Cold War," in *Corporations and the Cold War*, ed. David Horowitz, pp. 173–204. New York: Monthly Review Press.

Piven, Frances Fox, and Richard A. Cloward, 1979. *Poor People's Movements*. New York: Vintage Books.

Radosh, Ronald, 1970. "The Corporate Ideology of American Labor Leaders from Gompers to Hillman," in *For a New America: Essays in History and Politics from Studies on the Left, 1959–1967*, ed. James Weinstein and David W. Eakins, pp. 125–52. New York: Random House.

Seidman, Joel, 1953. *American Labor from Defense to Reconversion*. University of Chicago Press.

Stein, Herbert, 1969. *The Fiscal Revolution in America*. University of Chicago Press.

Sundquist, James L., 1983. *Dynamics of the Party System: Alignment and Realignment of Political Parties in the United States*. Washington, D.C.: The Brookings Institution.

Thorelli, Hans, 1954. *The Federal Antitrust Policy: Origination of an American Tradition*. Baltimore: Johns Hopkins University Press.

Van Alstyne, Richard W., 1960. *The Rising American Empire*. Chicago: Quadrangle.

van Parijs, P., 1980. "The Falling-Rate-of-Profit Theory of Crisis: A Rational Reconstruction by War of Obituary," *Review of Radical Political Economies*, 12(1): 1–16.

Weinstein, James, 1969. *The Corporate Ideal in the Liberal State: 1900–1918*. Boston: Beacon Press.

Williams, William Appleman, 1962. *The Tragedy of American Diplomacy*, revised edn. New York: Dell.

Wolfe, Alan, 1979. *The Rise and Fall of the 'Soviet Threat': Domestic Sources of the Cold War Consensus*. Washington, D.C.: IPS Books.

— 7 —

The financial system and the social structure of accumulation

MARTIN H. WOLFSON

The theory of the social structure of accumulation (SSA) has been advanced to explain in general the alternating periods of long-term boom and bust in advanced capitalist economies and in particular the current problems of US capitalism. A social structure of accumulation consists of the institutional environment affecting capital accumulation. Over a period of roughly fifty years, a given social structure of accumulation initially promotes capital accumulation, but ultimately winds up hindering that process.

The theoretical model of the social structure of accumulation posits that the financial system plays a central role in the institutional environment affecting capital accumulation. As argued by Gordon *et al.* (1982, pp. 23, 25):

> Among the most important institutions [that make up the social structure of accumulation] are *the system ensuring money and credit*, the pattern of state involvement in the economy, and the structure of class struggle ... it is not unreasonable to distinguish between those institutions that directly and demonstrably condition capital accumulation and those that touch it only tangentially. Thus, for example, *the financial system* bears a direct relation whereas the character of sports activity does not. (emphasis added)

Nonetheless, the specific analysis of the role of the financial system in the postwar social structure of accumulation in the United States has remained relatively undeveloped. This chapter is an attempt to contribute to that analysis.

The theoretical framework

The financial system that promoted capital accumulation in the United States in the postwar period comprised the institutional arrangements that governed the way in which financial transactions would take place. It was created during the 1930s and 1940s and had both a domestic and an international dimension.

It was based upon two fundamental aspects of the concrete conditions of the time: the structural characteristics of the financial system, and the relationship of class forces. The financial component of the postwar social structure of accumulation contributed to strong economic growth in the United States in three important ways: by promoting stability, by enhancing profitability, and by managing class conflicts.

Successful capital accumulation over the course of the early postwar period, however, changed the initial conditions upon which the financial component of the social structure of accumulation was built. In other words, it changed the structural characteristics of the system and the relationship of class forces. As a result of these changes, the institutional arrangements which had promoted growth no longer did so. In particular, stability gave way to instability, profitability eroded, and class conflict intensified.

These institutional arrangements which formed the financial component of the postwar social structure of accumulation now became a barrier to further capital accumulation. They were subsequently dismantled, by private market participants who sought to profit from the changed conditions, and by governmental authorities who attempted to ameliorate the instability, conflict, and worsening profitability that accompanied these changed conditions.

The actions of private market participants resulted in both financial innovation and speculation. On the government level, the postwar social structure of accumulation was dismantled by deregulation (domestically) and by negotiation (internationally).

The financial system and the postwar SSA

Domestically the financial component of the postwar social structure of accumulation comprised the framework for regulation and government support for financial institutions established in the 1930s; internationally, it consisted of the Bretton Woods monetary system created in 1944.

The domestic financial system

The early 1930s during the Great Depression were the most turbulent time in US banking history. During 1930–33, 9,096 banks suspended operations (Board of Governors, 1943, p. 283).[1] Mounting bank difficulties culminated in the closing of all banks on a national banking holiday on March 6, 1933. In addition, failures of nonfinancial businesses were widespread.

Out of this turmoil came landmark legislation such as the Banking Act of 1933 (sections 16, 20, 21, and 32 of which are known as the Glass–Steagall Act of 1933), the Securities and Exchange Act of 1934, and the Banking Act of 1935. This legislation produced sweeping changes in the financial system. These changes included the separation of commercial and investment banking; the prohibition of the payment of interest on demand deposits and ceiling interest rates on time deposits; the creation of the Federal Deposit Insurance Corporation, the Federal Home Loan Bank Board, and the Securities and Exchange Commission; and, perhaps the most significant change, the introduction of federal insurance of deposits.

These changes modified significantly existing ways of doing business in the financial system. They resulted in a new institutional structure which sought to limit the chaos that excess competition and a *laissez-faire* government policy had produced. This structure had two defining characteristics: a restriction of competition among financial institutions, and government protection to limit further failures.[2]

The restriction of competition took several forms. Ceilings on interest rates paid by commercial banks were established (and promulgated by the Federal Reserve by means of Regulation Q). These provided for maximum interest rates that could be paid on savings deposits, and prohibited the payment of interest on demand deposits altogether. These ceiling rates were created in reaction to what was perceived to be a destructive competitive bidding war for deposits.

A second form was the continuation and extension of the "compartmentalization" of financial institutions. In the legislation of the 1930s, commercial and investment banking were separated. Thus depository intermediaries were more sharply differentiated from nondepository financial institutions, to correspond to the already existing delineations among depository intermediaries: the specialization of savings and loan associations in home mortgages, commercial banks in business lending, and credit unions in consumer finance. Each benefited from a degree of monopoly and a restriction of competition. In addition, other financial institutions such as investment banks and insurance companies were not allowed to take deposits or to intrude upon the lending activities of the depository intermediaries.

A third type of restricted competition was the limitation on interstate banking.[3] Banks were not allowed to establish branches in states other than those in which they were chartered, and many states prohibited banks from having more than one branch (the "unit-banking" states).

The most important form of government protection for financial institutions was the introduction of federal deposit insurance and the creation of the Federal Deposit Insurance Corporation (FDIC) in 1933. The federal insurance of deposits was unquestionably the most important step taken to restore confidence in the banking system following the Banking Crises of 1931–33 and the widespread runs on banks throughout the country. In addition, government support for the safety and stability of the banking system was enhanced with the expansion of the governmental regulatory and supervisory role that the creation of the FDIC provided.

A second form of government support for financial institutions was provided by banking legislation which expanded the powers of the Federal Reserve system. Power was centralized in the Federal Reserve Board and control over open-market operations was consolidated, the collateral acceptable for lending through the discount window was liberalized, lending to non-member banks was permitted and, in general, the Federal Reserve's ability to act as a lender of last resort was strengthened.

The institutional structure which emerged from the turmoil of the 1930s took a

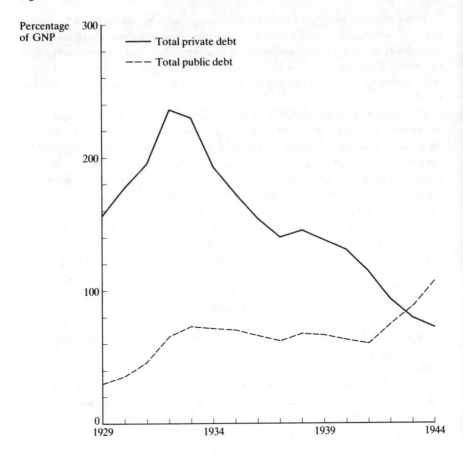

Fig. 7.1. Debt levels outstanding, 1929–44. (*Source*: US Department of Commerce [1975, series 398, 394].)

particular form, one based upon the concrete conditions of the time: the structural characteristics of the financial system and the relationship of class forces. The most important structural characteristic was the low level of private debt. The conditions of the Depression had dramatically reduced debt levels: many firms failed, many repudiated their debt, and asset values fell. (In addition, the domination of financial markets during World War II by the government's need to finance the war left little room for private debt creation.) See Figure 7.1. During the Depression, prices declined and the demand for credit was stagnant. These conditions influenced the design of the new institutional structure, which was created to function in the environment of low and stable interest rates made possible by the low debt levels and low level of inflation.

The relationship of class forces was such that significant reforms were instituted despite the opposition of the large banks. Public indignation over scandals in the stock market involving large banks helped the passage of the Glass–Steagall legislation separating commercial and investment banking. A coalition of forces representing labor and popular movements (including those whose savings disappeared during the bank failures of the early 1930s), business interests, and some small banks insured the passage of federal deposit insurance.[4] Congress, by enacting deposit insurance in 1933, at the same time rejected the proposed alternative to the failure of large numbers of small banks: state-wide and interstate branching. The branching restrictions prevented the large banks from expanding into territory occupied by small community banks. In general, the restriction of competition that was enforced by the reforms of the 1930s did much to protect the small financial institutions from the competitive pressures of larger institutions. As a result, small banks survived the 1930s and continue in large numbers today.[5]

This institutional structure supported economic growth in the postwar US economy in three ways: by promoting stability, by enhancing profitability, and by moderating class conflict.

Stability was assured by the renewed confidence in financial institutions made possible by the system of government support and protection, and by the environment of low and stable interest rates made possible by the low levels of debt and inflation.[6]

The profitability of financial institutions was enhanced by the monopoly rents provided by "compartmentalization," by the subsidy implicit in federal deposit insurance,[7] and by the assured profits made possible by the positive spread between long-term and short-term interest rates. In an environment of stable interest rates, thrift institutions in particular could make guaranteed profits simply by financing long-term mortgage loans with short-term deposits.

The profitability of nonfinancial corporations was enhanced by the postwar housing boom promoted by financing from subsidized and protected thrift institutions, and by the low and stable cost of borrowed funds (see Figure 7.2).

Class conflict, and also intraclass conflict, was moderated in several ways. Among financial capitalists, competition was limited by "compartmentalization," by the monopoly power and restricted entry characterizing the various financial industries. Conflict between financial and industrial capitalists was moderated by high absolute levels of profitability, which eased pressures over the relative division between the two groups. Also, the institutional structure in finance was such that financial institutions could make high profits while at the same time extending relatively low-cost loans to workers, consumers, and homeowners.

The increased stability, profitability, and moderation of class conflict all helped to provide an environment conducive to rapid economic growth. Thus, by promoting accumulation, the institutional structure of the domestic financial system functioned as an integral component of the postwar social structure of accumulation.

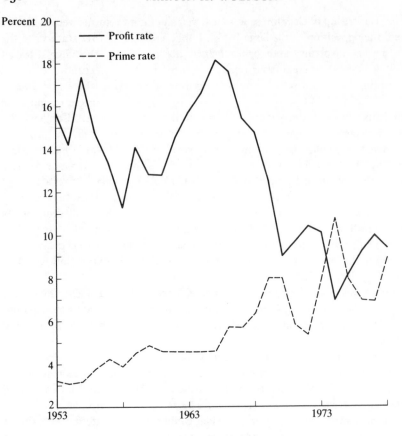

Fig. 7.2. Interest rates and profitability, 1953–78. Profit rate is calculated as profits before tax as a percentage of capital stock. (*Sources:* Board of Governors of the Federal Reserve System [1976, p. 707; 1981, p. 159]; US Department of Commerce [annual, table 1.16; 1987].)

The international financial system

The international financial system in the postwar period was the one established at Bretton Woods, New Hampshire in 1944.[8] Negotiations there created the conditions for a fixed-exchange rate monetary system based upon the dollar as a reserve currency, expanded international trade, and a structure of international financial organizations (such as the International Monetary Fund and the World Bank).[9]

The structural condition upon which this system was based was the need for international liquidity following World War II. The class relationship was US hegemony: the overwhelming superiority of US military, economic, and political power following World War II.[10]

Not surprisingly, then, the dollar was established as the center of the new international monetary system. The arrangement of the dollar as the reserve currency of the new system solved the problem of international liquidity. At the same time it provided important benefits for US corporations.

The international financial system functioned, as did the domestic system, as part of the postwar social structure of accumulation because it promoted stability, enhanced profitability, and moderated class conflicts.

It promoted stability by establishing a system of fixed exchange rates, which was a welcome change from the competitive devaluations and trade wars of the 1930s. Fixed exchange rates reduced uncertainty and promoted international trade. The annual average compound growth rate in export volume of the OECD countries was 1.0 percent from 1913 to 1950, but increased to 8.6 percent from 1950 to 1973 (Maddison, 1989, p. 67).

The Bretton Woods system also enhanced the profitability of US corporations. The role of the dollar as a reserve currency allowed the United States to spend freely around the world to establish military bases, influence foreign governments, and improve conditions for US foreign investment. Reducing barriers to world trade (as was done in 1947 by the General Agreement on Tariffs and Trade) enabled US corporations to take advantage of their dominant position in world markets.

Conflicts among capitalists from different nation-states were moderated because international economic and financial relationships were carried out under the umbrella of US hegemony. Capitalists in other nations did not have the strength (at the time) to challenge the dominance of the United States.

Economic growth and the financial SSA

Capital accumulation is a dynamic process. Economic growth in the postwar period in the United States and in the world economy resulted in changes in the initial conditions – the structural characteristics of the financial system and the relationship of class forces – upon which the institutional structure of the financial system had been built. Under changed conditions the institutional arrangements that had supported growth in the early postwar period now became obstacles to further successful capital accumulation.

The international financial system

By the 1960s the need for dollars to serve as international reserves had changed dramatically. As a result of continual US balance-of-payments deficits, the shortage of dollars in the early postwar years had become an oversupply.

In addition, the relationship of class forces had changed. Unquestioned US hegemony was being challenged on a number of fronts. The recovered capitalist economies of Western Europe and Japan were now challenging the United States in world trade and production. Opposition by Third World countries to US policies was increasing. The Vietnam War, the most dramatic form of that opposition, was disastrous for the US economy and the international financial system. The inability to finance an unpopular war by taxation resulted in an "overheated" economy, which worsened the profitability of US corporations and resulted in strong inflationary pressures. Inflation, along with the direct foreign exchange costs of waging the war, significantly worsened the US balance of payments.

The dollar shortage had become a dollar glut. US hegemony, which underlay the use of the dollar as a reserve currency, was being challenged. The Bretton Woods system came under increasing pressure, exacerbated by foreign-exchange specu- lation by multinational banks and corporations (Moffitt, 1983), and was finally dismantled in the early 1970s.

The domestic financial system

Domestically, conditions had also changed. The low level of debt and general robustness of the financial system, the structural conditions upon which the postwar financial system had been built, had begun to change. The 1960s and subsequent years were ones of increasing financial fragility in the US economy (Figure 7.3), which contributed to financial crises and increasing financial instabi- lity (Minsky, 1986; Pollin, 1987; Wolfson, 1986, 1990).

Two other factors – inflation and technological change – changed the conditions upon which the success of the postwar institutional structure was based.[11] Inflation combined with increasing debt and financial fragility (and also Federal Reserve tight monetary policy in the early 1980s) to raise the level of interest rates. Higher and more volatile interest rates destroyed the viability of interest rate ceilings and led to disintermediation, especially of thrift institutions.[12] Technological change, by dramatically increasing the ability to move money electronically, contributed to the financial innovation of money market mutual funds, led to disintermediation on a massive scale, and helped to break down the walls among financial institutions created by "compartmentalization."

Successful capital accumulation had also changed the relationship of class forces. The development of the Eurodollar market and the globalization of finance in the 1960s and 1970s led to opportunities for expansion and growth of US multinational banks. The increased global presence of these banks gave them advantages over their domestic counterparts. On the other hand, globalization also resulted in increasing competition from the expanding role in the United States of the branches and agencies of foreign banks. Increased competition was further heightened by technological change and financial innovation, which enabled nonbank financial institutions to challenge areas of banking formerly the province of banks and thrifts.

These developments broke down the walls separating financial institutions (Wojnilower, 1985), increased the power (but also the financial difficulties) of the larger institutions, and disrupted the balance of class forces which had helped to create the unique US financial system.

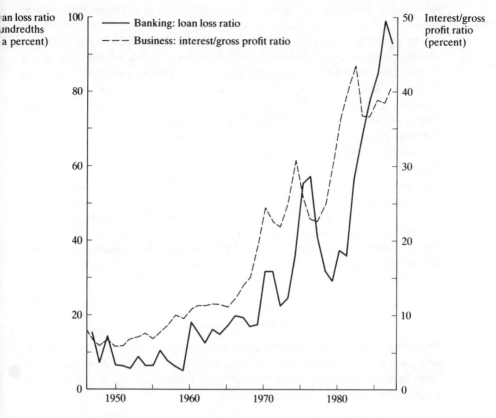

Fig. 7.3. Financial fragility, 1946–87. (*Source*: See Wolfson [1990].)

Conclusion

The financial system which had been a part of the postwar social structure of accumulation has been significantly changed. In the international arena, the Bretton Woods monetary system has given way to a system of floating exchange rates. Domestically, the regulatory structure which had restricted competition in the early postwar period has mostly been dismantled. The support which the institutional structure of the financial system had given to accumulation has mostly disappeared. In particular, the instability of exchange rates that accompanied the collapse of the Bretton Woods system, and the increase in financial fragility and volatility of interest rates that accompanied the dismantling of the regulated domestic financial system, have been unfavorable for accumulation and constitute barriers to the revival of rapid accumulation.

The demise of the financial component of the social structure of accumulation has come from the pressure exerted by the contradiction between, on the one hand, an institutional structure developed in the 1930s and 1940s and, on the other hand, the changed structural conditions and relationship of class forces of the recent period.

The government protection for financial institutions which was part of the postwar institutional structure (deposit insurance, lender of last resort) has expanded to prevent sharp crashes of the financial system, but at the expense of increasing financial fragility (Minsky, 1986; Wojnilower, 1980). Government attempts at stabilizing the financial system may indeed be facing increasing difficulties (Wolfson, 1989). Whether efforts to deregulate completely the domestic financial system constitute a new financial component of a new SSA, or whether they simply constitute the removal of the remaining vestiges of the old system, is an important question to which the answer is not yet clear.

In any event, successful capital accumulation has not yet been restored. An understanding of how a new SSA will be created will depend on an understanding of the concrete conditions of the present: the structural characteristics of the present financial system as it has evolved, and the relationship of class forces. It will also involve an understanding of how different programs for financial reform reflect the interests of the proponents, and what an agenda for progressive financial reform would be.

Acknowledgments

The author is grateful for extensive discussion concerning the issues in this chapter with Jill Krus, Michele Naples, and Reynold Nesiba; and for helpful comments from Teresa Ghilarducci, Mark Greer, Doug Koritz, and editors David Kotz, Terrence McDonough, and Michael Reich.

Notes

1 The number of commercial banks dropped from 23,251 on June 30, 1930 to 13,949 on June 30, 1933 (Board of Governors, 1943, p. 16). Bank suspensions are defined to comprise (p. 281)

> all banks closed to the public, either temporarily or permanently, by supervisory authorities or by the banks' boards of directors on account of financial difficulties, whether on a so-called moratorium basis or otherwise, unless the closing was under a special banking holiday declared by civil authorities.

2 This restriction of competition should not be viewed as the elimination of competition, but rather the management of the particular manifestations of competition.

3 These restrictions were established by the McFadden Act of 1927 and the Banking Act of 1933.

4 Large banks were strongly opposed to deposit insurance. They viewed the deposit premiums as an unnecessary and unwanted financial drain (Kennedy, 1973). Interestingly, though, despite the fact that deposit insurance was very important to the continued survival of small banks, there was significant opposition by small banks to the deposit insurance legislation. Partly this was due to the negative experience of deposit insurance on the state level. Partly it was due to the general conservatism of the small banks. Partly it was due to specific features of the deposit insurance legislation which the small banks opposed: the requirement to join the

Federal Reserve System, and the lack of a cap on the amount of premiums per year (Keeton, 1990). As it turned out, the banks were successful in changing the unwanted provisions: premiums were capped, and the requirement to join the Federal Reserve was postponed and eventually dropped. Due to these changes, and due to the success of deposit insurance, small bank opinion on deposit insurance became more supportive. In Missouri in 1934, "a total of 476 non-member state banks decided to follow a policy [deposit insurance] that not one year previously they had condemned as 'opposed to all principles of sound banking'" (Hubbard and Davids, 1969, p. 174).

5 As noted above, the number of commercial banks in the United States numbered 13,949 on June 30, 1933. Federal deposit insurance was established with the passage of the Banking Act of June 16, 1933. More than fifty-seven years later, on December 31, 1990, there were still 12,316 insured commercial banks in the United States; of these, 9,469 were small banks with assets of less than $100 million (Board of Governors, 1991, p. A73).

6 In addition, the way in which the federal government financed World War II re-emphasized the environment of stable interest rates. Given the importance of the success of the government's funding efforts, the Federal Reserve pegged the level of interest rates at which the government borrowed. This policy was continued until the Federal Reserve–Treasury Accord of 1951.

Despite the suspension of the official pegging policy, interest rates remained low and stable throughout the 1950s and into the 1960s. An important source of this stability was the financing of World War II. As a result of the domination of credit markets by the federal government during the war, private corporations built up a portfolio of safe and highly liquid assets. Because of the broad and deep market for government securities, sales to meet liquidity needs could be accomplished without significant effect on interest rates.

7 By reducing the risk of deposits, federal deposit insurance allows financial institutions to pay less to attract deposits.

8 As Kotz (1987) has pointed out, some aspects of the Bretton Woods system were not put in place until after 1944.

9 The description of the postwar international monetary system is limited here because of space considerations and because of its extensive treatment elsewhere. Interested readers can consult the many excellent references (Block, 1977; MacEwan, 1978; Moffitt, 1983; Solomon, 1977; Wachtel, 1990).

10 US hegemony is taken to be a class relationship because it involved the exploitation of the people (and resources) of the world for the benefit of a wealthy business and financial elite in the United States.

11 Both developments may be taken as exogenous to the analysis of change in the domestic financial system. However, inflation can be considered endogenous to a broader analysis which includes the international financial system (see above) and which incorporates conflict over declining profit rates due to the overall deterioration of the postwar social structure of accumulation (Kotz, 1982; Bowles et al., 1986).

12 Disintermediation is the process whereby depositors withdraw funds from depository intermediaries in order to take advantage of higher interest-rate returns from direct investment in securities markets.

References

Block, Fred L., 1977. *The Origins of International Economic Disorder*. Berkeley: University of California Press.

Board of Governors of the Federal Reserve System, 1943. *Banking and Monetary Statistics: 1914–1941.* Washington, D.C.

1976. *Banking and Monetary Statistics, 1941–1970.* Washington, D.C.

1981. *Annual Statistical Digest, 1970–79.* Washington, D.C.

1991. *Federal Reserve Bulletin,* 77(5), special table 4.20.

Bowles, Samuel, David M. Gordon, and Thomas Weisskopf, 1986. "Power and Profits: The Social Structure of Accumulation and the Profitability of the Postwar U.S. Economy," *Review of Radical Political Economics,* 18(1&2): 132–67.

Gordon, David M., Richard Edwards, and Michael Reich, 1982. *Segmented Work, Divided Workers: The Historical Transformation of Labor in the United States.* Cambridge University Press.

Hubbard, Timothy W., and Lewis E. Davids, 1969. *Banking in Mid-America: A History of Missouri's Banks.* Washington, D.C.: Public Affairs Press.

Keeton, William R., 1990. "Small and Large Bank Views of Deposit Insurance: Today vs. the 1930s," *Federal Reserve Bank of Kansas City Economic Review,* 75(5): 23–35.

Kennedy, Susan Estabrook, 1973. *The Banking Crisis of 1933.* Lexington: University Press of Kentucky.

Kotz, David, 1982. "Monopoly, Inflation, and Economic Crisis," *Review of Radical Political Economics,* 14(4): 1–17.

1987. "Long Waves and Social Structures of Accumulation," *Review of Radical Political Economics,* 19(4): 16–38.

MacEwan, Arthur, 1978. "The Development of the Crisis in the World Economy," in *U.S. Capitalism in Crisis,* ed. Bruce Steinberg *et al.,* pp. 45–54. New York: Union for Radical Political Economics.

Maddison, Angus, 1989. *The World Economy in the Twentieth Century.* Paris: Development Center of the Organization for Economic Cooperation and Development.

Minsky, Hyman P., 1986. *Stabilizing an Unstable Economy.* New Haven: Yale University Press.

Moffitt, Michael, 1983. *The World's Money: International Banking from Bretton Woods to the Brink of Insolvency.* New York: Simon and Schuster.

Pollin, Robert, 1987. "Structural Change and Increasing Fragility in the U.S. Financial System," in *The Imperiled Economy,* ed. Robert Cherry *et al.,* vol. 1, pp. 145–58. New York: Union for Radical Political Economics.

Solomon, Robert, 1977. *The International Monetary System, 1945–1976: An Insider's View.* New York: Harper and Row.

United States Department of Commerce, 1975. *Historical Statistics of the United States: Colonial Times to 1970.* Washington, D.C.

United States Department of Commerce, Bureau of Economic Analysis, 1987. *Fixed Reproducible Tangible Wealth in the United States.* Washington, D.C.

United States Department of Commerce, Bureau of Economic Analysis, annual. *National Income and Product Accounts.* Washington, D.C.

Wachtel, Howard, 1990. *The Money Mandarins: The Making of a Supranational Economic Order,* revised edn. Armonk, N.Y.: M. E. Sharpe.

Wojnilower, Albert M., 1980. "The Central Role of Credit Crunches in Recent Financial History," *Brookings Papers on Economic Activity,* 2: 277–326.

1985. "Financial Change in the United States," paper presented at the conference on *The Origins and Diffusion of Financial Innovation* at the European University Institute, Florence, Italy, October 7–9.

Wolfson, Martin H., 1986. *Financial Crises: Understanding the U.S. Experience.* Armonk, N.Y.: M. E. Sharpe.

1989. "The Stock Market and Recession," *Review of Radical Political Economics*, 21(3): 40–4.

1990. "The Causes of Financial Instability," *Journal of Post-Keynesian Economics*, 12(3): 333–55.

8

Alternative social structure of accumulation approaches to the analysis of capitalist booms and crises

THOMAS E. WEISSKOPF

My primary purpose in this chapter is to explore the theoretical foundations of alternative social structure of accumulation (SSA) approaches to the analysis of booms and crises in advanced capitalist economies. A secondary purpose is to consider some of the strengths and limitations of the particular type of SSA theory that Samuel Bowles, David M. Gordon, and I have applied in our own work on the post-World War II United States economy.

In the first part of this chapter I formulate simplified models of two quite different SSA-based theories of capitalist accumulation and crisis – one based on the kind of "neo-Marxian" analysis that Bowles, Gordon, and I have helped to develop, and the other based on an alternative kind of "neo-Keynesian" analysis that reflects work that has been done by other non-neoclassical political economists working on the same range of issues. In the second part I compare and contrast the neo-Marxian and neo-Keynesian models and discuss how each of them can be embedded in an SSA framework. In the final part, I discuss our SSA-based neo-Marxian analysis of the postwar boom and crisis in the US economy in the light of the comparative theoretical issues raised in the first two parts of the chapter.

Modeling alternative SSA theories of boom and crisis

The concept of an SSA was developed as part of an approach to analyzing successive booms and crises in capitalist economies (see Gordon [1978] and Gordon et al. [1982]). The SSA approach suggests that each boom period of rapid capital accumulation is grounded in the historically contingent establishment of certain critical socioeconomic institutions. Increasingly serious problems arise during the course of a boom, and these problems ultimately bring the boom to an end and precipitate a crisis. There is nothing automatic in the dynamics of the crisis to assure the emergence of institutions that will sustain a new boom; instead, the outcome of a period of crisis is highly uncertain and depends on the course of political struggles and concrete historical events.

Within the context of this general approach there are a variety of ways in which an SSA-based theory of capitalist boom and crisis can be developed. Bowles,

Gordon, and I have advanced a particular SSA theory that is "neo-Marxian" in the sense that it is based on the Marxian notions of profit-driven accumulation and power-determined profits.[1] The neo-Marxian theory that we have applied to the postwar US economy focuses on class conflict and the exercise of class power in the realms of production and distribution; a boom is associated with an SSA that sustains a strong capitalist class and a high rate of profit, while a crisis is associated with the erosion of such an SSA, the weakening of the capitalist class, and a squeeze on the profit rate.

There is an important alternative theoretical framework, focusing on demand more than supply conditions, which can also readily be embedded in an overall SSA approach to the study of booms and crises. This "neo-Keynesian" alternative emphasizes the importance for capitalist prosperity of maintaining sufficient market growth to sustain demand for the output that can be produced with available productive capacity.[2] A boom is associated with an SSA that generates a high rate of growth of market demand, while a crisis reflects erosion in the ability of the SSA to sustain the growth of demand.

In order to bring out clearly the essential features of the neo-Marxian and the neo-Keynesian theories, I will formulate each of them in terms of a simple set of equations reflecting the essential determinants of profitability, accumulation and growth. To highlight the differences between the two alternative theories, I will develop the two models in parallel rather than in sequence.

Alternative determinants of the rate of accumulation

An SSA approach to the analysis of economic booms and crises must clearly provide some kind of social-structural explanation for the rate of accumulation in a capitalist economy. From a neo-Marxian perspective, capitalists are assumed to undertake capital accumulation to the extent that they expect investment to yield future profits; and expected profitability is in turn considered to be primarily a function of rates of profit actually experienced in the recent past. It follows that investment is largely profit-driven, and that the overall rate of capital accumulation will depend (with a lag) on the average rate of profit. Taking into account also the argument that the need to invest will be greater the more fully current capacity is being utilized, I specify a simple neo-Marxian accumulation function as follows:

$$k = k_M(u, r_{-t_1}), \tag{1a}$$

where k is the rate of increase in the capital stock, the subscript M refers to a neo-Marxian function, u denotes the rate of utilization of capital stock, r denotes the rate of profit, and the subscript $-t_1$ reflects the lag between profitability and accumulation.

In the alternative neo-Keynesian model of accumulation, the rate of accumulation is dependent on the "animal spirits" of investors or – more generally – on certain characteristics of the overall economic environment that affect business's willingness to invest, which can be described as the "investment climate". Further, many neo-Keynesians suggest that investment is influenced by the expected rate of growth of market demand, which in turn can be regarded as a function of the rate of market growth experienced in the recent past. I therefore specify a simple neo-Keynesian accumulation function as follows:

$$k = k_K(\Phi, u, g_{-t_2}), \tag{1b}$$

where the subscript K refers to a neo-Keynesian function, Φ represents the investment climate, g represents the rate of growth of output, and the subscript $-t_2$ reflects the lag between output growth and accumulation.

Alternative determinants of the rate of profit

To analyze the rate of profit, it will be useful to begin with a simple accounting decomposition. Defining the rate of profit as the ratio of a measure of profits to a measure of invested capital stock, I write:

$$r = R/K = (R/Y)(Y/K_U)(K_U/K) = szu, \tag{2}$$

where R denotes the volume of profits, Y the level of income or output, K the value of the capital stock, and K_U the value of actually utilized capital stock (all in nominal terms); while s and z refer to the profit share and the average nominal output/(utilized-)capital ratio, respectively.

Consider first the neo-Marxian approach to the determination of the profit share s. To illustrate this approach I distinguish four distributive shares in total income:

$$Y = R + W + N + T, \tag{3}$$

where Y is defined gross of imported inputs and taxes, W is the wage bill, both R and W are measured after taxes, N is the imported material input bill, and T is the tax bill. I can then write:

$$s = R/Y = 1 - W/Y - N/Y - T/Y. \tag{4}$$

Expressing the wage bill W as the product of the nominal wage w and labor-hour input L, the imported material input bill N as the product of the (domestic-currency) price of a unit of imported inputs p_M and the real quantity of those inputs M, and nominal gross income Y as the product of the gross output price deflator p and the corresponding real output measure Q, equation (4) can be rewritten as follows:

$$s = 1 - wL/pQ - p_M M/pQ - t$$
$$= 1 - (w/p)/q_L - (p_M/p)/q_M - t, \tag{5}$$

where t is the ratio of the tax bill to (gross) income, and q_L and q_M denote the average productivity of labor and imported material inputs, respectively.

The essence of the neo-Marxian approach to the analysis of profit-share determination is that the distribution of income is fundamentally determined by the balance of power between capitalists and other competing income claimants.

Equation (4) above suggests a simple fourfold class structure with which to illustrate the neo-Marxian approach. Corresponding to each distributive share there is a class with a claim on income – capitalists claiming (after-tax) profits, workers claiming (after-tax) wages, foreign suppliers of material inputs claiming the imported import bill, and beneficiaries of state spending claiming the tax share of income. Profits are viewed as "the spoils of a three-front war fought by capital in its dealings with workers, foreign buyers and sellers, and the state (or indirectly with the citizenry)";[3] and the ability of capitalists to fight that war depends on the power they can bring to bear in the struggle. This formulation suggests that capitalist power relative to that of the other competing classes determines the size of the capitalist profit share in the distribution of income.

The full neo-Marxian analysis of income distribution and profitability is somewhat more complex; it relates capitalist power to the profit share in ways that can best be illustrated with reference to equation (5). First of all, neo-Marxian analysis of the labor process suggests that the real output produced by any given bundle of inputs depends not simply on the state of technology (which I will denote by T) but also significantly on the "intensity of work," i.e., the effort and care expended by workers on the job. The level of work intensity, in turn, is theorized to be a function of the power exercised by the capitalist class in its dealings with the working class – on the presumption that capitalists' interest in maximizing work intensity conflicts to a significant degree with workers' interest in the structure and pace of work. It follows that the two productivity variables in equation (5), q_L and q_M, will be positive functions of both technology (T) and the power of the capitalist class vis-à-vis the working class (which I will denote by Π_L).

The remaining terms in equation (5) can also be related to the balance of power in fairly obvious ways. The real wage (w/p) can be modeled as the outcome of a bargaining process in which the power of labor (to push up the nominal wage w) is pitted against the power of capital (to raise output prices p) in such a way that the real wage becomes a negative function of Π_L. Similarly, the real cost of a unit of imported material inputs (p_M/p) can be modeled as the outcome of a political process in which the power of foreign material input suppliers (to raise p_M) is pitted against the power of domestic purchasers of those materials (to raise p), in such a way that real material import costs becomes a negative function of the power of (domestic) capitalists vis-à-vis foreign material suppliers – to be denoted by Π_F.[4] And the tax ratio t can be seen as in part a function of the power of the domestic citizenry to induce the state to levy taxes in order to support public spending on programs benefiting noncapitalists, which will be pitted against the power of capitalists to resist taxes whose ultimate impact is on profits and whose benefits do not accrue to themselves; thus t becomes a negative function of the power of capital vis-à-vis the general public – to be denoted by Π_C. Additionally, one can argue that some or all of the productivity variables in equation (5) will be positive functions of Π_C, on the grounds that the capitalist class has a conflict of interest with the general public over social and environmental regulations which have the effect of lowering measured output, or increasing measured input, but which improve the quality of the workplace or the environment.

In sum, all of the variables on the right-hand side of equation (5) can be expressed in part as functions of the power of the capitalist class, in such a way that increases in each dimension of relative capitalist power – Π_L, Π_F, and Π_C – serve unambiguously to increase the profit share s. The neo-Marxian analysis of the determination of the profit share can thus be characterized by a reduced-form equation:

$$s = s_M(\Pi, T), \tag{6a}$$

where the single variable Π represents an overall measure of capitalist power relative to each potentially contending class, T reflects the influence of technology on the productivity variables affecting the profit share, and the partial derivatives of s with respect to Π and T are both positive.

Consider now the neo-Marxian approach to the determination of the average output–capital ratio z. Starting from equation (2) I write:

$$z = Y / K_U = (pQ) / (p_K K_U) = (p/p_K)q_K, \tag{7}$$

where p_K denotes the price index for capital stock and q_K is the average productivity of (utilized) capital stock. Ignoring the relative price term as a secondary issue, we can equate z with q_K, which, for the same reasons given earlier for the other two productivity variables q_L and q_M, will be a positive function of both technology (T) and the power of the capitalist class vis-à-vis the working class (Π_L). Thus the neo-Marxian analysis of the determination of the output–capital ratio can be characterized by a reduced-form equation:

$$z = z_M(\Pi, T), \tag{8a}$$

where the partial derivatives of z with respect to both independent variables are positive.

Returning finally to the rate of profit itself, I substitute equations (6a) and (8a) into equation (2) to obtain a reduced-form equation reflecting the neo-Marxian model of profitability determination:

$$r = r_M(\Pi, T, u), \tag{9a}$$

where all partial derivatives are positive.

The essence of the alternative neo-Keynesian approach to the analysis of profit-rate determination is that profitability is most fundamentally a function of the growth of aggregate demand; but the relationship between demand growth and profitability is somewhat indirect and requires careful specification. The neo-Keynesian model involves first of all an analysis of income distribution developed initially by Kalecki, in which the profit share depends mainly on the ability of capitalist firms to mark up prices over unit variable costs.[5] More precisely, oligopolistic firms operating in a context of excess capacity and constant unit variable costs are assumed to set prices by marking up unit variable costs by an amount of which the average level in any given industry is a positive function of the "degree of monopoly" prevailing in that industry. Thus I write:

$$p = m(M)c = m(M)(W/Q + N/Q + T/Q), \tag{10}$$

where m denotes the mark-up, M is the degree of monopoly, c is unit variable costs, and each variable represents an average value for a particular industry. Recalling that $pQ = Y$, equations (10) and (4) (at the industry level) can be manipulated to show that the profit share in industry gross income is given by:

$$s = R/Y = 1 - 1/m(M). \tag{11}$$

Cowling (1982) has shown that each industry's degree of monopoly can be expressed as a positive function of the degree of concentration and the degree of collusion among firms in the industry, and a negative function of the industry price elasticity of demand; thus M depends on product-market structural characteristics of a given industry. Equation (11) applies also at the aggregate level, provided that m and M are defined as the suitably weighted average mark-up and the corresponding average degree of monopoly for the economy as a whole. Thus, I write the following neo-Keynesian equation for the economy-wide profit share:

$$s = s_K(M), \tag{6b}$$

where M reflects product-market structural characteristics as opposed to the capitalist power variable Π that appears in the corresponding neo-Marxian equation (6a).

Consider now the neo-Keynesian approach to the determination of the average output–capital ratio z. Ignoring as before the relative price term in equation (7), I equate z with the average productivity of (utilized) capital stock q_K. From a neo-Marxian perspective q_K is a function of both technology T and capitalist power Π; from a neo-Keynesian perspective, however, Π plays no role; so:

$$z = z_K(T). \tag{8b}$$

Returning finally to the rate of profit itself, I need to substitute equations (6b) and (8b) into equation (2) to obtain a reduced-form equation reflecting the neo-Keynesian model of profitability determination:

$$r = r_K(M, T, u), \tag{9b}$$

where all partial derivatives are positive. The only difference between equations (9a) and (9b) is that the neo-Keynesian variable M is substituted for the neo-Marxian variable Π. But the two approaches differ in their analysis of the determinants of T, and this is where the neo-Keynesian emphasis on demand growth will come to the fore.

The dependence of profitability on capacity utilization and output growth

Consider first the neo-Marxian variable Π, which is a vector made up of three elements reflecting capitalist power vis-à-vis the domestic working class (Π_L), foreign suppliers of material inputs (Π_F), and the domestic citizenry (Π_C), respectively.[6] According to Marx's theory of short-run cyclical fluctuations in a capitalist economy, the bargaining power of the working class *vis-à-vis* the capitalist class varies inversely with the size of the reserve army of labor. This suggests that the relative power of the capitalist class *vis-à-vis* the working class (Π_L) varies positively with the rate of unemployment and hence negatively with the rate of capacity utilization *u*. This argument can be generalized to the relative power of capitalists *vis-à-vis* foreign sellers of material inputs (Π_F) and *vis-à-vis* the general public (Π_C), since the bargaining position of the foreign sellers is strengthened by high levels of demand for their products, and citizens' influence on state policy is likely to rise in times of greater overall economic prosperity. It follows that Π should be modeled as a negative function of *u*.

This line of reasoning points to an analogous relationship between capitalist power Π and the long-term past rate of growth of output. The logic of the Marxian reserve army analysis of short-run cyclical fluctuations has been extended in the neo-Marxian literature on accumulation and crisis to theories of "over-accumulation,"[7] in which rapid accumulation and employment growth over a long period of time strengthen the bargaining power of the working class. In a similar way, long periods of rapid accumulation and high employment can be expected to raise the ability of other contending classes to challenge capitalist power and control. Thus, I formulate a neo-Marxian equation for capitalist power as follows:

$$\Pi = \Pi(\Pi^*, -u, -g_{-t_3}),\qquad(12)$$

where Π^* represents the "underlying" relative power of capital, g_{-t_3} denotes the long-term rate of growth of output over a period centered t_3 years in the past, and a minus sign in front of an independent variable in a functional expression signifies a negative partial derivative. The underlying power variable Π^* reflects the basic underlying structural element in actually exercised relative capitalist power Π – an element that is independent of the level and growth of economic activity and is grounded in fundamental long-term characteristics of the institutional environment.

Consider now the neo-Keynesian variable *M*, the average degree of monopoly across industries, which varies directly with the extent of firm concentration and firm collusion and inversely with the price elasticity of demand. There is little reason to expect either concentration or collusion to vary one way or the other with the rate of capacity utilization *u* or the rate of output growth *g*; but it is plausible to argue that effective industry price elasticities of demand will tend to fall at high levels of *u*, so the effective degree of monopoly (and the mark-up) will be correspondingly higher.[8] On the other hand, there is no reason to expect a period of rapid output growth to have the same kind of effect on demand elasticities as a high current level of *u*, since over a longer period productive capacity can be expanded to meet additional demand. Thus, I write the neo-Keynesian equation for the average degree of monopoly as follows:

$$M = M(M^*, u), \qquad (13)$$

where M^* represents the "underlying" degree of monopoly that is grounded in fundamental long-term characteristics of the institutional environment, such as the degree of firm concentration and the extent of firm collusion in different industries.

The variable T, reflecting the state of technological development, appears in both the neo-Marxian and the neo-Keynesian equations for the profit rate. From a neo-Marxian perspective, T is a variable of lesser importance than relative capitalist power Π determining profitability, and it can be treated as exogenous. From a neo-Keynesian perspective, however, T is a function not only of exogenous technological forces but also of the rate of growth of output. An important strand of neo-Keynesian analysis, associated with the work of Kaldor and Verdoorn, suggests that productivity growth is a positive function of output growth.[9] Therefore differing neo-Marxian and neo-Keynesian equations should be formulated for the technology variable as follows:

$$T = T_M(T^*), \qquad (14a)$$

$$T = T_K(T^*, g_{-t_4}), \qquad (14b)$$

where T^* reflects the underlying exogenous element in T and the subscript $-t_4$ reflects the lagged relationship between output growth and its effect on the state of technological development.

The neo-Marxian and neo-Keynesian equations for the rate of profit may now be rewritten in terms of the more basic underlying variables introduced in this section. Substituting equations (12) and (14a) into equation (9a), and equations (13) and (14b) into equation (9b), I get:

$$r = r_M(\Pi^*, T^*, +/-u, -g_{-t_3}), \qquad (15a)$$

$$r = r_K(M^*, T^*, u, g_{-t_4}), \qquad (15b)$$

where the $+/-$ in front of u in equation (15a) reflects the dual effect of capacity utilization on profitability in the neo-Marxian model – which deserves closer scrutiny.

On the one hand, higher u means higher r in the neo-Marxian model because of the direct effect of u as a component of r in equation (2); this effect is shared with the neo-Keynesian model. On the other hand, higher u means lower r in the neo-Marxian model because of the indirect effect of u on r via Π in equation (12); this effect is unique to the neo-Marxian model (for in the neo-Keynesian model the positive direct u effect is augmented by a positive indirect effect of u on r via M in equation (13). To explore the relationship between r and u in the neo-Marxian model I substitute equation (12) directly into equations (6a) and (8a) for s and z, and then substitute the latter into equation (2) to get:

$$r = s_M(\Pi^*, T^*, -u, -g_{-t_3})z_M(\Pi^*, T^*, -u, -g_{-t_3})u. \qquad (16)$$

Differentiating r with respect to u in equation (16):

$$dr/du = + (sz) - (uz)|\partial s_M/\partial u| - (us)|\partial z_M/\partial u|. \qquad (17)$$

At low levels of u the positive first term will dominate the negative second and third terms; but as u rises it becomes increasingly likely that the two negative terms will dominate the positive first term. Thus r first rises and then falls with u; whether it reaches its maximum value before u reaches a level corresponding to full employment depends on the precise specification of the s_M and z_M functions and the precise relationship between employment and capacity utilization.

It is in fact a characteristic feature of neo-Marxian analyses of profitability that there does exist a "high-employment profit squeeze." Thus neo-Marxian theory posits that there is a profit-maximizing level of u below the full-employment level of u, and hence that there is a range of (relatively high) values for u at which $\partial r/\partial u$ is negative. By contrast, in the neo-Keynesian model $\partial r/\partial u$ is positive for all values of u. A second point of sharp contrast between the neo-Marxian and neo-Keynesian analyses of profitability involves the effect of the long-term past rate of output growth. Equations (15a) and (15b) show clearly that lagged g has a negative effect on the profit rate in the neo-Marxian model (via its effect on Π in equation (12)) but a positive effect on the profit rate in the neo-Keynesian model (via its effect on T in equation (14b)).

Alternative determinants of capacity utilization and output growth

The rate at which available productive capacity is actually utilized clearly depends on the level of aggregate demand in relation to potential output. The chief distinction between the neo-Marxian and neo-Keynesian analyses of the rate of capacity utilization is that the former stresses the role of government macroeconomic policy as the ultimate determinant of aggregate demand, while the latter focuses on the effect of private consumption propensities and investment decisions on aggregate demand. From a neo-Marxian perspective aggregate demand is determined in part by random (mostly short-run) events that must be treated as exogenous, and in part by deliberate (mostly medium-run) government policies. Thus I will write a simple neo-Marxian capacity utilization equation as follows:

$$u = u_M(u^*, m^*), \qquad (18a)$$

where u^* represents the exogenous non-policy forces affecting the level of aggregate demand, and m^* reflects the influence of government macropolicy – also treated as exogenous.

The neo-Keynesian model of the determination of the level of aggregate demand and capacity utilization focuses attention on the level of private consumption and investment demand. Consumption demand is related to the class distribution of income on the reasonable presumption that wage-earners consume most of their income and profit-recipients save most of theirs. Thus consumption demand is modeled as a negative function of the profit share of income, slightly lagged to allow for the passage of time between the receipt and the expenditure of income. Investment demand is a function of the same variables that determine the rate of capital accumulation in equation (1b); hence I can write the following neo-Keynesian equation for capacity utilization:

$$u = u_K (u^*, k, -s_{-t_5}),$$ (18b)

where the exogenous variable u^* reflects the influence of forms of spending other than (endogenously determined) consumption and investment, and the subscript $-t_5$ reflects the (short) lag between the receipt of income and the corresponding expenditure on consumption.

The neo-Marxian and the neo-Keynesian analyses of the determination of output growth differ sharply over whether output growth is primarily a function of the growth of potential output or the growth of aggregate demand. From a neo-Marxian perspective the growth of actual output g is primarily a function of the growth of potential output, as aggregate demand is assumed to adjust over time to the available aggregate supply. Potential output, in turn, depends on the rate of growth of the capital stock (k) and the rate of technological progress (which affects the rate of growth of output per unit of capital stock). I therefore write the neo-Marxian output growth equation as follows:

$$g = g_M(T, k).$$ (19a)

From a neo-Keynesian perspective the growth of actual output g is primarily a function of the growth of aggregate demand, as potential output is assumed to adjust over time to aggregate demand. The growth of aggregate demand is itself a function both of exogenous market growth forces (which will be denoted by Δ) and of the distribution of income. Whereas the neo-Keynesian perspective suggests that a high profit share has a relatively short-lagged negative effect on the level of consumption demand and hence on the rate of capacity utilization u, it seems reasonable to model its effect on the growth of consumption and hence on the growth of aggregate demand as a longer-lagged one in which high profit shares over a period of time discourage consumption and demand growth. I therefore write the neo-Keynesian output growth equation as follows:

$$g = g_K(\Delta, -s_{-t_6}),$$ (19b)

where the subscript $-t_6$ reflects the lagged effect of the profit share on the growth of aggregate demand.

Comparing the neo-Marxian and neo-Keynesian models

In order to explore the contrasting ways in which neo-Marxian and neo-Keynesian models can be embedded in an SSA framework to explain economic booms and crises, I display the equations of each model in the form of path diagrams in

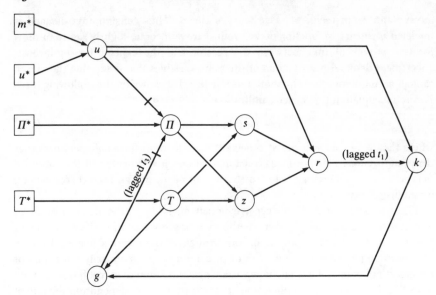

Fig. 8.1. The neo-Marxian model.

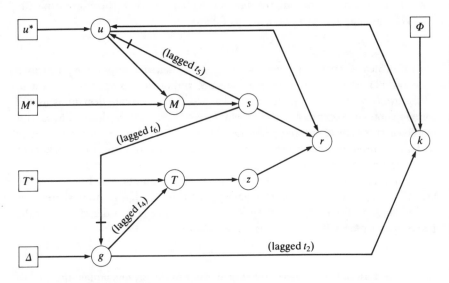

Fig. 8.2. The neo-Keynesian model.

Figures 8.1 and 8.2.[10] Exogenous variables are shown in boxes, and endogenous variables in circles.

Consider first the neo-Marxian model in Figure 8.1. The most distinctive exogenous variable is the underlying (relative) power of the capitalist class Π^*; the remaining exogenous variables are the underlying state of technology T^*, government macroeconomic policy m^*, and the residual exogenous forces affecting aggregate demand u^*. The primary chain of causation runs from Π^* via actual capitalist power Π to the rate of profit r and (with a lag) to the rate of accumulation k. Ignoring for the moment the negative effects of u and g on Π, the remaining exogenous variables T^*, m^* and u^* also have positive effects on the profit rate r and on the accumulation rate k. The accumulation rate in turn contributes positively to the rate of output growth g.

The neo-Marxian model contains two key elements of negative feedback. The first is associated with the short-run "high-employment profit squeeze": as the rate of capacity utilization u rises (beyond its profit-maximizing level), the level of capitalist power Π falls, and this in turn leads to a lower profit rate r. The second is associated with long-run "over-accumulation": higher rates of output growth lead (with a lag) to lower levels of capitalist power Π, which in turn lead to lower profitability.

Consider now the neo-Keynesian model in Figure 8.2. Here the most distinctive exogenous variables are the investment climate Φ and the forces generating market growth Δ; the remaining exogenous variables are the underlying degree of monopoly M^*, underlying technology T^*, and the residual forces affecting the level of aggregate demand u^*. The primary chains of causation run from Φ (directly) and from Δ (indirectly via output growth g) to the rate of accumulation k, and then from k via capacity utilization u to the profit share s and the profit rate r. Additional positive lines of causation run from M^* and from u^* to the share as well as the rate of profit, and from T^* to the rate of profit.

The neo-Keynesian model also contains two elements of negative feedback, involving – as in the case of the neo-Marxian model – the rate of capacity utilization and the rate of output growth. But here the direction of (negative) causation runs *to* these variables rather than from them: a high profit share s is presumed to lower the level of aggregate demand and hence also the rate of capacity utilization u (with a short lag), and to lower the rate of growth of aggregate demand and hence also the rate of output growth g (with a longer lag).[11]

Among the most important differences between these (simplified) neo-Marxian and neo-Keynesian models are the following:

(1) In the neo-Marxian model higher profitability leads to higher accumulation, while higher accumulation (with a considerable lag) leads to lower profitability. In the neo-Keynesian model, higher accumulation leads to higher profitability, while higher profitability has no effect on accumulation.

(2) In the neo-Marxian model output growth is supply-determined and is positively influenced by accumulation; in the neo-Keynesian model output growth is demand-determined and positively influences accumulation.

(3) In the neo-Marxian model output growth has a negative (lagged) impact on both profitability and accumulation; in the neo-Keynesian model output growth has a positive (lagged) effect on profitability and accumulation.

(4) In the neo-Marxian model a high profit share is favorable to profitability,

capital accumulation and output growth; in the neo-Keynesian model a high profit share is favorable to profitability but unfavorable to output growth and capital accumulation.

(5) In the neo-Marxian model the capacity utilization rate has a negative impact on profitability (above the profit-maximizing level of u); in the neo-Keynesian model capacity utilization always has a positive impact on profitability.

(6) In the neo-Marxian model the rate of capacity utilization is determined solely by exogenous variables, reflecting government macropolicy and short-run disturbances; in the neo-Keynesian model capacity utilization is significantly influenced by endogenous variables, specifically the profit share and the accumulation rate.

Embedding the models in an SSA framework

The SSA approach takes as its point of departure the institutional structure of a capitalist economy (the SSA itself) and then develops a theoretical framework linking this structure to the long-term rate of capital accumulation. To see how the neo-Marxian and the neo-Keynesian models can be embedded in an SSA framework, it will be helpful to generate for each model a single reduced-form equation for the rate of capital accumulation (which is closely associated with the long-term rate of output growth).

In the case of the neo-Marxian model, substitution of all the relevant equations into equation (1a) yields:

$$k = k_{\mathrm{M}}(\Pi^*_{-t_1}; \; T^*_{-t_1}, \; -T^*_{-t_1-t_3}; \; u^*, \; +/-u^*_{-t_1}; \; m^*, \; +/-m^*_{-t_1}; \; -k_{-t_1-t_3}),$$
$$(20a)$$

where, as before, minus signs reflect negative partial derivatives. In the case of the neo-Keynesian model, substitution of the relevant equations into equation (1b) yields:[12]

$$k = k_{\mathrm{K}}(\Phi; \; \Delta_{-t_2}; \; -M^*_{-t_2-t_6}; \; -u^*_{-t_2-t_6}; \; -k_{-t_2-t_6}).$$
$$(20b)$$

Equations (20a) and (20b) express the rate of accumulation in terms of the exogenous variables of each model and (via the relevant feedback loops) in terms of the long-term lagged rate of accumulation itself.

Equation (20a) indicates that in the neo-Marxian model the rate of accumulation is unambiguously a positive function of (lagged) underlying capitalist power. Underlying technology T^*, government macroeconomic policy m^* and the exogenous element in the rate of capacity utilization u^* have ambiguous effects on accumulation, depending both on the relative strength of positive and negative effects and on the lag structure of those effects. Finally, the rate of accumulation has a long-run negative feedback effect on itself; in the neo-Marxian model a high rate of accumulation, by weakening actual capitalist power Π and reducing profitability, ultimately slows down the rate of accumulation.

Equation (20b) indicates that in the neo-Keynesian model the rate of accumulation is unambiguously a positive function of both the investment climate Φ and (lagged) market growth forces Δ. Both the underlying degree of monopoly M^* and the exogenous element in the rate of capacity utilization u^* have (lagged) negative effects on accumulation. Finally, the rate of accumulation here too has a long-run negative feedback effect on itself; in the neo-Keynesian model a high rate of accumulation, by raising capacity utilization and the profit share, ultimately slows down the rate of accumulation.

Since the SSA represents the broad institutional structure that defines the external environment within which an economy's accumulation process takes place, the logical way to characterize an SSA from the perspective of each model is in terms of the most important exogenous variables in its reduced-form accumulation equation. From a neo-Marxian perspective, one would therefore characterize an SSA in terms of its ability to promote and sustain the key neo-Marxian exogenous variable – underlying capitalist power Π^*.[13] Attention should be focused on the evolution of institutions affecting the balance of class power between capitalists and their potential challengers; one would expect economic booms to be associated with institutional structures that maintain capitalist power and economic crises to be associated with the erosion of such institutions and the consequent weakening of capitalist dominance.

From a neo-Keynesian perspective, one would characterize an SSA primarily in terms of its ability to promote the key neo-Keynesian exogenous variables – the investment climate Φ and market growth forces Δ.[14] In this case, attention should be directed to institutions that affect consumers' and investors' propensity to spend; one would expect economic booms to be associated with institutional structures that promote investors' "animal spirits" and the growth of markets, and economic crises to be associated with the failure of such institutions.

Thus far I have stressed the fact that basic SSA institutions are defined in terms of variables exogenous to the accumulation process itself, so that turning points come about when the key exogenous variables reflecting the strength of an SSA themselves turn about – for political-historical reasons that must be analyzed independently of the variables that are endogenous to the economic system. But I have not yet addressed the fact that both of the reduced-form accumulation equations do include an endogenous long-term cyclical mechanism in the form of a lagged accumulation rate term with a negative sign. This suggests the possibility of long cycles being generated endogenously by the negative feedback effects characterizing each model.

In the case of the neo-Marxian model, a high rate of accumulation eventually weakens actual capitalist power Π, which in turn serves to reduce the rate of profit and ultimately also the rate of accumulation itself. If the lags are long enough, and if the rest of the system is stable enough, this mechanism could explain a cyclical pattern in which a boom period of high profitability r and high accumulation k is followed in succession by a pre-crisis period of lower r and (still) high k, a crisis period of low r and low k, and a pre-boom period of high r and (still) low k.[15] In the case of the neo-Keynesian model, a high rate of accumulation raises capacity utilization and the profit share s, which in turn eventually slows down the rate of growth of demand and ultimately also the rate of accumulation itself. Here, if the lags are long enough and the system stable enough, this negative feedback mechanism could explain a cyclical pattern in which a boom period of rapid growth g and rapid accumulation k is followed in succession by a pre-crisis period of slow g and (still) rapid k, a crisis period of slow g and slow k, and a pre-boom period of rapid g and (still) slow k.

While long cycles based on either of these endogenous feedback mechanisms are plausible, at least theoretically, it would appear empirically doubtful that the structure of either system would remain stable over a long enough time period to warrant such an explanation of any actually observed long cycles. SSA analysis explicitly emphasizes that exogenous political-historical developments, not endogenous mechanisms, shape the construction of a new SSA on the basis of which a crisis yields to a new boom. However, SSA analysis does allow for the possibility that an economic boom might be turned into a crisis because of endogenous contradictions involving the negative feedback effect of a high rate of accumulation.

In the neo–Marxian model such a negative feedback effect would take the form of a long-run profit squeeze, induced by a boom period characterized by rapid accumulation and high employment. In the neo–Keynesian model, it would take the form of a long-run failure of demand, induced by a boom period characterized by rapid accumulation and excessive profitability. Each of these scenarios is theoretically plausible, and each has in fact been applied to the analysis of actual long-run crises.[16] SSA analysis, however, does not rely solely on endogenous long-run feedback mechanisms to explain the critical turning points from boom to crisis. Instead, it devotes much attention to political-historical processes of institution building, institutional contradictions and institutional demise – processes that must be analyzed in their own terms as well as in interaction with the behavior of such economic variables as employment, growth, profitability, and accumulation.

A neo-Marxian SSA analysis of the postwar US economy

The available evidence on profitability, accumulation, and output growth suggests that the US economy experienced a long-wave pattern of boom and crisis from the late 1940s through the mid-1980s. To explain this pattern of boom and crisis Bowles, Gordon, and I have developed an SSA-based approach to the study of the post-World War II US macroeconomy. Our work rests fundamentally on the logic of the neo-Marxian model summarized in Figure 8.1; we treat capitalist power as the most critical focus of analytical attention. However, we have modified and extended the neo-Marxian model in a number of respects in an effort to render it more useful for the analysis of developments in the US economy.[17]

Since World War II the US economy has experienced a characteristic long-wave pattern of boom and crisis; the available evidence on profitability, accumulation, and output growth suggests that the boom lasted for roughly two decades, peaking in the second half of the 1960s, and that the subsequent crisis has continued well into the 1980s. To explain this pattern of boom and crisis we advance a neo-Marxian variant of the SSA approach to long-wave analysis, which treats capitalist power as the most critical focus of analytical attention. Thus we begin with the new social structure of accumulation that was established in the aftermath of the crisis of the Great Depression and the disruption of World War II; and our characterization of that SSA is grounded in the neo-Marxian conception of an SSA as the institutional environment conditioning the power of the capitalist class relative to potential challengers.

More specifically, we have described the postwar US SSA in terms of three sets of institutions affecting the power of the US capitalist class vis-à-vis the US domestic working class, foreign buyers and sellers, and (potentially anti-business coalitions among) the US domestic citizenry, respectively.[18] The three corresponding institutional pillars of the postwar SSA are (1) the "capital-labor accord," assuring management control over enterprise decision-making and relative labor peace in exchange for rising real wages, benefits, and job security; (2) "Pax Americana," assuring overall international economic stability and favorable terms for US capital in dealing with foreign buyers and sellers; (3) the "capital-citizen accord," protecting the priority of capitalists' pursuit of profits while meeting some basic citizen needs through government demand management, public programs, and transfers. In more recent work we have taken account also of a fourth important dimension of the postwar US SSA: (4) the "moderation of intercapitalist rivalry," involving the maintenance of domestic oligopoly structures and limited foreign competition with US firms. This institutional dimension of the postwar SSA is seen as supporting the (relative) power of the US capitalist class by promoting intracapitalist class cohesion and limiting the intensity of intercapitalist competition.[19]

Our SSA-based argument proceeds in three steps, corresponding to three distinct subperiods in the postwar development of the US economy. The first subperiod includes the two decades of the boom itself; the second subperiod involves the onset and initial phase of the economic crisis, from the mid-1960s to the early 1970s; and the third subperiod covers the subsequent evolution of the crisis, from the mid-1970s to the mid-1980s. Our analysis of each of the first two of these subperiods is based on the primary neo-Marxian line of causation shown in Figure 8.1. This is the causal chain that runs from (1) the strength of the SSA, as reflected in institutions sustaining underlying (relative) capitalist power Π^*, to (2) actually exercised (relative) capitalist power Π to (3) the rate of profit r to (4) the rate of accumulation k. Our analysis of the third subperiod invokes some of the additional neo-Marxian relationships shown in Figure 8.1.

Beginning with our analysis of the postwar boom, we argue that the new postwar US SSA provided the institutional basis for a high degree of US capitalist class power and control vis-à-vis all three of its major potential challengers. This high degree of capitalist class power was translated into high rates of profit; and the high rates of profit in turn induced high rates of accumulation and thus the economic boom from the late 1940s to the mid-1960s. During the 1960s, however, we argue that the SSA institutions began to erode and that the US capitalist class therefore found it more difficult to maintain its position of power and control. Increasingly successful challenges from competing classes and groups reduced the relative power of the US capitalist class and led to a squeeze on profits by the late 1960s, which in turn led to reduced rates of accumulation and thus precipitated the economic crisis.

The continuation of the crisis in the 1970s and (at least the early) 1980s poses an apparent problem for such a power-based analysis, for there is a great deal of evidence that the (relative) power of the US capitalist class was on the rise again by the mid-1970s and reached new heights with the accession to power of the Reagan administration in the 1980s. If the weakening of US capitalist power (associated with the erosion of the postwar SSA) contributed to falling profitability and the onset of an economic crisis by the late 1960s, why didn't the apparent strengthening of US capitalist power from the mid-1970s on lead to rising profitability and a new boom? Our answer is based on the critical analytical distinction between underlying capitalist power and actually exercised capitalist power.

In order to apply the neo-Marxian analysis to this third subperiod of postwar US macroeconomic history we must go beyond the primary neo-Marxian causal chain outlined above to take into account the way in which actual capitalist power Π can vary independently of underlying capitalist power Π^*. As shown in Figure 8.1, the level of Π is not only a positive function of Π^* but also a negative function of the rate of capacity utilization u and the (past) rate of output growth g. From the mid-1970s on, and especially in the early 1980s, US government policy-makers pursued a considerably more restrictive macropolicy than they had during the 1960s and early 1970s (this is represented by a lower value for m^* in Figure 8.1). As a consequence, rates of capacity utilization u (and indirectly also rates of output growth g) were lowered, and this served to increase actual capitalist power Π without any improvement in underlying capitalist power Π^*. However, because of the direct positive effects of u on r and k, the restrictive macroeconomic policy also had counter-productive effects on both profitability r and accumulation k. Thus, what we have labeled the "contradictions of conservative economic policy" resulted in augmented capitalist power Π but, in the absence of any comparable improvement in the underlying strength of the SSA Π^*, no significant improvement in the profit rate r or the accumulation rate k.

From the perspective of this analytical approach, a new boom could be generated in the US economy only as a consequence of fundamental institutional change that would generate a strengthened SSA associated with significantly increased underlying capitalist power Π^*. But in our most recent analysis of the period of "business ascendancy" during the 1980s (Bowles et al., 1991, ch. 10), we have found little evidence of such an increase in underlying capitalist power.

Empirical evidence on our neo-Marxian SSA approach

Much of our work in recent years has been concerned with empirical estimation and testing of various aspects of the neo-Marxian SSA-based model that we have applied to the analysis of macroeconomic trends in the postwar US economy. Indeed, we have sought to respond to the challenge of translating an institutionally based theoretical approach into precisely specified models made up of quantifiable variables, in such a way that our hypotheses can be subjected to rigorous statistical testing. Our efforts have not surprisingly generated a certain amount of tension between the desire to ground our work in an understanding of socioeconomic institutions, and the need to utilize variables for which statistical measures can be compiled on a systematic basis.

In our description of trends in the postwar US SSA itself, we have necessarily been limited to qualitative historical evidence on the evolution of key institutions. Thus we have provided (most recently in Bowles *et al.* [1991, especially chs. 5 and 6]) narrative accounts of how the "capital–labor accord," "Pax Americana," the "capital–citizen accord," and the "moderation of intercapitalist rivalry" were established and functioned effectively in the first two postwar decades, but then began to erode significantly in the 1960s. We have associated this erosion with increasingly effective challenges to capitalist control from the domestic working class, from foreign buyers and sellers, from domestic citizens' movements, and from a rising degree of competition faced by US firms both at home and abroad. Thus we have sought to link the rise and decline of the strength of the postwar US SSA with a corresponding rise and decline of the (relative) power of the US capitalist class.

Most of our empirical work, however, has been devoted to econometric analysis of the relationships between (relative) capitalist power, profitability, and accumulation in the US economy – designed to test some of the critical elements of the neo-Marxian model described in Figure 8.1. It is relatively easy to obtain measures of the profit rate and the accumulation rate for US nonfinancial corporate business; what is much more difficult is to develop quantitative indicators of the relative power of the US capitalist class. Accordingly, we have had to devote a great deal of attention to the construction of measures of various aspects of capitalist power for which annual time series can be compiled.

For each of the four dimensions of US capitalist power (corresponding to the four principal sets of institutions by which we characterize the postwar US SSA), we have developed statistical indicators of relative capitalist power for which we have been able to compile the needed annual observations.[20] Thus, capitalist power *vis-à-vis* the working class is reflected in a measure of the "cost of job loss" and (inversely) in a measure of "workers' resistance"; capitalist power *vis-à-vis* foreign buyers and sellers is reflected in a measure of "trade power"; capitalist power *vis-à-vis* the domestic citizenry is reflected (inversely) in measures of "government regulation" and "capital's tax share"; and the degree of intracapitalist class cohesion is reflected in a measure of "product market tightness" and (inversely) in

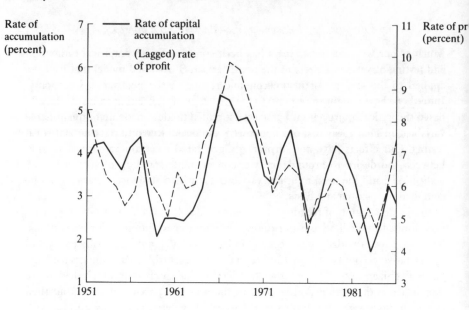

Fig. 8.3. Profitability and accumulation, 1951–86. (*Source*: See Bowles *et al.* [1989].)

a measure of "import penetration." Each of these indicators reflects an element of *actually exercised* capitalist power *Π*; as we will discuss below, further work is needed to derive estimates of the elements of *underlying capitalist power Π**.

To test the neo-Marxian relationship between power and profitability, we have undertaken regression analyses of the after-tax rate of profit in US nonfinancial corporate business in which the key independent variables are our quantitative indicators of (relative) capitalist power. In the most recent such regression (reported in Bowles *et al.* [1989, table 3]) we regressed annual observations on the profit rate from 1955 to 1986 on:

(1) the seven capitalist power indicators described above, representing *Π*
(2) the rate of capacity utilization *u*
(3) a measure of technological innovation, representing *T**, and
(4) a dummy variable for the wage-price controls applied in the early 1970s.

The first three sets of independent variables reflect all of the influences on the profit rate *r* shown in the diagram of the neo-Marxian model in Figure 8.1; the fourth was added because of the presumption that wage-price controls will have an independent exogenous effect on profitability. This regression analysis, like earlier such efforts, yielded estimated coefficients of the expected sign and in almost every case with a very high degree of statistical significance; the equation as a whole tracks the postwar behavior of the profit rate very closely.

In investigating the neo-Marxian relationship between profitability and accumulation, it is instructive to consider first a simple time-series graph of the rate of accumulation and the rate of profit (lagged two years) in the US nonfinancial corporate business sector from the early 1950s to the mid-1980s. It is obvious from such a graph (reproduced here as Figure 8.3) that these two key variables are highly correlated. To test the relationship more rigorously, we have undertaken econometric analyses of the net rate of capital accumulation in US nonfinancial corporate business in which the key independent variable is the corresponding rate of profit; the most recent such analysis is reported in Bowles *et al.* (1989, table 3). We regressed annual observations of the accumulation rate from 1955 to 1986 on:

(1) the profit rate r (with a distributed lag averaging roughly two years)
(2) the capacity utilization rate u (lagged one year), and
(3) a measure of the real cost of capital (lagged two years).

The first two of these independent variables reflect the influences on the accumulation rate k shown in Figure 8.1; the third was added because of the theoretical presumption that it is the expected return to capital *relative* to the cost of capital that will motivate firms' decisions to invest. This regression analysis yielded estimated coefficients of the expected sign and in every case with a very high degree of statistical significance; and the equation as a whole tracks the postwar behavior of the accumulation rate quite well.

An important additional quantitative task we set outselves was to generate an indicator of the *underlying* relative power of the US capitalist class Π^*, which can serve to reflect the strength of the SSA itself. As we have noted above, our quantitative indicators of capitalist power reflect the actually exercised relative power Π – which varies with the rate of capacity utilization u and the (past) rate of output growth g as well as with Π^*. To derive measures for underlying capitalist power Π_i^* corresponding to each measured element of actual capitalist power Π_i, it is therefore necessary to "purge" the actually observed levels of Π_i of their covariance with u and g. This we have done (in Bowles *et al.* [1989]) by regressing each of the seven time series Π_i in turn on time series for u and g, and then computing the corresponding Π_i^* time series as the values of Π_i which would have obtained at fixed benchmark levels of u and g.[21] We than aggregated these estimates of the individual power elements Π_i^* (with weights determined by their coefficients in a profit rate regression) to obtain a single overall quantitative index of underlying capitalist power Π^*. The postwar time pattern of this index of Π^* is shown in Figure 8.4, along with a correspondingly aggregated index of actual capitalist power Π.[22]

The rising level of our index of Π^* from the mid-1950s to the mid-1960s, followed by a long declining trend into the early 1980s, is quite consistent with our historical account of the rise and demise of the postwar US SSA. Moreover, the growing gap between the index of Π and the index of Π^* from the mid-1970s to the mid-1980s reflects our analysis of the second phase of the economic crisis in terms of the "contradictions of conservative economic policy." Deviations of Π from Π^* reflect (inversely) deviations in capacity utilization u and (past) output

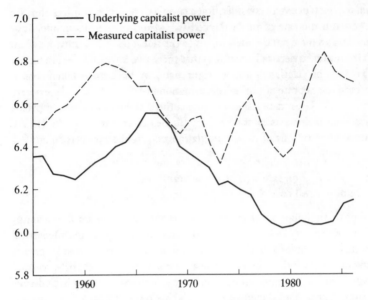

Fig. 8.4. Indices of capitalist power, 1955–86. (*Source:* See Bowles *et al.* [1989].)

growth *g* around their benchmark levels. Figure 8.4 shows clearly that the rising trend in actual capitalist power *Π* after the early 1970s did not reflect any significant rise in underlying capitalist power *Π**, but was instead due to the lower rates of capacity utilization and output growth associated with an increasingly restrictive government macropolicy.

It is nonetheless the case that the long-term decline in our index of underlying capitalist power *Π** appears to have bottomed out in the 1980s. Thus our quantitative analysis cannot rule out the possibility that the underlying power relationships have begun to shift back in favor of the US capitalist class in recent years. But our analysis does caution against concluding that such a turnaround has occurred on the basis of evidence about trends in actually exercised capitalist power, as reflected in our index of *Π*. And more compelling evidence of an increase in underlying capitalist power *Π** would be required before one could conclude that a stronger SSA had emerged again in the United States.

The explanatory power of the neo-Keynesian approach

In this chapter I have drawn a sharp contrast between the type of neo-Marxian SSA analysis Bowles, Gordon, and I have applied to the postwar US economy and an alternative neo-Keynesian SSA analysis that has been explicitly or implicitly adopted by other political economists in explaining capitalist booms and crises. The juxtaposition of these two theoretical approaches raises the question of whether the experience of the postwar US economy could be better understood in terms of a neo-Keynesian model. We have not done a systematic investigation of the relative explanatory power of the two models; but some of our empirical work does allow at least for some preliminary judgments on this question.

One of the sharpest points of contrast between the two models involves the relationship between profitability r and accumulation k: in the neo-Marxian model k is a lagged function of r, while in the neo-Keynesian model k is quite independent of r (and indeed r is a function of k). The evidence from the postwar US economy that we have compiled on this relationship clearly favors the neo-Marxian approach. Figure 8.3 demonstrates that k is closely correlated with r lagged by two years (the simple correlation coefficient is 0.78); and the simple correlation coefficient diminishes as the lag is reduced and turned into a lead. The hypothesis that profitability affects accumulation with a lag receives further support from our regression analysis of the rate of accumulation in the postwar US economy.

A second important point of contrast between the two models involves the determination of the rate of profit r. In the neo-Marxian model it is the elements of (relative) capitalist power Π which play the most critical role in affecting r (positively); while in the neo-Keynesian model it is the rate of output growth g which is most distinctive in influencing r (positively). Our econometric analysis of the determinants of the after-tax profit rate in the US nonfinancial corporate business sector provides support for the neo-Marxian view, since the estimated coefficients on all of the capitalist power variables proved significant with the hypothesized sign and these results were quite robust to a variety of alternative specifications and statistical tests (Bowles et al., 1986). Moreover, a neo-Keynesian approach to profitability determination in the US economy would find it difficult to explain the most dramatic drop in the profit rate in the postwar period – the one that occurred as the boom turned to crisis in the late 1960s – because the decade of the 1960s as a whole was one of unusually rapid growth in aggregate demand and total output.

The analysis of profitability determination in the two models differs sharply with respect to the effect of both output growth g and capacity utilization u on the rate of profit r. In the neo-Keynesian model both g and u have unambiguously favorable effects on r. By contrast, in the neo-Marxian model g and u (beyond a profit-maximizing level of u below full employment) have negative effects on r; these represent the distinctive over-accumulation and high-employment profit squeeze features of the neo-Marxian model. The case for at least a short-run cyclical high-employment profit squeeze in the postwar US economy has received empirical support from Weisskopf (1979); but the relationship between longer-run output growth and profitability remains to be tested in a systematic and rigorous fashion.

Concluding observations

An SSA approach to the analysis of long-term trends in a capitalist economy calls for two different types of empirical study. On the one hand, one must investigate the evolution of the institutions comprising the SSA itself: how do they come into being, how do they evolve, and, in particular, how do the institutions that have sustained a viable SSA and an economic boom lose their vitality, so that the SSA is weakened and a boom turns into an economic crisis? On the other hand, one must investigate the links between the SSA institutional framework and the performance of the capitalist macroeconomy: what are the causal chains by which particular SSA institutions affect key economic variables and ultimately the rate of accumulation?

The empirical work that Bowles, Gordon, and I have carried out in the context of our neo-Marxian SSA approach to analyzing the post-World War II US economy has focused primarily on the second of these two broad tasks. We have explored in great detail the way in which the institutions characterizing the SSA affect the rate of accumulation, applying a neo-Marxian line of causation running from the institutions of the SSA through capitalist power and profitability to the rate of accumulation. In pursuing our empirical analysis we have identified and described what we believe to be the key institutions comprising the postwar US SSA; we have linked these institutions conceptually to the underlying (relative) power of the US capitalist class; we have developed quantitative measures of various elements of underlying (relative) capitalist power and of actual (relative) capitalist power; and we have linked our power variables econometrically to the determination of the rate of profit and the rate of accumulation in the postwar US nonfinancial business sector. Our quantitative analysis has yielded, among other things, an index of underlying (relative) capitalist power Π^* that is designed to trace the rise and subsequent demise of the postwar US SSA; the time pattern of this index is clearly displayed in Figure 8.4.

While we have done much to illuminate the relationships between SSA institutions, capitalist power, profitability, and accumulation in the postwar US economy, we have for the most part treated the SSA itself as essentially exogenous to our empirical analysis. We have described and quantified the evolution of the SSA in great detail; but we have not done much to explain *why* the SSA evolved as Figure 8.4 suggests it did – why it developed increasing strength through the mid-1960s, why it then began to lose strength and continued on a downward course through the early 1980s, and why it began to turn up again in the mid-1980s. In other words, we have not yet addressed ourselves sufficiently to the first of the two main tasks of empirical SSA analysis outlined above. In this concluding section I will offer some suggestions about directions for further research on the evolution of the SSA itself.

In introducing the overall SSA approach to analyzing long waves, I noted that it is based on the idea that SSA institutions are established as a consequence of historically contingent political actions in the wake of an economic crisis, but that there is no endogenous mechanism assuring the generation of a new SSA or the transition from crisis to boom. On the other hand, the SSA approach does suggest that the transition from boom to crisis is endogenous – that a viable SSA becomes increasingly subject to problems during the course of the boom which it sustains, problems which eventually became serious enough to bring the boom to an end and precipitate a crisis.

More work is required on the nature of the contradictions that weakened the US SSA and turned the postwar boom into an economic crisis. The logic of the neo-Marxian analysis (as depicted in Figure 8.1) suggests two possible types of explanation for a transition from boom to crisis, one of which involves contradictions associated with the experience of an economic boom, and the other of which involves contradictions in the SSA institutions themselves.

The first of these possible neo–Marxian explanations of the onset of economic crisis is based on the long-run negative feedback loop running (in Figure 8.1) from the rate of accumulation via the rate of output growth to the level of (relative) capitalist power. If the lag in the effect of output growth on capitalist power is sufficiently long, then this negative feedback effect could by itself explain why a period of rapid accumulation (and high employment) would eventually turn into a period of slow accumulation (and low employment). This line of argument suggests that the very success of the postwar US SSA in generating two decades of economic boom brought about the economic crisis by increasing the relative power of challengers to capitalist control. For example, one could argue that the experience of relatively high employment over an extended period of time reduced the effectiveness of the threat of job loss as a labor-disciplining device; that rapid economic growth in the world capitalist economy as a whole improved the bargaining position of foreign raw material suppliers; that the buoyant national economy facilitated expansion of government welfare state programs; and that the buoyant world economy increased the strength of foreign competition with US-resident producers.

This type of explanation of the origins of the economic crisis in the United States is quite plausible; the experience of high employment, rapid accumulation, and rapid output growth in the preceding years does appear to have contributed to the sharp drop in profitability of the late 1960s. But the over-accumulation argument implies no change in the strength of the SSA itself (as represented by Π^* in Figure 8.1); it involves a long-term cycle of boom and crisis that occurs independently of any changes in the external environment set by the SSA institutions.

Yet the index of underlying power Π^* that I have displayed in Figure 8.4 suggests clearly that the transition from economic boom to crisis in the postwar US economy had much to do with changes in underlying capitalist power and hence with changes in the SSA itself. Thus we need to explore the second possible type of explanation for the onset of an economic crisis – contradictions whereby a successful SSA generates forces that undermine the strength of its own institutions.

What kind of internal contradictions may have arisen to weaken the postwar US SSA? It can be argued that rising wages and greater job security led to more concern about the quality of working conditions and the structure of authority at the workplace, helping to undermine the capital–labor accord; that the over-valued dollar inherent in Pax Americana proved contradictory by facilitating foreign competition with US producers; that the capital–citizen accord ultimately encouraged popular movements demanding ever greater regulation of business; and that the oligopolization of US domestic industry weakened its ability to defend itself against increasing competition from abroad. These are only examples of the kinds of internal contradictions that may have arisen within the SSA institutions; further work is needed to explore other possibilities.

In conclusion, our neo-Marxian SSA-based analysis suggests that the postwar boom in the United States gave way to crisis both because of the negative effects on capitalist power of over-accumulation and high employment (within the context of given SSA institutions) and because of internal contradictions arising from the logic of the SSA institutions themselves (which led to the weakening of their ability to sustain capitalist power).

Acknowledgments

In writing this chapter I have drawn on joint work with Samuel Bowles and David M. Gordon: I am indebted to both of them for many of the ideas developed herein, but responsibility for the chapter is solely mine. I am also grateful to David Kotz, Terrence McDonough, and Michael Reich for their constructive comments on earlier versions of this chapter, which was originally presented as a paper at the International Conference on the Theory of Regulation held in Barcelona, June 16–18, 1988.

Notes

1 The first formulation of our SSA approach is in Bowles et al. (1983); subsequent elaborations and extensions are presented in Bowles et al. (1986, 1989, 1991).

2 The reason for characterizing this approach as "neo-Keynesian" rather than simply "Keynesian" is that the analysis to be developed below goes beyond purely Keynesian elements to include theoretical propositions advanced by such "post-Keynesians" as Kalecki, Kaldor, and Verdoorn.

3 The quotation is from Gordon et al. (1988, p. 47).

4 This analysis in terms of the supply of imported material inputs can easily be generalized to apply to all transactions between foreigners (exporters and importers) and domestic capitalists (importers and exporters), so that the relative price p/p_M is a function of the relative power Π_F of domestic capitalists vis-à-vis foreign buyers and sellers. (This is in fact the way in which the issue is treated in Bowles et al. [1986].)

5 This analysis is set out in Kalecki (1971); for a modern version, see Cowling (1982).

6 As noted in the previous section, one can easily generalize the analysis of the international power dimension to include foreign buyers as well as foreign sellers vis-à-vis domestic capitalists.

7 See, for example, Armstrong et al. (1991, ch. 11).

8 The reason is that when the rate of capacity utilization in an industry is relatively high, at least some firms will begin to experience constraints on the expansion of their output; as a result,

the demand for the output of the remaining firms will be less likely to fall in response to higher output prices than would be the case in the absence of any quantity constraints.

9 This argument is based on the proposition that there are dynamic economies of scale to technological change, so that periods of rapid economic growth (especially in manufacturing) will yield more rapid improvements in the state of technology; see Thirlwall (1983) for a review of the literature on what has come to be labeled the "Verdoorn Law" or "Kaldor Law."

10 It should be stressed again that I have deliberately formulated each of the models in a highly simplified form, so as to bring out most sharply the differences between them.

11 See Dutt (1984, pp. 30–1), for a mechanism whereby a rise in the profit share can cause the rate of growth of output (and accumulation) to fall.

12 In deriving this equation I have suppressed a positive effect of s on k (operating via u, M, s and g with a lag of $t_5 + t_6 + t_2$) because it serves merely to dampen the negative effects of M^* and u^* on k which are shown in the equation.

13 The remaining exogenous variables in the neo–Marxian accumulation equation (20a) can be considered of secondary importance because of their ambiguous effects on accumulation.

14 Since the underlying degree of monopoly M^* and the exogenous element in capacity utilization u^* both have unambiguously negative effects on accumulation, a case could be made for a neo–Keynesian characterization of an SSA that included its ability to restrain these two exogenous variables; however these effects are relatively indirect and long-lagged, so it would seem appropriate to consider them of secondary importance.

15 This kind of model is developed in Weisskopf (1988).

16 The neo–Marxian model has most often been applied to the most recent economic crisis, while the neo–Keynesian model has more often been applied to that of the 1930s.

17 The initial statement of our basic argument is in Bowles *et al.* (1983), especially chapters 4 and 5. In subsequent joint work (Weisskopf *et al.*, 1985; Bowles *et al.*, 1986; Gordon *et al.*, 1988; Bowles *et al.*, 1989), we have developed the argument further and subjected it to more rigorous quantitative testing. Our most recent formulation of the analysis is in Bowles *et al.* (1991).

18 Note that these three potential challengers correspond to the three dimensions of relative capitalist power (represented by Π_L, Π_F, and Π_C) in the neo–Marxian analysis of the "three-front war" for profits discussed in the second part of this chapter.

19 To pursue the neo–Marxian analogy of the "three-front war" for profits that the capitalist class wages with its potential challengers, the fourth dimension of capitalist power reflects the ability of the capitalist class to organize its troops for battle.

20 Our work along these lines began with Bowles *et al.* (1983) and has continued since then; during the course of our work we have redefined and remeasured some variables and added others. For a detailed specification and documentation of our most up-to-date quantitative indicators of the various dimensions of US capitalist power, see the data appendix to Bowles *et al.* (1989).

21 The method we actually used for the purging exercises reported in Bowles *et al.* (1989) differs in some minor details from the method outlined here, but the principle is precisely the same.

22 To bring out more clearly the long-term trends, Figure 8.4 shows three-year centered moving averages rather than single-year observations on each index.

References

Armstrong, Philip, Andrew Glyn, and John Harrison, 1991. *Capitalism Since 1945*. Oxford: Basil Blackwell.

Bowles, Samuel, David M. Gordon, and Thomas E. Weisskopf, 1983. *Beyond the Waste Land: A Democratic Alternative to Economic Decline*. New York: Doubleday.

1986. "Power and Profits: The Social Structure of Accumulation and the Profitability of the Postwar U.S. Economy," *Review of Radical Political Economics*, 18(1–2): 132–67.

1989. "Business Ascendancy and Economic Impasse: A Structural Retrospective on Conservative Economics, 1979–1987," *Journal of Economic Perspectives*, 3(1): 107–34.

1991. *After the Waste Land: A Democratic Economics for the Year 2000*. Armonk, N.Y.: M. E. Sharpe.

Cowling, K., 1982. *Monopoly Capitalism*. London: Macmillan.

Dutt, Amitava K., 1984. "Stagnation, Income Distribution and Monopoly Power," *Cambridge Journal of Economics*, 8(1): 25–40.

Gordon, David M., 1978. "Up and Down the Long Roller Coaster," in *U.S. Capitalism in Crisis*, ed. Union for Radical Political Economics, pp. 22–35. New York: Union for Radical Political Economics.

Gordon, David M., Richard Edwards, and Michael Reich, 1982. *Segmented Work, Divided Workers*. Cambridge University Press.

Gordon, David M., Thomas E. Weisskopf, and Samuel Bowles, 1988. "Power, Accumulation and Crisis: The Rise and Demise of the Postwar Social Structure of Accumulation," in *The Imperiled Economy*, ed. R. Cherry *et al.*, pp. 43–57. New York: Union for Radical Political Economics.

Kalecki, Michal, 1971. *Selected Essays on the Dynamics of the Capitalist Economy*. Cambridge University Press.

Thirlwall, A. P., 1983. "A Plain Man's Guide to Kaldor's Growth Laws," *Journal of Post-Keynesian Economics*, 5(3): 345–58.

Weisskopf, Thomas E., 1979. "Marxian Crisis Theory and the Rate of Profit in the Postwar U.S. Economy," *Cambridge Journal of Economics*, 3(1): 341–78.

1988. "The Analytics of Neo-Marxian Crisis Theory: An Illustrative Model," *Keizai Kenkyu* (*The Economic Review*, Hitotsubashi University, Tokyo), 39(3): 193–208.

Weisskopf, Thomas E., Samuel Bowles, and David M. Gordon, 1985. "Two Views of Capitalist Stagnation," *Science and Society*, 49(3): 259–86.

— 9 —

The politics of the US industrial policy debate, 1981–1984 (with a note on Bill Clinton's "industrial policy")

JIM SHOCH

Introduction

As the contributions to this volume show, the emerging social structures of accumulation (SSA) approach to political economy has begun to provide a comprehensive, middle-range theory of capitalist development that can be fruitfully used to better understand American economic and political history. The approach has been employed to explore the construction, unraveling, and reconstruction of the institutional foundations of capital accumulation during various stages of American history.

My aim in this chapter is twofold: to contribute to a clearer understanding of the political and cultural/ideological dimensions of SSA theory, and to show that the theory can be used to explain *failed* attempts at institutional change or innovation during periods of SSA crisis. I hope to accomplish this through a case study of the wide-ranging debate that took place in the United States in the early 1980s on the need for an American "industrial policy" in response to growing competitive challenges from Japan, Europe, and various newly industrializing countries. Many analysts at that time – including certain SSA theorists – saw industrial policy as the necessary and probable next step in the rationalization of American capitalism, in other words, as a "core" institution of a new SSA. Yet industrial policy faded as an issue in the early 1980s almost as rapidly as it had arisen.

Bill Clinton's announcement of a new "technology policy" in early 1993 – the term "industrial policy" was not used – might appear to indicate that the adoption of the concept was only delayed in the 1980s. But as I will demonstrate in a brief note at the end of this chapter, Clinton's program is not the radical departure that industrial policy supporters hope for and critics fear.

I will argue that a properly constructed version of SSA theory, one that gives adequate weight to political and cultural factors, can explain *both* the rise and rapid demise of the industrial policy debate in the early 1980s, as well as the incremental character of Clinton's technology policy initiative.

Deepening SSA theory

Briefly, a social structure of accumulation is a historically and nationally specific complex of all the formal economic, political, and ideological institutions and, I would add, more informal norms that impinge on a given nation's capital accumulation process at a given time.[1]

SSA institutions and norms of this sort are "middle level" theoretical concepts and are to be distinguished from what might be termed more fundamental or abstract "deep structures" of the economy, the state, and the culture. Such deep structures, irreducible to one another, are more fixed or invariant in character than are SSA institutions and norms and limit the scope of institutional and normative variation, just as institutions and norms constrain the practices of individual and collective actors or agents.[2]

Structures, institutions, and norms do more than merely constrain actors, however; they enable or empower them, as well. Structures, institutions, and norms all provide actors with resources, while institutions and norms also help to constitute individual and collective identities and interests through processes of socialization. They facilitate agents' decisions and actions in a complex and uncertain environment through the transmission of stabilizing traditions, customs, habits, routines, rules of thumb, and standard operating procedures. And, while it is not easy, actors can in turn through their various practices transform structures, institutions, and norms (although it is more difficult to transform "deep structures" than it is to change middle level institutions and norms).

To return to SSA theory, a given SSA is a product of earlier struggles and compromises among rival social forces and coalitions that "congeal" to assume over time a degree of autonomy from those forces. The SSA serves in a variety of ways to facilitate rapid capital accumulation in a specific country. The SSA comes to shape the interests of various economic actors, routinize and regularize various social practices, and provide information to reduce uncertainty, thus creating a stable, predictable economic climate. This in turn improves business expectations and induces steady investment and a relatively long period or "swing" of economic growth.

At some point, however, successful accumulation itself disrupts prevailing institutions and norms, or the SSA begins to fetter the accumulation process. In either case, accumulation slows, and a period of uncertainty and crisis opens. Existing compromises and coalitions are disrupted by a variety of social and political conflicts, which existing institutions and norms can no longer channel and contain. Actors struggle to redefine their interests and search for solutions to the newly emergent economic tensions. This period of conflict and search is also usually quite lengthy, due to the "inertial" or "sticky" character of institutions and norms.[3] In fact, existing institutions and norms are sufficiently resilient despite their growing dysfunctionality that a depression or crash is usually necessary before these obstacles to growth can be swept away and a set of core institutions of a new SSA constructed to underpin a new upswing of accumulation.

There is no singular, functionally determined resolution of an SSA crisis. The nature of the new SSA is the contingent outcome of a variety of social conflicts and search processes.[4] In particular, dynamics within the party and state systems, involving the formation of new political coalitions and institutions, will be of great importance in the resolution of the crisis and in the construction of a new SSA. SSA theorists, however, have paid relatively little attention to these expressly political dynamics (although shifts in the substance, if not the politics, of macro-economic policy have been explored), an imbalance I hope to help correct in the case study presented here.

Industrial policy: the Democrats' "big idea"

The industrial policy debate emerged in the early 1980s in the wake of Ronald Reagan's election to the Presidency, as the Democratic Party sought an alternative to "Reaganomics" in an effort to retake the White House.

Reagan took office with the country mired in stagflation and the postwar SSA – including the Keynesian welfare/warfare state – under great pressure. Buoyed by his landslide victory, and amidst Republican claims of political "realignment" and policy "mandate," Reagan moved quickly in 1981 to implement his "supply-side" program, actually a hybrid combining the continuation of the tight money policy begun under the Carter administration, personal tax cuts (tilted toward the top brackets), corporate tax reductions, deregulation, social spending cuts, and major military spending increases.

While supply-side economics was backed by some Reagan supporters principally as a viable new "accumulation strategy," for Reagan and his closest backers, supply-side was promoted primarily as an ideological and political doctrine. This "hegemonic project" would be capable, it was hoped, of uniting various sectors of business and much of the working- and middle-class electorate on behalf of a program of painless, inflation-free growth.[5] While the Reaganite reworking of "Americanist" ideology also included traditional patriotic, militarist, individualist, and familialist themes, it was mainly by attacking the role of government in the economy in order to seize from the Democrats the mantle of the party of growth that the Republicans hoped to hold power in the 1980s.

The initial results of Reaganomics, however, were disastrous. The tight money policy plunged the country into a sharp recession. At the same time, the value of the dollar was driven up as rising interest rates attracted foreign capital, needed to finance growing budget deficits. This worked to slash US exports and boost imports, compounding pre-existing problems of American trade competitiveness. This was to become one of the pre-eminent economic problems of the 1980s.

As factories closed throughout the Northeast and Midwest, a new term was coined to describe the consequences of the country's economic decline – "deindustrialization." As Reagan's support among nationally based industrial interests and the wider electorate began to weaken, a Democratic alternative to supply-side economics emerged – "industrial policy."

Defining industrial policy and its political utility

Industrial policy has been broadly defined by Chalmers Johnson as "a summary term for the activities of government that are intended to develop or retrench various industries in a national economy in order to maintain global competitiveness" (Johnson, 1984, p. 7). Such sectoral or firm-level policies – including subsidies, loans and loan guarantees, tax incentives, government procurements, research and development support, infrastructure development, workers assistance programs, trade policies, regulations, etc. – are used in Japan and Europe. They are employed to (1) move resources from declining basic to growing high-technology industries, (2) modernize basic industries, (3) aid adjustment from old to new industries by easing worker and community dislocation, and (4) protect older industries from decline.

The United States, of course, has any number of programs that impact specific industries and firms. Defense spending is most often cited, but there are many others. However, as industrial policy proponents pointed out as the debate began, these programs are *ad hoc* in character, with little attempt to coordinate them in the overall interest of improved national competitiveness.

Industrial policy was presented by some of its academic supporters principally as a component of an accumulation strategy. It would be a "left" supply-side economics, cognizant of the deficiencies of demand-oriented Keynesianism and designed to help reinvigorate the economy by providing at least one core institution of what we have called a new SSA. But for most Democratic political entrepreneurs, industrial policy was to serve mainly as a political program. It would be part of a new hegemonic project, able to reunite the fractured Democratic coalition – including labor, the middle class, and even sectors of domestically oriented industrial capital – around a new and positive view of the role of government in promoting growth.[6]

Thus, after the 1980 election, the Democrats went looking for a new "big idea" that could do for them what they believed supply-side economics had done for Ronald Reagan. They thought they found it in industrial policy. As Senator Edward Kennedy put it, "Historically, the unifying issue for the Democratic Party has been the economic issue. We need the restoration of our economy. The basis of the restoration is the development of an industrial policy" (quoted in Blumenthal, 1983, p. 40).[7]

The debate begins: setting the agenda

The earliest exchanges in the industrial policy debate among Democrats really began in the late years of the Carter administration, as the long-term competitive weakness of the American economy began to surface. The real struggle over industrial policy, however, was still to come, launched mainly by a number of individuals and organizations closely tied to the Democratic Party: (1) academics and policy entrepreneurs mostly outside the policy mainstream, (2) the labor movement, (3) several Democratic presidential aspirants, (4) a number of Congressmen, and (5) a small group of maverick capitalists by no means representative of their class on this issue.

The policy entrepreneurs kick off the debate

For the most part, the earliest phase of the ensuing industrial policy debate, in 1980–81, was dominated by policy analysts and entrepreneurs. Most of the participants agreed that US economic problems were structural, not just macroeconomic, in character. They were also influenced by the impressive successes of the Japanese "developmental state." They believed that more, not less, state intervention was required to raise investment and productivity levels and to improve competitiveness.[8]

Even in this early state, however, two broad streams of industrial policy thinking began to emerge: there were those who stressed reviving the nation's existing industrial base, and those who emphasized the promotion of new high-technology industries. This division did not emerge sharply until late 1982 or early 1983, and there were those who tried to develop a synthetic position, stressing the importance of both kinds of industries. But the differences were real, nonetheless, and they would ultimately prove crippling.

The leading early advocate of what might be called the "reindustrialist" position, stressing the importance of reviving basic industry, was Felix Rohatyn of Lazard Frères. As early as 1974, Rohatyn first advanced the idea of a new Reconstruction Finance Corporation (RFC), modeled on the New Deal era institution of the same name, to make loans to troubled industries.[9]

Also in the "reindustrialist camp" should be placed the *Business Week* team that authored the magazine's influential report, "The Reindustrialization of America," which appeared in late June, 1980 (*Business Week*, 1980). The report focused on the competitive problems of basic industry, proposing corporate tax incentives, export promotion, research and development support, and a "tripartist" advisory body to make policy recommendations.

Also among the "reindustrialists, on the left end of the political spectrum, were Barry Bluestone and Bennett Harrison, authors of *Capital and Communities*, published by the United Auto Workers (UAW)-backed Progressive Alliance , and the later *The Deindustrialization of America* (Bluestone and Harrison, 1981, 1982). Bluestone and Harrison proposed "truly democratic economic planning," as opposed to the "corporatist" models of Rohatyn, *Business Week*, and the "neoliberals," to be discussed below.

Not surprisingly, the American labor movement began to embrace these reindustrialist perspectives and started consulting with leftist industrial policy advocates like Bluestone, Robert Kuttner, Kennedy aide David Smith, and others. In 1982 the UAW began to develop its own industrial policy proposal, as did the Machinists Union and the AFL-CIO's Industrial Union Department. Labor would come to play a pivotal role in the unfolding industrial policy debate.

The second strain of industrial policy thinking developed as a component of a wider and newly emergent political tendency – "neoliberalism." Neoliberals acknowledged an important part of the conservative critique of Keynesianism and traditional Democratic liberalism, i.e., that those doctrines favored redistribution and consumption over growth and investment. While not abandoning traditional Democratic commitments to equality and justice, new means would have to be found to achieve these ends in a world of scarcity. Above all, this meant restoring growth, and the key to fostering growth in the new global economy was investment, especially in new technologies and new, "high value-added" industries.[10]

An early neoliberal "bible" was Lester Thurow's *The Zero-Sum Society* (Thurow, 1980). Thurow stressed the importance of rapidly moving resources out of declining basic or "sunset" industries into new high-technology "sunrise" industries better able to compete in world markets. Thurow thought this would require a form of national planning, including the "national equivalent of a corporate investment committee," which he would later specify as an RFC-like bank.

Another pivotal neoliberal analyst and industrial policy proponent was Robert Reich, of Harvard's Kennedy School for Public Policy, who had learned about European and Japanese industrial policies while working for the Federal Trade Commission in the 1970s. Reich wrote extensively about industrial policy in journals like *Foreign Affairs*, *The Harvard Business Review*, *The New Republic*, and elsewhere, and published two influential books in the early 1980s that included calls for such a policy.[11] To improve competitiveness, Reich, like Thurow, advocated the promotion of new high-tech industries. But he also advocated the use of advanced technology to modernize existing basic industries. To facilitate these changes, Reich proposed a range of coordinated industrial policies, including a government-subsidized lending institution and policies to ease the adjustment process and thus reduce opposition from the established business, labor, and regional interests.

The labor movement had little enthusiasm for these neoliberal analyses and programs, which it felt were either too quick to write off basic industry entirely or to sacrifice jobs in those industries via automation. This tension between labor-backed and neoliberal industrial policy proposals would later severely undermine the industrial policy campaign.[12]

Enter the politicians

Later in 1981 and 1982, spurred by the writings and advocacy of the industrial policy entrepreneurs, the politicians got into the act, attracted by the concept's potential to unite labor, the middle class, and sectors of business in a rejuvenated, pro-growth Democratic coalition. Edward Kennedy, with his ties to labor, was closest to the reindustrialists, but in late 1981 he began talking with Reich and Thurow as well. Walter Mondale became an industrial policy convert after reading the manuscript of Reich's new book, *The Next American Frontier*. Mondale found Reich's argument on behalf of both old and new industries politically appealing (although he rejected Reich's strict free-trade position).

The emerging block of Congressional neoliberals – including in particular Senators Gary Hart of Colorado and Bill Bradley of New Jersey, and Representatives Tim Wirth of Colorado and Richard Gephardt of Missouri – also embraced industrial policy, but the kind that emphasized shifting resources from "sunset" to "sunrise" industries. Such an industrial policy was viewed by these neoliberals as an alternative to the labor-driven protectionist sentiment that was growing in the Congress, support for which they felt would doom the Democrats to be viewed popularly as a captive of a "special interest."

Building support and creating controversy

With Reagan's high interest rate, strong dollar accumulation strategy continuing to lay waste American industry, and with the Democrats holding a working majority in the House of Representatives, serious movement toward the development of specific industrial policy proposals began in late 1982 and early 1983. In addition, all the leading Democratic presidential contenders with the exception of John Glenn, i.e., Mondale, Hart, Alan Cranston, Ernest Hollings, and Reuben Askew, embraced some form of industrial policy in the first half of 1983. Although their proposals at this stage were very undefined, most spoke of government aid for both hard-hit basic industries like auto, steel, and rubber, as well as for rapidly growing high-tech industries. Active labor movement support for industrial policy grew in the first part of 1983, too. The UAW released a proposal calling, among other things, for a National Strategic Planning Board and a bureau to help declining industries (Arenson, 1983). The AFL-CIO's Industrial Union Department was also working on an industrial policy proposal, with the express purpose of making it an issue in the 1984 presidential campaign.

Also important in this period in building momentum for industrial policy were changing business attitudes. Throughout the first half of 1983, a number of reports and proposals concerning the competitive decline of the US economy were published by business organizations, associations, and coalitions (Phillips, 1984).

The debate gets serious and Reagan responds

Activity intensified in the Congress in May.[13] From June through October, the Subcommittee on Economic Stabilization of the House Committee on Banking, Finance, and Urban Affairs, chaired by John LaFalce from upstate New York, held exploratory field hearings. While some thirty bills related to industrial policy would eventually be introduced into the 98th Congress, the principal focus of the subcommittee debate was on two bills: the National Industrial Strategy Act (HR2291), co-authored by New York Representative Stanley Lundine and Michigan Representative David Bonior; and another bill (HR3443) co-sponsored by Wirth and Gephardt. The differences between the two bills reflected deepening regional cleavages within the Democratic Party.

Lundine and Bonior were from industrial states hard-hit by the recession and

foreign competition, and their bill reflected Frost Belt priorities. They proposed a
National Industrial Development Bank, with a $12 billion loan capitalization and a
$24 billion loan guarantee capability, the money to be allocated evenly between
basic and high-tech industries (Lundine and Bonior's priorities clearly lay with the
former). An Economic Cooperation Council (ECC), with representation from
business, labor, government, and the public, would analyze the problems and
prospects of specific industries and propose specific policies.

The centerpiece of the Wirth–Gephardt bill was their version of the ECC, to be
governed by a board representing no particular constituencies (labor felt it would
be underrepresented in this plan). The council would function strictly to build
consensus proposals; it would have no independent power to initiate policy of its
own. Representing a high-tech state, Wirth saw the council as working principally
to promote dynamic new industries. The Wirth–Gephardt proposal again omitted
any mention of a bank, as the authors remained fearful that bank loans and
guarantees would be disproportionately allocated to politically entrenched declining industries in the Northeast and Midwest.

As the hearings unfolded during the summer, opposition mounted, focused on
the proposed bank. In particular, business leaders who had earlier been open to
new, general proposals to expand the role of government in the economy now
moved into opposition to the idea of a bank designed expressly to pick "winners"
and "losers" and to channel capital toward targeted sectors. Testimony from
high-tech and even hard-hit basic industry executives was almost uniformly
opposed to the proposed bank.

As the debate swirled, Democratic presidential aspirants became more vocal in
their support for various industrial policy schemes. Feeling vulnerable to Democratic criticisms that his administration was doing too little to restore American
competitiveness, Reagan in June proposed the establishment of a Department of
International Trade and Industry. In late July, in what one White House aide
called a "pre-emptive strike" against the Democrats, he announced the formation
of a Commission on Industrial Competitiveness, to be chaired by John Young,
president and chief executive officer of Hewlett-Packard. (*Business Week*, July 25,
1983). In August, the administration formed a tripartite steel-industry task force
and escalated its attacks on Democratic proposals as a step toward a planned
economy. On September 12, Reagan announced the National Productivity Act of
1983, designed to spur the development of new technology by reducing legal
barriers to cooperative research among competitors.

The "Fall offensive" and the beginning of the end for industrial policy

The attack of the "killer" economists

Perhaps most important in turning the tide of elite and public opinion against
industrial policy in the Fall of 1983 was the offensive against the doctrine mounted
from within the economics profession, especially by economists affiliated with

conservative and liberal think-tanks. In the first organized effort, Clemson University economist Richard McKenzie headed a Heritage Foundation task force that was eventually to commission more than two dozen papers critical of industrial policy, at a cost of over $200,000 (*Fortune*, October 31, 1983; McKenzie, 1983). On August 23–24, in Jackson Hole, Wyoming, the Federal Reserve Bank of Kansas City sponsored a small but widely publicized conference of respected economists which was critical of industrial policy (Berry, 1983).

The most damaging of the economists' attacks on Democratic industrial policy thinking came from within the ranks of the liberal Brookings Institution. While the Brookings analysts, many of whom had been long-time Democratic advisors, had been moving steadily toward fiscal conservatism since the stagflation of the 1970s, they became almost apoplectic on the issue of industrial policy, turning the Institution, in *Fortune*'s words, into a "hotbed of anti-industrial policy work" (Bartlett, 1983).

The tide begins to turn

In late September intra-Democratic fighting intensified over the issues of the bank, the possible use of the Economic Cooperation Council to plan and pick winners, and the degree to which the policy would tilt on labor's behalf. At the behest of House Democratic Caucus chairman Gillis Long, former Democratic National Committee chair Robert Strauss began to assemble a high-powered group of eighty-one businessmen and politicians to develop a moderate industrial policy plank for inclusion in the 1984 Democratic platform, one that would help, not hurt the party in the election (*Business Week*, September 26, 1983).

The conflict only heightened in October, however. On October 1, the AFL-CIO Executive Council unanimously adopted the strong industrial policy proposal it had been developing for months. The plan called for the creation of a National Industrial Policy Board and a National Development Bank. While aid was envisioned for both old and new industries, the Frost Belt tilt of the proposal was clear in the provision that the bank should "direct its resources to specific geographic areas of the country that are most in need" (Serrin, 1983).

Meanwhile, opposition to industrial policy hardened further, particularly within the business community. A spate of articles in the business and popular press included a flood of critical comments from leaders of virtually every sector of American industry.

During October attacks on industrial policy from the Reagan administration, the economics profession, and the mass media intensified. By late in the month, the regional splits between Frost Belt and Sun Belt Democrats, the academic, business, Republican, and media attacks, fears of labor domination of any industrial policy apparatus, and the polling analyses of public doubts about national planning had all combined to seriously undermine Congressional support for an RFC-like bank. As Robert Reich acknowledged at a press conference on October 19, industrial policy had arisen "from obscurity to meaninglessness" in just a few months, and he predicted – correctly, as it turned out – that it would not be an issue in the 1984 election.[14]

The Democratic retreat

The tide had indeed turned; the Democratic retreat from an interventionist industrial policy began in earnest in November. On November 16, the Senate Democratic Task Force on Industrial Policy, formed a year earlier by Edward Kennedy, finally issued its report. The term "industrial policy" appeared nowhere in the document, nor did the concept of a bank (Baker, 1987; Russell, 1986). Meanwhile, the House Democratic Caucus, working with Robert Strauss' group of notables, was putting the finishing touches on a similarly weak report. It was released on January 8 and also omitted any mention of a bank, calling only for an Economic Cooperation Council and some other relatively uncontroversial policies.

In some sense, these tepid proposals were the dying gasps of the industrial policy debate. From here the once furiously contested issue slowly faded away. Despite the early hopes of industrial policy advocates, the issue in the end played almost no role in the presidential election, in either the primaries or the general election.

Analyzing the fall of industrial policy

The concept of industrial policy seemed initially to many Democrats to have great promise as an accumulation strategy and even more so as a hegemonic project (our terms, of course, not theirs). Why, then, was the industrial policy debate of the early 1980s such a brief one?

Republican control of the Presidency and the Senate

With Reagan in the White House and the Republicans in control of the Senate, chances that industrial policy legislation would be passed during Reagan's first term were always remote, a fact that was of course recognized by Congressional industrial policy supporters, who hoped to provide a key campaign issue for the 1984 election.

But with Republican control of the Presidency and the Senate, our initial question should really be reformulated: why did proposed industrial policy legislation never even make it to the floor of the Democratic-controlled House for a vote? Why did the Democrats themselves back off from the issue? The following proximate and background factors can help answer these questions.

Proximate factors: labor, business, and public opinion

The Democrats backed off industrial policy in part because of the balance of social forces and public opinion surrounding the issue that was ultimately struck.

The strongest social force supporting industrial policy was the American labor movement. But in the early 1980s, the US labor movement was in woefully bad shape. Structural shifts from goods to service production, capital flight, automation, restrictive macroeconomic policy, foreign competition, the overvalued dollar, an "employers offensive," and inadequate organizing had all combined to badly weaken the labor movement during the previous thirty years. This in turn had weakened its political power. In the early 1980s labor had insufficient strength to compel Democratic legislators and candidates to remain firm in their commitment to industrial policy.

On the other side of the class divide, as the industrial policy debate unfolded, and as proposals became more specific, American business – a minority of which had been at least open to the idea – became steadily more opposed to the concept. Business became an important force in the lobbying and wider campaign against industrial policy.

Beyond the level of organized social forces, public opinion was mostly indifferent or opposed to industrial policy. For most Americans industrial policy was too technical in character to become a burning issue. Others found it unnecessary with the recovery of 1983–84 (see below). Among those who did follow the debate, most were convinced by the opponents of the concept. They worried that industrial policy, or at least more interventionist proposals like a bank, would lead to the growth of bureaucracy, waste, or both. The Democrats thus came to fear that their support of industrial policy would cost them at the polls.

It should be noted that the configuration of interests and opinion surrounding industrial policy had a distinctly geographical or regional dimension. Support for more interventionist forms of industrial policy was largely concentrated in the Frost Belt, with its declining firms and unions. Support was decidedly weaker in the Sun Belt, where it was felt that any industrial development bank would be dominated by politically entrenched Frost Belt interests. This led to intra-Democratic regional splits which eroded the party's advocacy of the concept.

Background factors: the economy, the state, and the culture

A number of contextual factors conditioned the preferences of actors involved in the industrial policy debate. First among these was the state of the American economy.

As "hegemonic stability" theorists argue, hegemonic nations in the world economy are generally free-traders and tend to oppose quasi-mercantilist programs like industrial policy as unnecessary. Such was the case for the US during most of the postwar period. As the US economy and competitive position weakened in the 1970s and during the recession of the early 1980s, sentiment for industrial policy grew. But the short-term success of Reaganomics undermined this drift. The tight money policy helped to drive down wages and oil prices, thus checking inflation and raising profits, while tax cuts and military spending increases boosted demand. The ensuing strong recovery of 1983–84 made industrial policy – and the return of the Democrats to the White House – seem unnecessary by the time the 1984 election rolled around.

The fragmented and decentralized nature of the American state also obstructed the adoption of industrial policy. The American state is fractured in a number of ways, including by (1) federalist divisions among local, state, and national levels of government, (2) the separation among executive, legislative, and judicial powers, (3) diversity within the executive branch, (4) fragmentation within the Congress, and (5) the single-member district form of electoral representation. The administrative capacity of the American state is also weakened by its internal fragmentation and the interest group cross-pressures this fragmentation encourages, as well as by the absence of a strong Treasury and strong, stable civil service (Heclo, 1986; Brady, 1988).

These aspects of state structure and capacity undercut the industrial policy movement in two ways. First, regional divisions between Frost Belt and Sun Belt Democrats, discussed above, were magnified by the fragmenting state-and-district-based character of Congressional representation, preventing the party from unifying around a single conception of industrial policy.

This difference among Democrats in turn highlighted for industrial policy critics a second problem with any form of industrial policy. The fragmented nature of the American state, it was argued, would prevent the kind of coherent, comprehensive policy-making necessary for an effective industrial policy because it allows strong interest groups access to the state at multiple points. In addition, it was further maintained, the American state bureaucracy lacked the internal cohesion, the independence of interest groups, and the administrative capacity and skill necessary to conduct an effective industrial policy.

Another important source of the positions of those actors among the public and within the business community who opposed industrial policy is to be found in the anti-statist character of American political and industrial culture. As argued earlier, although SSA crises involve the reconstruction of institutions and norms, such restructuring is not easy; SSA institutions and norms are quite "sticky," usually requiring an actual depression to uproot them. What I have termed "deep structures" are even "stickier," even more resistant to the transformational struggles of individual and collective actors. Following Robert Lane, I would argue that the individualist and anti-statist American political and industrial culture is just such a "deep structure," one that profoundly constrains the development of public policy in the US (Lane, 1986; see also Merelman, 1989).

In the case of the industrial policy debate, I would maintain first, following Jeffrey Freyman, that popular opposition to industrial policy stemmed to an important degree from "America's *pervasive liberal ideology*, which culturally conditions a limited role for the state in social and economic spheres" (Freyman, 1987, p. 61).

Second, American business has long held a historic "distrust" of the state, to borrow David Vogel's term, rooted in a number of factors related to the nature of the nation's processes of industrialization and democratization.[15] While individual firms may have "rationally" calculated that industrial policy would have damaged their particular interests or even the overall health of the economy, much of the business antagonism to the concept of industrial policy must be attributed to the United States' anti-statist industrial culture, which predisposed American business to oppose Democratic industrial policy proposals designed expressly to help business.

The role of middle-class policy experts

The role of policy experts and intellectuals in the industrial policy debate was pivotal. Given the complexity and uncertainty that often surrounds important policy questions, such experts, often driven by their own conceptions of the "national interest," can sometimes enhance their autonomy and influence by actively shaping the perceived interests and policy positions of other actors via various educational efforts. Such was the case during the industrial policy controversy, during which various policy intellectuals struggled to interpret or construct the nature or effects of some of the background factors discussed above for other actors involved in the debate.

In this struggle, the industrial policy entrepreneurs, mostly non-economists, were bested by a phalanx of mainstream economists. Some of these economist-opponents of industrial policy were funded by or housed at conservative think tanks, but the most influential of the critics were those associated with the traditionally more liberal Brookings Institution.

The Brookings economists and their co-thinkers influenced the industrial policy debate by advancing two main arguments. First, they provided a persuasive interpretation of the sources of the nation's economic difficulties that differed in crucial ways from the "causal story" (Stone, 1989) told by industrial policy supporters. The critics argued that the country's economic problems were merely macroeconomic and cyclical, not structural, in character, necessitating the use only of traditional fiscal and monetary tools to deal with the recession of 1981–82. The recovery of 1983–84 gave credibility to this interpretation, enabling the economists to construct for the American public and business interests a picture of an economy in no need of anything as drastic as an interventionist industrial policy.

Second, the economists successfully argued that the fragmented and porous character of the American state, described above, would result in the capture of any industrial policy planning board by politically powerful but inefficient "sunset" industries and their unions. Capital would thus likely be wasted in subsidizing "losers" rather than "winners."

Whether motivated by purely "objective" assessments of the weaknesses of the arguments advanced on behalf of industrial policy or by their own anti-statist cultural biases, mainstream American economists were both active and effective in persuading others that industrial policy was either unnecessary or likely to prove harmful.

The various factors discussed above combined to make the industrial policy debate of the early 1980s a brief one.

A note on Clinton's "industrial policy"

While "industrial policy" as such was driven off the American political agenda by 1984, the underlying problem of American industrial "competitiveness" remained and was debated throughout the rest of the decade and into the 1990s.

With the economy stagnant throughout most of George Bush's term of office, Bill Clinton made the revival of American economic growth and competitiveness central to his presidential campaign. In September 1992, at the urging and with the help of Silicon Valley executives, who had reversed their earlier position and were now calling for federal help, Clinton announced the broad outlines of a "technology policy" designed to "restore America's economic leadership" by aiding key industries.

After his election, Clinton seemingly fulfilled his promise to his high-tech supporters, returning in February 1993 with much fanfare to Silicon Valley to unveil his new technology initiative. It appeared to be the "second coming" of industrial policy.

Yet, as Marc Levinson of *Newsweek* observed, "If you're a critic of Clinton's controversial technology policy, rest easy. There's much less to the new plan than meets the eye." Noting that under Clinton's plan, industry would get support for high-tech research, small manufacturers would get some help applying technical innovations, and everyone else would be urged to curb pollution and use less energy, Levinson concluded, "If this is industrial policy, free-market purists can rest easy" (Levison, 1993, p. 42).

Clinton's original sketchy proposals were never on the scale of those forwarded in the early 1980s, nor did they envision helping declining basic industries, whose problems were viewed as self-inflicted and whose political power was also in decline.

Between the announcement of the outlines of Clinton's plan in September and its unveiling in February, the most far-reaching of those ideas that had been under discussion quietly disappeared. Clinton's campaign promise to establish a civilian agency to promote selected cutting-edge technologies was dropped. "There was no support for that from industry," said a White House aide (quoted in Levinson, 1993, p. 42). Nor was high-tech industry to be provided with help in raising venture capital, as Silicon Valley executives had requested. Clinton proposed no industrial policy "czar," nor even a centralized effort to coordinate government research programs. Instead, the administration planned to increase funding for existing programs in agencies from the Commerce Department to the National Aeronautics and Space Administration. The Defense Advanced Research Projects Agency, which fostered new technologies for military use, would remain in the Defense Department but would give higher priority to projects with civilian uses. Government labs would take on projects with commercial applications, but they would remain in their current agencies. Clinton's proposal to create 170 manufacturing extension centers, modeled after the Agricultural Extension Service, was revised so that much of the money would be funneled to outreach programs already in place at universities and community colleges.

While Clinton did plan to shift the government's research emphasis from military to civilian projects, with a special focus on clean cars and fast computer networks, there was little money attached. Government spending on civilian research and development was scheduled to rise only 15 percent over the next five years after inflation, less than a billion new dollars each year. "There's a lot of pruning back of what they're going to do," said a Congressional technology expert (Levinson, 1993, p. 43).

Why did Clinton back off from some of his already modest proposals? Part of the explanation lies in the recovery of the American semiconductor and other electronics industries and in the perceived failures of Japanese and European high-tech industrial policy. But the factors that undermined industrial policy proposals in the early 1980s were also at work. White House fears of eventual public opposition to new big-spending, bureaucratic programs; business, media, and academic criticism of proposals thought overly interventionist; concern over the possibility of Congressional "pork-barreling"; and the lack of centralized state administrative capacity all led the Clinton administration to scale back its technology policy initiative.

Conclusion

In early 1987, *Business Week*, the journal that gave a big boost to the industrial policy debate with its special "reindustrialization" issue, observed that "Unless a dire economic crisis radically shifts public attitudes, the best we can probably expect is to muddle through with our present ad hoc planning" (Welles, 1987).

This may seem to be an unduly pessimistic position, given one of the arguments of this chapter that the outcome of an SSA crisis and restructuring period is usually the result of an indeterminate process of social and political conflict. I certainly would not want to maintain that only one accumulation or hegemonic project was possible in the early 1980s (or remains possible now). In fact, Bill Clinton's overall economic strategy – with its emphasis on "public investment" in education and training, infrastructure, and to a modest degree, new technologies – differs significantly in its pro-government orientation from the largely *laissez-faire* strategy deployed by the Reagan and Bush administrations.

But I do not believe that the kind of limited technology policy Bill Clinton has proposed is sufficiently radical in nature that it can be said to constitute a "core" institution of a new social structure of accumulation. As I have argued at a number of points, SSA institutions and norms are not easy to change, and "deep" economic, political, and cultural structures are still more difficult to transform. The restructuring involved in the establishment of a truly non-incremental, interventionist industrial policy may well require a truly severe economic crisis as a facilitating condition, as *Business Week* acutely observed.

In the absence of a truly system-shaking crash during Reagan's tenure in office, the "deep" structural constraints of American political and industrial culture, perceptions of similarly limiting aspects of American state structure, and the more conjunctural opposition of important political forces combined to make the industrial policy debate of the early 1980s a brief one.

During the Clinton years, various social and political forces will continue to struggle over the shape of a new SSA. Short of a true economic collapse, however, Clinton's "industrial policy," as Robert Kuttner once predicted in a similar context, will likely be "minimalist art" (Kuttner, 1988, p. 18).[16]

Notes

1 See the first part of this volume for a full discussion of the SSA theoretical literature.
2 On the distinction between deep structures and institutions see Thompson (1989, p. 70). For a related discussion, see Mouzelis (1991, pp. 40–3).
3 As against the views of neoclassical economists who view institutions and norms as at best epiphenomenal, and "new neoclassical institutionalists" (Williamson, the "early" North, etc.), who see interests and norms as adapting rather rapidly and efficiently to changed incentive structures.
4 For a discussion of search processes during periods of institutional change see Bianchi (1990).
5 The concepts of "accumulation strategy" and "hegemonic project" have been developed by Bob Jessop. See Jessop (1990).
6 For other statements of this view see Galbraith (1989, p. 136) and Ginsberg and Shefter (1990, pp. 57–8).
7 See also the discussion in Baker (1987).
8 See the early, influential academic work on Japan by Ezra Vogel (1979) and Johnson (1982).
9 See the writings collected in Rohatyn (1983).
10 On Neoliberalism, see Rothenberg (1984).
11 See, for example, Reich (1982a, 1982b). The books were Magaziner and Reich (1982) and Reich (1983).
12 On this tension, see Lazarus and Litan (1983).
13 The account in the next four paragraphs is based on Baker (1987), Clark (1983), Corrigan (1983), and Murray (1983).
14 Reich, quoted in Clark (1983).
15 See Vogel (1978). See also McCraw (1984), and Orloff and Parker (1990).
16 Writing during the 1988 presidential campaign, Kuttner was discussing the prospects for industrial policy under a Democratic administration led by then Massachusetts Governor Michael Dukakis.

References

Arenson, Karen, 1983. "Debate Grows Over Adoption of National Industrial Policy," *New York Times*, June 19.

Baker, Ross, 1987. "The Bittersweet Courtship of Congressional Democrats and Industrial Policy," *Economic Development Quarterly*, 1(2): 111–23.

Bartlett, Bruce R., 1983. "Industrial Policy: Crisis for Liberal Economists," *Fortune*, November 14.

Berry, John M., 1983. "Leading Economists Dispute the Case for an 'Industrial Policy'," *Washington Post*, September 4.

Bianchi, Mariana, 1990. "The Unsatisfactoriness of Satisficing: From Bounded Rationality to Innovative Rationality," *Review of Political Economy*, 2(2): 149–67.

Bluestone, Barry and Bennett Harrison, 1981. *Capital and Communities: The Causes and Consequences of Private Disinvestment*. Washington, D.C.: The Progressive Alliance.

1982. *The Deindustrialization of America: Plant Closing, Community Abandonment, and the Dismantling of Basic Industry*. New York: Basic Books.

Blumenthal, Sidney, 1983. "Drafting a Democratic Industrial Plan," *New York Times Sunday Magazine*, August 28.

Brady, David W., 1988. *Critical Elections and Congressional Policy Making*. Stanford University Press.

Business Week, 1980. Special Issue: "The Reindustrialization of America," June 30.

1983. "The Point Man for 'Industrial Policy'," July 25.

1983. "Democrats Try Again on Industrial Policy," September 26.

Clark, Timothy B., "An Industrial Policy Get-Well Card," *National Journal* (May 28): 1129.

Corrigan, Richard, 1983. "Democrats Seek an Industrial Policy in time for the Next Election Campaign," *National Journal* (June 11): 1221–2.

Fortune, 1983. "The Attack on Industrial Policy," October 11.

Freyman, Jeffrey B., 1987. "Industrial Policy: Patterns of Convergence and Divergence," in *Political Economy: Public Policies in the United States and Britain*, ed. Jerold L. Waltman and Donley T. Studlar, pp. 44–68. Jackson: University Press of Mississippi.

Galbraith, James K., 1989. *Balancing Acts: Technology, Finance and the American Future*. New York: Basic Books.

Ginsberg, Benjamin, and Martin Shefter, 1990. *Politics By Other Means: The Declining Importance of Elections in America*. New York: Basic Books.

Gurwitt, Rob, 1983. "Unions Hope Endorsement of Mondale Will Advance Labor's Legislative Goals," *Congressional Quarterly Weekly Report* (October 8): 2080–1.

Heclo, Hugh, 1986. "Industrial Policies and the Executive Capacities of Government," in *The Politics of Industrial Policy*, ed. Claude E. Barfield and William S. Schambra, pp. 292–317. Washington, D.C.: American Enterprise Institute.

Jessop, Bob, 1990. "Accumulation Strategies, State Forms and Hegemonic Projects," in *State Theory: Putting Capitalist States in their Place*, ed. Bob Jessop, pp. 196–219. University Park, Pa.: Pennsylvania State University Press.

Johnson, Chalmers, 1982. *MITI and the Japanese Miracle: The Growth of Industrial Policy, 1925–1975*. Stanford University Press.

1984. "Introduction: The Idea of Industrial Policy," in *The Industrial Policy Debate*, ed. Chalmers Johnson, pp. 3–26. San Francisco: Institute for Contemporary Studies Press.

Kuttner, Robert, 1988. "Dukakonomics," *The New Republic*, July 18 and 25.

Lane, Robert, 1986. "Market Justice, Political Justice," *American Political Science Review*, 80(2): 383–402.

Lazarus, Simon, and Robert E. Litan, 1983. "The Democrats' Coming Civil War Over Industrial Policy," *The Atlantic*, September.

Levison, Marc, 1993. "Cutting Edge?" *Newsweek*, March 8.

McCloskey, Herbert and John Zaller, 1984. *The American Ethos: Public Attitudes Toward Capitalism and Democracy*. Cambridge University Press.

McCraw, Thomas K., 1984. Business and Government: The Origins of the Adversary Relationship," *California Management Review*, 26(2): 33–52.

McKenzie, Richard, 1983. "NIP in the Air," *Policy Review*, Fall.

Magaziner, Ira C., and Robert B. Reich. 1982. *Minding America's Business: The Rise and Decline of the American Economy.* New York: Harcourt Brace Jovanovich.

Merelman, Richard M., 1989. "On Culture and Politics in America: A Perspective from Structural Anthropology," *British Journal of Political Science*, 19(4): 465–93.

Mouzelis, Nicos, 1991. *Back to Sociological Theory: The Construction of Social Orders.* London: Macmillan.

Murray, Alan, 1983. "With an Eye on '84 Elections, Democrats Lay Foundations for National Industrial Policy," *Congressional Quarterly Weekly Report* (August 20): 1679–87.

Orloff, Ann Shola, and Eric Parker, 1990. "Business and Social Policy in Canada and the United States, 1920–1940," in *Comparative Social Research*, vol. XII: Business Institutions, ed. Craig Calhoun, pp. 295–339. Greenwich, Conn.: JAI Press.

Phillips, Kevin, 1984. *Staying on Top: The Business Case for a National Industrial Strategy.* New York: Random House.

Reich, Robert, 1982a. "Making Industrial Policy," *Foreign Affairs*, 60(4): 852–81.

1982b. "Why the U.S. Needs an Industrial Policy," *Harvard Business Review*, 60(1): 74–81.

1983. *The Next American Frontier.* New York: Times Books.

Rohatyn, Felix, 1983. *The Twenty-Year Century: Essays on Economics and Public Finance.* New York: Random House.

Rothenberg, Randall, 1984. *The Neo-Liberals: Creating the New Politics.* New York: Simon and Schuster.

Russell, Robert W., 1986. "Congress and the Proposed Industrial Policy Structures," in *The Politics of Industrial Policy*, ed. Claude E. Barfield and William Schambra, pp. 318–31. Washington, D.C.: American Enterprise Institute for Public Policy Research.

Serrin, William, 1983. "Firm U.S. Policy to Guide Growth of Industry Urged by Labor Chiefs," *New York Times*, October 3.

Stone, Deborah, 1989. "Causal Stories and the Formation of Policy Agendas," *Political Science Quarterly*, 104(2): 281–300.

Thompson, John B., 1989. "The Theory of Structuration," in *Social Theory of Modern Societies: Anthony Giddens and His Critics*, ed. David Held and John B. Thompson, pp. 56–76. Cambridge University Press.

Thurow, Lester, 1980. *The Zero-Sum Society: Distribution and the Possibilities for Economic Change.* New York: Basic Books.

Vogel, David, 1978. "Why Businessmen Distrust Their State: The Political Consciousness of American Corporate Executives," *British Journal of Political Science*, 8(1): 45–78.

Vogel, Ezra, 1979. *Japan As Number One: Lessons for America.* New York: Harper and Row.

Welles, Chris, 1987. "The 'Competitiveness' Craze: A New Name, An Old Idea," *Business Week*, January 17.

III

CLASS, RACE, AND GENDER

__ 10 __

Shopfloor relations in the postwar
capital–labor accord

DAVID FAIRRIS

The postwar years are generally described as a period of relative stability in mass-production industrial relations. It is often claimed that a set of mutual understandings and a web of rules and regulations guided the actions of employers and organized workers during this period toward the maintenance of industrial peace through the attainment of mutual prosperity. A particularly concise description of this view is contained in the account of the postwar capital–labor accord found in social structures of accumulation (SSA) theory. SSA theorists argue that under the accord workers in the unionized sector gave up their bid for greater control over the labor process (a goal originating in the 1930s' organizing drives) in exchange for wages tied to productivity, employment security, and better working conditions (Gordon *et al.*, 1982; Bowles *et al.*, 1983, 1986).

I will argue that this description of postwar capital–labor relations does not square with the reality of shopfloor practice. The postwar industrial relations system may have offered a stable set of institutional arrangements for determining wages, hours, and fringe benefits, but it never encompassed a similar set of arrangements for determining shopfloor conditions. A closer look at postwar shopfloor relations reveals that collective bargaining agreements and grievance procedures were initially unutilized and ultimately inadequate mechanisms for shopfloor dispute resolution, and that the set of mutual understandings concerning the bounds of collective bargaining was struck between employers, the state, and the labor leadership, without the consent of the rank and file. Within this rather unstable set of institutional arrangements there was in fact much jockeying for position and institutional adjustment at the shopfloor level.

It is commonly accepted that the postwar industrial relations system is currently in the midst of rather dramatic changes, if not outright institutional demise. One of the more interesting attempts to analyze these developments is contained in the work of SSA theorists, where shopfloor relations play a prominent role and pressures for institutional change are seen to be the result of contradictory tendencies inherent in postwar institutional arrangements (Weisskopf *et al.*, 1983; Bowles *et al.*, 1986). Oddly, though, most of the research of SSA theorists has focused on exogenous, as opposed to endogenous, forces promoting change. For example, the 1960s' expressions of rank-and-file discontent over shopfloor conditions are seen to be the result of such exogenous forces as the decline in the unemployment rate and the increase in the social wage. The internal, historical/ institutional unraveling of the postwar industrial relations system remains largely unexplored terrain.

I will argue that the postwar industrial relations system represented not only an unstable set of institutional arrangements for determining labor's shopfloor conditions, but that it represented a contradictory set as well. As the government, the labor leadership, and employers pursued their interests within the rather loose confines of the postwar accord, shopfloor relations became highly bureaucratic, and rank-and-file shopfloor power became increasingly compromised. The result was a deterioration in working conditions and growing rank-and-file militancy in expressions of discontent over this deterioration. The ensuing crisis on the shopfloor had an important impact on employers' designs for the future of capital–labor relations, designs that have played a prominent role in recent institutional challenges to the postwar industrial relations system.

The outline of this chapter is as follows: in the first section I provide a brief historical overview and discuss the determinants of mass-production shopfloor relations from roughly the mid-1930s through the 1960s. I concentrate in this section on three institutional forces that were crucial in shaping and delimiting rank-and-file control over working conditions in the period from roughly 1950 to 1970: the technology and organization of production, labor law, and the internal organization of union structures. The discussion reveals both the instability of the postwar industrial relations system as well as its contradictory nature. In the second section I draw out briefly the implications of the analysis for an understanding of the recent shopfloor initiatives of employers: quality of worklife programs and team production.

Postwar shopfloor relations[1]

The technology and organization of mass production which emerged in the United States around the turn of the century produced a rather homogeneous lot of semi-skilled machine-tenders, whose fate lay largely in the hands of a supervisory elite with a great deal of discretionary authority. The feelings of solidarity engendered by the workers' common predicament helped to foster both the empowerment of industrial work groups on the shopfloors of many core sector manufacturing firms, and workers' collective demands for change (Gordon et al., 1982).

Organizing drives begun as early as the 1910s in steel, meatpacking, and other mass-production industries appeared with renewed vigor in the Depression years. The newly emerging industrial unions rested upon the mass support of workers at the shopfloor level and the active participation of unpaid staff members from shop stewards on up. This created a decentralization of power in these early union structures, one consequence of which was a significant amount of rank-and-file control over union goals, especially at the shopfloor level. Indeed, in the days before World War II, labor–management disputes were settled largely through collective shopfloor power brokering, sometimes with workers simply "knocking off" until the dispute was favorably resolved (Lichtenstein, 1982).

By the decade's end an informal and rather vague understanding had emerged among significant segments of capital, the state, and the labor leadership. Capital would willingly enter into negotiations with labor over wages, hours, fringe benefits, and their distribution to workers in the plant (through the definition of job titles, job evaluation schemes, and seniority agreements). The government would support, through legislation and various government-financed agencies, the process of responsible collective bargaining. As for the "other conditions of employment," labor would not dictate to capital how it should market its products or where it could invest its profits, and in turn employers would not refuse to discuss a wide range of shopfloor conditions (e.g. safety, speed-up, technology). Contract language and the grievance procedure would serve as adequate mechanisms for the orderly resolution of shopfloor disputes.[2]

The United Auto Workers' historic 1948 agreement with General Motors appeared to seal the deal in the auto industry, and the so-called postwar accord was then to have spread quickly throughout the rest of manufacturing. Shortly after the turn of the decade, the accord seemed to be well in place and the future looked rather rosy. However, the rank and file were not informed of the larger set of intentions concerning shopfloor control, and since the goals and actions of the labor union bureaucracy are no clear guide to those of the rank and file, the appearance of shopfloor relations conveyed by contract language turned out to be a relatively poor indicator of actual shopfloor practice.

It is true that compared with the situation a decade earlier the process of workplace dispute resolution had by the late 1940s grown less openly conflictual. The "quickie strike" was less common in day-to-day shopfloor relations, and although the slowdown was still employed in those industries and departments whose production processes left some control over pace in the hands of workers, these older expressions of shopfloor power had become integrated with a new form of dispute resolution referred to as "fractional bargaining" (Chamberlain, 1948). Fractional bargaining was a decentralized and strategic form of workplace dispute resolution involving foremen, shop stewards, and industrial work groups. Its existence rested upon the power, though not necessarily the right as defined by either company or union, of foremen and shop stewards to strike extra-contractual deals governing shopfloor conditions. Fractional bargaining has therefore been aptly described by Hyman (1972, p. 62) as "the unauthorized pursuance of demands backed by unofficial sanctions."

Kuhn (1961) notes that most extra-contractual workplace issues were handled in this fashion well into the mid-1950s, and that even contractual rights of management were often won by workers through this technique. Through fractional bargaining unionized workers were able both to win new improvements in working conditions in the immediate postwar period and to protect past gains. This form of shopfloor power served as an adequate mechanism for policing contractual agreements on job descriptions and seniority rules, as well as an important source of rank-and-file empowerment in influencing those work standards which were largely noncontractually determined.

Though the postwar accord did not successfully extend to the shopfloor, the larger understanding forged in the late 1940s nonetheless had an important impact on the direction of future developments on shopfloor relations. The state was constantly refashioning bits and pieces of labor law in the hopes of realizing the industrial peace and enhanced productivity the accord seemed to promise. Unions shifted their focus to bureaucratic, centralized bargaining structures in order to insure the monetary gains the accord made possible. And employers were freed, subject to the rank-and-file's shopfloor power, to enlarge their control over the labor process, allowing them the possibility of offsetting the monetary gains which the accord effectively conceded to labor, and of reappropriating those shopfloor gains which workers had won in past struggles. The result of these developments was a gradual bureaucratization of shopfloor relations, leading to the slow erosion of rank-and-file power at the point of production and increased appropriation of working conditions by employers in the labor process.[3]

Fractional bargaining thus slowly gave way in the late 1950s and early 1960s to increased reliance on contract language and use of the grievance procedure. These, however, proved almost immediately inadequate to the task of legislating and adjudicating shopfloor conditions. By the early 1960s, signs of institutional stress in capital–labor relations were evident in the large number of unresolved grievances and in workers' demands that "local issues" be addressed in contract negotiations. By the mid-1960s, signs of systemic decay could be seen in the intensity of shopfloor conflict, the effort to adjust the legal framework of collective bargaining, and the number of contract rejections. I turn now to the role of the technology and organization of production, labor law, and the structure of unions in this emerging contradiction.

The technology and organization of production

Fractional bargaining was most successful where strong industrial work groups were able, through their power in production, to force their will on foremen, or where shop stewards could do the same by using the threat of collective slowdown or wildcat strike. Developments in the technology and organization of mass production in the late 1950s and early 1960s addressed both of these sources of shopfloor power. Companies' conscious attempts to capture control of the process of shopfloor dispute resolution represented one aspect of the strategy to eliminate fractional bargaining, and further advances in mechanization and automation of production represented the other.

Procedures governing the hiring, firing, and promotion of workers, the extensive classification of jobs and their duties, and the internal resolution of labor–management disputes expanded enormously in the years following the war. Rules and regulations governing the allocation of labor allowed workers to eliminate some of the deleterious effects of arbitrary behavior by supervisors. They also reduced the need for a constant mustering of workers' shopfloor power for daily dispute resolution. But, as Edwards (1979) points out, there was clearly a flip side. The proliferation of job categories created divisions among workers in the plant, and the web of rules and regulations that soon became known as "company policy" served to institutionalize the power of the company by making the use of its power less arbitrary and interpersonally visible, but no less controlling in its effects. The system of internal grievance procedures took a bit longer to become fully incorporated into "company policy," but when finally accomplished, it, too, contained both costs and benefits for the rank and file.

Formal mechanisms for the resolution of workplace disputes date back to the "welfare capitalist" movement of the 1910s and 1920s, where they were part of a larger effort by employers to reduce labor mobility and prevent the unionization of industrial workers. These mechanisms died out during the early days of the Depression, but were revived during the organizing drives of the 1930s, once again as an attempt by employers to stave off unionization. The War Labor Board during World War II gave further impetus to their development as a means by which to maintain industrial peace. And employers' own attempts to grapple with the enormous shopfloor power held by the newly organized and empowered rank and file suggested the need for some formal procedures for workplace dispute resolution. By the late 1940s and early 1950s, the prevalence of grievance procedures had reduced the extent of spontaneous shopfloor activity, but what emerged in its place was a decentralized system of informal shopfloor bargaining in which the grievance procedure became a weapon strategically wielded by the rank and file.

Kuhn's (1961) survey of twenty major manufacturing firms during the mid-1950s revealed that the internal grievance procedure was being used by workers as a mechanism to facilitate shopfloor bargaining over workplace concerns. Fractional bargaining often operated as a strategic process of grievance filing, shopfloor slowdowns, and occasional shutdowns, through which the rank and file were able, with the support of shop stewards, to bring their power to bear over the conditions of production in the labor process. In his interviews with foremen and shop stewards, Kuhn found that roughly 80 percent of all grievances were resolved by the give-and-take efforts of these two groups of actors (1961, p. 27).

The significant postwar expansion contained management's frustration with its lack of control over shopfloor conditions. The brief downturn in economic activity in 1957–58, however, caused management's concern to turn away from stability in production to the now more important issue of unit labor costs. This shift in emphasis, combined with the often bitter struggles with workers surrounding the introduction of automated technologies, convinced management to go on the offensive (Strauss, 1962). While the ensuing assault was highly touted to be on the restrictive work rules contained in labor contracts, Livernash (1962) argues convincingly that the real target was the noncontractual shopfloor practices labor had been able to establish over the years following unionization.

Much of managements' energy in the years that followed was spent on extending bureaucratization to internal grievance procedures. This was accomplished by increasing the size of industrial relations departments, by hiring young, recently educated industrial relations experts with an exceedingly legalistic approach to the resolution of workplace disputes, and by the schooling of foremen and supervisors in the proper, bureaucratic approach to dispute resolution (Strauss, 1962). The advantages were clear. Not only were the decisions of rationally minded industrial relations experts, union leaders, and arbitrators preferable to those of foremen and the rank and file, but in committing a large number of disputes to the grievance procedure management gained the right to act unilaterally until – or, rather, when and if – some resolution was reached.

The growing bureaucratization of workplace dispute resolution over the late 1950s reduced the ability of rank-and-file workers to win working conditions concessions from management and to protect past workplace gains. But as long as the technological conditions which gave form and shape to informal work groups remained unchanged, certain kinds of appropriative moves in the labor process would simply be ruled out for employers. The technology of production rarely remains constant, however; nor does it evolve in a neutral, socially efficient manner. As Noble (1977) and others have so convincingly argued, technology bears the imprint of the social relations under which it evolves.

Technological developments during the 1950s and 1960s came in the form of further increases in the degree and scope of mechanization and the introduction of automated technologies.[4] A number of case studies have revealed the enhanced control over the labor process that capital is able to achieve as a result of automation (see, for example, Noble [1979]; Shaiken [1985]). These, however, have tended to concentrate on the deskilling of highly skilled workers, who possess significant power in the shop by virtue of their craft skills. Automation's impact on informal work groups composed of semi-skilled workers – a group equally if not more inclined towards the use of fractional bargaining – is less-explored territory. One can draw some very general and tentative conclusions on this subject by building on the research of sociologists and industrial relations experts from the 1950s.

Although automation has had different effects on production processes across industries, scholars of technological change point to a number of important similarities.[5] A close reading of the four most cited studies of automation's impact on the workplaces of the 1950s – in automobiles (Faunce, 1958), steel (Walker, 1957), chemicals (Blauner, 1964), and electric power (Mann and Hoffman, 1960) – suggests that automation is likely to (1) decrease the amount of team production, (2) reduce the ease of communication between workers, as it tends to increase the distance between work stations, (3) diminish workers' control over the pace of production, (4) lessen the amount of physical effort and increase the level of attention required, (5) increase the intensity of supervision, since a breakdown at one job location can often put a halt to the entire production process, (6) decrease the differentiation of tasks, thereby leveling the occupational structure of the plant, reducing the number of job titles, and limiting the size of job ladders for promotion, and (7) blur the distinction between white- and blue-collar jobs, particularly in continuous-process technologies.

Some conjectures about the impact of automated technologies on the power of industrial work groups can be developed by integrating these findings with Sayles' (1958) study on the link between technology and the form and extent of work group behavior. From his field investigations in the mid-1950s, Sayles characterized four types of industrial work groups – apathetic, erratic, strategic, and conservative – all so named for the kinds of behavior they exhibited. The apathetic and conservative work groups represented the very bottom and very top, respectively, of the occupational hierarchy, and are therefore of less interest to us in the task at hand.

Erratic work groups – characterized by small assembly or work crew forms of production, involving dirty, dangerous, and physically tedious tasks – are prone to spontaneous outbursts of discontent, the intensity of which is often, Sayles argues, in direct disproportion to the subjectively felt level of dissatisfaction. (An example is wet sanders in the auto industry.) Strategic groups, on the other hand – characterized by individual production jobs, involving self-pacing and critical judgment factors – are those most enthusiastically engaged in fractional bargaining. (Examples are welders, metal polishers in autos, or wire drawers in steel.) It is these strategic groups that systematically use the grievance procedure and their shopfloor power in a deliberate and calculated attempt to further their workplace interest.

Utilizing Sayles' taxonomy and the workplace impact of automated technologies described above, one can hazard some tentative generalizations about the altered shopfloor power position of informal work groups. Erratic work groups gained some added prestige and responsibility as a result of automation, in that their jobs became physically less demanding and safer, and their worksites became somewhat cleaner and less cluttered. Strategic work groups, on the other hand, faced a clear diminution of shopfloor power in the form of deskilling; as their jobs became automated these workers were integrated into the larger processing network, thereby losing control over the pace and quality of their output as well as their craftsmen-like identity. Both groups faced decreased possibilities for communication and increased supervision.

Arguably, the sum total of these changes was to decrease the power of semi-skilled labor on the shopfloor by reducing its informal work group identification. In addition to providing the basis for appropriative activity by employers, these changes also, it would seem, decreased the likelihood of "strategic" behavior and increased the likelihood of militant, "spontaneous" actions as the means by which workers express workplace discontent. If typical work group forms of collective action got subverted, workers would be forced, depending on the responsiveness of union structures, to return to wildcats and quickie work stoppages for exerting power on the shopfloor.

The ultimate effect of these changes in both the technology and the organization of production on the realized shopfloor power of the rank and file is, of course, difficult to chart. However, several studies indicate that the management offensive was at least partly successful. Derber *et al.*, (1961) surveyed company managers and local labor officials in forty-one manufacturing firms in 1955 and then again in 1959. The survey results suggest that union members faced important reductions in their ability to participate in decisions concerning the content of jobs and the safety rules governing the plant. Interestingly, a majority of the managers surveyed in 1959 viewed the union as a favorable institution for cooperating in worker discipline and maintaining harmony – a view that was not widely shared by management in the earlier survey results.

The Board, the courts, and labor law

Labor legislation and common-law developments proceeding from the National Labor Relations Act (NLRA) of 1935 have been seen as part of an overall philosophy of "industrial pluralism," which envisioned the establishment of industrial peace through the construction of a rational and efficient structure for the private resolution of labor–management disputes requiring minimal continuous state intervention (e.g. Klare, 1981). The architects of industrial pluralism believed, early on, in the private resolution of worker–employer disputes through the process of collective bargaining, even for those disputes concerning the conditions of production.

However, this position contained a number of ambiguities. First, it did little to establish the line separating managerial prerogative from those "other conditions of employment" over which labor had been granted the right to collectively bargain by the NLRA. Second, it displayed a certain naïvety about the process by which the parties were to achieve resolutions to day-to-day shopfloor disputes. When, in the late 1950s and increasingly in the 1960s, outward signs of institutional stress in industrial relations began to emerge, the National Labor Relations Board (NLRB) and the Supreme Court took the lead in addressing these ambiguities. The ambiguities concerning managerial prerogatives and bargainable workplace issues were addressed in attempts to set out the proper subjects of collective bargaining. In the famous *Borg-Warner*[6] decision of 1958, the Supreme Court stipulated some things as "mandatory subjects" of bargaining and others as only "permissible subjects." The distinction was an important one (even though the range of issues covered under each category remained unclear) in that permissible subjects of bargaining carried no duty for either party to bargain to impasse, and therefore accorded no protection to labor should it choose to strike over such issues.

In a series of Board rulings in 1961 and 1962, and upheld by the Supreme Court in its *Fireboard*[7] decision, there was an attempt to set out "meaningful limits." Certain issues, such as technological change, were deemed within the realm of managerial prerogative, and should be considered only permissible subjects of bargaining. Establishing the limits of proper subjects of bargaining was important not only for its substantive effect on the kinds, and therefore amounts, of power parties could bring to bear on the relationship, but also for its ideological effect on workers. These rulings took place at a time when workers' diminished shopfloor power caused them to turn increasingly to contractual stipulations for determining working conditions.

A second set of ambiguities in industrial pluralist philosophy concerned the resolution of day-to-day workplace disputes. The grievance procedure, culminating in binding arbitration, was a mechanism for dispute resolution employed by the War Labor Board during World War II and bolstered as a source of insuring industrial peace by the Taft–Hartley amendment. Both the Board and the Court moved, over the course of the late 1950s and 1960s, to shore up this method of dispute resolution as a cornerstone of the industrial relations system guiding capital and labor. These actions were spurred, at least in part, by employers' increasing efforts over the late 1950s to move dispute resolution from the shopfloor to the professional and rational decision-making capacities of industrial relations experts.

The Board's *Spielburg*[8] decision of 1955 stated that the Board would not consider unfair labor practice charges after a "fair and regular" arbitration hearing had reviewed the incident. A series of Board rulings over roughly the next two decades allocated enormous powers of adjudication to private arbitrators (Stone, 1981). The Supreme Court also abdicated to the rulings of private arbitration hearings. In its *Lincoln Mills*[9] decision of 1957, the Court argued that the Taft–Hartley Act disclosed a Congressional policy of committing disputes to arbitration. Moreover, it argued that the federal courts were only to be involved in developing the new body of law which would guide arbitrators, not act as the judiciary themselves. In the famous *Steelworkers' Trilogy*[10] of 1960, the Court found that the courts should not review an arbitrator's decision, but should instead confine themselves solely to the question of whether or not the issue was indeed an arbitrable one. For many important working-conditions issues of concern to workers, then, the newly bureaucratized grievance procedure, culminating in arbitration, had become the dominant method for shopfloor dispute resolution by the early 1960s.[11]

The grievance procedure grants employers two important sources of power. First, the bureaucratic nature of the process allows more rationally minded, level-headed experts, divorced from the day-to-day realities of the shopfloor, to resolve disputes. This lends an air of legitimacy and anonymity to the procedure, while simultaneously sending workers the message that their direct participation in resolving disputes is unworkable. The second source of power is the "obey now, grieve later" aspect of the procedure. In giving management the unilateral right of immediate shopfloor governance subject only to later review by grievance committees or arbitrators, this feature of the grievance procedure offends even traditional notions of due process (Stone, 1981). Both of these sources of power were important for re-establishing "managerial prerogative" during the period of fractional bargaining.

Bureaucratization of the industrial unions

The Congress of Industrial Organizations unions emerged during the 1930s with much grass-roots support and reasonably decentralized power structures. Because

the emerging US industrial relations system required workers to privately negotiate most of the benefits they won from employers, centralization of union power
at the level of the international, multi-plant and multi-employer bargaining agreements, and contract negotiations conducted by well-trained experts became important factors in winning wage and fringe benefits demands from firms within an
industry.

However, the bureaucratization of union structures served one set of workers'
interests at the expense of another. As the power to affect wages and fringes grew,
the ability to control shopfloor conditions diminished (Weber, 1967). It is tempting
to explain this process of bureaucratization, and the loss in rank-and-file shopfloor
power which resulted, as the natural evolution of an institutional structure that
efficiently responds to the most important demands of workers. But such a view
ignores the important influence of larger forces attempting to shape the societal role
of unions in general, and the extent of rank-and-file shopfloor power in particular.[12]

The evolution towards longer contract periods, for example, was an important
factor contributing to bureaucratization and centralization of power in union
structures over the postwar period. The growth in contract length – from the
annual contract in the 1940s, to an average of two years in the mid-1950s (US
Department of Labor, 1956, pp. 810–11), and to a three-year average in the
mid-1960s (US Federal Mediation and Conciliation Service, 1969) – brought
about apathy and disillusionment among the rank and file. Annual contract
negotiations not only helped to sustain debate over union goals at the shopfloor
level, they were also effective devices for preventing employer appropriation of
working conditions, as any such moves were certain to bring retaliation by workers
in the form of monetary demands by year's end.

It is often forgotten precisely how important the NLRB's "contract-bar"
doctrine was to the emergence of longer contract periods, and to the ossification of
labor union structures. The doctrine, which originated in the 1940s but took on
increasing breadth and scope in the 1950s, protected an existing union from rivals,
both internal and external, for either the length of the contract period or for a
"reasonable proportion" thereof (Tomlins, 1985, p. 322). Union leaders lobbied
with great effort over these years for extensions in the contract-bar protection
period, arguing that such extensions be viewed as a *quid pro quo* for the labor
leadership's maintenance of industrial peace through the increased use of no-strike
clauses in contracts of much longer duration (Tomlins, 1985). In addition to its
contribution to the growing length of contract periods, the contract-bar doctrine
also, and perhaps most obviously, served to protect the labor leadership from
internal insurrection by the rank and file.

The emergence of "bureaucratic control" in firm policy also had an effect on the
structure of unions, primarily through its disempowerment of the shop steward's
position. The bureaucratization of shopfloor dispute resolution made the shop
steward's job an exercise in fairly routine company policy. Companies and unions
reduced the power of shop stewards on the plant floor even further by shifting the

job of grievance handling over to business agents and committeemen – full-time, nonproduction positions paid by the union, or in some cases by the company, to address workers' grievances.

During the 1960s the growing bureaucratic structure of industrial unions came under increasing strain.[13] Workers' first inclination upon their loss of shopfloor power was to seek working conditions protection through contract language. As a result largely of these rank-and-file initiatives, more working conditions issues began to appear in contracts, but as Livernash (1967) makes clear, the issues of deep concern to workers were largely non-contractual in nature; their resolution required decentralized forms of power and decision-making on the shopfloor, and neither the firm nor union bureaucracy was in a position to grant this.[14]

When contract language failed them, workers turned to the grievance procedure wherever possible to address their workplace concerns. The number of grievances rose, but, to the extent they got resolved at all, either took too long to resolve, were far too biased in their results, or involved a process that was too narrow in the kinds of issues it could address.[15] Workers' experience using the mainstays of industrial pluralism to resolve shopfloor issues was in fact a brief and, for the most part, bitter lesson.

The contradiction inherent in union structures manifested itself in the growing separation and tension between the rank and file and the labor leadership. Contract rejections by the rank and file, an event unheard of before the early 1960s, jumped from 8.7 percent of FMCS "joint-meeting cases" in 1964 to 14.2 percent in 1967 (US Federal Mediation and Conciliation Service, 1970, p. 37). And between 1964 and 1969 significant movements developed to depose union leaders in steel, electrical equipment, and rubber, all of them successful. This challenge filtered down with even more vigor to the local level. For example, in the steelworkers' union new local presidents were elected in 1,100 of the union's 3,800 locals in 1970 (Mkrtchian, 1973, p. 146). Important changes emerged from these struggles. However, in all too many cases the centralization of power held firm.

When the conventional institutions failed them, workers turned to more desperate measures. The proportion of strikes over working conditions, for example, rose from an average of roughly 16 percent in the period 1953–60 to almost 30 percent in the period 1968–73, with disproportionate growth occurring between the intervening and later period. The proportion of wildcat strikes, over half of which generally involve working conditions issues, also increased over the 1960s, from 32 percent of all strikes in 1961–67 to 40 percent in 1968–73 (Naples, 1981, p. 38).

While the bureaucratization of shopfloor dispute resolution beginning in the late 1950s was successful in eliminating the source of workers' rank-and-file shopfloor power, and producing a short-lived spurt in productivity and profits in the early 1960s, the long-run consequences for capital were clearly negative. The expressions of rank-and-file discontent with shopfloor conditions beginning in the second half of the 1960s produced significant losses for employers in the form of declining productivity growth and reduced profits rates (Naples, 1986; Bowles et al., 1986; Norsworthy and Zabala, 1985).

The 1973–74 recession brought an abrupt end to the rank-and-file shopfloor revolts, but not to the underlying worker discontent nor to the bureaucratic structures for shopfloor dispute resolution that partially fueled this discontent. The elimination of fractional bargaining meant that workers were less successful in protecting contractual rights, and much less successful in winning rights surreptitiously. Workers responded to this alienation with a defensive shopfloor posture and a "work-to-rule" mentality with respect to work. The negative impact on labor productivity, even in periods of greater unemployment, has been significant. McKersie and Klein (1985) found in a survey of management that the most important constraints to productivity increases facing firms were, in management's view, employee motivation, work rules, and general resistance to change on the part of workers and supervisors. Such things as general business conditions (including technological development), government regulations, and worker skill levels ranked much lower on the list of constraints.

Employers' recent shopfloor initiatives[16]

Employers' recent shopfloor experiments are an attempt to address these remaining aspects of the productivity slowdown in manufacturing. Quality of worklife (QWL) programs can be directly traced to attempts by management to solve problems associated with the jammed grievance procedure and the workplace discontent of the 1960s. Team production and pay-for-knowledge schemes were often introduced in these settings as ways of decentralizing shopfloor decision-making. However, there is an additional, ulterior motive in employers' continued interest in shopfloor issues. Employers saw in the 1960's rank-and-file revolts against bureaucratic shopfloor relations a possible inroad for weakening workers' allegiance to unions. More decentralized forms of shopfloor organization, even if they give only the appearance of addressing workers' working conditions grievances, might undermine rank-and-file commitment to unions by attacking the very Achilles' heel of union structures – their inability to grant workers control over shopfloor conditions (Wells, 1987).

Quality of worklife committees typically consist of regular meetings of rank-and-file workers and management, taking place on company time, to solve problems encountered in production. They have no direct power, as implementation of proposals almost always requires approval by the normal chain of command. QWL programs, or their equivalents, grew at a healthy clip throughout the 1970s, but witnessed a tremendous surge in the early 1980s (Parker, 1985).[17]

The early experiments were credited with reducing grievance rates and absenteeism and with improving some shopfloor conditions, but the committees were severely constrained in their scope and they received little support from industrial relations departments and local union officials. Interest in participation schemes reappeared in the late 1970s and early 1980s, this time with a slightly different focus. There was still the emphasis on resolving workers' noncontractual shopfloor concerns, but increasingly management turned its attention to cost-cutting measures and the unions' interest turned to job security. Many of the new participation programs were explicitly designed as joint labor–management "cost study teams." In most cases, one of the stated management goals was to decentralize shopfloor decision-making in the hopes of increasing worker participation and making better use of the knowledge of production possessed by the rank-and-file worker.

In situations in which the progress of participation schemes had not been stalled or blocked entirely by entrenched bureaucracies, cracks appeared in the institutional structure of postwar industrial relations. The labor leadership's efforts to maintain a separation between issues discussed in QWL programs and in contract negotiations generally failed. Local agreements – which are independent of the national contract, but procedurally determined by collective bargaining – witnessed a proliferation of work-rule practice changes in many industries over these years. In many, perhaps even most, cases these were concessionary moves by unions to enhance productivity without a concomitant increase in shopfloor power. But, the trajectory of these changes was toward the further devolution of shopfloor decision-making to workers and supervisors directly concerned with production in a setting absent of formal contract language. What remained to be worked out, then, was the institutional form for joining participation schemes to workplace practice. This is where team production entered the scene.

A number of alternative development paths towards team production emerged in US manufacturing during this period. This diversity of experience makes it difficult to describe team production in general terms. Most team production systems, however, contain the following attributes: a dramatic reduction in job classifications, often to a single classification for all production workers; workers becoming skilled in a much fuller range of production activities; work teams composed of between ten and fifteen workers who meet weekly to discuss such issues as efficiency, quality of product, and the job assignments of team members; a team leader (typically a union member in union plants) from the ranks of workers and a group leader (a salaried, non-union employee) from the ranks of management as coordinators of team activity; and a pay-for-knowledge system which encourages workers to acquire different skills in the plant by awarding increased wages for skill acquisition. Workers and supervisors are encouraged (indeed forced) by this structure to resolve shopfloor disputes speedily, with a minimum of bureaucracy.

Team production builds on workers' natural desires to produce a quality product in surroundings that are reasonably pleasant and under conditions of relative autonomy. While the team concept acknowledges these desires, it never truly fulfills them. It is properly viewed as a system of management control in which the *responsibility* for producing is squarely placed on workers' shoulders while the production goals and job standards are dictated by management. Experience to date suggests that in exchange for an increase in the intensity of labor effort, decreased safety, the attenuation of seniority as a criterion for labor allocation, and an ideological structure that promotes competition between workers (across teams, plants, and firms) workers receive the promise of limited job security, wage increases for newly acquired skills, a quicker turnround time for the resolution of workplace disputes, and limited – in some cases bordering on the truly superficial – say in the nature of work (Parker and Slaughter, 1988; Brown and Reich, 1989).

The downside of team production for workers stems from the fundamental fact that an institutional void has been both created and filled by management's initiative. That work-teams primarily focus on, and allow for the realization of, management's concerns in production should therefore be no great surprise. What management has essentially done is to replace a system of shopfloor regulation and dispute resolution that contained significant (contractual) rights for workers, little rank-and-file responsibility, and few shopfloor freedoms with a system that contains significantly fewer contractual rights, much more rank-and-file responsibility, and arguably less shopfloor freedom. In essence, team production restores the decentralized atmosphere of shopfloor relations during the days of fractional bargaining, but severely constrains the rank-and-file's ability to act.

The search for new institutional arrangements of shopfloor governance may, however, provide an opening for progressive forces to establish a more participatory form of workplace decision-making. The long-run goal should be workplace democracy. The short-run goal should be the adoption of shopfloor institutions that grant workers limited rights of participation while simultaneously bolstering the attainment of genuine democratic participation in the future. As the working class and its supporters struggle toward the realization of these goals, we should build on the history of workers' experiences and the strength of past organizational forms. The decentralized shopfloor organization of the 1940s and 1950s was flexible, efficient, and empowering for workers. Something akin to this system of shopfloor governance would be far superior from workers' perspectives to the recent shopfloor initiatives of employers; it may also be a significant social improvement.

Conclusion

This analysis of postwar shopfloor relations poses a number of challenges to the account of the postwar capital–labor accord found in SSA theory. First, the accord appears to be a better statement of the hopes and intentions of influential actors than of the actual unfolding of events. The rank and file were never "signatories" to the agreement, and, at least with respect to shopfloor conditions, rarely confined their actions to the accepted rules of the game. Explicit in the notion of the accord is the claim that the rank-and-file sold away their hopes for greater shopfloor power for a bit more cash. A closer look at postwar shopfloor relations reveals that this was simply not the case.

Second, this analysis suggests that, at least with respect to shopfloor conditions, rank-and-file power decreased over the postwar period. This is in direct contrast to the claim of increasing worker power – owing to the tight labor markets and increasing social wage of the 1960s – found in SSA theory. Tight labor markets no doubt allowed workers to vent their anger and frustration over the loss of shopfloor power in ways – e.g. wildcat strikes – that they could not have otherwise. And it is certainly plausible that the labor leadership responded to this rank-and-file frust-ration by demanding and winning better wages and fringe benefits for organized workers during the 1960s than in previous bargaining rounds, thereby increasing workers' power with respect to monetary compensation. But, if the analysis of this chapter is correct, workers' expressions of workplace discontent during the late 1960s and early 1970s were acts of desperation, not the calculated moves of the increasingly empowered rank-and-file.

These challenges do not, however, form a devastating critique of SSA theory. They force upon the theory more subtlety in its notion of the accord and more complexity in its notion of the power configuration between capital and labor. In other respects, the analysis appears to support and even bolster the SSA descrip-tion of postwar capital–labor relations. There was indeed a contradiction in the institutional arrangements and set of understandings surrounding postwar indus-trial relations. The unfolding of this contradiction produced an institutional crisis in shopfloor relations that is quite plausibly linked to the emergence of a decline in productivity growth in the late 1960s and an accompanying decline in the rate of profit.

This analysis also offers compelling evidence for the claim of SSA theorists that workplace democracy can enhance productivity growth and lead to a social improvement over existing workplace institutions. The period of fractional bar-gaining in US shopfloor relations reveals that an organization of production in which there exists an empowered rank and file engages the active participation of workers in improving both working conditions and workplace practice, in addition to eliminating bureaucratic layers of management and countering managerial ineptitude. The history also suggests, however, that instituting a system of shopfloor governance akin to that of the immediate postwar period will not be accomplished without a struggle.

Notes

1 This section of the paper is a slightly revised version of Fairris (1990).
2 For a description of this emerging form of "job control unionism," as well as a discussion of why postwar industrial relations took on this form, see Piore and Sabel (1984).
3 Objective measures of working conditions improvements in the early period following unionization and their deterioration in the late 1950s are not easy to come by. The trajectory of injury rates, however, follows a telling path. Injury rates in the late 1920s were roughly twice those of the immediate postwar period (US Bureau of the Census, 1975, series D-1029). Injury rates in manufacturing continued to decline in the immediate postwar years, reaching a low of 11.4 work injuries per million employee-hours in 1958, but turned upward thereafter, increasing rapidly in the years between 1963 and 1967, from roughly 12.0 to 14.0. Sizeable increases in injuries occurred over this period in meatpacking, chemicals, rubber, primary metals, and electrical equipment, in ascending order of injury rate increases (US Department of Labor, 1963, 1967).
4 Henceforth, I refer to these two interchangeably, or merely as automation, since automated technologies are only a more advanced stage of mechanization.

5 There are two broad types of automated technologies that affected production processes in the major manufacturing industries of the postwar period. The first, more common to the automobile and steel industries, is the "transfer technology" type of automated technology, in which a product is produced primarily through automatic transfer between machines that in some cases may also automatically do the processing. The second, more common to the oil and chemical industries, is "continuous process" technologies, in which the level of automation is carried even further to include automatic inspection and feedback mechanisms with both quality and quantity control.

6 *NLRB* v. *Wooster Division of Borg-Warner Corp.* (1958), 356 US 342, 348.

7 *Fireboard Paper Products Company* v. *NLRB* (1964) 379 US 203, 211–12.

8 *Spielburg Manufacturing Co.* v. *Harold Gruenberg* (1955) 112 NLRB 1080.

9 *Textile Workers Union* v. *Lincoln Mills* (1957) 353 US 448.

10 *United Steelworkers* v. *American Manufacturing Co.* (1960) 363 US 564; *United Steelworkers* v. *Warrior and Gulf Navigation Co.* (1960) 363 US 574; and *United Steelworkers* v. *Enterprise Wheel and Car Corp.* (1960) 363 US 593.

11 Since many working conditions are noncontractual issues, the ability to commit such disputes to grievance and arbitration is clearly relevant here. Derber *et al.*'s (1961, p. 88) survey results revealed that 20 percent of firms allowed only contractual issues to be grieved, and only half allowed any issue to be grieved.

12 The growing bureaucracy made communication between the rank-and-file and the union leadership more difficult, and the centralization of power allowed labor leaders to be less than fully responsive to workers' demands. But ideological factors were also responsible for the labor leadership's skewed response to workers' economic versus shopfloor demands. The slow drift away from the principles of "social unionism" toward those of "business unionism" was accompanied by a narrower, more material definition of collective bargaining goals (Lens, 1959; Davis, 1986). The anti-communism of the 1940s and 1950s not only removed many progressively minded shopfloor militants from positions of influence in the labor movement, but also made shopfloor demands themselves appear insurrectionist by association. Of course, there were also economic incentives for the labor leadership to clamp down on workers' expressions of shopfloor demands, as, for example, in the provision of the Taft–Hartley Act which held labor leaders responsible for work stoppages in violation of the bargaining agreement – a majority of which are generally over working conditions.

13 The relative size of the labor union bureaucracy in the United States can be gleaned from Lipset's (1962, p. 93) estimate that in the early 1960s there were 60,000 full-time, salaried union officials in the US (one for every 300 workers), as compared to 4,000 in Britain (one for every 2,000) or 900 in Sweden (one for every 1,700).

14 Contract language governing working conditions increased significantly over the postwar period. But, with the exception of some of the smaller firms, contract provisions mainly addressed workplace issues through detailed job descriptions, job ladders, and seniority rights, along with an occasional provision governing relief time. Industrial relations scholars saw in these provisions – and not completely mistakenly, of course – increased worker power in the production process (see, for example, Slichter *et al.*, 1960). For a more balanced view of these developments, see the excellent essay by Brody (1980).

15 At GM, for example, the number of written grievances per 100 blue-collar workers rose from 50.4 in 1960 to 71.9 in 1973 (Kochan *et al.*, 1986, p. 39). Lichtenstein (1985, p. 370) notes that unresolved local grievances which got raised during contract negotiations at GM amounted to 11,600 in 1958, but had grown to 39,000 by 1970. Herding found from interviews with management and labor representatives in a steel plant in the late 1960s that "the (grievance)

load has increased at a rapid pace in about a decade ... [T]he speed of the procedure is 'definitely stalled'" (1972, p. 188). Arbitration cases, for example, took an average of sixteen months to resolve. In this same plant during the period 1948–52, an average of 6 percent of all grievances appealed to arbitration were still pending at year's end. By 1967, this number was 49 percent!

16 For further elaboration on the material in this section, see Fairris (1991).

17 Worker participation schemes go by different names in different firms. Employee involvement, quality circles, and labor–management participation teams are some examples. I will use the QWL label throughout my discussion.

References

Blauner, Robert, 1964. *Alienation and Freedom: The Factory Worker and His Industry.* University of Chicago Press.

Bowles, Samuel, David M. Gordon, and Thomas E. Weisskopf, 1983. *Beyond the Waste Land: A Democratic Alternative to Economic Decline.* New York: Anchor Press/Doubleday.

1986. "Power and Profits: The Social Structure of Accumulation and the Profitability of the Postwar U.S. Economy," *Review of Radical Political Economics*, 18(1–2): 132–67.

Brody, David, 1980. "The Uses of Power I: Industrial Battleground," in *Workers in Industrial America: Essays on the Twentieth Century Struggle*, pp. 173–214. Oxford University Press.

Brown, Clair, and Michael Reich, 1989. "When Does Union–Management Cooperation Work? A Look at NUMMI and GM-Van Nuys," *California Management Review*, 31(4): 26–44.

Chamberlain, Neil W., 1948. *The Union Challenge to Management Control.* New York: Harper & Brothers.

Davis, Mike, 1986. *Prisoners of the American Dream.* London: New Left Books.

Derber, Milton, W. E. Chalmers, and Milton T. Edelman, 1961. "Union Participation in Plant Decision-Making," *Industrial and Labor Relations Review*, 15(1): 83–101.

Edwards, Richard, 1979. *Contested Terrain: The Transformation of the Workplace in the Twentieth Century.* New York: Basic Books.

Fairris, David, 1990. "Appearance and Reality in Postwar Shopfloor Relations," *Review of Radical Political Economics*, 22(4): 17–43.

1991. "The Crisis in U.S. Shopfloor Relations," *International Contributions to Labour Studies*, 1 (1): 133–56.

Faunce, William A., 1958. "Automation in the Automobile Industry; Some Consequences for In-Plant Social Structure," *American Sociological Review*, 23(4): 401–7.

Gordon, David M., Richard Edwards, and Michael Reich, 1982. *Segmented Work, Divided Workers: The Historical Transformation of Labor in the United States.* Cambridge University Press.

Herding, Richard, 1972. *Job Control and Union Structure.* Rotterdam University Press.

Hyman, Richard, 1972. *Strikes.* Glasgow: Fontana.

Klare, Karl E., 1981. "Labor Law as Ideology: Toward a New Historiography of Collective Bargaining Law," *Industrial Relations Law Journal*, 4(3): 450–82.

Kochan, Thomas A., Harry C. Katz, and Robert B. McKersie, 1986. *The Transformation of American Industrial Relations.* New York: Basic Books.

Kuhn, James, 1961. *Bargaining in the Grievance Settlement.* New York: Columbia University Press.

Lens, Sidney, 1959. *The Crisis of American Labor.* New York: Sagamore Press.

Lichtenstein, Nelson, 1982. *Labor's War at Home: The CIO in World War II.* Cambridge University Press.

1985. "UAW Bargaining Strategy and Shop-Floor Conflict: 1946–1970," *Industrial Relations*, 24(3): 360–81.

Lipset, Seymour Martin, 1962. "Trade Unions and Social Structure II," *Industrial Relations*, 1 (2): 89–110.

Livernash, E. Robert, 1962. "The General Problem of Work Rules," in *Proceedings of the 14th Annual Meeting, Industrial Relations Research Association* (Madison), pp. 389–98.

1967. "Special and Local Negotiations," in *Frontiers of Collective Bargaining*, ed. John T. Dunlop and Neil W. Chamberlain, pp. 27–49. New York: Harper & Row.

McKersie, Robert B., and Janice A. Klein, 1985. "Productivity: The Industrial Relations Connection," in *Productivity Growth & U.S. Competitiveness*, ed. William J. Baumol and Kenneth McLennan, pp. 119–59. Oxford University Press.

Mann, Floyd C., and Richard L. Hoffman, 1960. *Automation and the Worker*. New York: Holt, Rinehart, and Winston.

Mkrtchian, A., 1973. *U.S. Labour Unions Today: Basic Problems and Trends*. Moscow: Progress Publishers.

Naples, Michele, 1981. "Industrial Conflict and its Implications for Productivity Growth," *American Economic Review*, 71(2): 36–41.

1986. "The Unraveling of the Union–Capital Truce and the U.S. Industrial Productivity Crisis," *Review of Radical Political Economics* 18(1–2): 110–31.

Noble, David, 1977. *America By Design*. Oxford University Press.

1979. "Social Choice in Machine Design: The Case of Automatically Controlled Machine Tools," in *Case Studies on the Labor Process*, ed. Andrew Zimbalist, pp. 18–50. New York: Monthly Review Press.

Norsworthy, J. R., and Craig Zabala, 1985. "Worker Attitudes, Worker Behavior, and Productivity in the U.S. Automobile Industry," *Industrial and Labor Relations Review*, 38(4): 544–57.

Parker, Mike, 1985. *Inside the Circle: A Union Guide to QWL*. Boston: South End Press.

Parker, Mike, and Jane Slaughter, 1988. *Choosing Sides: Unions and the Team Concept*. Boston: South End Press.

Piore, Michael J., and Charles F. Sabel, 1984. *The Second Industrial Divide: Possibilities for Prosperity*. New York: Basic Books.

Sayles, Leonard R., 1958. *Behavior of Industrial Work Groups*. New York: Wiley.

Shaiken, Harley, 1985. *Work Transformed: Automation and Labor in the Computer Age*. New York: Holt, Rinehart, and Winston.

Slichter, Sumner H., James J. Healy, and E. Robert Livernash, 1960. *The Impact of Collective Bargaining on Management*. Washington, D.C.: Brookings Institution.

Stone, Katherine, 1981. "The Post-War Paradigm in American Labor Law," *Yale Law Journal*, 90(7): 1509–80.

Strauss, George, 1962. "The Shifting Power Balance in the Plant," *Industrial Relations*, 3(1): 65–96.

Tomlins, Christopher L., 1985. *The State and the Unions: Labor Relations, Law, and the Organized Labor Movement in America, 1880–1960*. Cambridge University Press.

US Bureau of the Census, 1975. *Historical Statistics of the United States: Colonial Times to 1970*. Washington D.C.: US Government Printing Office.

US Department of Labor, Bureau of Labor Statistics, 1956. "Characteristics of Major Union Contracts," *Monthly Labor Review*, 79(7): 805–11.

1963, 1967. *Injury Rates*, reports nos. 295 and 360. Washington, D.C.: US Government Printing Office.

US Federal Mediation and Conciliation Service, various years. *Annual Report*. Washington, D.C.: US Government Printing Office.

Walker, Charles R., 1957. *Toward the Automatic Factory*. New Haven: Yale University Press.

Weber, Arnold, 1967. "Stability and Change in the Structure of Collective Bargaining," in *Challenges to Collective Bargaining*, ed. Lloyd Ulman, pp. 13–36. Englewood Cliffs, N.J.: Prentice-Hall.

Weisskopf, Thomas E., Samuel Bowles, and David M. Gordon, 1983. "Hearts and Minds: A Social Model of U.S. Productivity Growth," *Brookings Papers on Economic Activity*, 2: 381–441.

Wells, Donald M., 1987. *Empty Promises: Quality of Working Life Programs and the Labor Movement*. New York: Monthly Review Press.

II

Towards a broader vision:
race, gender, and labor market segmentation in the social structure of accumulation framework

RANDY ALBELDA AND CHRIS TILLY

Introduction

The social structure of accumulation (SSA) framework has brought new clarity to analysis of labor markets. The integration of neo-Marxian class analysis with labor market segmentation (LMS) models marks a major contribution of the SSA approach, as developed in the late 1970s and early 1980s (Edwards, 1979; Weisskopf, 1981; Gordon *et al.*, 1982; and Bowles *et al.*, 1983). While Marxist and institutional labor market segmentation analysis had convincingly described labor markets (Doeringer and Piore, 1971; Edwards *et al.*, 1975), this description lacked a theoretical and historical basis. The SSA framework, through its integration of long waves of economic activity with class-based economic crisis theory, provided that foundation.

This accomplishment is substantial, since LMS theory gives Marxist analysis important insights into economic and political outcomes. First, LMS has provided a coherent and empirically testable alternative approach to neoclassical human capital theory (Dickens and Lang, 1985; Reich, 1984). Second, LMS provides a consistent explanation for the absence of class politics and solidarity in the postwar period – particularly during the downswing, roughly 1968 to the present – as suggested by the title of the first full-scale work using the SSA framework, *Segmented Work, Divided Workers* (Gordon *et al.*, 1982).

SSA theorists identify the development of labor markets and the labor process as the central focus of the model. Choosing labor's role in capitalist development as the primary lens to examine economic behavior is a hallmark of Marxist analysis and coincides with the stated political project of the model's framers: undermining capitalist relations in favor of more democratic and egalitarian ones.

Yet, by over-emphasizing class relations in interpreting changes in labor markets and in the labor process, authors in the framework submerge the importance of race and gender relations. While SSA theorists acknowledge in principle the importance of race and gender, for the most part they have relegated these categories to a subsidiary role, neglecting their centrality in the economic and political dynamics of United States society. This omission limits SSA-based research on labor markets.

In this chapter we discuss the flaws that result from the theory's lack of attention to the role that race and gender play in the US post-World War II capitalist economy. The problems we identify come mainly from two sources. First, by relegating race and gender relations to a "segmented" status, the SSA authors have not identified one of the important labor market processes of the period – that being the sustained integration of women and men of color into industrial capitalist production. Second, race and gender divide workers in ways that go beyond labor market segmentation. That is to say, in societies divided by race and gender, non-class relations play an essential role in shaping the contours of both economic institutions and popular struggle. Thus, incorporating race and gender more fundamentally into SSA analysis would offer both a more complete and robust theory *and* a better handle on strategy for social change.

SSA theorists present economic development as a series of linked stages: the consolidation of an SSA, the decline of that SSA, political and economic struggles over the direction for future development, and finally the construction of a new SSA. Taking the post-World War II economic regime as our object of inquiry, we argue that at each of these stages, incorporating race and gender analysis enriches understanding of economic change – and specifically the evolution of labor markets. We direct our critique primarily to the two most ambitious presentations of SSA theory: Gordon *et al.* (1982) and Bowles *et al.* (1983). Furthermore, we argue for the importance of race and gender analysis based on evidence *in the labor arena*. It is in this critical arena that the blind spots of SSA theory are most visible.

Expansion of SSA

The capital–labor accord and labor market segmentation

One of the three pillars of the postwar SSA is the "limited capital–labor accord" (Bowles *et al.*, 1983; Kotz, 1987). Under this accord, newly organized unions and workers – primarily those in manufacturing – guaranteed labor peace in exchange for job security and a share in the growing economic pie.[1] This accord provided a basis for stably expanding production coupled with continuously growing mass consumption. The capital–labor accord provided the grease for the three components of the accumulation process: it helped structure the ways in which labor was hired (M–C), it provided rules for the smooth operation of the production process (C–C′), while increased wages helped boost realization (C′–M′). The glue of the accord was economic growth. And for a time, with the help of newly opened world markets and state assistance to business, that growth was forthcoming.

The accord, to be sure, was "limited": different sections of workers obtained different guarantees from capital, and a large group of workers were excluded altogether from the benefits of the accord. Thus, Gordon *et al.* identify the distinctive labor market feature of the current long wave as *segmentation*. They note two axes of segmentation: the divide between "core" firms (large firms with market power) and "peripheral" firms, and divisions between privileged and less-privileged jobs within firms. Such segmentation contrasts sharply with the "homogenization" of the United States workforce that characterized the late nineteenth and early twentieth centuries.

Building on earlier work by Doeringer and Piore (1971) and Edwards (1979), Gordon *et al.* describe two broad categories of jobs – primary and secondary – but identify three distinct labor segments, since primary jobs include independent and subordinate jobs. These job classes are "segmented" in that each has different characteristics and there is little mobility for workers between segments. Independent primary jobs are largely white-collar, professional ones with well-defined job ladders, considerable flexibility in work rules, and relatively high pay. The subordinate primary sector jobs also offer workers job ladders (or at least wage advances with seniority), relatively high pay but considerably less work-rule flexibility. These jobs are most often associated with blue-collar, skilled and semi-skilled manufacturing jobs located in core firms. The secondary labor market contains jobs with few opportunities for job advancement, relatively low pay, high turnover, and little or no control over work rules.

While LMS theory describes the characteristics of jobs (not people), the segments have a striking racial and gender complexion to them. Independent primary sector jobs tend to be filled mostly by white workers, while the subordinate primary jobs are filled mostly by men. Secondary labor market jobs tend to be largely populated by white women, women of color, and men of color. Gordon *et al.* recognize these patterns, noting:

> The development of tendencies toward segmentation interacted with growing participation by [women and members of various racial and ethnic groups] in the labor force. In one direction, labor segmentation influenced and limited employment opportunities for women and minority workers. In the other direction, the mechanisms reproducing discrimination and occupational segregation helped reproduce segmentation ... (1982, p. 204)

But from the eyes of a gender or race analyst of labor history in the US, this account falls short on two scores. First, the emphasis on *segmentation* as the new feature of labor markets accurately describes the experience of white men only. Second, explanatory power of the tripartite taxonomy of labor market segments is weakened when race and gender enter the picture. We discuss the former of these points at length, before returning briefly to the latter.

Segmentation for whom?

Labor market segmentation, as it unfolded in the postwar period, was hardly a new experience for white women, women of color, and men of color. Even ninety years ago, in the midst of the earlier period identified by Gordon *et al.* as one of "homogenization," gender and race formed strict dividing lines in the workplace.

At the turn of the century, white women in the wage labor force were concentrated in domestic labor and small, labor-intensive manufacturing enterprises (see

Table 11.1. *Occupational distribution for white and black women,*
1900–1990 (percent)

	1900	1930	1960	1990
White women				
Agriculture	9.8	4.1	1.5	1.1
Manufacturing	32.6	21.2	18.5	9.9
Private household service	29.8	12.0	4.4	1.2
Service (other than private household)	3.8	8.1	13.2	15.2
Sales	4.1	9.3	9.2	13.6
Clerical	6.9	25.3	34.5	28.2
Professional and technical	10.2	16.2	14.6	19.1
Managerial, administrative, and official	2.9	3.6	4.3	11.6
Black women				
Agriculture	44.2	24.7	3.7	0.3
Manufacturing	2.6	8.4	15.5	14.5
Private household service	43.5	53.5	39.3	3.1
Service (other than private household)	7.9	7.5	23.0	24.2
Sales	0.1	0.6	1.6	9.4
Clerical	0.1	0.6	8.0	26.1
Professional and technical	1.2	3.4	7.8	14.8
Managerial, administrative, and official	0.5	1.2	1.1	7.5

Source: Census data compiled by Amott and Matthaei (1991, pp. 125, 158); US Bureau of Labor Statistics (1991). Occupational categories are not strictly comparable over time.

Table 11.2. *Labor force participation rates for white and black women,*
1900–1990 (percent)

	1900	1930	1960	1990
White	16.0	20.3	33.6	57.5
Black	40.7	38.9	42.2	57.8

Source: Census data compiled by Amott and Matthaei (1991, p. 403); US Bureau of Labor Statistics (1991).

Table 11.1). All women's jobs were, by definition, dead-end. As historian Alice Kessler-Harris (1982, p. 128) points out, "The labor market denied women of every ethnic and class reference group self-directed ambitions toward upward mobility." Even more important, the work of the vast majority of white women consisted of non-wage labor in the home (Table 11.2) – a work role that sharply demarcated them from men. While this labor was not waged, it often involved participation in the market for goods and services: for example, taking in laundering, sewing, or other work, and cooking and cleaning for boarders.

African-Americans (and, for that matter, Mexican-Americans, Native Americans, and Puerto Ricans), although no longer slaves, remained concentrated in agriculture at the turn of the century (Tables 11.1 and 11.3). Baron (1971) describes their situation:

Table 11.3. *Occupational distribution for black men, 1890–1990 (percent)*

	1890	1910	1930	1950	1970	1990
Farmers	26	26	23	14	1 ⎫	
Farm workers	35	32	21	11	4 ⎭	3
Manufacturing	30	31	41	54	61	48
Private household service	5	3	2	1	0	0
Service (other than private household)	2	6	9	14	16	18
Sales and clerical	1	1	2	4	10	15
Professional and managerial	1	2	3	4	9	16

Source: Census data compiled by Reich (1981, p. 24); US Bureau of Labor Statistics (1991, pp. 164–6, 184). Farmers and farm workers are combined (along with forestry and fishery workers) after 1970. Occupational categories are not strictly comparable over time.

[The black worker] was basically confined to a racially-defined agrarian labor status in which he [*sic*] was more exploited than any class of whites, even the landless poor ... Outside of agriculture the vast bulk of black workers were to be found either in domestic and personal service or in unskilled menial fields that were known in the South as "Negro jobs." (pp. 13, 16)

Like white women, black male workers remained largely cut off from the jobs in large-scale manufacturing, construction, and transportation that white men had access to. Black women were further segregated from white women's manufacturing work and most often found in domestic work.

This segregation by race and gender that characterized the workforce of 1900 has been the rule rather than the exception throughout United States history. Since capitalism's inception in the United States the role of white supremacy and patriarchal control have limited the ways in which white women, women of color and men of color have been able to participate in labor markets. Women of color, men of color, and white women have always faced largely different or segmented labor market opportunities, largely different work rules and means of control, patterns of participation, compensation for skills and education, and lower pay from those faced by white men. The relevant jobs may have changed, but the pecking order – and the lack of job mobility at the bottom – remain strikingly unchanged. In short, segmentation is not new or even the salient labor market experience for many workers once we widen our field of vision to include the entire labor force.

This is not to say the postwar period simply represents the same old story for workers – quite the contrary. Two important, but distinct, changes remolded postwar labor markets: (1) the change in the job amenities/characteristics for overwhelmingly male blue-collar manufacturing workers which constitutes the change described by Gordon *et al.* as segmentation and (2) the large-scale integration of workers of color and white women into a new set of capitalist work sites, as capitalist relations expanded their reach in the postwar period while maintaining social and patriarchal control.

When Gordon *et al.* discuss the rise of segmentation, they are referring to a set of changes in job amenities for blue-collar production workers that constitute the development of the subordinate primary sector. Prior to the "American Plan" experiments of the 1920s and, more importantly, the union victories of the 1930s and 1940s, blue-collar production jobs fit the definition of a secondary labor market, as laid out above. By the 1940s, most of these workers had gained job stability and significant wage improvements tied to productivity growth, thus transforming the jobs. This change affected a set of mainly white, mostly male workers.

The second major change – the integration of white women and people of color into new capitalist work sties – has received considerably less attention in the SSA literature (Albelda, 1985). In 1930, at the onset of the Great Depression, four out of five white women were absent from the paid labor force, for the most part performing unpaid labor in the home (Table 11.2). The remaining 20 percent were mainly unmarried women, participating in the paid labor force prior to marriage; of these white women, 13 percent worked in domestic service. A larger 40 percent of women of color took part in the paid labor force; 54 percent of these wage workers toiled as domestic servants and almost one quarter in agriculture (Amott and Matthaei, 1991; see also Table 11.1). Men of color were crowded in agriculture and extractive industries. Thus, these groups still stood largely apart from industrialized capitalist labor markets.

Contrast this picture with that at the end of the 1980s. White women have come out of their homes, and women of color have come out of white women's homes. Well over half of all women – 57.5 percent in 1990 (U.S. Council of Economic Advisors, 1991) – are in the paid labor market. White women and women of color share a similar occupational distribution, with the largest numbers of women concentrated in clerical, service, professional, and sales jobs (Table 11.1). Domestic service and agriculture have virtually vanished as areas of employment, even among black women: the two areas of employment combined (along with forestry and fisheries) account for only 4 percent of black women's jobs.

Men of color have exited from agriculture as well: fewer than 4 percent of black men work in agriculture, forestry, and fishing occupations, although almost 10 percent of Latino men remain in these jobs. Instead, black men are concentrated in blue-collar and service jobs (Table 11.3).

In short, over the last fifty years, women of all races and men of color were rapidly sucked into new capitalist worksites – ending up disproportionately in secondary labor markets in service, sales, clerical, and laborer jobs. Why? One half of the story is the tremendous economic expansion of the postwar period: employment grew rapidly, and grew most rapidly of all in retail trade, services, and government employment. The other half is the relative absence of immigrant labor that had stoked secondary labor markets in earlier long waves. Despite a substantial influx from Mexico, Puerto Rico, and, later, other Caribbean countries and Asia, immigration simply did not provide enough labor for the explosion of new jobs.

In fact, the capital–labor accord itself, in addition to stimulating the creation of the subordinate primary sector, fueled the demand for low-paid workers in the service, sales and clerical sectors. The ascendancy of rule-bound bureaucratic control in the workplace (see Edwards [1979]) and the rise of the state sector heightened demand for clerical workers. Higher wages for male household heads translated into increased demand for workers in personal services and retail sales. The mass production/mass consumption had not only transformed the means of production, it had also transformed the means of consumption, most notably by promoting virtually universal automobile ownership, which in turn powered the demand for more places to shop, eat, and be entertained. Finally, capitalists bound by the accord sought to contain wage costs by expanding the use of workers visibly excluded from the accord. Race- and gender-stratified labor markets existing prior to the mid-twentieth century provided employers with the needed sources of low-wage labor.

Thus, for most white women the rise of the postwar SSA can be described as a period of *proletarianization* rather than segmentation. For women and men of color, who were already proletarianized but had been concentrated in peripheral sectors, the appropriate characterization may be *integration* into the mainstream of the capitalist economy. Gordon *et al.* overlook these crucial complements to segmentation within the white, male workforce. They do so by defining the workforce of interest as a manufacturing workforce, and relegating agricultural labor, domestic service, unpaid housework, and the growing service sector to an unexplored periphery – a focus that imposes racial and gender blinders.

We would argue not just that the postwar labor market experiences of white women and people of color were different from those of white men, but that they were equally or perhaps even more important in providing the institutional base for capital accumulation. While manufacturing provides a central engine of economic growth in the United States economy, it has not been the main source of job growth over the last several decades. Even in 1940, the majority of the workforce was outside of goods production; by the late 1980s less than a quarter of workers were employed in goods-producing industries. The most phenomenal growth industries of the postwar era are retail trade, finance, services, and government – employment in which grew by amounts ranging from 226 percent (retail trade) to 501 percent (services) between 1946 and 1990, compared to 30 percent growth in manufacturing over the same period. Differences in output growth over these decades are not as dramatic, but services GNP growth at 315 percent (in constant dollars) has clearly outstripped goods GNP growth of 251 percent (US Council of Economic Advisors, 1991). The white women and people of color who filled the lower ranks of these industries were the foot-soldiers of the new economy. Indeed, by the late 1980, women and people of color made up a majority of the workforce.[2]

An incomplete framework

A somewhat separate critique of the SSA model raises a question about the labor market taxonomy itself. The tripartite taxonomy adopted by Gordon *et al.*, while powerful, does not do a good job of characterizing the jobs held by women and by men of color in the postwar period (Albelda, 1985). The taxonomy cannot account for a central fact: that female and non-white faces fill the worst jobs in the postwar period.[3] Indeed, within a given labor market segment (as defined by industry, occupation, and/or firm characteristics), gender or race distinctions often overwhelm common job features.

These problems are especially apparent with gender differences. Within the primary labor market, for example, women's jobs do not share the privileges of men's jobs. Predominantly female professions such as nursing and teaching, classified as independent primary jobs, do not offer the flexibility, control over work, or payoff to experience of the mainly male professions. General Motors' secretaries receive wages markedly below GM's production workers, even though both fall in the subordinate primary segment. Empirical attempts to meaningfully specify the difference between primary and secondary labor markets, while successful for men, have not succeeded for women (Dickens et al., 1988).

Decline of the SSA

SSA theorists list a wide variety of causes for the breakdown of the postwar SSA – some domestic, some international. In the area of labor they emphasize the breakdown of the capital–labor accord as workers became unruly and demanded more, particularly when growth had slowed. The demands of people of color and women are cited separately from the demands of workers within the accord; thus, in Bowles et al.:

> The exclusion of many workers from the [capital–labor] accord proved [very] problematic ... Protest against the racism, sexism, and distributive injustice of the growth coalition emerged through four different but effective movements: the civil rights movement, the welfare rights movement, the organization of the elderly, and the women's movement. These movements all led to government efforts at accommodation ... (1983, pp. 85, 87)

On the surface, this discussion appears to give white women and people of color due attention as actors in the decline of the SSA. But again, blind spots mar the analysis presented by Bowles et al. First, in emphasizing these movements' demands on the state, they downplay the movements' demands on capital. Second, they argue that the movements were sparked by exclusion from the accord – i.e. segmentation – when in fact they were in large part due to proletarianization and integration of these groups. Finally, they implicitly discount the importance of struggles by all women and people of color. We address each flaw in turn.[4]

Demands on the state or on capital?

Mention the civil rights movement and the women's movement, and many of the first images that spring to mind are government actions: the Civil Rights Act of

1964; integration of buses, schools, and public accommodations; affirmative action; abortion rights. Demands on the state, and state concessions to these demands, have indeed formed a central part of the dynamics of these movements. But a closer look affirms that in many cases these movements have featured demands by people *as workers*, demands *on capital*, and concessions *by capital* rather than the state.

While the movements of people of color and women appropriate the language of liberal democratic values (as did the labor movement in the 1930s), they were and are based on racial and gender identities that bridge workplace and community. The feminist movement's 59 cent campaign, comparable worth, and the demand for women's access to non-traditional occupations all point to concern about women's inequality as wage-earners. African-Americans and other people of color have demanded access to the closed building trades and have picketed and boycotted businesses that failed to hire people of color. (For a narrative that explains how these demands arose as part of black mobilization in particular city, see King [1981].) A recurrent theme in black community development is ensuring that black consumers can and do buy from businesses owned by blacks and employing blacks. As Malcolm X liked to point out (Epps, 1968, p. 141),

> Whenever you take money out of the neighborhood and spend it in another neighborhood, the neighborhood in which you spend it gets richer and richer, and the neighborhood from which you take it gets poorer and poorer. This creates a ghetto ... We have to teach our people the importance of where to spend their dollars.

In addition to a strong labor component in the movements of woman and people of color, there are powerful race and gender components in the labor movement in the current SSA. Consider the most dynamic elements of the labor movement from the 1960s onward (particularly in the area of organizing non-unionized workers): public employees, health-care workers, and clerical workers. All three groups are disproportionately black and/or female. Indeed, District 1199's East Coast hospital organizing drives of the 1960s and early 1970s built explicitly on the Civil Rights movement and black pride. Clerical organizing drives by 9to5, the Service Employees International Union, and District 65 have incorporated women's demands for respect and equal treatment. The largest union in the country is no longer the Teamsters, but the National Education Association – and even the Teamsters have turned to organizing teachers, nurses, and service workers as their traditional base erodes.

Furthermore, in many cases the distinction between a demand on the state and a demand on capital is unclear. In affirmative action, the state intervenes to constrain the action of employers. In other cases, employers may act first. For example, the personnel director of a large insurance company told one of us why the company was changing its personnel policies to accommodate working mothers (Tilly, 1989):

> The working parents issue is gaining much more national attention. There's a feeling in companies that if we don't respond, some state or federal regulations will be imposed. Companies like us don't tend to like to be regulated in this way. We prefer to be proactive. (p. 197)

Roots of the movements: segmentation or proletarianization/integration?

Why did the civil rights and women's movements arise when they did? Bowles *et al.* attribute the explosion of these movements to exclusion from the capital–labor accord. Again, we note that white women and people of color were always excluded from the benefits extended to white males – there was nothing new about this state of affairs. What *was* new was the accelerated proletarianization and integration of these groups.

The strategies and demands of the movements reflect this. The Montgomery bus boycott originated precisely because Southern blacks had become an integral part of an urban workforce – and was effective for the same reason. Concern over rights to abortion and birth control reflect in large part women's increased participation in the regular workforce (and the interruption that child-bearing represents); demands for child care and parental leave represent the other side of this coin. Affirmative action and equal employment opportunity law emphasize access to upper-level jobs within a firm – rather than simply any jobs – because people of color and women were already working in the relevant firms, but remained trapped at the bottom of the job hierarchy.

Despite their roots in proletarianization and integration, the demands of women and people of color generally have not been part of a broad-based class movement. This is where segmentation *does* matter. In many cases, particularly early on, women workers and workers of color have been unorganized and hence not directly affiliated with the self-proclaimed voice of the working class – unions. They have been concentrated in peripheral industries, occupations, and firms. On the whole, their relationship to core sectors of the workforce has always been uneasy. For example, while the AFL-CIO supported the civil rights struggle, craft unions resisted entry by people of color.

How important?

Bowles *et al.* imply, without stating it explicitly, that the demands of women and people of color threatened the postwar SSA far less than the demands of those – mainly white men – who fell within the purview of the capital–labor accord. They offer a half-page nod to the impact of the women's and civil rights movements (1983, p. 87), followed by a four-page discussion of how accord beneficiaries' demands shook the SSA (pp. 87–91). In general, they maintain that the capital–labor accord was undermined from within.

This treatment understates the importance of race- and gender-based contradictions. As noted above, women of color, men of color and white women inhabit the most dynamic (though not the most powerful) sections of the labor movement, and are concentrated in the most rapidly growing industries. Although the capital–labor accord certainly crumbled within many of the firms and industries where it had once reigned, it was also rendered increasingly irrelevant as sectors where the accord had never applied outgrew the sectors where it had.

We do not claim that the demands of women and people of color were the main force toppling the postwar SSA. Indeed, our sense is that heightened international competition and conflict (to which Bowles *et al.* accord five pages, 79–84) were most decisive. But we do hold that the changing position of white women and people of color was quite central to the SSA's decline, and correspondingly are central to current conflicts over the economy, a subject to which we now turn.

Current conflicts and political consequences

Grounding labor market analysis in race and gender sheds additional light on mass political responses to the *current* economic restructuring. Much left-wing discourse on current economic problems stresses the shrinking of the "middle class," the replacement of good jobs by bad jobs, and a falling average standard of living (Tilly, 1990). At the level of LMS analysis, these observations correspond to a reduction of the size of the subordinate primary labor market segment. As this segment shrinks, the workforce is increasingly polarized into independent primary and secondary segments – with the secondary segment growing most quickly.

What are the expected political consequences of these changes? We detour through economic theory to arrive at political conclusions. Gordon *et al.* and Bowles *et al.* argue that segmentation has kept workers divided, reducing their capacity for unified economic and political contention. If segmentation were the major division among workers, the contraction of the subordinate primary segment, then, might appear to be a "rehomogenization" of much of the working class and an opportunity for common ground between former core sections of the working class and peripheral sections. Harrison and Bluestone (1988) express this view:

> A broader and more diverse "rainbow" of Americans – including many in the middle class – are being victimized by the stagnation and growing inequality that characterize the emerging postindustrial society. This sets up the objective conditions for the formation of a new political coalition that could begin to demand progressive change. (p. 195)

But despite the promise of the Rainbow Coalition formed around Jesse Jackson's 1984 and 1988 campaigns, nothing resembling a broad, powerful, working–class-centered coalition has emerged. We believe the reasons have a great deal to do with the continuing importance of race and gender in United States economics and politics. Here we discuss three such reasons: the disproportionate impact of the economic crisis on people of color and their communities; the ability of married-couple families to buffer the economic effects of the current crisis by increasing wives' labor force participation; and a historical legacy of politics based on race and gender divisions rather than class ones.

The crisis's disproportionate impact on people of color

The deterioration of the postwar SSA clearly has a much more devastating impact on people of color than on whites. The white/black wage gap has widened (for men and women) since at least the early 1980s. Median family income ratios of both black and Latino families to white families have dropped since the mid-1970s. Median black family income stood at 62 percent of white family income in 1975, but had tumbled to 58 percent by 1989; the ratio for Latinos slid from 71 percent in 1974 to 63 percent in 1989 (US Bureau of the Census, 1990).

Similarly, whereas the ratio of black to white unemployment rates fell during recoveries in the 1950s and 1960s, beginning in the 1970s blacks have *lost* ground over business cycle peaks, suggesting that they are further marginalized with every short-run economic recovery. For example, the 1981–82 recession saw unemployment rates of blacks rise to 18.9 percent – a rate 2.2 times as high as whites; the "recovery" resulted in a lower unemployment rate of 11.7 percent for blacks in 1988, but the ratio of black to white unemployment rose to just under 3. The growing black disadvantage in unemployment is compounded by increasing non-participation in the labor force by black men.

In short, people of color, their families and communities disproportionately bear the burden of the accumulation regime's demise: the workforce and the population remain highly segmented by race. This has spurred mobilization of black and Latino communities, often through electoral coalitions. But white workers – at least on average – are not only insulated from the worst of the economic impacts, they are most often physically removed from the carnage. Black men are three times as likely to be robbed as white men; black women are three times as likely to be raped as white women (US Justice Department, 1987, table 3.7). Because of the growing chasm between white and non-white, whites regrettably have an incentive to set themselves apart from blacks, Latinos, and Asians, economically and politically, rather than seeking common cause.

Growing female labor force participation

A second mediating factor in the postwar SSA's downward arc is women's increased labor force participation rates. Women's economic contributions to families have had important economic and political effects, which cannot be understood without an explicit analysis of women's proletarianization. Proliferation of both the two-earner family and the female-headed family can be attributed to women's growing participation in paid work – in the latter case, economic independence leads to marital independence (McCrate, 1987).

What are the consequences of women's proletarianization? Increasing paid work by women has *not* heightened overall income inequality among families, in part because women from low-income families are those most likely to work (Tilly, 1990). But women's heightened participation has generated two other effects: one powered by the growth of two-earner families, the other by the growth of female-headed families. Among two-earner families, women's wages have counteracted the economic impact of the current economic crisis within families, holding off income decline. Thus, while average real wages have fallen (or at best stagnated) since the early 1970s, real family income has improved slightly. The improvement comes as men have withdrawn their labor, while women have increased it. But since women make considerably less than men, it has taken more family hours of wage work to maintain family incomes (Albelda and Tilly, 1992).

As for single-mother families, they are caught between the prospect of economic autonomy for women and the reality that women raising families without male incomes have always been poor. Growing numbers of single mothers has meant growing numbers of women dependent on the state. Because women are now "expected" to work for wages, the state has proven increasingly reluctant to protect these families without putting the mothers to work. Women's proletarianization, then, has had a two-edged effect in the current economic impasse. It has bought time for one set of families, while sharpening the deprivation of another set. In both cases, the impetus for a broad class coalition is blunted.

The vacuum of class politics

A third reason for the lack of a new class-based political surge is the lack of an old one. The United States – as opposed to her European industrial counterparts – has never had a lasting, bona fide labor party. The closest approximation was the New Deal Democratic coalition that included organized labor but also embraced (as non-workers) Jews, Catholics, blacks, and farmers. That coalition, forged in the Depression but cemented by growth during the war years and the 1950s, began to unravel as economic growth faltered, and now stands in absolute disarray.

Interestingly, many of the most creative efforts to construct a new progressive politics have come out of the black and women's movement. At the national level, presidential candidates Jesse Jackson, Pat Schroeder, and Sonia Johnson picked up the progressive banner. At the local level, black candidates such as Harold Washington, David Dinkins, and Boston's unsuccessful mayoral candidate Mel King galvanized city-wide rainbow coalitions. But race and gender splits have limited the impact of these initiatives. The shunning of Jesse Jackson by the Democratic Party establishment highlights the Party's failure to embrace a new social democratic or populist alternative. With the high tide of economic growth gone, progressivism and even liberalism lie grounded on the reefs of gender and particularly racial division.

Conservatives, on the other hand, have been able to exploit economic shifts that fracture class alliances and at the same time cohere identities based on racial and gender domination. Two of the most successful mobilizing issues for conservatives have been tax-cutting (and accompanying service-cutting) and crime. Since the main weight of the crisis falls heavily on people of color and on female-headed households, many white working-class families (especially those with two wage-earning adults) resent paying for a welfare state that is carrying a growing burden of other people's problems. At the same time they demand to have the external effects of the crisis (crime) contained. These discourses generated two of the most potent images of the victorious 1988 Republican presidential campaign: escaped black rapist Willie Horton (and the implication that Democrats were "soft" on crime), and Bush's slogan "Read my lips: no new taxes."

Women's proletarianization has also evoked a set of divisive discourses from the right. While some right-wing spokespeople champion work requirements for welfare mothers, others (and in some cases the same ones) call for married women's exit from the workforce, for the sake of the "family." The hysterical edge of the latter tendency is the movement against abortion rights, which seeks to rehabilitate child-bearing by force.

But one does not have to turn to the far right to find a yearning for the nostalgically imagined family of yore. Male-dominated sections of organized labor tend to support economic and political measures designed to restore a male-earned "family wage" that would allow women – at least those with husbands in certain economic brackets – to return to the home. In particular, voices from the AFL-CIO have argued for limiting part-time and temporary work and other "flexible" forms of work, since they undermine the earnings of (mainly male) regular workers. States AFL-CIO economist John Zalusky,

> This nation sorely needs more jobs, not different ways of pulling people into the labor market, or repackaging the 40-hour workweek, or redefining the relationship of employee/employer and work. What is being created is a new sub-class of workers. (Bureau of National Affairs, 1986, p. 98)

The argument is reminiscent of the nineteenth-century British labor movement's advocacy of the family wage (Humphries, 1977). Like that earlier campaign, this strategy seeks to defend the working class's standard of living – but also maintain women's subordination. Support for this strategy contrasts with calls from other parts of the labor movement (particularly unions with large female memberships, such as the Service Employees and the American Federation of State, County, and Municipal Employees) to *improve* part-time and temporary jobs, and *increase* flexibility for employees.

In summary, people's experience of the current economic crisis is radically shaped by race and gender divisions, and their actions grow from identities rooted at least as much in race and gender as in class. How one assesses the clashes generated by the current SSA's decline will certainly condition one's choice of strategies to shape a new set of new institutions and structures. It is to the likely choices we now turn.

Constructing a new SSA

The left, in its analysis of SSAs, needs to bring an understanding not just of class but also of race and gender. In its vision for the future, it must remove its blinders, it must imagine not only how to reshape the firm and the state but also the family and community. An unobstructed view of the possible strategies will matter.

While theories have not yet clearly articulated the way that a new SSA is constructed (see, for example, McDonough [this volume, ch. 4]), it is generally assumed that constructing a new SSA will require a new engine of economic growth. The postwar Fordist regime of mass production and mass consumption relied on the expansion of a vast "middle class'" to propel economic growth in the postwar SSA. But the middle strata are now shrinking. What will be the new engine of growth and which labor segments will most likely provide the source of growth?

Consolidate the top?

The choice of conservatives is clear: consolidate the position of the top of the income distribution, in what Mike Davis (1984) has called "overconsumptionism." Such a strategy relies on growth in the size of the independent primary sector (yuppies and entrepreneurs) to generate sufficient consumption to fuel the economy. This solution would require industrial policies that boost high tech, business services, and luxury consumption as well as macroeconomic and public finance policies that continue redistributing wealth from the "have-nots" to the "haves."

But so far, the fruits of "overconsumption" have been meager indeed. While the number of entrepreneurs has grown, most of them are actually low-wage individual contractors: among the self-employed, median nonfarm self-employment income in 1987 was $7,000 (US Bureau of Census, 1989).[5] And though professional and technical workers make up a larger proportion of the workforce, almost three-quarters of full-time, year-round professional/technical workers earned less than $35,000 in 1990 (US Bureau of the Census, 1991). Consumption growth in the 1980s was propelled by debt, not income. At its best, consolidating the top smacks of the 1920s. Now, as then, this solution is unlikely to yield sufficient consumption to sustain prolonged growth.

Rebuild the middle?

A progressive alternative to this conservative strategy could take one of two forms: rebuild the middle, or bring up the bottom.

Perhaps the most obvious political response to the atrophy of the subordinate primary sector is to try to recapture economic prosperity for the traditional working class. The goal would be to rebuild the middle and restore political prosperity through mass production/consumption. This solution argues the necessity of a revitalized manufacturing sector as the backbone of the economy, and an updated New Deal coalition as the key political actor. This describes the agenda of much of organized labor, as well as a collection of advocates ranging from liberal to left in persuasion.

Yet this path also seems unlikely to work. First, the economic basis of the strategy is questionable. The changed international competitive climate has placed severe limits on manufacturing, and those limits will persist – unless displaced by protectionism that itself would curtail growth. Second, the political foundation is also shaky. The New Deal coalition appears exhausted. Neither the Democrats nor the AFL-CIO as currently constituted seems likely to become the cornerstone of a new progressive coalition. Finally, a rebuilt middle would no doubt be constructed on the backs of those at the bottom, reproducing the race and gender divisions that currently exist. Rather than a replay of postwar growth, it could end up as what Peter Glotz (1986), national secretary of the German Social Democratic Party, calls the "two-thirds society": the bottom third marginalized and stigmatized by race and female headship, the middle third scrambling to stay out of the bottom third but identifying with the top third, and only the top third enjoying economic security.

Bring up the bottom?

A final strategy would be to bring up the bottom. Advocates of this approach would push to transform unsatisfactory service jobs into good jobs through a combination of unionization, legislation, and employer investment in more advanced technology; they would seek to consolidate service industries into the leading sectors of the economy. They would also demand an enlarged and redefined welfare state, to boost consumption of the lowest economic strata. The political agent of this strategy would be an expanded "rainbow coalition" bringing together movements of labor, women, people of color, and many other groups. Such a coalition would contest for political power by, in the words of Manning Marable (1990, p. 20), "expanding the electoral base to include millions of non-voting blacks, Hispanics, poor, and working class voters, and advancing an American version of leftist social democracy, attacking the power of corporations." As Marable adds, the movement must extend beyond electoralism to include a wide range of approaches to protest and the construction of counter-institutions.

This strategy combines economic justice with a potential formula for economic and political success. It uses large, growing but currently low-productivity service industries as engines of growth. This focus holds out the possibility of winning the political support of capital in the service sector as well. As reports such as *Workforce 2000* (Johnson and Packer, 1987) and *America's Choice; High Skills or Low Wages* (National Center on Education and the Economy, 1990) demonstrate, substantial sections of United States capital are already disturbed by the expansion of the secondary labor market, and are searching for alternatives. Management guru Peter Drucker (1991) identifies raising service-job productivity as a key economic objective, and white-collar and service sector employers across the country are experimenting with total quality management, employee involvement, and continuous improvement. Schlesinger and Heskett (1991) of the Harvard Business School point to a potential virtuous cycle for service employers: reward and train employees more; gain more skilled, committed, long-term employees; consequently gain the ability to attract and keep more customers.

Management theory and practice to boost service-sector productivity have conflicting elements: both intensified Taylorism and a possible new capital–labor accord in which workers gain compensation, respect, and even power. Progressives could help shift the balance toward a new, more favorable accord by supporting policies that subsidize or reward some employer responses (such as expanded research and development or genuine worker participation) while penalizing or restricting others (for example, by requiring equal pay and benefits for part-time workers). A revitalized labor movement would play a key role in any progressive outcome. To this end, unions need legislation to facilitate union organizing and banning permanent replacement of strikers.

By funneling economic resources downward, a strategy of raising the bottom bids to expand total consumption, since marginal and average consumption propensities are highest among low-income groups. Expansion of the welfare state will probably have to be built around universal "family income policies" such as universal (but progressively structured) child allowances and child-care provision, in order to appeal to wide sectors of the workforce. Since such income support will raise the wage floor, it will complement firm-centered policies to improve secondary labor market jobs.

Finally, this strategy provides the basis for expanding democracy through increased participation by previously "locked out" groups – the lowest-paid workers and those without work, especially communities of color.

Conclusion

Race and gender matter a great deal in United States labor markets – both as bases of unified identities and as dividing lines. They mattered in the upswing of the postwar social structure of accumulation, and in its downswing. They matter in the current configuration of political struggle, and in attempts to push for a more just and stable economy in the decades to come.

Because race and gender matter much, SSA theory will be strengthened to the extent that it gives these categories their due. The necessary recasting of the SSA framework is an extensive project; in this chapter, we have simply sketched out one part of the project. For those who use the social structure of accumulation as a concept to frame economic change and stability, remedying the theory's blind spots of race and gender represents a continuing challenge.

Notes

1 The other two pillars of the SSA are the capitalist–citizen accord (which establishes an expanded role for the state both in aiding business and in assuring economic security to citizens), and United States hegemony in international economic, political, and military relations.

2 While we have limited our discussion to the postwar SSA, the logic of different labor force experiences by gender and race could be extended to earlier SSAs. For example, the SSA from 1820 to 1890 could be characterized by homogenization for white women workers in manufacturing – taking their skills in the home in textile production and mechanizing it, akin to the process male craft workers underwent in later decades. That SSA also formed a period of domestication for white married women, as commodity production was removed from the

home/land into the industrial sector. From the viewpoint of African-American workers, it is difficult to class 1820–1890 as a single period, given the dramatic break emancipation and Reconstruction represented; a similar argument could be made for Native Americans.

3 This is by no means a new or original critique of (neo)-Marxist theory, e.g. see Hartmann (1981).

4 Other problems can be found in the empirical evidence used by Bowles et al. (1983) to support their claim. First, they frequently (e.g. in chapter 6) discuss changes in average labor market and firm indicators as if they represented longitudinal changes in a fixed set of firms. But in fact, an important source of change is the shifting industrial composition of the economy which, in turn, is linked to race and gender changes in the workforce composition. Second, they use the ratio of white male earnings to the weighted mean of female and black male earnings as an index of earnings inequality, and find that the index climbed dramatically between 1948 and 1966. But this climb is entirely due to the growing ratio of white male to female earnings; the ratio of white men's earning to those of black men remained essentially unchanged over this period. Giving a complete and accurate picture of workforce changes requires diasggregation.

5 The mean of nonfarm self-employment income was $15,000; it is a highly right-skewed distribution.

References

Albelda, Randy, 1985. "'Nice Work If You Can Get It': Segmentation of White and Black Women in the Post-War Period," *Review of Radical Political Economics*, 17(3): 72–85.

Albelda, Randy, and Chris Tilly, 1992. "All in the Family: Family Types, Access to Income, and Family Income Policies," *Policy Studies Journal*, 20(3): 388–404.

Amott, Teresa L., and Julie A. Matthaei, 1991. *Race, Gender, and Work: A Multicultural Economic History of Women in the United States*. Boston: South End Press.

Baron, Harold, 1971. "The Demand for Black Labor: Historical Notes on the Political Economy of Racism," *Radical America*, 5(2): 1–46.

Bowles, Samuel, David Gordon, and Thomas Weisskopf, 1983. *Beyond the Waste Land: A Democratic Alternative to Economic Decline*. Garden City, N.J.: Anchor Press/Doubleday.

Bureau of National Affairs, 1986. *The Changing Workplace: New Directions in Staffing and Scheduling*. Washington, D.C.: Bureau of National Affairs.

Davis, Mike, 1984. "The Political Economy of Late-Imperial America," *New Left Review*, no. 143: 6–38.

Dickens, William T., Rachel Friedberg, and Kevin Lang, 1988. "Is the Relation Between Gender and Labor Market Segmentation Changing?" Mimeo.

Dickens, William T., and Kevin Lang, 1985. "A Test of Dual Labor Market Theory," *American Economic Review*, 75(4): 792–805.

Doeringer, Peter, and Michael Piore, 1971. *Internal Labor Markets and Manpower Analysis*. Lexington, Mass.: Lexington Books.

Drucker, Peter, 1991. "The New Productivity Challenge," *Harvard Business Review*, 69(6): 69–78.

Edwards, Richard, 1979. *Contested Terrain: The Transformation of the Workplace in the Twentieth Century*. New York: Basic Books.

Edwards, Richard, Michael Reich, and David Gordon (eds.), 1975. *Labor Market Segmentation*. Lexington, Mass.: Lexington Books.

Epps, Archie (ed.), 1968. *The Speeches of Malcolm X at Harvard*. New York: Morrow.

Glotz, Peter, 1986. "Forward to Europe," *Dissent*, 33(3): 327–39.

Gordon, David M., Richard Edwards, and Michael Reich, 1982. *Segmented Work, Divided Workers*. Cambridge University Press.

Harrison, Bennett, and Barry Bluestone, 1988. *The Great U-Turn*. New York: Basic Books.

Hartmann, Heidi, 1981. "The Unhappy Marriage of Marxism and Feminism: Toward a More Progressive Union," in *Women and Revolution: A Discussion of the Unhappy Marriage of Marxism and Feminism*, ed. Lydia Sargent, pp. 1–41. Boston: South End Press.

Humphries, Jane, 1977. "The Working Class Family, Women's Liberation and Class Struggle: The Case of Nineteenth-Century British History," *Review of Radical Political Economics*, 9(3): 25–41.

Johnson, William B., and Arnold E. Packer (project directors), 1987. *Workforce 2000: Work and Workers for the 21st Century*. Indianapolis: Hudson Institute.

Kessler-Harris, Alice, 1982. *Out to Work: A History of Wage-Earning Women in the United States*. Oxford University Press.

King, Mel, 1981. *Chain of Change: Struggles for Black Community Development*. Boston: South End Press.

Kotz, David, 1987. "Long Waves and Social Structures of Accumulation: A Critique and Reinterpretation," *Review of Radical Political Economics*, 19(4): 16–38.

McCrate, Elaine, 1987. "Trade, Merger, and Employment: Economic Theory on Marriage," *Review of Radical Political Economics*, 19(1): 73–89.

Marable, Manning, 1990. "A New Black Politics." *The Progressive*, 54(8): 18–23.

National Center on Education and the Economy, 1990. *America's Choice: High Skills or Low Wages*. Rochester, N.Y.: National Center on Education and the Economy.

Reich, Michael, 1981. *Racial Economic Inequality: A Political Economic Analysis*. Princeton University Press.

    1984. "Segmented Labour: Time Series Hypotheses and Evidence," *Cambridge Journal of Economics*, 8: 63–82.

Schlesinger, Leonard, and James Heskett, 1991. "The Service-Driven Company." *Harvard Business Review*, 69(5): 71–81.

Tilly, Chris, 1989. "Half a Job: How U.S. Service Firms Use Part-time Workers," Ph.D. dissertation, Departments of Economics and Urban Studies and Planning, MIT, Cambridge, Mass.

    1990. "The Politics of the New Inequality," *Socialist Review*, 20(1): 103–20.

US Bureau of the Census, 1983. *1980 Census of Population*, vol. I, ch. C, "General Social and Economic Characteristics," part 1, "United States Summary," PC80–1–C1. Washington, D.C.: Government Printing Office.

    1989. *Current Population Reports*, series P–60, no., 162, "Money Income of Households, Families, and Persons in the United States: 1987." Washington, D.C.: Government Printing Office.

    1990. *Current Population Reports*, series P–60, no. 168, "Money Income and Poverty Status in the United States: 1989." Washington, D.C.: Government Printing Office.

    1991. *Current Population Reports*, series P–60, no. 174, "Money Income of Households, Families, and Persons in the United States: 1990." Washington, D.C.: Government Printing Office.

US Bureau of Labor Statistics, 1991. *Employment and Earnings*, 38(1).

US Council of Economic Advisors, 1991. *Economic Report of the President*. Washington, D.C.: Government Printing Office.

US Justice Department, 1987. *Sourcebook of Criminal Justice Statistics: 1987*. Washington, D.C.: Government Printing Office.

Weisskopf, Thomas, 1981. "The Current Economic Crisis in Historical Perspective," *Socialist Review*, 11(3): 9–53.

IV

THE INTERNATIONAL DIMENSION

___ 12 ___

Accumulation and crisis in a small and open economy:
the postwar social structure of accumulation in Puerto Rico

Introduction

The mid-1970s' economic slowdown in industrialized economies brought the renewed attention of economists to the long-term determinants of growth. At first, most research on the economic crisis focused on theoretical issues, but, pressed by the political implications of different arguments and by the advent of conservative economics, scholars quickly turned to empirical and historical analyses. Despite the growing research on crisis theory and empirical work, very few scholars have paid attention to the international dimension of the crisis. Although many acknowledge the increasing importance of "countertendencies" pertaining to the global economy, few identify the internationalization of production as a critical element in the crisis. Most theoretical constructs begin with a closed economic system in which long-term profitability largely determines the rate at which the economic surplus is reinvested. In a similar vein, in spite of the fact that empirical research has focused on assessing the factors inducing long-term trends in the profit rate, only very occasionally do international factors play a principal role in such an analysis.[1]

Recent research, however, offers new ground from which to understand the relationship between economic crisis and the globalization of production. The object of this chapter is to develop a model of capital accumulation in a small and open economy considering a high degree of economic integration with a larger and politically powerful country. Following Gordon (1980) and Bowles *et al.* (1983, 1986), I will extend the theory of the social structure of accumulation (SSA) to explain the postwar expansion and crisis in Puerto Rico. The SSA approach emphasizes the critical roles of class relations, domestic and international competition among capital, and the limits of state intervention in explaining long-term trends in profitability and consequently in the rate of reinvestment of the surplus. I will show that in a small and open economy reinvestment of the economic surplus by foreign capital is determined largely by profit rate differentials between two regions, and that long-term trends in the domestic profit rate are determined by the stability or deterioration of the SSA.[2]

During the 1950s and 1960s, the Puerto Rican economy experienced rapid industrialization, showed impressive rates of growth, and generated a rapid rise in per capita income. Economists referred to this period of economic expansion and development as the "Puerto Rican miracle." Foreign investment and government incentives directed toward the private sector were credited as the key elements inducing prosperity and social stability. Inspired by the success of the Puerto Rican model, economists and other social scientists prescribed foreign investment and export-led industrialization as antidotes to nationalist revolutions in Latin America.

The situation today is dramatically different. In the mid-1970s, the island's economy entered a period of crisis and there is no reasonable indication that the economy will regain in the foreseeable future the strength of past decades. Unemployment reached a postwar record low of 10.3 percent in 1970, but in 1977, at the trough of the mid-1970s recession, it reached 20.0 percent, and in 1983, the trough of the next cycle, it jumped to 23.4 percent (Puerto Rico Planning Board, 1989). In contrast to the 1950s and 1960s, when the impact of the United States business cycle upon the island's economy was mild, the last two recessions have had cumulative adverse effects. Even at the peak of the current cycle, unemployment remains above 17 percent.

Rising unemployment was associated with declining living standards and increasing government transfers to individuals. In the early postwar period, average family income (as measured in 1954 dollars) had increased from $1,802 in 1951 to $3,107 in 1963, and to $5,279 by 1973. In contrast to these impressive gains between 1951 and 1973, average family income increased only slightly to $5,513 in 1979, and declined, for the first time in the postwar period, to $4,994 by 1986. This dramatic stagnation in family income would have been worse in the absence of government transfer payments to individuals, most of these transfers coming directly from the Federal government. The percentage of transfer payments from personal income grew from 20.4 to 35.8 between 1973 and 1986 (Puerto Rico Planning Board, 1989). In short, as indicated by unemployment and income trends, the long wave of expansion of the early postwar period had been reversed and the late 1970s and early 1980s were characterized by long-term stagnation.

To explain the economic crisis in Puerto Rico, I have developed a model of capital accumulation based on a foreign investment equation and a profit equation in which flows of foreign capital and foreign reinvestment of the surplus are assumed to be positive functions of relative profitability. After explaining the determinants of the profit rates, I shall examine how the different variables defining the profit rate are related to the social structure of accumulation in Puerto Rico. Then, following a historical analysis of *Populismo*, the postwar SSA in Puerto Rico, I shall present an econometric estimation of the model. Finally, I shall draw some conclusions on how international factors affect the long-term dynamics of capital accumulation in a small and open economy.

Capital accumulation in a small and open economy

The aim of this section is to develop a model of capital accumulation for a small and highly open economy that explains the postwar long wave of expansion and the mid-1970s crisis in Puerto Rico.[3] The model explains the reinvestment of the economic surplus as a function of United States–Puerto Rico profit rate differentials in the context of highly integrated capital, labor, and commodities markets. Movement of resources between the small economy and the large economy are constrained mostly by transportation or information costs and not by policy instruments such as tariffs, quotas, exchange rates, or immigration laws. Asymmetry in the sizes of the economies and in political power makes the key variables in the smaller economy highly sensitive to exogenous fluctuations of the larger economy.

This model takes into account important institutions that determine the stability of the accumulation process. First, the model focuses on the crucial role of class conflict in determining key variables such as the wage rate, labor productivity, and the profit rate. Second, it accounts for competition among different capitals, for the postwar integration of the industrialized economies under the US hegemony, and for the important and decisive role of foreign investment, migratory flows, trade, and Federal government policies for the Puerto Rican economy. Finally, the model accounts for the importance of government policies that influence capital accumulation in Puerto Rico. I will refer to these institutions which are determinants of the stability of capital accumulation as the social structure of accumulation. The long-term trends in profits and investment are determined by the consolidation, reproduction, or deterioration of these institutions.

Investment

In an industrialized economy, the accumulation of capital takes the form of net investment, representing the use of the economic surplus for the expansion of both productive capacity and employment. In a small open economy net investment depends on domestic accumulation and net flows of foreign capital. In the Puerto Rican case, foreign capital is the more dynamic economic sector.[4] In 1975, foreign investment in public corporations accounted for 43 percent of the total government-owned capital stock and 64 percent of the private sector capital stock. Considering investment in both sectors, foreign investment represented 58 percent of the capital stock (Melendez, 1985, p. 204). In 1984, foreign investment accounted for 77 percent of the total sources of capital funds. Furthermore, foreign capital is concentrated in the most important financial and manufacturing industries. According to the US Department of Commerce, in 1979 foreign stockholders' equity as a percentage of total equity was almost 100 percent in ten industries that accounted for half of that year's total manufacturing output in Puerto Rico (US Department of Commerce, 1979). Assuming that domestic capital is of secondary importance, the expansion of productive capacity is determined largely by net capital flows and the reinvestment of foreign property income in the

Table 12.1. *Foreign and domestic investment*

Cycle	F/FPY	I/GNP	GI
1951–55	2.37	0.19	0.16
1956–62	1.99	0.22	0.14
1963–72	1.68	0.27	0.13
1973–78	1.12	0.21	−0.00
1979–84	0.55	0.12	0.03

F/FPY = Foreign investment to foreign property income ratio
I/GNP = Net fixed domestic investment to gross national product ratio
GI = Net fixed domestic investment rate of growth
Source: Calculated by author from data published by Puerto Rico Planning Board (1981b).

domestic economy. Thus, net fixed investment constitutes a positive function of net foreign capital flows.[5]

The dependent variable in the investment function is defined as the ratio of net foreign investment (or net import of capital) to foreign property income (profits and interest paid to foreign individuals or corporations) represented as F/FPY. Normalization of foreign investment is necessary to avoid the National Income Accounts' double-counting of foreign profits and interest. Foreign property income is considered first as an outflow and then as an inflow, as net import of capital.[6] The F/FPY ratio accounts for the fact that there is reinvestment of a portion of the economic surplus generated in the island's economy and controlled by transnational capital. If $F/FPY > 1$, there is a net inflow of foreign capital; if $F/FPY < 1$, then there is a net outflow.

Table 12.1 shows F/FPY means for the four postwar business cycles for which complete data are available. During the first two business cycles, capital inflows remained about twice the share of foreign property income. F/FPY began to decline in the mid-1960s, and by the 1973–78 business cycle, the first cycle during the crisis, foreign capital inflows were negligible. In fact, in 1976 F/FPY was 0.90 – the first time during the postwar period in which the island experienced net foreign capital outflows. Since 1978, F/FPY has remained below 0.80 and the average for the 1979–84 cycle is 0.55. These trends in foreign reinvestment of the economic surplus in Puerto Rico induced a decline both in net fixed domestic investment as a proportion of gross national product (I/GNP) and in the rate of growth of that investment (GI). During the 1973–78 cycle, GI was negative for the first time during the postwar period. Similarly, I/GNP remained below 0.17 after 1977, the lowest ratio since the 1940s.

The main determinant of the reinvestment of the surplus is relative profitability; other determinants include the cost of capital, and expectations about future demand and the long-term risk of investment in a given country. A behavioral equation for F/FPY can be represented thus:

$$F/FPY = F(r^*, i, D)$$

where

r^* = relative profitability ($r_{PR} - r_{US}$), the Puerto Rican profit rate (r_{PR}) minus the
US profit rate (r_{US})
i = cost of capital
D = expectations of future demand

Foreign reinvestment of the surplus is a function of international and domestic factors: cost of capital and US profitability are exogenous to the Puerto Rican economy, while the Puerto Rican profit rate, and expectations of social stability are locally determined. Expectations of future demand are affected by both international and domestic factors. To the extent that foreign investment of the surplus is a measure of capitalist strategies to cope with changing domestic and international conditions, the model is an explanation of the social consequences, in terms of macroeconomic stability, of foreign capital decisions about the reinvestment of the surplus.[7]

Investors' expectations are not formed exclusively by current profit levels but also depend on the expected direction of profit margins in the context of international market conditions. Given a high integration of capital markets, investors will compare the domestic profit rate to profitability in other countries. Investors' comparison of relative profitability is assumed in both the short and the long run, since reinvestment of the surplus can expand existing production or take the form of new capital ventures. The profit rates differential is a simple way to measure the relative return of alternative capital investment opportunities. United States investors, for example, look at the difference between the Puerto Rican and the US after-tax profit rates when considering an investment project.

Profit rates

Given the centrality of the process of capital accumulation as a basis for understanding the dynamics of a small and open economy, we must look at the role of profits as the regulator of the accumulation process. Profit rates, proportional returns to capital invested, are important for several reasons. First, they are an index of how successfully capital is reproduced. To the extent that the ratio of property income to the value of resources advanced in the production process increases, there is a greater incentive to reinvest the surplus and, thus, to expand or renovate the productive capacity. Second, profit rates play a major role in determining the allocation of resources among different industries, regions, and countries. Given no barriers to capital mobility, capital will flow to industries and geographical areas where higher returns are expected. Finally, advantageous profit rates induce technical innovation and the transfer of technology between countries.

Table 12.2 presents the historical data for profit rates in Puerto Rico and the United States.[8] During the first postwar business cycle, the Puerto Rican profit rate (r_{PR}) was almost three times the United States profit rate (r_{US}) declining to about twice by the 1973–77 cycle. This decline amounted to a 42 percent decline in

Table 12.2. *Puerto Rican and United States profit rates*

Cycle	r_{PR}	r_{US}	$r_{PR} - r_{US}$
1951–55	0.19	0.07	0.12
1956–62	0.17	0.07	0.10
1963–72	0.14	0.07	0.07
1973–78	0.12	0.05	0.07
1979–84	0.12	0.04	0.08

r_{PR} = profit rate, Puerto Rico
r_{US} = profit rate, United States
Source: Calculated by author (see text).

the average profit rate differential ($r_{PR} - r_{US}$) between the first and the fourth postwar business cycle. The relationship between a decline in the profit rate differential and foreign reinvestment of the surplus (F/FPY) can be appreciated in Figure 12.1. In a grouping of the data by business cycle ("1" corresponding to 1947–50 up to "6" corresponding to 1979–84), there is a clear positive relationship between F/FPY and $r_{PR} - r_{US}$. A lower profit rate differential corresponds to lower reinvestment of the economic surplus.

The profit rate is defined as

$$r = (\Pi/Y)(Y/Z)(Z/K)(1 - t)$$

where

$$\Pi/Y = \text{profit share}$$
$$Y/Z = \text{rate of capacity utilization}$$
$$Z/K = \text{ratio of potential output to capital}$$
$$t = \text{effective corporate tax rate}$$

and

$$\Pi/Y = (1 - ULC)$$

where

$$ULC = (W/L)/(Y/L) = \text{unit labor cost}$$
$$W/L = \text{average labor compensation}$$
$$Y/L = \text{average labor productivity}$$

The above definition allows us to assess the forces influencing the reinvestment of the surplus and the accumulation of capital in a small and open economy.[9] Movements in unit labor cost (ULC)[10] represent capital–labor struggles over the extraction of labor from labor power and over the distribution of the product. Other things being equal, an increase in wages or a decrease in productivity reduces profitability. ULC is affected by institutions that regulate labor markets and the structure of class relations such as the organization and use of technology in the workplace, industrial structure, labor unions, the industrial reserve army, and

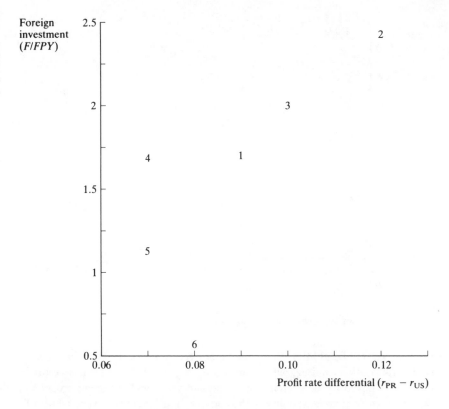

Fig. 12.1.   Foreign investment vs. profit rate differential. (*Source*: See Table 12.1 and text.)

migratory flows (Schor and Bowles, 1983; Boddy and Crotty, 1975; Weisskopf *et al.*, 1983).

Long-term movements in Z/K are determined by technological changes which are in turn associated with the crucial role of foreign capital flows. The use of capital-intensive technology by transnational corporations has had a decisive influence on the long-term trends in Z/K. Foreign investment induces a higher organic composition of capital to the extent that transfers of production technologies induce a higher than average volume of capital per worker. Two historical periods in which technological transfers were important are the transition from the sugar economy to light manufacturing to capital-intensive industries during the 1960s. Short-term or business cycle fluctuations in Z/K are induced by fluctuations in capacity utilization. Although the precise forces behind this relation are in dispute, a rising level of capacity utilization is associated with falling Z/K and vice versa (Sherman and Evans, 1984, pp. 212–21).

State policies have a direct impact upon profitability through tax policies (t), market regulations, and direct subsidies to capital (training of workers, physical

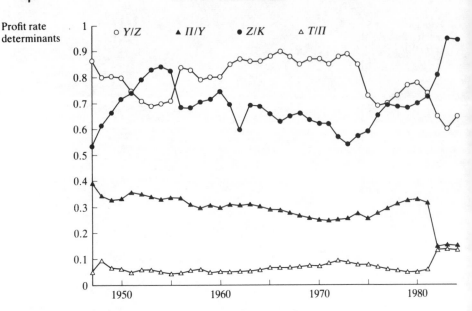

Fig. 12.2. Profit rate determinants, 1947–84.

plant, low-cost public utilities, etc.), and an indirect influence through the regulation of class relations and aggregate demand management. Long-term investors' confidence is linked to the overall effectiveness of social and economic programs and to the history of social stability in the country. The longer the expected life of the investment venture and the larger the amount of capital invested, the more these long-term risk factors influence the decision to invest.

The historical data for the ratios defining the Puerto Rican profit rate are given in Figure 12.2. The tendencies in these ratios, and consequently in the Puerto Rican profit rate, can be divided into three periods. The first period corresponds to the first three postwar business cycles, between 1947 and 1962, when the Puerto Rican profit rate was relatively high and so were profit rate differentials. In the second period, between 1963 and 1973 there was a sharp decline in profitability. Finally, the profit rate has remained at relatively low levels beginning with the 1973–78 business cycle. These long-term tendencies in the Puerto Rican profit rate are determined by movements in the ratios defining the profit rate. Between 1947 and 1962, the period corresponding to the expansion, increases in capacity utilization (Y/Z) offset the decline in potential output to capital ratio (Z/K) while the profit share ($\Pi/Y = 1 - ULC$) was stable and the share of corporate taxes (t) remained low. During the second period the sharp decline in Z/K induced the decline in the profit rate. At the beginning of the current crisis, Z/K and Π/Y show an upturn, but Y/Z remains very low keeping r_{PR} at a low level. These tendencies in the ratios defining the profit rate could be associated with the consolidation and deterioration of key social institutions affecting the accumulation process in Puerto Rico.

The rise and fall of *Populismo*[11]

The postwar period in Puerto Rico was characterized by an initial phase of continuous economic expansion, in which business cycle downturns were mild and output growth rates were high by international standards. Beginning in the early 1960s, however, the expansion gave signs of deterioration and by the mid-1970s the island entered a period of long-term economic stagnation. *Populismo*, the postwar social structure of accumulation (SSA)[12] in Puerto Rico, was characterized by stability in labor markets, sizeable flows of foreign capital, export-oriented industrialization, and strong state support for this mode of accumulation; but these pillars of stable accumulation deteriorated, giving way to a period of crisis and redefinition of the institutions crucial to the accumulation process. In this section, I will discuss the correspondence between *Populismo*, and the early postwar expansion, the 1960s' deterioration of economic stability, and the eventual mid-1970s' crisis.

Stability in labor markets

Industrial peace was an important element of the expansion. Stability in capital–labor relations was the product of three major processes: a weakened trade-union movement, a rising standard of living, and population control.

Labor militancy during the war years was perceived by the emerging political coalition represented by the Popular Democratic Party (PPD) as a destabilizing factor in the government attempt to attract foreign capital to the island. The PPD controlled the trade-union movement by cooptation and recruitment of militant labor leaders. The imposition of the Taft–Hartley Act in 1947 and the expansion of AFL-CIO unions at the expense of independent unions also contributed to a weak trade union movement. The Taft–Harltey law imposed a bureaucratic structure that greatly benefited the expansion of more conservative AFL-CIO unions. As a result, the trade-union movement was highly fragmented during the 1950s and 1960s, and labor militancy decreased significantly. Industrial peace was also maintained by the continuous labor migration and rising standard of living. The expansion of industrial employment and migration to the US combined to reduce unemployment, a trend which was translated into better working conditions and earnings (Caban, 1984; Quintero, 1983; Centro de Estudios Puertorriquenos, 1979).

The 1960s were years of transition in the structure of capital–labor relations: the development of new labor leaders in the independent sector undermined both the AFL-CIO and the PPD's influence in the labor movement, and relatively low levels of unemployment created the conditions for labor activism (North American Congress on Latin America, 1976). These factors combined to increase the labor militancy of private and public workers, so that the average number of workers on strike per year in the 1963–1972 cycle was double what it had been in the preceding cycle. The state responded with increased repression of strikes and organizational drives; consequently, the duration of strikes more than doubled in the 1970s (Melendez, 1985, p. 197). Particularly after the 1974–75 recession, many strongholds of the new labor movement were defeated in long and bitter strikes. Industrial peace, one of the key elements inducing the early postwar period expansion, was gone.

Export-led industrialization

A second foundation of *Populismo* was massive flow of US capital and export-led industrialization. There was more US direct investment in Puerto Rico during the first decades of the postwar era than in any other developing country. By 1970, the island had about one-fifth of the total US direct investment in Latin America, and by 1980 this portion had jumped to nearly one-third (Melendez, 1985, p. 198). The massive flow of foreign capital displaced local capital and oriented industrial production toward US markets. By 1970, 37 percent of the private capital stock was owned, and 33 percent of the public capital stock was financed, by transnational capital (p. 204). The flows of foreign capital and the consequent transfer of technology was a key element increasing labor productivity and income through the expansion.

Foreign capital flows allowed higher rates of economic growth than those possible in a closed economy, and induced a rapid expansion of productive capacity in industry. Industrialization stimulated also other sectors of the economy and allowed the rapid expansion of public utilities and other government services. The open economy embodied a latent contradiction, however: foreign investment allowed foreign investors to gain control over the economic surplus. When financial resources were withdrawn from the economy, mobility of capital became a force against macroeconomic stability. Transnational corporations define strategies and respond to changing market conditions not solely on the basis of local interest nor with the domestic economy as their primary concern. Economic stability thus became a residual product of foreign corporate headquarters' decisions.

State policies

State policies played a critical role in enforcing industrial peace and creating political conditions for multinational capital investments, but also in directly subsidizing foreign capital through tax exemptions, low-cost public utilities, and training of the labor force. Through state support of the accumulation process, but also through income maintenance programs and government employment, state expenditures became an increasingly important component of aggregate demand. The expansion of government expenditures was possible, given low levels of corporate taxes, by increasing federal funds, taxing the working class, and increasing public debt (Castillo, 1981).

The structure of state finances fueled the expansion but then collapsed with the impact of the mid 1970s' recession. Eventually, subsidization of foreign capital built the public debt and adversely affected credit conditions for the Commonwealth. Stagnant income and rising public debt forced the Federal government to increase transfers to the Puerto Rican government and to individuals. During the 1970s, the share of Federal funds in the Commonwealth government revenues grew from 22.8 percent to 28.7 percent, and the share of transfers to individuals grew from 53.9 percent to 69.3 percent (Melendez, 1985, p. 209). The impact of the 1974–75 recession was so severe in part because state policies supporting accumulation and legitimizing the system were constrained by the structure of state finances inherited during the expansion (i.e. direct subsidization of foreign capital and rising public debt).

Economic integration with the United States

The internal logic of the SSA must be considered in a broader international perspective. Economic and politico-military domination of the capitalist world, in the form of the United States international hegemony, became an important characteristic of the accumulation process in the postwar period. The United States' economy depended upon an international finance system based on the dollar, on secure export markets, and on low prices for foreign raw materials, manufactured imports, and energy. Military expenditures and international "aid" became the main disciplinary mechanism to sustain an international hierarchy that benefited industrialized countries. Hegemony in international markets allowed higher levels of capacity utilization, low cost of capital, and favorable terms of trade. The erosion of these conditions in international markets was evident during the 1960s.

In this context, there is an articulation of the conditions limiting accumulation in Puerto Rico and the United States. Throughout the first two decades after World War II, the accumulation process in one country reproduced that in the other. A long wave of capitalist expansion in the island rested upon United States' hegemony in international markets and its strong domestic economy and vice versa. Similarly, the economic crisis characteristic of the 1970s was partially spurred by the contradictions between the two accumulation processes: as the United States' hegemony over international markets decreased, competition in domestic markets became more intense; as military and welfare expenditures increased, the fiscal crisis of the state became more acute, and transfer payments to the island's economy became less politically viable; as profitability was undermined and social instability increased, outflows of foreign capital increased.

Empirical model

Previous sections have outlined a model of the accumulation of capital which explains long-term trends of expansion and decay in a small, open economy. In this section, I will use the model to provide an econometric analysis of variations in foreign investment and profitability in the Puerto Rican economy during the postwar period. The data for the model were taken from the Puerto Rico Planning Board (1963, 1981a, 1981b, 1981c, 1989, and unpublished data for the capital stock) and the United States Department of Commerce (1979 and 1989, p. 32, table 2) for the years 1947–84.

The previously explained definition of the after-tax profit rate as the product of three ratios allows us to focus on a set of social processes that are of crucial theoretical importance in explaining the economic crisis that began in the mid-1970s. Thus, to understand the postwar trend in profitability, I shall begin with an assessment of the empirical proxies of the variables determining each of these ratios. The estimated profit rate equation is a function of the different factors determining profit shares or cost conditions, utilization of the capital stock, and the aggregate productivity of the capital stock. Then I will present and discuss an investment equation where F/FPY is the dependent variable, in order to focus on the determinants of net flows of foreign capital, the critical variable explaining long-term expansion and stagnation in the Puerto Rican economy.[13]

The profit rate

The after-tax profit rate is defined as the product of three ratios: profit share $(\Pi/Y = 1 - ULC)$, potential output to capital (Z/K), and capacity utilization (Y/Z). A system of equations for the determinants of the profit rates is as follows:

$$ULC = f(U), \qquad \partial ULC/\partial U > 0 \tag{1}$$

$$Z/K = g(F, Y/Z), \qquad \partial(Z/K)/\partial F < 0 \text{ and } \partial(Z/K)/\partial(Y/Z) < 0 \tag{2}$$

$$Y/Z = h(Y_{US}/Z_{US}), \qquad \partial(Y/Z)/\partial(Y_{US}/Z_{US}) > 0 \tag{3}$$

Unemployment (U) is included as a proxy for the reserve army effect. During expansions, wages will increase and productivity will decrease as the reserve army is depleted. Conversely, labor's weaker position during downturns will tend to reduce costs. The unemployment variable is lagged one period to avoid multicollinearity with the rate of capacity utilization. The potential output to capital ratio is a negative function of foreign capital investment (F) and the rate of capacity utilization (Y/Z). F is operationalized as the cumulative sum of the net import of capital, beginning in 1947.

Finally, the rate of capacity utilization has a more complex influence on profit rates. Short-term fluctuations in aggregate demand in Puerto Rico are highly correlated to similar movements in the United States. Since capacity utilization is one of the defining ratios of the profit rates, it has a direct and positive influence on profit rates. However, capacity utilization has an inverse correlation to Z/K and consequently affects profitability indirectly. These two effects work in opposite directions and there is no theoretical expectation of which effect will be dominant.

Substituting equations (1) to (3) into the after-tax profit rate:

Table 12.3. *Beta coefficients for* r_{PR}, 1948–84 (*t*-values are in parentheses)

	a	b	c
Constant	−0.000	0.000	0.000
	(−0.19)	(0.07)	(0.84)
U_{t-1}	0.469	0.710	0.439
	(2.37)**	(3.49)**	(2.53)**
F	−0.599	−1.761	−1.60
	(−3.21)**	(−5.39)**	(−4.68)**
Y/Z	0.354	0.278	
	(2.08)**	(1.76)**	
Y_{US}/Z_{US}			0.173
			(1.43)
Cycle7378		0.267	0.237
	(1.42)	(1.24)	
Cycle7984		0.850	0.796
		(2.72)**	(2.52)**
Summary statistics			
Adjusted R^2	0.27	0.58	0.56
Durbin–Watson	1.74	1.81	1.78
Rho	0.68	0.33	0.34

**Significant at the 0.95 level.

$$r = r(U, F, Y_{US}/Z_{US}) \tag{4}$$

where,

$$\partial r/\partial U < 0$$
$$\partial r/\partial F < 0$$
$$\partial r/\partial (Y_{US}/Z_{US}) > 0$$

Equation (4) allows estimation of the effects of the structure of capital–labor relations, foreign investment, and economic integration on the profit rate. Empirical results for three alternative models correcting for serial correlation using Cochrane–Orcutt estimation are given in Table 12.3.

The specified equations explain 27 to 58 percent of the variance in the profit rate. All coefficient signs are as expected, and all variables except Y_{US}/Z_{US} in the third model have a significant explanatory power. I have included two dummy variables, corresponding to the 1973–78 and 1979–84 business cycles respectively, to control for unexplained factors during the period of crisis. The positive and significant coefficient for the 1979–84 cycle dummy in the second and third equations indicates that the profit rate increased during this period as a result of factors not captured by the effects of the variables included as regressors. However, this increase in the profit rate is consistent with theoretical expectations after a period of crisis (See the earlier explanation regarding the tendencies in the ratios that define the profit rate and Figure 12.2.)

Foreign investment

The previously defined equation for flows of foreign capital is

$$F/FPY = F(r_{PR} - r_{US}, i, D)$$

Net flows of foreign investment depend on relative profitability as measured by $(r_{PR} - r_{US})$, cost conditions in international capital markets, and expectations about future demand. Let these variables be represented as follows:

$$r_{PR} - r_U = \text{after-tax profit rates differential lagged one period}$$
$$i = \text{prime interest rate, US}$$
$$D = \text{rate of capacity utilization, lagged one period}$$

Then

$$\partial(F/FPY)/\partial(r_{PR} - r_{US}) > 0$$
$$\partial(F/FPY)/\partial i < 0$$
$$\partial(F/FPY)/\partial D < 0$$

An increase in real profitability or expectations of future demand increases flows of foreign capital. Conversely, increases in the cost of capital decrease flows of foreign capital. Beta coefficients for this equation, using Cochrane–Orcutt estimation to correct for serial correlation, are as follows:

$$(F/FPY) = \; -0.610 \; + \; 0.298\,(r_{PR} - r_{US}) - \; 0.601i \quad + \; 0.288D$$
$$(-0.610) \quad (2.55)^{**} \qquad\qquad (-5.08)^{**} \quad (2.43^{**})$$

Adjusted R^2 = 0.52
Durbin–Watson = 1.60
Rho   = 0.23

**Significant at 0.95 level.

The specified equation explains 52 percent of the variance in foreign capital flows. All the coefficient signs are as expected and significant at the 0.95 level.

The econometric estimations of the model lend support to the explanation of the crisis in terms of the social structure of accumulation. Looking first at the investment equation, one sees from the empirical estimates of the model that (a) foreign investors based their reinvestment decision on relative profitability, and (b) international capital market conditions and expectations about domestic demand are also important factors affecting the reinvestment of foreign capital. The estimates of the profit rate have shown that long-term trends in this rate can be explained by (a) the structure of class relations, (b) capacity utilization, and (c) the impact of technology transfers as a constitutive aspect of foreign investment. With this general idea of the logic of the argument, and with an empirical model that supports the interpretation of the crisis previously presented, I shall draw some of the implications of the analysis.

Conclusions

The theory and the empirical analysis presented in the previous sections represent an alternative interpretation of the economic crisis that began in Puerto Rico in the mid-1970s. I have identified two alternative explanations of the crisis in a previous study (Melendez, 1988). Neoclassical economists emphasize deteriorating cost conditions inducing the loss of comparative advantages as the main underlying cause of the economic crisis. Their major policy prescription is to restore profitability, given their beliefs that low production costs are the most important determinant of profitability and that high profit rates will induce economic growth. The dependency school argument emphasizes the high degree of economic integration with, and dependence on, the US as the main factors leading to the crisis. The massive influx of foreign investment during the early years of the postwar period induced production for US markets based on the import of raw materials, and eventually induced a surplus drainage from the Puerto Rican economy. The SSA approach and the empirical model estimated in previous sections allowed me to assess the historical relevance of both explanations. In contrast to neoclassical and dependency analyses, I have explained the crisis as resulting from the erosion of key institutions that allowed the long-term expansion of the 1950s and 1960s.

The highly open character of the Puerto Rican economy was a critical factor in both the expansion and the crisis. The conditions for long-term economic and social stability at the beginning of the postwar period created net inflows of foreign capital, migration of unemployed labor, state support to transnational capital, access to foreign markets, and other factors pertaining to the economic integration between Puerto Rico and the United States. During this period the impact of the US business cycle upon the island's economy was negligible. By the early 1970s, however, the favorable conditions of the open economy had changed. The reinvestment decisions of multinational corporations, determined largely by relative profitability, became critical to the stability of the island's economy as a significant proportion of the productive capital and financial resources came under their control. It is in this context that the mid-1970s' recession triggered a period of long-term decline.

The importance of international factors must be assessed in the context of other institutions composing the postwar social structure of accumulation. The cooptation of the labor movement and strong state support for transnational capital were crucial elements of the postwar expansion. During the early 1970s, a long period of relatively low unemployment and the appearance of a new trade union leadership spurred a wave of labor militancy. Capitalist control over labor was restored only after the disciplining effect of the recession and a wave of government repression, but the defeat of labor was at the expense of capitalist confidence in long-term stability. The collapse of private investment induced by declining profitability, lower expectations, and unstable demand could not be compensated by state policies. These policies were constrained by high levels of debt, deteriorated credit margins, and lenders' pressures for conservative fiscal policies. When the recession of the mid-1970s pushed unemployment to a record high, social stability was preserved only by the massive transfer of Federal monies.

The interplay of internal and external factors affecting profitability and capital flows is evident from the preceding discussion. However, these factors were more or less important at different times and in relation to different processes. The long-term decline in Z/K, induced largely by foreign investment and the transfer of technology, was a leading factor in the long-term decline in the profit rate. The long-term decline in Z/K, however, was compensated by high levels of capacity utilization during the economic expansion and the consolidation of the SSA characteristic of the early postwar period. To the extent that conditions in international markets changed and domestic factors could not induce high levels of capacity utilization, the effects of declining Z/K led to a rapid decline in profitability. Declining profitability, unused capacity, and deteriorating capital–labor relations induced lower reinvestment of foreign capital. Thus, although external factors are very important, it is a mistake to reduce the crisis in the smaller economy to a simple reflection of the larger economy. Class relations and state policies, largely a consequence of conflicts confined to national boundaries, are as important as other factors pertaining to the international political economy.

The current economic crisis represents a transitional period. Structural change, the appearance and consolidation of a new set of institutions conditioning the accumulation of capital, is necessary to induce a new period of expansion. Within the context of a small and open capitalist economy, profitability and investors' confidence could be restored through changes in the structure of capital–labor relations, state policies, and the articulation of the Puerto Rican economy to the United States economy. An important lesson derived from this period of crisis is that a development model based upon foreign investment and overseas markets will eventually face the consequences of capital mobility. The power of capital strike – lower reinvestment of the surplus and eventually a surplus drainage – becomes a strong mechanism disciplining workers and local authorities through its impact upon the average rate of unemployment. Indeed, more than a decade of economic stagnation has produced favorable cost conditions and the electoral victories of pro-business administrations. The area that has remained without significant changes is the economic integration to the US Reforms that are aimed at solving the economic crisis but that ignore the important role of transnational capital and the export-led character of the economy are likely to fail.

Acknowledgments

I am especially indebted to Samuel Bowles and Bennett Harrison for their guidance and support. I have also benefited from comments by Jim Devine, Frank Thompson, and Victor Lippit.

Earlier versions of this chapter were presented at the annual meetings of the Allied Social Sciences Association, December 28, 1985, New York City, and of the Asociacion de Economistas de Puerto Rico, May 4, 1989, San Juan. This chapter was first published in 1990 in *Review of Radical Political Economics*, 22(2–3): 237–57.

Notes

1 I am making a distinction between international case studies on economic crisis (e.g. Canada, West Germany, and France) and theories and empirical work assessing the articulation between economic systems, and the effects of such articulation on domestic profits and capital accumulation. The neglect of international aspects of the economic crisis is particularly evident regarding the articulation between industrialized economies and the Third World.

2 This chapter is concerned with the articulation of two economic systems in a very limited way. First because it is a study which pertains to only two countries, Puerto Rico and the United States; and, second, because I make the unrealistic assumption that there is no significant feedback from the Puerto Rican economy to the United States. Thus, I am limiting the analysis to only half of the problem: the effects of the economic crisis in industrialized economies on smaller, Third World economies.

3 The process of capital accumulation is the repetition of a cycle in which capitalists buy inputs for the productive process (including labor power), organize these inputs in the labor process to produce commodities, and finally sell their commodities to realize surplus value. Crises are, in this context, interruptions in the process of capital accumulation when considering the reproduction of all capitals within a given social formation.

4 I have argued before (Melendez, 1988) that explanations of the crisis in Puerto Rico can be grouped into "rising cost" or "dependency" arguments. The dependency argument rests on the hypothesis that foreign investment is critical to developing countries' macroeconomic stability. Capital outflows or "surplus drainage" may induce instability and long-term economic stagnation. The aforementioned focus on foreign investment and the reinvestment of foreign capital allows one to test directly the surplus drainage hypothesis.

5 Results for a simple empirical model in which the capital stock in Puerto Rico at current prices ($KPRCP$) between 1947 and 1984 is explained as a function of the cumulative sum of foreign investment ($CSUMNMK$) are as follows:

$$KPRCP = \underset{(-0.79)}{1082} + \underset{(2.53)^{**}}{0.15\ CSUMNMK} + \underset{(2.55)^{**}}{0.17\ KPRCP(t-1)} + \underset{(2.29)^{**}}{79\ TIME}$$

Adjusted R^2 = 0.97
Durbin–Watson = 1.66
Rho = 0.61

Results for a similar model in which gross domestic investment of fixed capital (IFK) is explained as a function of foreign investment (NMK) are as follows:

$$IFK = \underset{(-0.27)}{-34} + \underset{(2.60)^{**}}{0.21\ NMK} + \underset{(3.21)^{**}}{0.34\ IFK(t-1)} + \underset{(1.71)^{*}}{20\ TIME}$$

Adjusted R^2 = 0.88
Durbin–Watson = 1.85
Rho = 0.53

Both equations were corrected for autocorrelation using Cochrane–Orcutt estimation; t-values are in parentheses;
**Significant at 0.95 level, and
*Significant at 0.90 level.

6 Double-counting of foreign property income results from the balance-of-payments accounting procedures. Foreign property income is first considered as an outflow because it is income paid to non-residents. Then the portion that was reinvested in domestic assets, plus additional investments from non-residents are considered as net import of capital. For an additional discussion of this procedure in the national income accounts in Puerto Rico see Tobin (1976), and in Latin America, see Ramsaran (1985).

7 The above specification assumes that $r_{PR} - r_{US}$ captures relative profitability in international markets. In reality, it only captures the effects of relative profitability with respect to US domestic investors but not to other Third World countries – particularly newly industrialized countries in direct competition with Puerto Rico in international capital markets. However, to the extent that Puerto Rico remains a US colony, US investors' risk is more comparable to domestic investments than to other international investments. Hence, specification error in the F/FPY equation regarding relative profitability in international capital markets is minimal.

8 The definitions used for profit rates in Puerto Rico and the United States are different. The US after-tax profit rate (r_{US}) is defined as after-tax corporate profits over non-residential all corporations capital stock. The Puerto Rican after-tax profit rate (r_{PR}) is defined as after-tax property income over private and public capital stock. Inclusion of all forms of property income in the numerator scales up r_{PR}, while inclusion of both private and public capital stock in the denominator will push it down. Since these effects tend to cancel each other out, empirical estimates based on different definitions of the profit rate are not significantly affected. But the reader should consider the explained differences in the comparisons that follow.

9 The profit rate is often presented in value terms as $r = s/(c + v)$, where s represents surplus value, and c and v refer to constant and variable capital, respectively. The equation implicitly assumes a one-period turnover for capital. The definition presented here allows us to discuss three different influences in the profit rate, each of which can be associated with a variant of Marxist crisis theory. A first stream of argument focuses on a rising organic composition of capital as the leading element inducing long-term decline in the profit rate. A second variant stresses the rising strength of labor, and the last one focuses on realization failures in the sphere of circulation. A discussion of these alternative views can be found in Wright (1979). Bowles et al. (1983, 1986) use a linear model to assess the factors determining the after-tax profit rate. Although there are some minor differences in the factors selected for observation between our two approaches, the basic argument about how the social structure of accumulation affects these factors is similar. See also Weisskopf (1979), Bowles and Edwards (1985), and Sherman and Evans (1984) for the derivation and discussion of this definition.

10 This definition of ULC is different from the one utilized by the United States Department of Labor and other commonly used definitions. The US Department of Labor defines unit labor cost as hourly compensations divided by output per paid hour. Gordon et al. (1983) defined unit labor cost as "$S_r = 1 - [(w/p)/qe]$ where w is the nominal wage, p is the price of output, q is output per unit of labor effort, and e is labor effort per hour." Limitations in the data available to estimate the model imposed the above variation in the definition.

11 I refer to this period as *Populismo* to highlight the importance of the populist movement that emerged in the late 1930s and served as the basis for the political dominance of the Popular Democratic Party up to 1968.

12 Political economists have developed the concept of social structures of accumulation to refer to the crucial economic, political or social institutions affecting and determining the reproduction of capital. Gordon et al. (1982, p. 23) define the SSA as "all the institutions that impinge

upon the accumulation process." The organizing force behind the exploration, consolidation, and eventual demise of a particular SSA is a stable and relatively high profit rate. The SSA concept is useful in an analysis of economic crises and long-term trends in capitalist economies. Long periods of economic expansion and long periods of decline and crisis are related to the exploration and consolidation of an SSA and to the eventual erosion of the institutions that constitute that SSA. Crises, in this context, are defined as transitional or conjunctural periods in capitalism in which a given SSA is replaced by a new set of institutions. The deterioration of an SSA is characterized by the instability of class relations, increased competition among factions of capitals, and the inability of state policies to induce economic stability. The institutionalization of a new set of power relations between capital and labor, international and domestic competitors, and state bureaucrats requires the transformation of the worn-out institutions. The emerging form of social organization is the object of struggle between different social classes; the emerging institutions ultimately represent the alliance of classes or sectors of classes behind a political-economic project (Bowles et al., 1983, 1986; Gordon, 1980; Bowles, 1984).

13 In contrast to other studies by Freire (1969, 1979) and Maldonado (1970), I will not attempt to explain gross domestic investment. Curet (1986) divides investment into domestic and foreign components and estimates equations for each sector, including changes in property income as an independent variable but excluding profit rates. The basic difference between the equation presented in this section and the above studies is the equation's emphasis on the profit rate as a determinant of investment. Sherman and Evans (1984, pp. 155–81) present a theoretical discussion of the role of profits in an investment equation and a comparison with neoclassical and Keynesian investment equations. Clark (1979) presents a comparison of neoclassical and Keynesian investment equations.

References

Boddy, R., and J. Crotty, 1975. "Class Conflict and Macro Policy: The Political Business Cycle," *Review of Radical Political Economics*, 7 (1).

Bonilla, F., and R. Campos, 1976. "Industrialization and Migration: Some Effects of the Puerto Rican Working Class," *Latin American Perspectives*, 3(3): 66–108.

1981. "Wealth of Poor: Puerto Ricans in the New Economic Order," *Daedalus*, 110 (Spring): 133–76.

Bowles, S., 1984. "Class Alliances and Surplus Labor Time," in *Economic Structure and Performance*, ed. H. B. Chenery. Orlando, Fla.: Academic Press.

Bowles, S., and R. Edwards, 1985. *Understanding Capitalism*. New York: Harper and Row.

Bowles, S., D. M. Gordon, and T. E. Weisskopf, 1983. *Beyond the Waste Land*. Garden City, N.J.: Anchor Press/Doubleday.

1986. "Power and Profits: The Social Structure of Accumulation and the Profitability of the Postwar U.S. Economy," *Review of Radical Political Economics*, 18(1/2): 132–67.

Caban, P. A., 1984. "Industrialization, the Colonial State, and Working Class Organizations in Puerto Rico," *Latin American Perspectives*, 11 (3).

Castillo, V. L., 1981. "La acumulacion de capital en Puerto Rico: 1960–1975." Doctoral thesis, Universidad Nacional Autonoma de Mejico.

Centro de Estudios Puertorriquenos, 1979. *Labor Migration Under Capitalism: The Puerto Rican Experience*. New York: Monthly Review Press.

Clark, P. K., 1979. "Investment in the 1970s: Theory, Performance and Prediction," *Brookings Papers on Economic Activity*, 1.

Curet, E., 1986. *Puerto Rico: Development by Integration to the U.S.* Rio Piedras, P.R.: Editorial Cultural.

Freire, J. F., 1969. *External and Domestic Financing in the Economic Development of Puerto Rico.* Rio Piedras, P.R.: University of Puerto Rico Press.

1979. *El modelo economico de Puerto Rico.* Rio Piedras, P.R.: Interamerican University Press.

Gordon, D. M., 1980. "Stages of Accumulation and Long Economic Cycles," in *Processes of the World System,* ed. T. Hopkins and I. Wallerstein, Beverly Hills, Calif.: Sage Publications.

Gordon, D. M., R. Edwards, and M. Reich, 1982. *Segmented Work, Divided Workers.* Cambridge University Press.

Gordon, D. M., T. E. Weisskopf, and S. Bowles, 1983. "Long Swings and the Nonreproductive Cycle," *American Economic Review,* 73(2): 152–7.

Maldonado, R. M., 1970. *The Role of the Financial Sector in the Economic Development of Puerto Rico.* New York: Federal Insurance Corporation.

Melendez, E., 1985. "Accumulation and Crisis in the Postwar Puerto Rican Economy," unpublished Ph.D. dissertation, University of Massachusetts.

1988. "Postwar Schools of Political Economy in Puerto Rico: Contrasting Views on the Open Economy and Economic Crisis," *Nature, Society, and Thought,* 1(2): 249–75.

North American Congress on Latin America, 1976. *NACLA,* 10(5) (May–June), special issue "Latin American and Empire Report: US Unions in Puerto Rico."

Puerto Rico Planning Board, 1963, 1981a. *Balance of Payments.* San Juan.

1981b. *Income and Product.* San Juan.

1981c, 1983, 1989. *Informe economico al Gobernador.* San Juan.

Quintero, A. G., 1983. "El movimiento obrero y el modelo puertorriqueno de desarrollo: algunos apuntes," paper presented at xv Congreso Latinoamericano de Sociologia, Managua, Nicaragua (October).

Ramsaran, R. F., 1985. *U.S. Investments in Latin America and the Caribbean: Trends and Issues.* New York: St. Martin's Press.

Schor, J., and S. Bowles, 1983. "Conflict in the Employment Relation and the Cost of Job Loss," Working Paper 6, Economics Institute of the Center for Democratic Alternatives, New York.

Sherman, H. J., and G. R. Evans, 1984. *Macroeconomics: Keynesian, Monetarist, and Marxist Views.* New York: Harper and Row.

Tobin, J., 1976. *Informe al governador del comite para el estudio de las finanzas de Puerto Rico: informe Tobin.* Rio Piedras, P.R.: Editorial Universitaria.

US Department of Commerce, 1979. *Economic Study of Puerto Rico,* vol. 1. Washington, D.C.: Government Printing Office.

1989. *Survey of Current Business,* October.

Weisskopf, T. E., 1979. "Marxian Crisis Theory and the Rate of Profits in the Postwar U.S. Economy," *Cambridge Journal of Economics,* 3: 341–78.

Weisskopf, T. E., D. M. Gordon, and S. Bowles, 1983. "Hearts and Minds: A Social Model of U.S. Productivity Growth," *Brookings Papers on Economic Activity,* 2.

Wright, E. O., 1979. *Class, Crisis and State.* London: Verso.

── 13 ──

Apartheid and capitalism:
social structure of accumulation or contradiction?

NICOLI NATTRASS

Introduction

Several recent radical studies of the South African political economy have drawn on social structures of accumulation (SSA) analysis. These contributions have an inadequate empirical basis, and suffer from the same functionalist leanings as earlier radical understandings of apartheid. This chapter argues that if SSA theory is applied in a meaningful way, the evidence suggests that no stable SSA existed in South Africa during the postwar period. Trends in the empirical data (most notably the rate and share of profit) do not reflect any balance between key economic variables.

Falling profitability, however, does not *necessarily* suggest a fundamental inadequacy in the institutional structure. If a credible explanation can be provided as to why profitability should be discounted as a key indicator of an SSA, then an exception can be made. As argued below, this is not the case as far as South Africa is concerned. Labor market and cost pressures (often exacerbated by apartheid policies) steadily eroded initially high levels of profitability. Trends in the share and rate of profit reflect the *absence* of any happy marriage of apartheid and capitalism in terms of a stable institutional structure, or a sustainable growth path.

Developments in the radical understanding of South Africa

Radicals found it relatively easy to argue that the institutions of apartheid (at least during the 1960s) were functional to capitalist development rather than a distortion of it.[1] Given the coexistence of apartheid with rapid economic expansion, these writers suggested that there was "something highly functional and causally significant about the relationship between the economic system and the system of radical domination" (Johnstone, 1976, p. 212). Wolpe made the point more strongly by claiming that apartheid was instituted "for the purposes of reproducing and exercising control over a cheap African industrial labour force" (1972, p. 450).

The agenda of the early radical writers was to expose and analyze the previously theoretically neglected class character of the South African political economy. Johnstone's (1976) detailed and subtle analysis of class struggle in the mining industry remains one of the best examples. However, as the popularity of Poulant-zian analysis grew, the radical project increasingly took the form of constructing arguments as to how state policies were functional to dominant "fractions" of capital and to capitalism in general (see below, for example, Davies *et al.* [1976], Morris [1977], and Kaplan [1977]).

This approach soon ran up against the limits inherent to functionalist analysis (Posel, 1983). Furthermore, the explanation was *post hoc* and, as Schumpeter reminds us, "there is no policy short of exterminating the bourgeoisie that could not be held to serve some economic or extra-economic short-run or long-run bourgeois interest, at least in the sense that it wards off still worse things" (1976, p. 55). More importantly, although the functionalist Marxists often mentioned the contradictory nature of capitalist development, little effort was made to investigate it, or the way state policies actually affected wages and profitbility.

The agenda of showing apartheid to be functional to capitalism eventually turned into a straight-jacket when, from the late 1970s, it became clear that the apartheid state was unable to generate conditions conducive to adequate capital accumulation. Disinvestment in response to low rates of profit, worker militancy and socioeconomic crisis, made the idea of a functional and reflexive relationship between apartheid and capitalism extremely unconvincing.

Saul and Gelb (1981) made the first attempt to recast the radical explanation by arguing that apartheid was a response to an "organic crisis" in the 1940s, but that by the mid-1970s, the system had itself degenerated into crisis. During the 1960s "soaring profits" and long-term expansion were allegedly guaranteed by apart-heid's driving down the black wage bill (Saul and Gelb, 1981, pp. 70-4). The dynamics (or contradictions) which eventually eroded this growth model were seen to be rising capital intensity and a restricted internal market.

For all its innovative ideas, the work of Saul and Gelb, like the early radical writings, was seriously flawed by a lack of supporting evidence. No substantive analysis of the dynamic relationship between wages, productivity, profitability and capital intensity was provided. They simply asserted that profit rates soared because they believed apartheid policies sufficiently depressed the wage share.

More recently, the ideas expressed in Saul and Gelb have been reformulated and elaborated with the aid of SSA[2] and "Regulation"[3] concepts. The central idea is that long waves in capital accumulation can be explained as a consequence of the successive creation and collapse of a supporting socioinstitutional structure or SSA (Kotz, 1990, p. 5). Accordingly, the heyday of apartheid has been represented as a distinct "Radical Fordist Regulation" (Gelb, 1987, 1991), an apartheid SSA (Morris and Padayachee, 1988), and as a form of "Peripheral Fordism" (Ramos and Cassim, 1989). State responses to the current crisis in the fields of privatization, deregulation and social reform, are seen as attempts to reconstruct conditions favorable to renewed accumulation (see, for example, Morris [1991]).

This work is empirically weak (see Nattrass [1988] for a critique). Nevertheless, it has placed potentially significant ideas on the South African theoretical terrain. Considering that SSA theory stresses the interrelationship between economic and sociopolitical processes, the approach has potential for contributing to a greater understanding of South Africa. Apartheid's labor-repressive role necessitates that economic developments are understood within the context of South Africa's racially discriminatory institutions and structures. The theory must, however, be applied in a meaningful way.

The major problem with the way in which SSA analysis has been utilized in South Africa, is that the authors were too quick off the mark to proclaim the existence of a racially repressive South African SSA. Rather than reasoning from empirical evidence, the old radical assumption that a favorable institutional structure must have underpinned the high rate of growth formed the basis of the argument.

This is a problem not only for those who favor empirically based arguments, but also for many writers in the tradition of SSA analysis who stress the highly contingent nature of SSAs and reject functionalist predetermination as a methodology. In this perspective, the economically favorable meshing of institutional and accumulation dynamics is regarded as far from inevitable. The essential point is that before an SSA can be deemed to exist, it is necessary to conduct substantial historical analysis of key institutional and social relations as well as of central empirical trends, most notably the rate of profit and accumulation.

The role of the rate of profit and accumulation in SSA theory

According to SSA theory, the importance of socioinstitutional structures lies predominantly in creating a stable and predictable environment in which capitalists can make "reasonably determinate calculations about their expected rates of return" (Gordon *et al.*, 1982, p. 23). Thus a more Keynesian concern with expectations of profitability is apparent (Kotz, 1990, p. 13), as opposed to a focus on actual trends in profit shares and rates.

Nevertheless, in the spirit of Marxian crisis theory, SSA theorists also place an emphasis on profitability as an indicator of the health of an SSA. According to Bowles, *et al.*:

> If the SSA perspective has merit, we would expect boom periods inaugurated by the establishment of a new and viable institutional structure to be characterized by rising and/or relatively high profitability, while we would similarly expect periods of crisis brought on by the demise of a SSA to be marked by falling and/or low profitability (1986, p. 134)

The immediate question that springs to mind is what does relatively high or low profitability actually mean? Presumably Bowles *et al.* are making a comparative point about the difference between long-wave periods of expansion and contraction, i.e. they mean that the average profit rate should be high in the expansion compared to that in the contraction[4] (see also Kotz [1987, pp. 22–3]). What is clear from the quotation, however, is that a viable capitalist SSA should not be characterized by *falling* profitability over a significant time period. Thus one can conclude that the establishment of a viable SSA should lead to a profit rate that either rises over time, or remains at a relatively high level compared to some long-term average.

Constant or gently rising profit rates characterized the postwar "golden age" boom in the advanced capitalist countries (ACCs). Writers in the SSA tradition argue that the institutional structures of the welfare state, coupled with incomes policies and Keynesian full employment strategies, allowed for a balance between the growth in output (aided by techniques of mass production) and purchasing power. In underlying economic terms, it is agreed that the institutional framework allowed for the rapid and parallel growth of productivity, real wages and capital stock per worker. The significance of this pattern was that it "guaranteed both a roughly constant profit rate, and roughly equal growth rates of consumption and production, thus pertaining the initial rate of accumulation" (Glyn et al., 1990, p. 48).

There is, however, a certain amount of tension between the empirical characterization of an SSA in terms of constant or rising profitability, and as a system conducive to a rapid rate of accumulation. Although profit rates are important as a source of investment funds, the relationship between the rate of accumulation and the rate of profit is far from clear.[5] Low or falling profit rates could coexist with high rates of accumulation if, for instance, investors are confident about the future. Furthermore, rapid accumulation in response to initially high rates of return, could eventually bring about a fall in the rate of profit as opportunities for high profit investment narrow with time.

It is thus not surprising that there is little agreement in the economic literature about the nature of the relationship between profitability and investment. In some approaches, a high historical rate of return is argued to be an important stimulus to investment (for example, Weisskopf [1979, p. 34]) while in others, a low historical rate of return is regarded as stimulating investment via the effect of profit squeeze on structural change (for example, van Duijn [1983]). Unresolved questions include whether investment boosts profitability by stimulating demand, or whether a rapid rate of accumulation generates diminishing returns via neoclassical processes of declining marginal efficiencies, or via Marxian mechanisms relating to capital intensity.

This uncertainty raises questions about the relevance of the rate of profit for SSA analysis. For example, viable SSAs probably existed in Germany and Japan, yet profit rates were on a declining trend in both countries (Hill, 1979). Under these circumstances, the rate of accumulation (which was high in both countries) is arguably a better empirical indicator for the purpose of SSA analysis.

But this immediately presents a theoretical quandary: if one can pick either the rate of profit or the rate of accumulation as the key empirical indicator, then the danger of tautological reasoning arises. One could end up with a facile argument to the effect that if rapid growth occurred, then there must, by definition, have been a facilitating institutional structure/SSA. Furthermore, one is plagued by the counterfactual: would growth have been faster if a more suitable SSA had been in place?

Focusing on the requirement of macroeconomic and socioinstitutional *balance* (rather than rapid accumulation) is theoretically neater. The concern clearly becomes whether there was a successful meshing of central economic trends such as productivity, wage and consumption growth (as manifested by constant or rising profitability). However, if SSA analysis is not to rule out cases like Germany and Japan, such empirical requirement needs qualifying in the following way.

In order to avoid the dangers of economism and tautology, SSA analysis should proceed on two fronts. First, a case must be made as to why certain institutional structures were likely to have promoted balanced, sustainable growth (as outlined above). Second, the hypothesis must be tested with reference to empirical data. If profitability and related variables manifest the expected balanced growth trends, then one can proceed with the argument that an SSA did indeed function.

If the data do not confirm the hypothesis, then a convincing case must be constructed as to why an exception should be made. It could, for example, be argued that in the case of Germany the joker in the empirical pack was simply the unsustainably high rate of accumulation during postwar reconstruction. Whatever the argument, the onus must rest on the analyst to make a case as to why the decline in the rate of profit should *not* be regarded as reflecting essential contradictions within an unhealthy and unsustainable institutional context.

This chapter explores whether adequate empirical support exists for the hypothesis that an apartheid SSA existed in postwar South Africa. Trends in South African net profitability are examined, with a prime focus on the manufacturing sector.

South African net profitability

If an analysis of profitability is to shed any light on the question whether an SSA existed in South Africa, then it is important that profitability be measured in the most appropriate or representative economic sectors. In the South African case, these would be manufacturing or mining.

The relationship between the mining sector (which needed to minimize the cost of black labour) and the migrant labour system (which did precisely that) is often pointed to as proof of the functionality of apartheid for capitalist expansion (see, for example, Johnstone [1986], Davies [1979]). Successful accumulation in the mining industry spurred on growth elsewhere in the economy by providing the import-intensive manufacturing sector with foreign exchange, as well as with a significant market for its output (Lombard and Stadler, 1980; J. Nattrass, 1981, ch. 7).

Nevertheless, despite the important role of mining, the manufacturing sector is a more crucial determinant of the long-run prosperity of the South African economy (Moll, 1988). Between 1948 and 1981, its contribution to the GDP rose from 18 percent to 24 percent, and its share of employment rose from 12 percent to 20 percent. This, coupled with the fact that most SSA analyses elsewhere focus on the manufacturing sector, makes manufacturing a more appropriate candidate for detailed study than mining.

However, to the extent that increases in the gold price have periodically alleviated crisis tendencies emanating from the manufacturing sector, it is useful to situate trends in manufacturing profitability in the context of those in mining, and in the economy as a whole. Accordingly, a summarized deconstruction of profitability trends in the mining and "core" economic sectors is also provided. The core sector, which comprises manufacturing, mining, construction, commerce, catering, and accommodation, and electricity, gas, and water, is the largest grouping of economic sectors for which adequate capital stock data exists (see Nattrass [1990b, data appendix]).

Deconstructing the share and rate of profits[6]

The (net)[7] rate of profit (measured in conventional national accounts price categories) can be expressed as the product of the profit share and the output:capital ratio. The profit share measures what proportion of total output (i.e. wages plus profits) accrues to capitalists. The output:capital ratio is a measure of the productivity of capital.

$$\frac{P}{K} = \frac{P}{Y} \cdot \frac{Y}{K}$$

P = profits (i.e. net operating surplus)[8]
K = net capital stock at replacement value[9]
Y = net value-added[10]

Given that value-added is the sum of wages and profits, the profit share can be expressed as 1 minus the wage share.

$$\frac{P}{Y} = 1 - \frac{W}{Y} \text{ where } \frac{W}{Y} = \frac{W}{P_q L} \cdot \frac{P_{yc} L}{Y} \cdot \frac{P_q}{P_{yc}}$$

W = remuneration of employees
P_q = price index of gross output (the production price index)
L = employment
P_{yc} = the net GDP deflator[11]

In growth rate terms this becomes:

$$\frac{\dot{W}}{Y} = \frac{\dot{W}}{P_q L} - \frac{\dot{Y}}{P_{yc} L} - \frac{\dot{P}_{yc}}{P_q}$$

In other words, the growth in the wage share can be approximated as the growth in product wages ($W/P_q L$) minus the growth in productivity ($Y/P_{yc} L$) adjusted for relative value-added input prices (P_{yc}/P_q). The latter term is included to pick up

Table 13.1. *The manufacturing, mining and core net profitability (average annual compound percentage growth rates)*

	1948–55	1955–60	1960–64	1964–70	1970–74	1974–81
Manufacturing						
Profit share	0.7	−0.7	−2.8	−2.2	−3.2	2.7
Output:capital	−2.5	−1.4	−0.3	−2.3	−5.7	−3.7
Profit rate	−1.8	−2.0	−3.2	−4.4	−8.4	−1.3
Mining						
Profit share	3.3	4.1	2.4	−0.8	6.7	−0.9
Output:capital	−3.3	2.9	1.9	0.3	10.8	−4.6
Profit rate	0.0	7.2	4.4	−0.5	18.0	−5.4
Core						
Profit share	1.1	0.1	0.4	−2.7	3.6	0.2
Output:capital	−3.9	−0.6	1.8	−0.7	−0.7	−4.7
Profit rate	−2.7	−0.6	2.2	−3.4	2.8	−4.6

Sources: Various editions of *South African Statistics*, the *South African Reserve Bank Quarterly Bulletin* and unpublished material from the South African Reserve Bank, the Central Statistical Services and the Institute for Futures Research, Stellenbosch University. See Nattrass (1990b) for a discussion of sources and adaptations to the data.

any input cost squeeze on profitability. It is assumed that the production price index reflects the price of inputs and that if these rise faster than value-added prices, the surplus available for distribution between wages and profits is squeezed as a result. Consequently, the rate of growth of productivity needs to be adjusted to take such price movements into account. The rate of growth of productivity minus that of relative value-added input prices equals the rate of growth of the surplus available for distribution.

Thus the wage share rises or falls depending on whether product wages rise faster or slower than the surplus. Product wages are used in preference to real wages as they provide a better indication of the real cost to capitalists of employing labor.

The deconstruction analysis has been conducted according to peak-to-peak periods on the business cycle between 1948 and 1981. The 1960s represent the high point of South Africa's growth performance. Between 1960 and 1970, the real GDP grew at 5.9 percent p.a. and manufacturing grew at 7.0 percent p.a. The 1970s saw a slowdown in growth which became much more pronounced in the 1980s.[12] 1981 has been selected as the end point of the analysis as it represents the last major peak on the business cycle before the apartheid social and economic system degenerated into clear crisis. As nobody argues that apartheid formed an efficient SSA for capitalism in the 1980s, the question of the application of SSA concepts is germane only to the period 1948–81.

As can be seen from Table 13.1, the manufacturing profit rate fell at an accelerating pace from 1948 (except for the slightly slower fall between 1974 and 1981). This was due to a falling output:capital ratio and, between 1955 and 1974, to

Table 13.2. *Deconstructing the South African manufacturing net rate of profit (average annual compound percentage growth rates)*

		1948–55	1955–60	1960–64	1964–70	1970–74	1974–81
1	Productivity	2.4	4.2	3.9	2.4	2.1	2.7
2	Effect of input costs	−2.4	−0.4	−1.0	−0.8	−2.3	−1.0
3	Surplus available (1 + 2)	0.0	3.8	2.9	1.6	−0.2	1.7
4	Product wage (3 + 5)	−0.4	4.2	4.5	2.6	1.0	0.6
5	Wage share	−0.4	0.4	1.6	1.0	1.2	−1.1
6	*Profit share*	0.7	−0.7	−2.8	−2.2	−3.2	2.7
7	*Output:capital*	−2.5	−1.4	−0.3	−2.3	−5.7	−3.7
8	*Profit rate* (6 + 7)	−1.8	−2.0	−3.2	−4.4	−8.4	−1.3

Note: Expressing certain growth rates as sums of other growth rates is only an approximation. They do not always add up exactly.
Sources: See Table 13.1

a declining profit share. The mining sector on the other hand, experienced only two periods of actual decline in profitability: the first between 1964 and 1970, when it fell slightly; and the second between 1974 and 1981 when it fell sharply. These compensating trends in mining contributed a great deal to the less severe decline of core sector profitability between 1955 and 1974 as compared to the manufacturing sector.

Despite the cushioning effect of mining, the steep fall in manufacturing profitability was reflected in the core sector, although to a lesser extent. One can thus safely conclude that the overall trend in profitability in the postwar period was downwards. The analysis of trends in manufacturing can thus be regarded as representative of the most important dynamics behind the decline in South African profitability.

South African net manufacturing profitability: 1948–81

As noted above, the rate of profit in manufacturing has been on a strong declining trend over the postwar period; falling from 44 percent in 1948, to 9 percent in 1986. However, it is important to note that although falling, profit shares and rates in South Africa were spectacularly high, and until 1981, consistently over twice those in Europe (Nattrass, 1990b, pp. 73, 219). Nevertheless the interesting question is not the comparably high absolute levels of profitability (which are difficult to measure accurately [Hill, 1979]), but rather why capitalists in manufacturing were unable to sustain them.

Table 13.2 presents a more detailed deconstruction of trends in manufacturing profitability. Interestingly, the wage share rose steadily between 1960 and 1974, despite declining productivity growth and increasing pressure of input costs. This indicates that the apartheid period was characterized more by a wage squeeze than by falling or constant wage shares (as assumed by radical analysts).

Table 13.3. *Racial differentiation in manufacturing*

	1948	1955	1960	1964	1970	1974	1981
Employment							
White share (percent)	32.3	28.4	27.0	25.5	24.0	22.3	22.2
Black share (percent)	48.5	53.0	53.7	53.3	52.9	55.1	54.4
White:black wage gap	4.0	5.2	5.5	5.4	5.8	5.1	4.2
Wage bill							
White share (percent)	61.7	63.2	63.4	61.7	61.7	56.0	52.3
Black share (percent)	23.4	23.1	23.1	24.4	23.9	28.0	31.2

Sources: See Table 13.1

Table 13.4. *Racial product wage growth in manufacturing (average annual compound percentage growth rates)*

	1948–55	1955–60	1960–64	1964–70	1970–74	1974–81
Surplus available	0.0	3.8	2.9	1.6	−0.2	1.7
Product wage						
Total	−0.4	4.2	4.5	2.6	1.0	0.6
Black	−2.1	3.9	6.3	2.3	4.2	2.3
White	1.9	5.3	5.3	3.7	1.0	−0.5
Coloured/Indian	−1.3	3.5	2.5	2.0	3.7	0.4
Wage share	−0.4	0.4	1.6	1.0	1.2	−1.1

Note: Average wages have been estimated so as to accord with the remuneration statistics in the national accounts (see Nattrass, 1990b, data appendix).
Sources: See Table 13.1.

These trends are discussed in more detail below. Given the stress in radical literature on black labor repression as a source of high profitability, the focus is primarily on trends in average product wages broken down according to racial groups (see Table 13.4).[13] The word "black" is used to describe the black African population. As such, it does not include "coloreds" (people of mixed descent) or Indians (Asians), who are referred to separately as one category. Table 13.3 provides some indication of racial differentiation in manufacturing between 1948 and 1981.

As can be seen from Table 13.3, the white share of employment fell steadily between 1948 and 1981, as did the white share of the wage bill from 1960. The main impetus behind the changing racial share of the wage bill from 1970 was the more rapid increase in black wages relative to white. Relative racial wage trends are reflected both in the changing white:black wage gap, and in product wage growth (see Table 13.4).

The rate of profit: 1948–60[14]

Between 1948 and 1955, the profit share rose at the cost of the wage share.[15] This is interesting for several reasons: firstly because the trend is in marked contrast with that during the war years (when wages *eroded* the profit share); and secondly, because the turnaround coincided with the coming to power of the nationalist government on an "apartheid" ticket.

During the war, when manufacturing expanded rapidly and there was a shortage of skilled and semi-skilled labor, black labor was able to secure wage gains at the cost of the profit share. White wage demands, and trade union complaints about the replacement of certain white skilled jobs by semi-skilled black jobs, met with little success (Nattrass, 1990a).

However, from the end of the war, and especially from 1948, the tables were turned. Continued rapid black urbanization,[16] coupled with the return of white servicemen, placed black labor in a far less favorable position. Institutional changes (such as the shift away from state intervention on the part of the unskilled worker) and the political repression of the black trade union movement added to – rather than generated – the hostile environment facing black workers.

White workers were in a very different position. The demand for skilled (predominantly white) labour continued unabated, and white workers were able to bargain significant wage increases. As shown in Table 13.3, the white:black wage gap widened between 1948 and 1960, and the white share of the wage bill rose in spite of a decline in the white share of employment.

These relative racial wage trends were, of course, consistent with the ideals of the apartheid government from 1948. However, to an important extent, the state was able to rely on the forces of supply and demand to do its dirty work.

Given that the surplus remained constant, whereas overall average product wages fell by 0.4 percent p.a., the rapid increase in white product wages was prevented from causing a profit squeeze by compensating declines in black and colored/Indian product wages. This extremely interesting development lends weight to the radical argument that white wage increases under apartheid were more than compensated for by the decline in black wages. However, as noted above, this was more a market-related phenomenon than as a result of apartheid institutional design. Furthermore, as can be seen from Table 13.2, such a state of affairs did not last beyond 1955.

Between 1955 and 1960, white wages continued to rise faster than black wages. White workers had their hand strengthened by the continued shortage of skilled labor, and by section 77 of the 1956 Industrial Conciliation Act (which provided for the reservation of certain jobs for whites only). Although job reservation only successfully took-off in the 1960s, the *threat* of applying to the state for job reservation was used by the white trade unions to good effect when bargaining for higher wages.

Despite the steady encroachment of apartheid into the labor market, black workers were nevertheless able to secure real wage gains. Between 1955 and 1960, black product wages rose faster (albeit by only 0.1 percent) than the surplus, thus contributing to the profit squeeze rather than alleviating the pressure caused by white wage increases. Factors behind this development included a more active and interventionist minimum wage policy on the part of the state, and growing demand for semi-skilled labor (Nattrass, 1990a).

It is interesting to note that between 1948 and 1955, the most important squeeze on profitability was the effect of input costs. As shown in Table 13.2, the increase in productivity was entirely neutralized by a more rapid rise in the cost of inputs relative to value-added prices.[17] Relatively high input costs were also an important factor behind the decline in the output:capital ratio (Nattrass, 1990b, pp. 228-31). Given that the output:capital ratio declined faster than the profit share was able to rise, the net effect was a fall in the rate of profit.

The rate of profit in the boom period, 1960-70

During the 1960s boom (when real GDP grew at 5.7 percent p.a.) the trend decline in the rate of profit became more pronounced. In the early 1960s, the main contributing factor was the sharp deterioration of the profit share, whereas by the latter part of the decade, the output:capital ratio decline was playing an equally important role.

It is illuminating to compare these trends with those in the ACCs,[18] where during the 1960s, profit rates *rose* by 2.6 percent p.a., due to *increases* (of 0.7 percent p.a.) in the profit share, and (of 2.0 percent p.a.) in the output:capital ratio (Glyn, 1988, p. 233). Thus in contrast to the ACC growth path, the South African boom was showing distinct signs of being unsustainable. Costs were increasing faster in South Africa, and workers were better able to make gains at the expense of the profit rate.

In the 1960s, the profit share was squeezed in both periods (although more severely between 1960 and 1964) by black and white product wages rising faster than the surplus available (see Table 13.4). Between 1960 and 1964, black wage growth was so rapid that the white:black wage gap fell slightly. However, this was reversed between 1964 and 1970.

In the absence of data relating to the relationship between race, skill structure and differential rates for the job, it is difficult to explain why the growth of black wages between 1960 and 1964 was so fast relative to white wages, and to its own growth in the previous and following periods. The answer probably lies in the particular political and economic circumstances of the early 1960s.

On March 21, 1960, police in the town of Sharpeville fired on a crowd demonstrating against the pass laws. Sixty-nine people were killed. A state of emergency was declared and the African National Congress (ANC) was banned. Investor confidence plummeted along with stock prices, and South Africa's gold and foreign exchange reserves were dangerously eroded. The state responded economically with capital controls, and politically by tightening and revamping its influx control policy. The policy pursued during the 1950s, of not interfering too drastically with the supply of black labor to urban industry (Posel, 1987), came to an abrupt end. The state dedicated itself to the task of attempting to reverse the process of black urbanization. Spending on defense and armaments was increased.

The state crackdown (which *inter alia* saw many ANC leaders jailed for life in 1963), and the boom in international markets, seemed to restore confidence. Between 1960 and 1964, investment in manufacturing grew at an incredible 25 percent p.a. Under these conditions, pressure on the labor market was unavoidable and probably accounts in large part for the rapid increase in black real wages. However, two further factors were operative which helped boost the growth of black wages relative to white.

First, certain businessmen were alarmed by the political unrest and recognized that black grievances had a definite material basis to them. Business lobbies (such as the Association for the Improvement of Bantu Wages and Productivity) argued for higher black wages. Foreign companies, under pressure from the nascent sanctions campaign, also increased black wages. This process was boosted by the upward revision of many unskilled minimum wages by the Wage Board and Department of Labour.

Second, the way in which capital and white labor adjusted to job reservation in the early 1960s, had implications for black upward mobility. Given that much of the early job reservation was designed to protect whites from skilled colored and Indian competition, the poor performance of colored/Indian wages can probably be attributed to this. Factors affecting black wages were, however, rather different. In return for white wage increases, capitalists were able to secure the cooperation of white trade unions when it came to fragmenting certain skilled jobs into black semi-skilled and operative jobs (Nattrass, 1990b, pp. 146–8).

By the late 1960s, however, the performance of black wages had slackened, relative both to white wages and to the previous period. Politically and economically, blacks were weakened by the strengthening of state intervention in the labor market, the tightening of influx control, and the effective annihilation of resistance to apartheid.

Although those workers with urban residential rights may have been protected in certain instances by restrictions on the supply of black labor to the towns, the fear of losing employment (and hence also the right to remain in urban areas) would have limited black bargaining power. Legislation such as the 1967 Physical Planning and Utilization of Resources Act (which limited black employment in certain industries and areas) would have had a further dampening effect on the urban black labor market (Nattrass, 1990b, pp. 162–4).

An additional factor was the slowdown in the climb of black workers up the occupational ladder. By the late 1960s, white trade unions were becoming increasingly wary of conceding further job fragmentation and rationalizations in return for higher wages. Where concessions were made by white trade unions, these were at an extremely high price in terms of white wage increases.[19]

Between 1964 and 1970, white workers were in a very powerful position because of strong market demand for skilled labor coupled with the state's policy of job reservation. Although job reservation affected a small percentage of the workforce (approximately 5 percent), it had significant implications because skilled and some semi-skilled occupations were targeted by the legislation. As noted earlier, the threat to its use also made employers more willing to concede to the demands of the white trade unions.

It is clear from Table 13.2 that the fall in the profit share was the major impetus behind the decline in profitability during the early 1960s. However, by the late 1960s, adverse trends in both the profit share and output:capital ratio lay behind the fall in the profit rate.

The reasons for the decline in capital productivity are unclear. It is possible that restrictions on black employment along with generous government investment subsidies, could have resulted in an economically irrational degree of capital intensification (Biggs, 1982). An additional factor might also have been the number of producers (encouraged into certain markets by tariff protection) in relation to the limited size of the domestic market. Production runs long enough to reduce unit costs were ruled out as a result (South Africa, 1972; Kleu Study Group, 1983). In other words, state policy in areas other than the labor market could have further contributed to the fall in profitability.

Gold-cushioned economic decline: 1970–81

Between 1970 and 1981, the manufacturing net profit rate showed very divergent tendencies. From 1970 to 1974 the profit rate dived at its fastest pace, and between 1974 and 1981 at its slowest, over the postwar period. The profit share continued its downward trend in the early period, but then recovered to rise at 2.7 percent p.a. between 1974 and 1981.

South African rates of profit were less affected by the economic slowdown and oil-shock which beset the ACCs.[20] South Africa was able to avoid major structural adjustment because her reserves were cushioned by the sharp increase in the gold price. As can be seen in Table 13.1, the mining net profit rate grew at 18 percent p.a. between 1970 and 1974.

However, to a great extent, South Africa failed to reap the full growth potential of the gold bonanza. Rather than channeling the additional foreign exchange into productive investment, consumption and inflation were stimulated. While the gold price rose at an average annual rate of 35 percent in the early 1970s, and 19 percent between 1975 and 1981, manufacturing investment over the decade grew at the relatively slow rate of just over 7 percent p.a. Growth in the latter part of the 1970s was constrained by imported inflation and the severe blow to business confidence of the Soweto uprising in 1976. It was only from 1979 onwards that the familiar constraints of labour shortage began reasserting themselves.

As shown in Table 13.4, the profit share was squeezed between 1970 and 1974 by product wages of all racial groups, especially blacks, rising faster than the surplus available. In the latter part of the decade, however, very different trends were evident. Black wages continued to rise faster than the surplus between 1974 and

1981. However, because white product wages actually *declined*, and colored/Indian wages rose slower than the surplus, the share of profit was able to *rise*. Thus if we compare this period with the only other postwar period which shows a falling wage share (i.e. 1948–55), we see that this time it was the erosion of *white* (and to a lesser extent colored/Indian) product wages that compensated for the rise in *black* product wages! The white share of the wage bill and the white:black wage gap fell at their fastest pace during the postwar period.

The decisive reversal in the relative fortunes of white and black workers from the early 1970s has to do with the growth of black trade union militancy, as well as with other institutional and economic reasons. Between 1970 and 1974, the South African economy prospered as the gold price soared, and capital flooded into the country. As usual, the shortage of skilled and semi-skilled labor was to become the most important constraint on growth during the period. This was one of the reasons why the spontaneous Durban strike wave of 1973 provoked a relatively moderate response from the state and employers, and why substantial wage increases followed (Institute for Industrial Education, 1976, p. 145).

The rapid rise in black wages stemmed ultimately from market demand, but also from institutional factors such as Wage Board interventions,[21] the shift in emphasis on the part of the government away from job reservations,[22] foreign pressure on South African subsidiaries to increase wages, and, most importantly, the use of strike muscle to force concessions for both skilled and unskilled workers.[23] The net result was the squeezing of the manufacturing profit share.[24] For the first time, concern began to be expressed about the faster rise in average wages relative to productivity.

Between 1974 and 1981, the profit share recovered dramatically. As noted above, negative white product wage growth more than neutralized the effects of rapid black wage growth. Recent studies indicate that this should be attributed to substantial black upward mobility, rather than to increases at all skill levels (Knight and McGrath, 1987; Hofmeyr, 1990). There is even some evidence that black unskilled wages may have fallen between 1976 and 1985 (Knight and McGrath, 1987; Hofmeyr, 1990). This trend is consistent with the cooling economy and growing levels of black unemployment (Simkins, 1982).

The output:capital ratio deteriorated markedly between 1970 and 1981 as investment remained high while output growth slowed down. Why investment growth continued apace is an interesting question. It probably had to do with negative real interest rates in the 1970s,[25] fiscal investment subsidies[26] and high levels of effective protection (which increased in the 1970s) leading to an over-valued exchange rate. All these had a price-distorting effect such that capital goods were substantially cheapened.

Conclusion

This chapter has shown that contrary to popular radical beliefs, the manufacturing rate of profit in South Africa was on a trend decline over the postwar period, as was the profit share (with the exception of the periods 1948–44 and 1974–81). For the mining (and core) sectors, rising profit rates occurred only during the periods 1960–64 and 1970–74. In manufacturing, the downward plummet of the profit rate actually *accelerated* during the "apartheid boom" of the 1960s.

Radicals assumed that profit rates were buoyant as a consequence of an allegedly depressed wage share, itself the outcome of a high rate of exploitation premised on the control, disorganization and repression of black labor. Such an interpretation predicts a constant or falling wage share. However, as shown above, with the exception of the periods 1948–55 and 1974–81, the manufacturing wage share *rose*.

Given that profit rates declined, largely as a result of increasing economic power of (initially white but later black) workers, there is a need for further empirically grounded investigation into the dynamics of the South African postwar economy. The historical account provided in this chapter argues that falling profitability reflects the build-up of severe pressures (or contradictions) in the system. While profit rates were *absolutely* high enough to help finance the boom periods, the growth/accumulation path was unsustainable. Capitalists in South Africa were able to obtain a relatively high proportion of the amount available for the distribution between wages and profits, both relative to workers and as a return on their investment, but they were unable to maintain this position.

At the same time, the institutional framework of the economy was far from constant and consistent. Apartheid policies, particularly with respect to interventions in the labor market, shifted in orientation and had a varying impact across the period: the 1950s were characterized by a fairly flexible, inconsistent, and largely ineffectual influx control policy (Posel, 1987); the 1960s saw the rise of a more hardline approach to racial segregation in the labor market, which nevertheless coincided with some black occupational mobility; and the 1970s saw the erosion of job reservation and the rise of a militant and effective black trade union movement.

The effect on black wages of labor market segmentation and differentiation was considerably more ambiguous than is generally acknowledged by radicals. Influx control limited black employment options, increased the costs of dismissal, and, together with direct constraints on trade unions, inhibited workplace organization. All of these served to reduce the bargaining power of black workers. However, labor market differentiation did not necessarily depress all wages. By dampening the rate of urbanization, influx control served also to protect the wages of "legal" black urban residents.[27]

Another commonly accepted radical belief is that although white workers were made more expensive by apartheid protectionist policies, the detrimental impact of the system on black wages more than compensated for this. Again, the only period in which the data support this view is 1948–55. From then onwards, increased black bargaining power not only squeezed profits, but also accelerated the erosion of radical distinctions in the labor market and set up pressures in the political sphere for change. These trends should be reflected in our theoretical understanding of the postwar South African political economy.

The development of, and fluctuations in, the economic power of black and white workers, was a subtle and complex function of both market and institutional forces. Very different political, economic, and administrative processes were at work at different times over the years from World War II to 1981.

In so far as state policies may have actively contributed to the fall in the output:capital ratio, the idea that the state acted in the interests of manufacturing and monopoly capital from the 1960s needs qualification. State economic strategies which encouraged the "overaccumulation" of capital by artificially cheapening it through taxation, exchange, and interest rate policies, had distinctly ambiguous effects. Whereas investment and growth may well have been stimulated, the rate of profit was undermined in so far as these policies contributed to a declining output:capital ratio. Furthermore, state price control policies (especially in the 1950s and 1960s), which prevented producers from passing rising input and capital costs on to the consumer, also contributed to declining profitability.

As noted earlier, even policies which were designed to protect and encourage industry backfired in important respects. High rates of tariff protection encouraged excessive numbers of firms into certain industries and hence restricted the size of production runs below economically rational levels. Similarly, economic pressures for the development of a capital goods sector were dulled by state policies which effectively subsidized the importation of advanced machinery imports (Kaplan, 1987). Consequently, it is possible that the government's import substitution policy indirectly created the conditions for a cost squeeze on profits.

In this way, one could make the case that despite the growth-stimulating effects of import substitution, the interests of capitalism (although not necessarily the short-term interests of individual capitalists) were undermined by the South African state – albeit unintentionally. Apartheid policies were often highly contradictory attempts to cater for a racially exclusive ideology, the requirements of economic growth, the demands of white workers, and calls for socioeconomic reform.

For the above reasons, it is incorrect to periodize the postwar South African political economy in terms of the rise and decline of a coherent, stable SSA. Trends in the empirical data (most notably the rate and share of profit) do not reflect any balance between key macroeconomic variables. Furthermore, the more detailed economic history suggests that labor market and cost pressures (often exacerbated by apartheid policies) steadily eroded the initially high levels of profitability. Trends in the share and rate of profit reflect the *absence* of any happy marriage of apartheid and capitalism in terms of a stable institutional structure, or a sustainable growth path.

As noted earlier, it is theoretically possible to have a stable SSA coexisting with falling profitability. However, for a convincing case to be made, it would have to be shown that the fall in profitability occurred for reasons unrelated to systemic tensions and contradictions.

In South Africa's case, falling profitability has been argued to reflect precisely such tensions and contradictions. An SSA analysis should thus conclude that apartheid institutions and policies did *not* constitute any part of an SSA. Any attempt to argue the opposite by pointing to rapid growth or high rates of accumulation will fall foul of acceptable theoretical criteria. It is tautological and incorrect to argue that an SSA *must* have existed because rapid accumulation took place. For SSA analysis to remain a useful theoretical tool, such arguments must be rejected.

Notes

1 Neoclassical writers such as Hutt (1964), Hobart Houghton (1964), and Horwitz (1967) argued that apartheid hindered development by distorting market forces – particularly those in the labor market.

2 See Gordon *et al.*, (1982) and Kotz (1987, 1990) for an introduction to the central themes in SSA theory.

3 See Jessop (1990) for a discussion of regulation school concepts.

4 I owe this insight to David Kotz.

5 In South Africa's case, there is not a strong relationship between the rates of profit in manufacturing and mining and their respective rates of accumulation (see Nattrass [1990b], ch. 6]). For manufacturing, the rate of accumulation was rather well maintained until after 1981, despite a strong downward trend in the profit rate. For mining, despite accumulation responding to the upsurges in profitability at times of gold price rises, this had been preceded by a long period of low accumulation despite relatively buoyant profitability.

6 This method of deconstruction of the profit rate is adapted from Glyn (1988) and Glyn *et al.* (1990). I am particularly grateful to Andrew Glyn for guidance during the statistical analysis.

7 The rate of profit is best measured net because "gross profits are seldom constant throughout the life of an asset" (Armstrong *et al.*, 1984, p. 459). As output declines over the life of an asset, linear depreciation of asset values allows for a better approximation of the true rate of return on capital.

8 Net profits are approximated by the national accounting concept of net operating surplus. Operating surplus corresponds to operating profit or trading profit in business accounts and as such, measures the surplus accruing in respect of real processes of production. The operating surplus of a producer unit is equal to its value-added minus the sum of compensation of employees (which includes cash and in kind wages, employers' contributions to social security schemes and private pension schemes, etc.), indirect taxes paid by the producer less subsidies received, and consumption of fixed capital (Hill, 1979, p. 89). For the purposes of the profit rate analysis, the net operating surplus series was inflated by an estimate of the income of working proprietors. In order to obtain the above estimate, the proportion of those employed who were working proprietors was obtained from various manufacturing censuses and, following Carlin (1987), the income of working proprietors was assumed to be equal to the average wage. The net profit series is thus a measure of the surplus in value-added as defined above, including the earnings of the self-employed.

9 The capital stock series (provided by the South African Reserve Bank) is estimated according to the perpetual inventory method.

10 This series is derived from the gross value-added series in the national accounts and the same series for depreciation (provided by the South African Reserve Bank) used in the calculation of the net capital stock and the net operating surplus.

11 The net GDP deflator is the current price net domestic product divided by the constant price

gross domestic product. It thus includes the effect of price changes and the changing weight of capital consumption.

12 South Africa experienced a period of stagnant growth in the 1980s. The GDP grew at a little over 1 percent p.a. and investment declined at 2 percent p.a. The decline in the gold price, the investor-confidence shaking effects of political crisis, economic sanctions, and disinvestment along with misguided government monetary policies were the key determinants of the sharply deteriorating economic situation.

13 The use of racial classification in no way implies acceptance of official racial classification.

14 A more detailed analysis of this period can be found in Nattrass (1990a)

15 Between 1948 and 1955, productivity rose by 2.4 percent p.a., but as input prices grew at 2.4 percent p.a. faster than value-added prices, the surplus available for distribution showed no growth. Because product wages fell by 0.4 percent p.a. over the period, the wage share fell by 0.4 percent p.a., thus allowing the profit share to rise.

16 Although apartheid policy from 1948 sought to constrain the level and rate of black urbanization, in reality the nationalists (until the early 1960s) lacked both the administrative capacity to do so and the will to interfere drastically with the labor market (Posel, 1987).

17 The rise in relative input prices (which was the sharpest in the entire postwar period) was probably related to the supply and transport bottlenecks of the late 1940s and early 1950s, and to the increased import prices following devaluation in 1949 and the Korean war. Price controls operative at the time probably prevented manufacturers from passing the rise in input prices on to the consumer in the form of higher value-added prices. South African manufacturing has a very high import content and it is also possible that the policy of import substitution and import licensing (which, according to Zarenda, was the main stimulus to production in the postwar period up to [1957, p. 110]) may have had more negative effects on average profitability (by exacerbating imported input price rises) than positive (by protecting industry from international competition).

18 Data on the ACCs refers to the weighted average of the seven largest capitalist economies, i.e. USA, UK, Canada, France, Germany, Italy, and Japan.

19 This implies that the "floating up" of the color bar in the 1960s was more a characteristic of the earlier than the later period (Nattrass, 1990b, pp. 164–70).

20 Between 1973 and 1975, ACC manufacturing profitability declined by 23.6 percent p.a. (Armstrong et al., 1984, pp. 464–6) whereas it fell by only 12.1 percent p.a. in South Africa.

21 According to the chairman of the Wage Board, it was "not the duty of the Board to keep unprofitable firms in business" (quoted in the [Johannesburg] Financial Mail, January 28, 1972). Following evidence presented to it by the National Union of Distributive Workers and the National Union of Commercial and Allied Workers, the Wage Board increased minimum wages in the retail and distributive trades by 44 percent (South African Institute of Race Relations, 1974, p. 246). After the 1973 Durban strikes, the Minister of Labour instructed the Wage Board to revise key wage determinations.

22 Very few job reservation determinations were passed in the 1970s, and with the adoption of the Wiehahn Commission recommendations in 1979, job reservation was finally scrapped.

23 Given that many of the increases in wage rates following the Durban strikes were across-the-board or specifically targeted at unskilled workers (South African Institute of Race Relations, 1974, p. 203), one can assume, at least for the earlier part of the 1970s, that workers at every level achieved real gains.

24 Input costs also squeezed the profit share – largely as a result of the oil shock and subsequent exchange rate devaluations.

25 Given the high inflation rates of the 1970s (which averaged 12.6 percent p.a. between 1970 and

1975 and 14.7 percent p.a. between 1975 and 1981) the average Reserve Bank discount rates (of 6.9 percent and 9 percent respectively) were clearly negative in real terms. Likewise, the real interest rates on long-term government stocks were −2.0 percent and 1.8 percent respectively over the two periods (Kleu Study Group, 1983, p. 157).

26 The 1962 Income Tax Act allowed for high initial machinery investment and rapid depreciation allowances (and from 1978 with respect to used assets as well). This artificially cheapened the cost of capital and led to uneconomically high rates of capital investment (see Biggs [1982, pp. 15–16]).

27 For instance, Bell argues that one of the major reasons for the decentralization of industry to growth points (where restrictions on black labor do not apply) was precisely to circumvent regional and racial forms of labor market segmentation which were eroding profitability by, *inter alia*, protecting urban labor (1986, pp. 285–9).

References

Armstrong, P., A. Glyn, and J. Harrison, 1984. *Capitalism Since World War Two*. London: Fontana.

Bell, T., 1986, "The Role of Regional Policy in South Africa," *Journal of Southern African Studies*, 12(2): 276–92.

Biggs, F., 1982. "Aspects of Combining Capital and Labour in South Africa," *Studies in Economics and Econometrics*, no. 13: 5–36.

Bowles, S., D. Gordon, and T. Weiskopf, 1986. "Power and Profits: The Social Structure of Accumulation and the Profitability of the Post-war U.S. Economy," *Review of Radical Political Economics* 18(1/2): 132–67.

Carlin, W., 1987. "The Development of the Factor Distribution of Income and Profitability in West Germany," D. Phil. thesis, University of Oxford.

Davies, R., 1979. *Capital, State and White Labour in South Africa, 1900–1960*. Brighton, Sussex: Harvester Press.

Davies, R., D. Kaplan, M. Morris, and D. O'Meara, 1976. "Class Struggle and the Periodisation of the South African State in South Africa," *Review of African Political Economy*, no. 7: 4–30.

Gelb, S., 1987. "Making Sense of the Crisis," *Transformation*, no. 5: 33–50.

1991. "South Africa's Economic Crisis: An Overview," in *South Africa's Economic Crisis*, ed. S. Gelb, pp. 1–32. Cape Town: David Philips.

Gordon, D., R. Edwards, and M. Reich, 1982. *Segmented Work, Divided Workers: The Historical Transformation of Labour in the United States*. Cambridge University Press.

Glyn, A., 1988. "Behind the Profitability Trends," *Keisai Kenkyu*, July: 230–42.

Glyn, A., A. Hughes, A. Lipietz, and A. Singh, 1990. "The Rise and Fall of the Golden Age," in *The Golden Age of Capitalism: Reinterpreting the Postwar Experience*, ed. S. Marglin, pp. 126–52. Oxford: Clarendon Press.

Hill, T., 1979. *Profits and Rates of Return*. Paris: Organization for Economic Cooperation and Development (OECD).

Hobart Houghton, D., 1964. *The South African Economy*. Oxford University Press.

Hofmeyr, J., 1990. "Black Wages: The Post-War Experience," in *The Political Economy of South Africa*, ed. N. Nattrass and E. Ardington, pp. 129–47. Oxford University Press.

Horwitz, R., 1967. *The Political Economy of South Africa*. London: Weidenfeld and Nicolson.

Hutt, W., 1964. *The Economics of the Colour Bar*. London: André Deutsch.

Institute for Industrial Education, 1976. *The Durban Strikes*. Durban and Johannesburg: Institute for Industrial Education.

Jessop, B., 1990. "Regulation Theories in Retrospect and Prospect," *Economy and Society*, 19(2): 153–216.

Johnstone, F., 1976. *Race, Class and Gold*. London: Routledge and Kegan Paul.

Kaplan, D., 1977. "Class Conflict, Capital Accumulation and the State," D. Phil. thesis, University of Sussex.

1987. "Machinery and Industry: The Causes and Consequences of Constrained Development of the South African Machine Tools Industry," *Social Dynamics*, 13(1): 60–7.

Kleu Study Group, 1983. *Report of the Study Group of Industrial Development Strategy*. Pretoria: Government Printers.

Knight, J., and M. McGrath, 1987. "The Erosion of Apartheid in the South African Labour Market," unpublished mimeo., Institute of Economics and Statistics, Oxford.

Kotz, D., 1987. "Long Waves and Social Structures of Accumulation: A Critique and Reinterpretation," *Review of Radical Political Economics*, 19(4): 16–38.

1990. "A Comparative Analysis of the Theory of Regulation and the Social Structure of Accumulation Theory," *Science and Society*, 54(1): 5–28.

Lombard, J., and J. Stadler, 1980. *The Role of Mining in the South African Economy*. Bureau for Economic Policy Analysis, University of Pretoria.

Moll, T., 1988. "Mishap or Crisis? The Apartheid Economy's Recent Performance in Historical Perspective," seminar paper presented at the African Studies Institute, University of the Witwatersrand (June).

Morris, M., 1977. "State Intervention and the Agricultural Labour Supply Post-1948," in *Farm Labour in South Africa*, ed. F. Wilson, A. Kooy, and D. Hendrie, pp. 62–71. Cape Town: Sprocas.

1991. "State, Capital and Growth: The Political Economy of the National Question," in *South Africa's Economic Crisis*, ed. S. Gelb, pp. 38–58. Cape Town: David Philip.

Morris, M., and V. Padayachee, 1988. "State Reform Policy in South Africa," *Transformation*, no. 7: 1–26.

Nattrass, J., 1981. *The South African Economy: Its Growth and Change*. Oxford University Press.

Nattrass, N., 1989. "Post-war Profitability in South Africa: A Critique of Regulation Analysis in South Africa," *Transformation*, no. 9: 66–80.

1990a. "Workers, Capitalists and Apartheid, 1939–60," paper presented to the History Workshop Conference, University of the Witwaterstand, Johannesburg (April).

1990b. "Wages, Profits and Apartheid," D. Phil. thesis, University of Oxford.

Posel, D., 1983. "Rethinking the Race Case Debate in South African Historiography," *Social Dynamics*, 9(1): 50–66.

1987. "Influx Control and the Construction of Apartheid, 1948–61," D. Phil. thesis, University of Oxford.

Ramos, M., and F. Cassim, 1989. "Beyond Dependency: Peripheral Fordism in South Africa," paper presented at the Lausanne Colloquium, University of Lausanne (July).

South Africa, 1972. *Report of the Commission of Enquiry into the Export Trade of South Africa* (Reynders Commission), RP–69–1972. Pretoria: Governmental Printers.

South African Institute of Race Relations, 1974. *Race Relations Survey 1973*. Johannesburg: South African Institute of Race Relations.

Saul, J., and S. Gelb, 1981. *The Crisis in South Africa*. New York: ZED Press.

Schumpeter, J., 1976. *Capitalism, Socialism and Democracy*. London: George Allen and Unwin.

Simkins, C., 1982. "Structural Unemployment Revisited," Fact Sheet, Southern African Labour and Development Research Unit, University of Cape Town.

van Duijn, J., 1983. *The Long Wave in Economic Life*. London: George Allen and Unwin.

Weisskopf, T., 1979. "Marxian Crisis Theory and the Rate of Profit in the Post-War U.S. Economy," *Cambridge Journal of Economics*, 3: 341–78.

Wolpe, H., 1972. "Capitalism and Cheap Labour Power in South Africa: From Segregation to Apartheid," *Economy and Society*, 1(4): 425–56.

Zarenda, H., 1977. "The Policy of State Intervention in the Establishment and Development of Manufacturing Industries in South Africa," M.A. dissertation, University of the Witwatersrand.

— 14 —

The social structure of accumulation approach and the regulation approach: a US–Japan comparison of the reserve army effect

TSUYOSHI TSURU

Introduction

Two recent alternative perspectives on the role of unemployment are the social structure of accumulation (SSA) approach in the United States and the regulation approach in France. Both approaches view unemployment not merely as a proxy for the excess labor supply, but as a reflection of the social and institutional conditions supporting the labor market. The argument that unemployment (the reserve army of labor) has a dual role can be traced back to Marx (1976 [1867]). Unemployment, he asserted, "compels those who are employed to furnish more labor" (p.793) and "puts a curb on their pretensions" to higher wages (p. 792). Kalecki (1943) went a step further: persistent full employment creates "political tension" over wage increases and improvements in working conditions. This leads to a growth of the political power of the working class and an eclipse in the social position of the employing class. Hence, from the employers' viewpoint, the pressure of the unemployed is indispensable as "an integral part of the 'normal' capitalist system" (Kalecki, 1943, p. 326). Recent years have seen the diffusion of this classical insight and its application to empirical studies on wages and productivity (Boddy and Crotty, 1975; Kahn, 1980; Oster, 1980; Green and Weisskopf, 1990).

This chapter examines the reserve army effect from a perspective that integrates propositions from the SSA and regulation approaches. These approaches suggest that the magnitude of the reserve army effect on the growth of unit labor costs ought to vary according to subperiod, and that the state of labor market institutions has a significant impact on the variation of the reserve army effect. Both of these hypotheses are tested by estimating a unit labor costs equation for heavily and lightly unionized sectors for the US and Japanese economies. The empirical results support the hypotheses. The chapter closes with an institutional evaluation of the results and a discussion of their implications.

The reserve army effect

The SSA approach

The SSA theorists regard unemployment as a disciplinary device to control the behavior of workers in both production and distribution. This regulatory role is captured in the notion of the reserve army effect, i.e., the reserve army is a threat to currently employed workers. A deterioration in labor discipline (leading to wage acceleration and/or productivity slowdown) will be checked by various pressures on the employed, especially the threat of job loss. In this sense, unemployment is the ultimate regulator affecting variations in wages and labor productivity, and thus it is considered a necessary condition for the normal functioning of a capitalist economy (Bowles, 1985; Rebitzer, 1987).

A significant aspect of the SSA theorists' contribution is the marshalling of empirical evidence to prove that the reserve army effect operated normally until the late 1960s and declined thereafter. According to Gordon et al. (1984) and Schor (1985a), the growth of unit labor costs during business cycle contraction switched from procyclical changes (1948–69) to countercyclical changes (1970–80) for the US nonfarm business sector. Schor's (1985b) study is limited to changes in real wage growth, but similar variations of the reserve army effect extend to a group of nine OECD countries, including the United States and Japan. These developments were correlated with the continuation of high employment in the late 1960s and the expansion of income-replacing social expenditure in the 1970s. This, it is argued, brought about a fundamental shift in bargaining position in favor of labor. Unemployment observed in the labor market no longer effectively disciplined the employed (Weisskopf et al., 1983; Schor, 1985b).

The SSA theorists clearly show that the impact of the reserve army effect on unit labor costs changed around the late 1960s, and that this change was associated with a shift in the underlying position of employees vis-à-vis employers.

What the above type of econometric analysis has not clarified, however, is the association of variations in the strength of the reserve army effect with the development of the institutional framework of the capital–labor relationship. For these theorists, the "labor accord" is the fundamental employment relation in the postwar social structure, and its core is the system of collective bargaining agreements. Under the labor accord, employers and unions focus on the determination of the level and structure of wages and benefits, as well as the regulation of working conditions, through a process of negotiations. According to Gordon et al. (1982) and Edwards and Podgursky (1986), the accord peaked in the 1960s and then began its steady unraveling due to such pressures as conflict between management and labor and non-union competition since the early 1970s. Because the labor accord ought to shape the basic framework for the determination of wages and productivity, its rise and demise logically should have a strong association with the operation of the reserve army effect on unit labor costs. Yet this line of institutional analysis is not effectively incorporated into econometric investigations of the reserve army effect.

In addition, the SSA writers tend to underestimate the impact of the increased threat of unemployment and the transformations of the collective bargaining system in the 1980s upon the reserve army effect. For example, Schor and Bowles (1987) argue that there have been no structural changes in labor relations in recent years. They reason as follows: first, in estimating the model in which the incidence of strikes is determined by the cost of job loss (the expected income loss associated with employment termination) for union members relative to costs for employers, most of the variations in the number of strikes can be explained by variations in the cost of job loss over the period 1955–81; and, second, extending the sample period to 1983, the result is unchanged and the dummy variable for the years after 1980 is not statistically significant. This argument, however, is not consistent with their own emphasis on subperiod variations in the reserve army effect. Moreover, it contradicts the findings concerning fundamental structural changes in labor relations in the 1980s in the process of wage negotiations, the organization of production, and the management structure of decision-making, all changes which have been widely documented (see, for example, Kochan et al., [1986]).

The regulation approach

These issues have received far more attention from the regulation theorists. Their argument regarding the changes in the strength of the reserve army effect can be summarized as follows.

First, regulation theorists emphasize the role of the collective bargaining system in eliminating the reserve army effect. They characterize the postwar experience of capital accumulation as Fordism, i.e., the system of mass production combined with mass consumption. Under Fordism, regularized wage increases translate into the stable growth of domestic demand for the consumption and related industries; increases in demand stimulate the further growth of investment and result in greater labor productivity as a result of economies of scale. Productivity growth, in turn, provides the resources necessary for regularized wage increases (Boyer, 1988a). In this Fordist "virtuous" circle, the collective bargaining system produces regularized wage increases, in spite of real economic conditions. Given this growth-regime model, wages and labor productivity need not respond to short-term fluctuations of labor demand. On the contrary, a less flexible "monopolistic regulation" of wages and productivity (and thus unit labor costs) is required to contribute to sustained economic growth in the Fordist regime. Accordingly, the reserve army effect is completely eliminated by the collective bargaining system associated with Fordism (Aglietta, 1979).

Second, regulation theorists analyze the directions of restructuring in industrial relations and labor markets from the late 1970s when the Fordist growth regime began to erode. In an environment of intensified international competition and supply shocks, the existing social institutions corresponding to Fordism in general and the collective bargaining system in particular began to restrain capital accumulation. Advanced capitalist economies have pursued labor flexibility in order to enhance their international competitiveness in the post-Fordist restructuring. This labor flexibility, in regulation theorists' conceptualization, includes changes at each level of the social reproduction of the labor force, ranging from the organization of production to the mobility of workers and developments affecting social security. But this flexibility typically has been sought through the expansion of new, less rigid types of employment beyond the bounds of the collective bargaining system (e.g., personnel supply services and part-time jobs). These developments have threatened the existence of the collective bargaining system and have created a situation in which organized rather than unorganized workers have been forced to accept substantial modifications of postwar union practices regarding wages and working conditions (Boyer, 1988b).

Regulation theorists, using the conceptualization of the erosion of Fordism and the post-Fordist restructuring toward greater labor flexibility, indicate that industrial relations and labor markets in the most advanced economies were transformed in the late 1970s and early 1980s.

The arguments advanced by regulation theorists are not without problems, however. First, it is an exaggeration to argue that the reserve army effect is entirely removed by the collective bargaining system. This is evident from standard empirical results on the effect of the collective bargaining system. The presence of unions significantly weakens but does not eliminate the responsiveness of wages to the demand pressure (for example, see Flanagan [1976] and Mitchell [1980]). Additionally, the assertion concerning the complete elimination of the reserve army effect neglects the SSA theorists' finding that this effect on unit labor costs operated until the late 1960s. Second, this aspect of the regulation theory may result in little or no analysis of the reserve army effect in the 1980s; regulation theorists do not analyze the key question of how the post-Fordist restructuring has affected the reserve army effect, despite their detailed institutional observation of various aspects of labor flexibility.

Hypotheses

Neither the SSA nor the regulation approach is successful in providing a complete explanation for the changes in the magnitude of the reserve army effect over the postwar period. However, both theories provide criteria for the division of the postwar development of the labor market into subperiods, and thus supply the elements necessary to construct a hypothesis regarding the subperiod variations in the reserve army effect. As noted by the SSA theorists, the reserve army effect on the variations of unit labor costs underwent a first turning point around the late 1960s, reflecting a shift in the underlying balance of power between capital and labor – the magnitude of the reserve army effect had been high in the 1950s and 1960s, but declined in the 1970s. As the regulation theorists suggest, the reserve army effect experienced the second turning point around the late 1970s, as a result of the weakening of the collective bargaining system in the post-Fordist restructuring toward labor flexibility – the magnitude of the reserve army effect was low in the 1970s, but was once again high in the 1980s.

These propositions from the SSA and regulation approaches suggest two hypotheses. The first states that the magnitude of the reserve army effect on changes in unit labor costs varied from subperiod to subperiod: it was high in the 1950s and 1960s, low in the 1970s, and high in the 1980s. The second hypothesis is that the type of collective bargaining system has a significant impact on the variation of the reserve army effect.

Toward a simple unit labor costs equation

To analyze the subperiod-to-subperiod variations in the magnitude of the reserve army effect, while also addressing the degree of coverage of the collective bargaining system, requires data on unit labor costs over the postwar period that take into account whether the unit labor costs are affected by collective bargaining. Such data are not available for either the US or Japanese economies. The data therefore were created using an indirect procedure. For the US economy, twenty-eight nonfarm industries were separated into a heavily unionized sector with a unionization rate of over 20.4 percent (the average unionization rate) and a lightly unionized sector with a rate under 20.4 percent, utilizing the estimates of unionization rates by industry in 1970 in the Current Population Survey. For the Japanese economy, eighteen nonfarm industries were classified into a heavily unionized sector with a unionization rate of over 35.0 percent (the average) and a lightly unionized sector with a rate under 35.0 percent, utilizing unionization rates by industry in 1970 estimated from the Basic Survey of Labor Unions.[1] The annual percentage changes in the unit labor costs, defined as annual percentage changes in average hourly earnings minus annual percentage changes in output per employee-hour, were calculated for the heavily and lightly unionized sectors, as well as for all industries combined.

The next step was to identify the appropriate subperiod divisions. For this purpose, the pattern of changes in unit labor costs during business cycle contractions was observed (for a more detailed discussion, see Tsuru [1991b, pp. 415–17]). For the United States, the growth of unit labor costs shows a strong pattern of deceleration in the recessions in the 1960s, but of acceleration in the 1973–75 and 1980 downturns. However, unit labor costs resume the strong pattern of deceleration in the 1981–82 recession. For Japan, unit labor costs decelerate sharply in the contractions in the 1960s. The 1970–71 and 1973–75 recessions, however, see a much smaller deceleration of the growth of unit labor costs. Then, unit labor costs resume the pattern of deceleration after 1977. From this observation, the full period (1959–87) is divided into 1959–69, 1970–79, and 1980–87 subperiods for the United States, and 1959–70, 1971–76, and 1977–87 subperiods for Japan. This division is based on the use of a business cycle trough to trough.

To test the reserve army hypothesis, it is necessary to estimate a unit labor costs equation to represent the magnitude of the reserve army effect. Because the view emphasizing the reserve army effect focuses on the ability of demand pressure in the labor market to regulate the growth of unit labor costs in the phases of the business cycle, it might be desirable to estimate an equation only for the phases of business cycle contraction and expansion (see Schor [1985b]). However, the number of observations for each subperiod and subsector prohibits this type of analysis; instead, the standard estimates on an annual basis are used in a time-series analysis.

There is no widely accepted functional form for unit labor costs. Therefore, a simple unit labor costs equation is specified in light of the underlying equations for nominal wages and real productivity (the determinants of unit labor costs), as well as for prices that are related to the wage and productivity equations.[2] The equations used for nominal wages, real labor productivity, and prices are standard ones. First, the wage equation is such that the nominal wage changes depend on the demand pressure in the labor market, lagged changes in the consumer price index, and changes in nominal labor productivity. Second, the growth of real labor productivity is determined by changes in real wages and the growth of real output. Third, the statistical relation between prices and unit labor costs is included. If these equations are assumed, then a type of reduced-form unit labor costs equation can be specified.

The focus of the analysis is on the coefficients of the demand pressure. They are interpreted as a measure of the strength of the reserve army effect. It is often claimed that the civilian unemployment rate (US) and the total unemployment rate (Japan) have shifted upward due to changes in the demographic composition of the labor force, and therefore provide a poor measure of demand pressure. To deal with this problem, the ratio of the index of "help wanted" advertisements to the number of unemployed in the United States and the ratio of job offers to applicants for Japan have been incorporated in an alternative equation.

According to the hypothesis of the reserve army effect, the unit labor costs equation should be estimated by subperiod and by subsector. This requires the construction of pooled cross-section and time-series data to secure a sufficient number of observations. From the above discussion, the unit labor cost equation is specified as follows.

$$\dot{ULC}_{it} = a_0 + a_1 DP_t + a_2 \dot{P}_{ct-1} + a_3 \dot{Y}_{it} + a_4 \text{ (Supply shock I)}_t$$
$$+ a_5 \text{ (Supply shock II)}_t + \text{Industry dummies} + u_{it'} \qquad (1)$$

where

$\dot{ULC}_{it}$ rate of change in unit labor costs in industry i at time t

DP_t measure of the demand pressure in the labor market[3]

$\dot{P}_{ct-1}$ rate of change of the consumer price index

$\dot{Y}_{it}$ rate of growth of real output in industry i at time t

(Supply shock I)$_t$, (Supply shock II)$_t$ dummy variables for the years 1973–74 and 1978–79, included to control the influence of external shocks

Industry dummies   dummy variables for the cross-sectional units

u stochastic error term with mean zero

Table 14.1. *Unit labor costs equations for total nonfarm industries, US and Japan, 1959-87[a] (dependent variable = annual rate of change in the nominal unit labor costs)*

Independent variable	1959-69 US		1959-70 Japan		1970-79 US		1971-76 Japan		1980-87 US		1977-87 Japan	
	(1)	(2)	(3)	(4)	(5)	(6)	(7)	(8)	(9)	(10)	(11)	(12)
1. Demand pressure												
a. Ratio of help wanted ads to the number of unemployed	4.368** (6.640)	—	—	—	-9.432** (-2.037)	—	—	—	8.181* (2.854)	—	—	—
b. Civilian unemployment rate	—	30.473** (6.750)	—	—	—	-84.181** (-4.796)	—	—	—	48.273** (2.641)	—	—
c. Ratio of job offers to applicants	—	—	4.672** (4.621)	—	—	—	-2.690 (-0.900)	—	—	—	24.241** (4.750)	—
d. Total unemployment rate	—	—	—	10.394** (2.748)	—	—	—	9.830* (1.729)	—	—	—	51.956** (7.456)
2. Lagged consumer price inflation	0.328 (1.550)	0.413** (2.050)	0.229* (1.672)	-0.006 (-0.028)	-0.367 (-1.213)	-0.810** (-3.282)	-0.390** (-2.539)	-0.135 (-1.074)	0.776** (8.259)	0.766** (8.158)	0.598** (5.109)	-0.389** (-2.948)
3. Growth of real output	-0.504** (-15.447)	-0.506** (-15.559)	-0.846** (-25.205)	-0.835** (-23.849)	-0.403** (-10.666)	-0.460** (-11.879)	-0.966** (-25.738)	-0.962** (-25.860)	-0.474** (-10.485)	-0.473** (-10.433)	-0.983** (-52.078)	-0.988** (-56.456)
4. Supply shock r[b]	—	—	—	—	3.475** (3.754)	3.034** (4.443)	11.759** (6.741)	10.089** (9.374)	—	—	—	—

5. Supply shock II[c]	—	—	—	—	6.333** (4.833)	5.120 (7.979)	—	—	—	—	0.203 (0.288)
6. Intercept	−3.059** (−3.448)	−6.642** (−5.915)	−1.567 (−1.121)	−4.607* (−1.854)	18.763** (4.266)	30.204** (6.862)	12.735** (2.728)	1.071 (0.207)	−6.921** (−3.049)	−9.636** (−3.054)	−15.936** (−4.252)
Summary statistics											
Adj. R^2	0.625	0.627	0.809	0.796	0.454	0.492	0.899	0.901	0.581	0.578	0.938
S.E.E.	2.686	2.680	3.874	4.003	4.000	3.858	4.912	4.851	4.552	4.565	3.661
Durbin–Watson	2.143	2.130	1.847	1.817	1.948	2.074	2.287	2.317	2.125	2.126	2.043
Number of observations	308	308	216	216	280	280	108	108	224	224	198

Last column (additional):

5. Supply shock II[c]	−0.769 (−1.142)
6. Intercept	−17.892** (−6.498)
Adj. R^2	0.947
S.E.E.	3.390
Durbin–Watson	1.936
Number of observations	198

Notes: [a]Numbers in parentheses are *t*-statistics. The symbol * denotes significance at a 90 percent confidence level. The symbol ** denotes significance at a 95 percent confidence level. All annual rates of change are calculated as $100(\log X_t - \log X_{t-1})$.

[b]Supply shock I is a dummy variable equal to one in years 1973 and 1974.

[c]Supply shock II is a dummy variable equal to one in years 1978 and 1979.

As is clear from this, equation (1) is a least-squares dummy variables model in which the time binary variables do not appear at all (see Kmenta [1986, pp. 630–5]). It has been estimated using the OLS technique.

Empirical analysis

Econometric results

The estimated coefficients of the unit labor costs equation for the US and Japanese economies are summarized in Tables 14.1–14.3. What follows focuses on the results of the demand pressure variables.

Table 14.1 exhibits the results for the set of all nonfarm industries of the United States and Japan. For the 1959–69/1959–70 period, estimates of the effect that changes in the measures of demand pressure have on the rate of change of unit labor costs are presented with the expected signs and a 5 percent level of significance. The coefficients of the demand pressure lose their predicted signs for the 1970–79/1971–76 period (except for column 8). However, the variables representing demand pressure recover the expected signs and statistical significance for the 1980–87/1977–87 period.

Table 14.2 contains the results for the heavily and lightly unionized sectors in the United States. For the 1959–69 period, the coefficients of the demand pressure for the heavily unionized sector are, by and large, equal to or smaller than those for the lightly unionized sector. The coefficients of the demand pressure lose the expected signs or statistical significance for the 1970–79 period. Yet, in the 1980–87 period, coefficients with the expected signs and significance at the 5 percent level are recovered for the heavily unionized sector, although coefficients for the lightly unionized sector still fall in the rejection area at the 10 percent level.

Table 14.3 displays the estimated results for the heavily and lightly unionized sectors in Japan. For the 1959–70 period, the effect that the demand pressure variables had on the growth of unit labor costs in the heavily unionized sector is weaker than or equal to that effect in the lightly unionized sector. In 1971–76, the coefficients of the demand pressure variables are not statistically different from zero. For the 1977–87 period, the effect of demand pressure is once again observed, but the heavily rather than the lightly unionized sector produces the greater coefficients.

Institutional evaluation

The regression results provide support for the hypothesis concerning the subperiod to subperiod variations of the strength of the reserve army effect on the US and Japanese economies. However, the results reveal that the impact of the collective bargaining system on the reserve army effect is quite different between the 1950s/1960s and 1980s. In the 1950s and 1960s, the heavily unionized sector yielded a relatively weak or at least similar reserve army effect in comparison with

Table 14.2. Unit labor costs equations for the heavily and lightly unionized sectors, United States, 1959–87[a] (dependent variable = annual rate of change in the nominal unit labor costs)

Independent variable	1959–69				1970–79				1980–87			
	Heavy		Light		Heavy		Light		Heavy		Light	
	(1)	(2)	(3)	(4)	(5)	(6)	(7)	(8)	(9)	(10)	(11)	(12)
1. Demand pressure												
a. Ratio of help wanted ads to the number of unemployed	4.399** (6.269)	—	4.936** (2.592)	—	−11.100** (−2.193)	—	1.368 (0.118)	—	8.306** (2.607)	—	7.605 (1.251)	—
b. Civilian unemployment rate	—	30.683** (6.375)	—	34.290** (2.618)	—	−91.122** (−4.766)	—	−38.243 (−0.846)	—	48.939** (2.409)	—	45.625 (1.177)
2. Lagged consumer price inflation	0.302 (1.337)	0.387* (1.805)	0.349 (0.573)	0.449 (0.775)	−0.408 (−1.226)	−0.841** (−3.105)	−0.029 (−0.039)	−0.536 (−0.880)	0.810** (7.711)	0.799** (7.618)	0.605** (3.118)	0.597** (3.078)
3. Growth of real output	−0.481** (−13.882)	−0.483** (−13.997)	−0.664** (−6.763)	−0.665** (−6.785)	−0.395** (−9.659)	−0.454** (−10.884)	−0.436** (−4.139)	−0.476** (−4.291)	−0.480** (−10.008)	−0.479** (−9.959)	−0.273* (−1.715)	−0.272 (−1.701)
4. Supply shock I[b]	—	—	—	—	3.500** (3.463)	2.910** (3.921)	3.254 (1.391)	3.779* (2.124)	—	—	—	—
5. Supply shock II[c]	—	—	—	—	6.631** (4.628)	5.104** (7.303)	4.300 (1.312)	5.128** (3.112)	—	—	—	—
6. Intercept	−3.109** (−3.505)	−6.715** (−5.822)	0.330 (0.227)	−3.693 (−1.542)	19.949** (4.169)	31.579** (6.608)	4.125 (0.386)	14.391 (1.302)	−7.198** (−2.961)	−9.945** (−2.891)	−2.401 (−0.655)	−5.035 (−0.850)
Summary statistics												
Adj. R^2	0.628	0.630	0.618	0.619	0.448	0.490	0.449	0.461	0.596	0.594	0.336	0.332
S.E.E.	2.645	2.639	2.913	2.908	4.041	3.883	3.820	3.777	4.684	4.698	3.647	3.660
Durbin–Watson	2.095	2.081	2.236	2.235	1.943	2.063	2.081	2.220	2.101	2.102	2.090	2.087
Number of observations	264	264	44	44	240	240	40	40	192	192	32	32

Notes: [a]Numbers in parentheses are t-statistics. The symbol * denotes significance at a 90 percent confidence level. The symbol ** denotes significance at a 95 percent confidence level. All annual rates of change are calculated as $100(\log X_t - \log X_{t-1})$.

[b]Supply shock I is a dummy variable equal to one in years 1973 and 1974.

[c]Supply shock II is a dummy variable equal to one in years 1978 and 1979.

Table 14.3. Unit labor cost equations for the heavily and lightly unionized sectors, Japan, 1959–87[a] (dependent variable = annual rate of change in the nominal unit labor costs)

Independent variable	1959–70 Heavy (1)	1959–70 Heavy (2)	1959–70 Light (3)	1959–70 Light (4)	1971–76 Heavy (5)	1971–76 Heavy (6)	1971–76 Light (7)	1971–76 Light (8)	1977–87 Heavy (9)	1977–87 Heavy (10)	1977–87 Light (11)	1977–87 Light (12)
1. Demand pressure												
a. Ratio of job offers to applicants	4.042** (2.937)	—	5.653** (3.845)	—	−2.885 (−0.698)	—	−2.720 (−0.620)	—	24.067** (3.747)	—	21.765** (2.516)	—
b. Total unemployment rate	—	10.137** (1.998)	—	10.896* (1.911)	—	10.959 (1.392)	—	8.191 (1.007)	—	53.799** (6.223)	—	46.102** (3.854)
2. Lagged consumer price inflation	0.244 (1.312)	−0.018 (−0.060)	0.207 (1.029)	0.016 (0.048)	−0.324 (−1.520)	−0.044 (−0.257)	−0.488** (−2.216)	−0.262 (−1.311)	0.635** (4.308)	−0.374** (−2.288)	0.474** (2.387)	0.402* (−1.803)
3. Growth of real output	−0.849** (−20.421)	−0.841** (−19.702)	−0.842** (−14.054)	−0.817** (−12.629)	−0.972** (−22.021)	−0.966** (−22.091)	−0.939** (−10.681)	−0.942** (−11.095)	−0.991** (−51.682)	−0.995** (−56.919)	−0.859** (−10.357)	−0.866** (−11.168)
4. Supply shock I[b]	—	—	—	—	11.745** (4.885)	9.936** (6.681)	12.017** (4.602)	—	—	—	—	—
5. Supply shock II[c]	—	—	—	—	—	—	—	10.381** (6.678)	0.174 (0.195)	−0.851 (1.020)	−0.019 (−0.016)	−0.855 (−0.746)
6. Intercept	−1.085 (−0.660)	−4.323 (−1.360)	5.335** (3.189)	2.405 (0.671)	12.289* (1.965)	−0.570 (−0.082)	19.813** (3.176)	9.536 (1.307)	−15.970** (−3.445)	−18.680** (−5.633)	−10.562* (−1.698)	−12.140** (−2.666)
Summary statistics												
Adj. R²	0.813	0.805	0.785	0.754	0.907	0.909	0.851	0.854	0.960	0.967	0.671	0.705
S.E.E.	4.121	4.199	3.511	3.754	5.335	5.252	4.354	4.311	3.607	3.285	3.780	3.575
Durbin–Watson	1.710	1.693	1.851	1.790	2.318	2.358	2.211	2.256	2.011	1.932	2.102	2.007
Number of observations	132	132	84	84	66	66	42	42	121	121	77	77

Notes: [a] Numbers in parentheses are *t*-statistics. The symbol * denotes significance at a 90 percent confidence level. The symbol ** denotes significance at a 95 percent confidence level. All annual rates of change are calculated as $100(\log X_t - \log X_{t-1})$.
[b] Supply shock I is a dummy variable equal to one in years 1973 and 1974.
[c] Supply shock II is a dummy variable equal to one in years 1978 and 1979.

the lightly unionized sector. In the 1980s, by contrast, the reserve army effect asserted itself more strongly in the heavily rather than the lightly unionized sector.

Empirical studies of the effect of unions in the US economy for the period before the 1980s have shown that the existence of a collective bargaining system weakens the responsiveness of wages to the demand pressure in the labor market (Mitchell, 1980), diminishes the effect of unemployment on labor productivity (Oster, 1980), and, more importantly, decreases the association of changes in unit labor costs with changes in labor market tightness (Rebitzer, 1989). These conclusions are consistent with the results obtained in Tables 14.2 and 14.3. Hence, the key issue is to determine why the heavily rather than the lightly unionized sector has contributed to the restoration of the reserve army effect on the growth of unit labor costs since 1980 for the United States and since 1977 for Japan. Although a conclusive answer to this question has not yet been derived from systematic empirical analyses, the following points are suggestive.

The US trajectory. In the United States, since the early 1980s, the increase in concession bargaining, including both the negotiation of wage cuts or freezes and drastic changes in work rules, has been crucial. It is not simply that employers have attempted to recover union wage premiums obtained in the 1970s and early 1980s, but rather that concession bargaining has transformed the structure of the capital–labor relationship.

In the distribution process, concession bargaining shifted the terrain of wage negotiations from the national level to the company or plant level. This has led to the eclipse of pattern bargaining, which had characterized wage determination in the union sector during most of the postwar period. Additionally, concession bargaining has transformed the criterion for wage determination by introducing contingent pay plans – such as lump-sum arrangements, bonus plans, and two-tier wage structures – which directly link the workers' wages with the firm's performance. This change drastically modified the standard wage formula based on cost-of-living adjustments and annual improvement factors (Kochan *et al.*, 1986; Tsuru, 1991a). In the production process, concession bargaining converted the traditional unionized regulation of work by "job control." In manufacturing industries, new contracts involving "cooperation" between management and unions include a significant reduction in the number of job classifications and a substantial simplification of work rules. Even in non-manufacturing industries such as the telephone communication industry, various programs for work redesign have also been implemented (Kassalow, 1988).

The results of concession bargaining are concentrated exclusively in the heavily unionized sector. According to Cappelli and McKersie (1985), there were fourteen industries in which more than 20 percent of union workforce were affected by concession bargaining in 1982. All of these industries are located in the heavily unionized sector. The factors often cited to explain the shift to concession bargaining include the economic stagnation associated with the 1981–82 recession for most industries, import penetration for the primary metal, machinery, and lumber industries, and deregulation for the construction and transportation industries (Mitchell, 1985).

The lightly unionized sector has faced a situation opposite to that of the heavily unionized sector, and thus it has not contributed to the restoration of the reserve army effect. First, while the heavily unionized sector is based on the secondary industries, the lightly unionized sector corresponds broadly to the tertiary industries. This section of the economy benefited from industrial shifts toward the service sector in the United States, and thus felt little of the impact of the recession in the 1980s. Additionally, the lightly unionized sector has escaped import penetration and deregulation. Second, while there are certainly unionized establishments within the lightly unionized sector, this sector is regarded as the non-union sector. The non-union sector has not witnessed the spread of concession bargaining nor the resultant institutional rearrangements that the unionized sector has experienced. Indeed, there is little evidence that non-union wage-setting practices have been altered by developments in the 1980s (Verma and Kochan, 1985; Mitchell, 1986).

The Japanese trajectory. In Japan, the heavily unionized sector contributed more to the restoration of the reserve army effect than the lightly unionized sector because of the particular behavior of employers and employees facing economic difficulty. In the early 1970s, employers in the heavily unionized sector suffered from a slowdown in economic growth and a rapid surge of wages and external input prices. As a result of mass overemployment stemming from the decline in capacity utilization, they hoarded redundant workers within the firms, and then undertook employment adjustment. When the employers began to adjust the level of employment, they followed a step-by-step procedure: restriction of overtime work; no replacements for vacant positions; a reduction in part-time workers; intrafirm transfer of regular employees; temporary transfer to a subsidiary company; and, as a last resort, the dismissal of regular employees. This procedure, however, led to substantial increases in labor costs, given the Japanese wage structure based on seniority. In order to deal with such labor cost pressures, employers responded as follows.

In the distribution process, they sought to alter the pattern bargaining typified by the spring offensive of the 1960s (Tsuru, 1992) by strictly linking workers' wages with the firm's performance rather than going wages, as implied in the notion of the "productivity-based principle of wage determination" proposed by Japan's Federation of Employers Associations. Further, employers reduced wage increases by keeping increases within the targets (so-called "guidepost") set by the above institution. This strategy was successfully applied by the mid-1970s. In the production process, employers have made substantial efforts in rationalizing the workplace: technologically, they have concentrated new investment on a system using microelectronics equipment; and organizationally they have developed small, informal work-group activities, such as total quality control, and the joint consultation system for information sharing between management and labor. This effort resulted in higher levels of productivity growth (Hashimoto, 1989).

Japanese unions usually cooperated in these actions, because they understood that in return they obtained relative employment security for union members, and because conditions for organized labor have deteriorated. For example, the unionization rate and the number of "good jobs" traditionally provided for unionized workers have both been declining.

In contrast, the relatively weak restoration of the reserve army effect in the lightly unionized sector can be attributed to the following factors. First, despite slow growth in the 1970s, industries in the lightly unionized sector experienced continuing employment growth, benefiting from the shift toward the service industries as in the United States. Specifically, the wholesale and retail industry, the most important element of the lightly unionized sector, has seen solid employment growth despite the economic slowdown since the early 1970s (Nakashima, 1980). This means that the lightly unionized sector has not faced the kind of employment adjustment problem observed in the heavily unionized sector. Second, the lightly unionized industries are free from the pressure of international competition. According to my computation, export dependence (exports as a percentage of output) was 5.0 percent for the lightly unionized sector in the period 1977–87, compared with 13.9 percent for the heavily unionized sector.[4] Further, some industries in the lightly unionized sector have been protected by government regulations and the restriction of competition. For example, the wholesale and retail trade industry is shielded from intense competition by the Large-Size Store Regulation Act (1974), the grouping of retail stores under a manufacturing company, and the system for the maintenance of resale prices. Thus, the lightly unionized sector does not face the massive competitive pressures that could lead to a strong renewal of the reserve army effect.[5]

Conclusion

This research was motivated by propositions concerning the reserve army effect that were derived from the social structure of accumulation and regulation approaches. With some modifications, these approaches provide a theoretical basis for specifying the transition points between subperiods with differences in the strength of the reserve army effect and also for indicating the significance of the transformation of the collective bargaining system.

The empirical analysis yielded evidence on the subperiod to subperiod variations of the reserve army effect on the growth of unit labor costs for the US and Japanese economies between 1959 and 1987. Further, the empirical analysis revealed a marked difference in the pattern of the reserve army effect between the 1950s/1960s and the 1980s. This difference is interpreted as the result of a fundamental transformation in the collective bargaining system brought about by the unequal competitive pressures which were imposed in each industry in recent years.

This research does not provide a direct comparison of the international competitiveness of the two economies, but a conclusion emerges from this investigation. For the United States and Japan, it is the heavily unionized sector that has led the relatively positive restoration of the reserve army effect in recent years. In the United States, concession bargaining since the early 1980s has had a significant impact. In Japan, by contrast, similar alterations had been achieved quite rapidly in the mid-1970s without concession bargaining. The heavily unionized sector in both the United States and Japan includes the key industries for international trade, such as the transportation equipment, electrical and electronics, and primary metal industries. Hence, this gap in the time and pattern of the restoration of the reserve army effect in the heavily unionized sector may contribute at least in part to differences in competitiveness and the resultant international imbalance between the United States and Japan.

Appendix: Data sources

Unionization rate. The unionization rates by industry are calculated by dividing the number of union members by the total number of employees for each industry. For the United States, the unionization rates by industry are from US Department of Labor (1972), and Freeman and Medoff (1979). For Japan, the number of union members by industry are from Japan Ministry of Labor (1971). The number of employees by industry are from Japan Economic Planning Agency, unpublished data tape.

Unit labor costs. Annual percentage changes in unit labor costs are calculated from annual percentage changes in real output per employee-hour and annual percentage changes in average hourly earnings. For the United States, data for gross national product by industry in 1982 constant dollars are from US Department of Commerce, Bureau of Economic Analysis, data diskette for *The National Income and Product Accounts of the United States*, 1988. Persons engaged in production by industry are from US Department of Commerce (1986), and US Department of Commerce, Bureau of Economic Analysis, *Survey of Current Business*, various issues. Average weekly hours of production workers or nonsupervisory workers by industry are from US Department of Labor (1979, 1983), and US Department of Labor, Bureau of Labor Statistics, *Employment and Earnings*, various issues. Average hourly earnings of production workers or nonsupervisory workers by industry are from US Department of Labor (1979, 1983), and US Department of Labor, Bureau of Labor Statistics *Employment and Earnings*, various issues. For Japan, data for gross domestic product by industry in 1980 constant yen are from Japan Economic Planning Agency (1985, 1988, 1989). Persons engaged in production by industry are from Japan Economic Planning Agency, unpublished data tape. Indices of total hours by regular employees by industry are from Japan Ministry of Labor (1988). Indices of average monthly cash earnings and total hours by regular employees by industry are from Japan Ministry of Labor (1988).

Implicit price deflator. Annual percentage changes of implicit price deflators are used to deflate the nominal unit labor costs. For the United States, indices of implicit GNP deflator by industry are from US Department of Commerce, Bureau of Economic Analysis, data diskette for *The National Income and Product Accounts of the United States*, 1988. For Japan, indices of implicit GDP deflators are from Japan Economic Planning Agency (1985, 1988, 1989).

Ratio of help wanted advertisements to the number of unemployed. Data for the ratio of the index of help wanted advertising in newspapers to the number of persons unemployed are from US Department of Commerce, Bureau of Economic Analysis, *Business Conditions Digest*, various issues.

Civilian unemployment rate. Data for unemployed as a percentage of the civilian labor force are from US Council of Economic Advisors (1989).

Ratio of job offers to applicants. Data for the ratio of job offers to applicants except new graduates for all industries are from Japan Economic Planning agency, *Keizai Hendo Kansoku Shiryo Nenpo* (*Annual Report on Business Cycle Indicators*), various issues.

Total unemployment rate. Data for the totally unemployed as a percentage of the labor force are from Japan Management and Coordination Agency (1988).

Lagged consumer price inflation. Lagged consumer price inflation is the annual percentage change in the consumer price index lagged a year. For the United States, the consumer price index for all items is from US Council of Economic Advisors (1989). For Japan, the consumer price index (general, excluding imputed rent) is from Japan Management and Coordination Agency (1989).

Growth of real output. The growth of real output is the annual percentage change in the real output by industry. For the United States, gross national product by industry in 1982 constant dollars are from US Department of Commerce, Bureau of Economic Analysis, data diskette for *The National Income and Product Accounts of the United States* (1988). For Japan, the gross domestic product by industry in 1980 constant yen is from Japan Economic Planning Agency (1985, 1988, 1989).

Notes

1 A list of the specific industries included in each sector for the US and Japanese economies is available from the author. Sources of the data used in this chapter are given in the appendix.
2 Concerning this procedure, see Ono (1973, 1985).
3 DP_t uses the ratio of help wanted advertisements to the number of employed and the inverse of the civilian unemployment rate for the United States, and the ratio of job offers to applicants and the inverse of the total unemployment rate for Japan.
4 Exports as a percentage of output are: 9.2 percent (1959–70) and 12.9 percent (1971–76) for the heavily unionized sector; 3.6 percent (1959–70) and 5.0 percent (1971–76) for the lightly unionized sector. The figures are calculated from Japan Economic Planning Agency (1985, 1988, 1989).
5 For the implication of these developments for the pattern of growth regimes in Japan, see Uemura (1992).

References

Aglietta, M., 1979. *A Theory of Capitalist Regulation: The U.S. Experience.* London: NLB.
Boddy, R., and J. Crotty, 1975. "Class Conflict and Macro-Policy: The Political Business Cycle," *Review of Radical Political Economics*, 7(1): 1–19.

Bowles, S., 1985. "The Production Process in a Competitive Economy: Walrasian, Neo-Hobbesian, and Marxian Models," *American Economic Review*, 75(1): 16–36.

Boyer, R., 1988a. "Formalizing Growth Regimes," in *Technical Change and Economic Theory*, ed. G. Dosi *et al.*, pp. 608–30. London: Pinter.

1988b. (ed.), *The Search for Labour Market Flexibility: The European Economies in Transition.* Oxford: Clarendon Press.

Cappelli, P., and R. B. McKersie, 1985. "Labor and the Crisis in Collective Bargaining," in *Challenges and Choices Facing American Labor*, ed. T. A. Kochan, pp. 227–45. Cambridge, Mass.: MIT Press.

Edwards, R., and M. Podgursky, 1986. "The Unraveling Accord: American Unions in Crisis," in *Unions in Crisis and Beyond: Perspectives from Six Countries*, ed. R. Edwards *et al.*, pp. 14–60. Dover, Mass.: Auburn House.

Flanagan, R. J., 1976. "Wage Interdependence in Unionized Labor Markets," *Brookings Papers on Economic Activity*, 3: 635–81.

Freeman, R. B., and J. L. Medoff, 1979. "New Estimates of Private Sector Unionism in the United States," *Industrial and Labor Relations Review*, 32(2): 143–74.

Gordon, D. M., R. Edwards, and M. Reich, 1982. *Segmented Work, Divided Workers: The Historical Transformation of Labor in the United States.* Cambridge University Press.

Gordon, D. M., T. E. Weisskopf, and S. Bowles, 1984. "Long-Term Growth and the Cyclical Restoration of Profitability," in *Nonlinear Models of Fluctuating Growth*, ed. R. M. Goodwin *et al.*, pp. 86–102. New York: Springer-Verlag.

Green, F., and T. E. Weisskopf, 1990. "The Worker Discipline Effect: A Disaggregative Analysis," *Review of Economics and Statistics*, 72(2): 241–9.

Hashimoto, J., 1989. "Kigyo Keiei to Roshi Kankei (The Management of Firms and Labor Relations)," in *Series Sekai Keizai IV Nihon (World Economy Series, IV: Japan)* ed. H. Baba, pp. 81–154. Tokyo: Ochanomizu Shobo.

Japan Economic Planning Agency, 1985. *Syowa 55 Nen Kijun Kaitei Kokumin Keizai Keisan Hokoku (Report on Revised National Accounts on the Basis of 1980)*, vol. II.

1988. *Choki Sokyu Suikei Kokumin Keizai Keisan Hokoku (Report on National Accounts from 1955 to 1969)*.

1989. *Kokumin Keizai Keisan Nenpo (Annual Report on National Accounts)*.

Japan Management and Coordination Agency, Statistics Bureau, 1988. *Rodo Ryoku Chosa Nenpo (Annual Report on the Labor Force Survey), 1987.*

1989. *Shohisya Bukka Shisu Nenpo (Annual Report on the Consumer Price Index), 1988.*

Japan Ministry of Labor, Bureau of Policy Planning and Research, 1971. *Rodo Kumiai Kihon Chyosa Hokoku (Basic Survey of Labor Unions), 1970.*

1988. *Maitsuki Kinro Tokei Chosa: Koyo, Chingin, Rodojikan Shisu (Indices of Employment, Wages, and Hours from Monthly Labor Survey).*

Kahn, L. M., 1980. "Bargaining Power, Search Theory and the Phillips Curve," *Cambridge Journal of Economics*, 4(3): 233–44.

Kalecki, M., 1943. "Political Aspects of Full Employment," *Political Quarterly*, 14(4): 322–31.

Kassalow, E. M., 1988. "Concession Bargaining: Towards New Roles for American Unions and Managers," *International Labour Review*, 127(5): 573–92.

Kmenta, J., 1986. *Elements of Econometrics*, 2nd edn. New York: Macmillan.

Kochan, T. A., H. C. Katz, and R. B. McKersie, 1986. *The Transformation of American Industrial Relations.* New York: Basic Books.

Marx, K., 1976 [1867]. *Capital*, vol. I, Harmondsworth: Penguin.

Mitchell, D. J. B., 1980. *Unions, Wages, and Inflation.* Washington, D.C.: The Brookings Institution.

1985. "Shifting Norms in Wage Determination," *Brookings Papers on Economic Activity*, 2: 575–608.

1986. "Explanations of Wage Inflexibility: Institutions and Incentives," in *Wage Rigidity and Unemployment*, ed. W. Beckerman, pp. 43–76. Baltimore: Johns Hopkins University Press.

Nakashima, H., 1980. "Daisanji Sangyo Koyo no Tokei Bunseki (A Statistical Analysis of Employment in Tertiary Industries)," in *Daisanji Sangyoka to Koyo Mondai (Tertialization and the Employment Problem)*, ed. G. Omiya, pp. 225–89. Tokyo: Nihon Rodo Kyokai.

Ono, A., 1973. *Sengo Nihon no Chingin Kettei (Wage Determination in Postwar Japan)*. Tokyo: Toyo Keizai Shinposha.

1985. "Rodo Shotoku no Bunpai to Keizai Seichoritsu (The Distribution of Labor's Share and the Rate of Economic Growth)," *Nihon Rodo Kyokai Zasshi*, 319: 37–48.

Oster, G., 1980. "Labour Relations and Demand Relations: A Case Study of the 'Unemployment Effect'," *Cambridge Journal of Economics*, 4(4): 337–48.

Rebitzer, J. B., 1987. "Unemployment, Long-Term Employment Relations, and Productivity Growth," *Review of Economics and Statistics*, 69(4): 627–35.

1989. "Unemployment, Long-Term Employment Relations and the Determination of Unit Labour Cost Growth in US Manufacturing Industries," *International Review of Applied Economics*, 3(2): 125–47.

Schor, J. B., 1985a. "Wage Flexibility, Social Welfare Expenditures, and Monetary Restrictiveness," in *Money and Macro Policy*, ed. M. Jarsulic, pp. 135–54. Boston: Kluwer-Nijhoff.

1985b. "Changes in the Cyclical Pattern of Real Wages: Evidence from Nine Countries, 1955–80," *Economic Journal*, 95: 452–68.

Schor, J. B., and S. Bowles, 1987. "Employment Rents and the Incidence of Strikes," *Review of Economics and Statistics*, 69(4): 584–92.

Tsuru, T., 1991a. "The Reserve Army Effect, Unions, and Nominal Wage Growth," *Industrial Relations*, 30(2): 251–70.

1991b. "Unit Labor Costs, the Reserve Army Effect, and the Collective Bargaining System," in *Making Economies More Efficient and More Equitable: Factors Determining Income Distribution*, ed. T. Mizoguchi, pp. 407–35. Tokyo: Kinokuniya and Oxford University Press.

1992. "Shunto: The Spillover Effect and the Wage-Setting Institution in Japan," Discussion Paper no. 51, International Institute for Labor Studies, Geneva.

Uemura, H., 1992. "Growth and Distribution in the Post-War Regime of Accumulation: A Theory and Realities in the Japanese Economy," *Mondes en Developpement*, 179/80: 135–51.

US Council of Economic Advisors, 1989. *Economic Report of the President*.

US Department of Commerce, Bureau of Economic Analysis, 1986. *The National Income and Product Accounts of the United States, 1929–1982*.

US Department of Labor, Bureau of Labor Statistics, 1972. *Selected Earnings and Demographic Characteristics of Union Members, 1970*.

1979. *Employment and Earnings, United States, 1909–1979*.

1983. *Supplement to "Employment and Earnings."*

Verma, A., and T. A. Kochan, 1985. "The Growth and Nature of the Nonunion Sector within a Firm," in *Challenges and Choices Facing American Labor*, ed. T. A. Kochan, pp. 89–117. Cambridge, Mass.: MIT Press.

Weisskopf, T. E., D. M. Gordon, and S. Bowles, 1983. "Hearts and Minds: A Social Model of U.S. Productivity Growth," *Brookings Papers on Economic Activity*, 2: 381–441.

The global economy:
new edifice or crumbling foundations?

DAVID M. GORDON

It is now virtually a commonplace among leftist observers and activists that we have recently witnessed the emergence of a New International Division of Labour (NIDL) and the Globalization of Production (GOP). For many, these twin tendencies manifest such deep structural transformations in the world economy that group or government efforts to swim against the currents are becoming increasingly ineffectual, if not futile. The power of labor, community and the state has seemed to wither as multinational corporations sweep irresistibly around the globe. The roots of these concerns, at least in the advanced capitalist countries, are obvious – manifested, for example, in rising unemployment, sectoral devastation in many traditional industries, and consistent corporate demands for concessions on wages, benefits and working conditions. Intensifying international competition appears to be casting its shadow more and more broadly across the economic landscape, chilling the spirit of growing numbers of organized and unorganized workers alike.

Some of these concerns are clearly warranted, since there have been striking changes in the dynamics of the world economy over the past fifteen years. But many others stem from a transposition of trend and long cycle, confusing the effects of continuing stagnation in the world capitalist economy with the auguries of a transformation of the global capitalist order. It is not always easy to discriminate between the decay of an older order and the inauguration of a new. I argue in this chapter, indeed, that widespread perceptions about the NIDL and the GOP have been significantly distorted and that much of the conventional wisdom prevailing on the left (and elsewhere) about recent changes in the global economy requires substantial revision. These changes are best understood not as a symptom of structural transformation but rather as a consequence of the erosion of the social structure of accumulation which conditioned international capitalist prosperity during the 1950s and 1960s.

Prevailing perceptions of a changing global economy

Distinguishing among secular, crisis, and transformational trends in the global economy would be difficult enough. Our task is further complicated by a difference between two somewhat divergent hypotheses about structural transformations, which I shall refer to respectively as the NIDL and the GOP hypotheses. The NIDL perspective stresses a new division of labor between the North and the South, the advanced and the developing countries.[1] In a critical review of this perspective, Dieter Ernst has usefully summarized its internal logic:

> According to the NIDL theory, a new capitalist world economy has emerged, its main feature being a massive migration of capital from major OECD countries to low-cost production sites in the Third World. The main purpose of establishing such a new international division of labour is to exploit reserve supplies of labour on a world scale. This type of an internationalization of capital requires the existence of world markets for labour and production sites, and of one global industrial reserve army of labour. (Ernst, 1981, p. 287)

The GOP perspective places much less emphasis on the movement of production from the North to the South and much more weight on the centralization and concentration of capital through two related developments: first, the spreading importance of decentralized production sites in both the advanced and the developing countries; and second, the increasingly centralized control and coordination by transnational corporations (TNCs) of these decentralized production units. These two trends have combined, according to the GOP, to foster both increasing international interdependence and enhanced TNC leverage over national governments and domestic unions.[2]

Global decay, not transformation

I am skeptical about the evidence supporting these views of structural transformation, and have provided a detailed empirical critique elsewhere (Gordon, 1988). If we are not yet experiencing a fundamental transformation in the global economy, how do we explain recent appearances? In what follows, I shall offer a very schematic alternative interpretation, arguing that we have been witnessing the decay of the postwar global economy rather than the construction of a fundamentally new and enduring system of production and exchange. This alternative account builds largely upon the analytic foundations of the general "social structure of accumulation" (SSA) approach.[3]

Applied to the period following World War II, this analysis emphasizes the challenges to capitalist control which by the 1960s had begun to undermine the long postwar boom in the advanced capitalist countries. Corporate profitability in the United States and in many other countries declined dramatically from the mid-sixties to the early seventies. Plunging profitability then dampened investment, resulting in increasingly stagnant accumulation after the early seventies. This stasis contributed to a corresponding stagnation in aggregate output. And, as corporations and their allies in the state began with intensifying vigor to take the offensive against their challengers from the mid-seventies on, both economic and political instability were amplified, leading to an increasing uncertainty of economic prospects and a heightened rabidity of neo-conservative assaults against the working majorities throughout many of the advanced capitalist countries.[4]

The postwar boom itself had depended on three crucial institutional features of the global economy.[5] (1) Both domestic growth in the advanced countries and their relative access to international trade were based on a tightly structured and carefully negotiated relationship between productivity growth and wage growth. (2) State policy during the expansion period, itself grounded in the security provided by the Bretton Woods system and the central role of the US dollar, encouraged trade growth among the advanced countries, leading to an increase in the share of international trade taking place among advanced countries from 40 percent in 1953–55 to 61 percent in 1973. (3) The combined effect of these first two trends contributed, other things being equal, to a close relationship between movements in the relative unit labor costs of advanced capitalist economies and changes in their relative shares of world markets and trade growth.

From the mid-1960s the foundations of this postwar system began to be eroded. Increasingly from the late 1960s and early 1970s, a sequence of interconnected global tendencies became more and more pronounced. (1) As corporate profits on fixed direct investment fell in most of the advanced countries, leading to increasing uncertainty and hesitation about real productive investment, there was a consequent tendency toward "paper investment" or what is otherwise called "increases in financial assets." (2) Because of movement toward flexible exchange rates after the collapse of the Bretton Woods system in 1971, there was an increasing synchronization of business cycles among the advanced countries after 1971, leading to increasingly volatile fluctuations of economic activity.[6] When one economy sneezed, others echoed. (3) Exchange rate fluctuations themselves became increasingly volatile, further reinforcing uncertainty about global conditions and expectations. (4) This prompted governments to pay more and more attention to money-market intervention in order to insulate their economies from exchange rate fluctuations. These interventions, in turn, led to increasing volatility and international variance over time in short-term interest rates. (5) This led, other things being equal, to further preoccupation with paper investment and to increasingly rapid movement of short-term financial capital across international borders.[7]

Global instability

This set of interrelated and mutually reinforcing tendencies obviously affected the investment horizons and global behavior of multinational capital. Three effects of this spreading global instability have been most important and have informed widespread perceptions of underlying international transformation. First, stagnation has spread everywhere and affected everyone's conditions and expectations. Perceptions of deindustrialization, at least in the United States, have resulted almost entirely from slower growth in final demand – and yet give rise to impressions of import competition. Second and consequently, multinational corporations have sought increasing protection from falling profits and spreading instability by searching for production enclaves where rates of profit on current investment could somehow be "protected" by special privileges and by higher rates of exploitation. Third, and probably most important in shaping recent perceptions, TNCs have sought stable and insulated political and institutional protection against the increasing volatility of international trade and the collapse of dollar-based "free-market" expansion of international trade growth. "Over the past ten years," a 1984 United Nations (1985, p. 11) survey concluded, "flexible exchange rates generated an erratic pattern in relative prices and made basic signals of resource allocation very noisy." In this respect, I would argue that the distinctive features of the newly industrializing countries (NICs) are not their low wages or their technical adaptations, since wages are low almost everywhere in the less developed countries (LDCs) and new technologies could be applied anywhere. Rather, what seems especially striking about the NICs is the increasingly political and institutional determinations of production and trading relationships. TNCs negotiate with each other and host countries for joint production agreements, licensing, and joint R&D contracts. They search among potential investment sites for institutional harbors promising the greatest protection against an increasingly turbulent world economy.

This is a highly schematic account and its generalizations can be adequately sub-stantiated only by much more detailed and quantitatively rigorous analysis than I have yet been able to pursue. I limit myself to a brief and purely illustrative review of some empirical trends which are at least consistent with and tend to support this institutional historical account.[8] First, foreign direct investment has become increasingly selective. Of the stock of total direct investments received by LDCs, the share received by tax havens and the NICs increased from 50.6 percent in 1967 to 70 percent in 1978, while the share of other non-OPEC LDCs fell from 21.7 percent to 13 percent over the same period (Andreff, 1984, table 4). By the end of the 1970s, nearly half of all manufacturing exports by majority-owned affiliates of US-based TNCs to the United States emanated from only four countries: Brazil, Mexico, Singapore, and Hong Kong. Of total employment in Export Promotion Zones in 1978, similarly, 72 percent was located in just seven countries: The Republic of Korea, Singapore, Malaysia, the Philippines, Hong Kong, Mexico, and Brazil (United Nations Centre on Transnational Corporations, 1983, pp. 160, 155).

Further, TNCs' investment and production for export in LDCs is now concentrated in highly specialized and institutionally particular economic sites. TNC affiliates in these protected offshore sites indeed enjoy a modern form of colonial trading privileges. Robert E. Lipsey and Merle Yahr Weiss (1981) report, for example, that US exports to LDCs are a positive function of the number of US-owned affiliates in those countries, indicating that foreign competitors are at least partly screened out of access to those countries by the presence of US-owned affiliates. Affiliates of firms from a single dominant home country, furthermore, now account for more than 50 percent of all affiliates located in 73 of 124 developing countries, while only 6 of 25 Developed Market Economies (DME) hold the same position of single-country dominance (United Nations Centre on

Transnational Corporations, 1983, table 11.10). This leads to the apparent corollary that NIC economic fortunes bear a relatively direct positive relationship to the degree of TNC involvement in, and trading relationships with, them.[9]

The net result, as several others have also stressed, is an increasingly differentiated "Third World." Instead of flowing more and more widely around the globe, capital is on the contrary settling down in a few carefully chosen locations. Four different kinds of LDCs can be distinguished, even at a superficial level. One category, best represented by the East Asian NICs, has received continually expanding investment (at least until the early 1980s) primarily for the purposes of financial services and production for export back to the advanced countries. A second category is best represented by the Latin American NICs, toward which foreign investment continues to flow predominantly for production aimed at the large home markets. A third comprises the oil-exporting countries whose fortunes increased dramatically during the 1970s and now vacillate with the cobweb cycles of price hikes and oil gluts. The fourth category includes at least 75–80 developing countries which have been shunted off to a side spur, virtually derailed in the drive for access to global resources.

This kind of differentiation is illustrated by the evident trend, reported in Lipsey (1982) and MacEwan (1982), that US-owned affiliates abroad are increasingly likely to direct their exports to the United States primarily or even exclusively if located in the Asian NICs: the ratio of exports to total sales of US majority-owned foreign affiliates in Asia had increased from 23.1 percent in 1966 to 61.9 percent in 1977, for example, and roughly half of this increase was accounted for by the rise in the share of exports to the US (out of total sales) over the same period.[10] In Latin American countries, by contrast, more than 90 percent of the sales of US manufacturing affiliates, in 1977, were still directed to local markets, and that percentage had scarcely changed since the mid-1960s.[11]

One consequence, apparently, is a significant shift in international trading patterns away from a trans-Atlantic to a trans-Pacific pattern of trading specialization.[12] In 1970, for example, 28.2 percent of European DMEs' exports went to the United States, but that portion fell to 20.9 percent in 1983. In 1970, similarly, 30.4 percent of US exports traveled to European DMEs but only 25.2 percent in 1983. The same reduction of trans-Atlantic flows affected the rest of the Americas: in 1970, 29.6 percent of Latin American exports traveled to the European DMEs; that share had dropped to 18.4 percent in 1983. In 1970, by contrast, 23.9 percent of US imports had come from Japan and other Asian countries; by 1983, that trans-Pacific share had increased to 33.8 percent. Out of total world trade, trans-Atlantic trade fell from 13.1 percent in 1970 to 8.7 percent in 1983 while Pacific Basin trade increased from 10.2 percent in 1970 to 14.2 percent in 1983.[13]

Commentary

Several critical points emerge from this analysis which deserve some further attention.

(1) *Determinants of foreign direct investment.* Popular impressions suggest that TNCs choose their investment sites in order to capitalize on low wages and surplus labor abroad. This factor has been much exaggerated and can be substantially clarified by some recent analyses of patterns of foreign direct investment. Two recent studies of foreign direct investment make possible some comparisons of the relative importance of these determinants. In a study of foreign direct investment (FDI) to fifty-four LDCs, Friedrich Schneider and Bruno S. Frey have found that labor-force wage and skill-level characteristics were by far the least important among factors affecting foreign direct investment in the period 1976–80. The combined importance of the size of the home market, price/exchange-rate stability, and political/institutional stability was fifteen times greater than the influence of relative wage costs and skill levels. Between 1976 and 1980, moreover, the relative influences of price stability and political/institutional stability each increased by nearly a third while the relative influence of wage/skill effects declined by about one-sixth (Schneider and Frey, 1985, pp. 167–75).[14] In a study of US FDI to a combined sample of twenty-four DMEs and LDCs, Timothy Koechlin (1989) has also found that the home market and political instability factors were very important. In pooled analysis for the period from 1966 to 1983, he estimates that wage differentials accounted for only about 11 percent of the explained variance in US foreign direct investment among those countries.[15]

How is it possible that relative wages matter so little in determining investment? There are three main reasons. First, in many commodities, labor costs are a relatively small proportion of total costs; proximity to large home markets will matter much more than variations in wage costs, at the margin, among possible investment sites. Second, particularly in recent years, exchange rates have shown much greater volatility than wages, so those countries with relatively stable price and trade horizons are much more exceptional than those with relatively low labor costs. Third, and probably most important, investments in plant and equipment must be amortized over the medium run, say ten years, while larger investments in infrastructure and distribution systems must be recouped over even longer periods. What matters most, for those kinds of investments, is the general institutional climate and its prospective evolution over the period of a decade, not simply current unit labour costs. Since, as we have all noticed, political and institutional instability has been bouncing all over the map in the Third World, these sets of influences are especially likely to play an important – and doubtlessly increasing – role in a fragile international environment.

(2) *Flows of productive and financial capital.* The preceding analysis suggests an interesting and important contrast between the dynamics of productive investment and of financial investment around the globe. I have argued that flows of productive capital have become increasingly selective, oriented more and more toward a few preferred havens in the stormy global seas. At the same time, many have observed that financial funds are flowing more and more easily and rapidly around the world in veritable torrents of liquid capital. How do these two developments fit

together? Do the trends in financial flows not support the NIDL/GOP perspective even if the increasing selectivity of productive investment seems somewhat inconsistent?

In this context, it is important to view productive and financial investments as either complementary or competing, depending on the circumstances. When economic conditions are prosperous and stable, financial capital flows help support and even foster productive investment. But when the economy has become stagnant and unstable, investors tend to move their capital out of productive investments – because of increasingly cloudy longer-term prospects – and into short-term financial investments. The investment climate becomes increasingly speculative. The past two decades appear to have illustrated the latter dynamic. As the rate of return on fixed investment in plant and equipment has declined and as global economic conditions have become increasingly volatile, firms and banks have moved toward paper investments. The new and increasingly efficient international banking system has helped to foster an accelerating circulation of liquid capital, bouncing from one moment of arbitrage to another. Far from stimulating productive investment, however, these financial flows are best understood as a symptom of the diminishing attractiveness and increasing uncertainty about prospects for fixed investment.

(3) *Different sources of import competition.* The NIDL/GOP hypotheses gain much of their plausibility from the phenomenon of intensifying import competition. But increasing import competition in the advanced countries over the past fifteen years has had various sources which need to be carefully distinguished. One source, of course, has been the other advanced economies and particularly the Japanese economy. The Japanese success story deserves careful attention. But it is not primarily or even significantly a story of low-wage competition. Relative wages in Japan have increased with great rapidity during the period of its continued ascendancy. The Japanese story, by and large, is a tale of corporatist collaboration between large corporations and the state, pushing for modernization and relative advantage in international markets. While this kind of competition is certainly a new and probably permanent feature of the international environment, its implications are substantially different from what some of the NIDL/GOP analyses would imply. We return to these implications in the next section.

A second source of import competition is from goods and services produced by the foreign affiliates of TNCs which choose to ship their capital overseas and produce for re-export rather than cope with production conditions in the domestic economy. This has become an important dimension of import competition. But it is not obvious that it is either as large or as rapidly accelerating as the NIDL/GOP hypotheses would suggest. Imports to the US from the majority-owned foreign affiliates of US TNCs comprised only 17 percent of total US imports in 1982 and had not increased since the mid-1960s.[16] It is useful once again to view these trends in perspective. In 1983, only 5 percent of all non-petroleum imports to the United States came from US TNC affiliates in developing countries.[17]

A third significant source of imports is enterprises in newly industrializing countries in which capital has been to a significant degree indigenously generated and enterprises are largely controlled domestically. South Korea is perhaps the best example of this type. Here too, however, the sources of relative expansion need to be interpreted carefully. The South Korean model is neither necessarily durable nor clearly replicable. It has not built principally on the advantages of low wages, as noted earlier, but on a particular conjuncture of state capital and state repression. Recent political developments in South Korea further underscore the risks in projecting that model forward as a permanent fixture in the global environment.

(4) *Multinational power.* It is common, finally, to assume that the power of TNCs has significantly increased throughout the world over the past decade or more. But it is not at all obvious, in light of the preceding analysis, that such increases have occurred. I noted earlier that there has been increasing competition among multinationals as a result of the declining relative power of US TNCs. This increasing intercorporate competition has been coupled with an increasingly assertive attitude toward multinationals by many governments, particularly in the Third World. Both outright nationalizations and joint ownership agreements have been imposed on multinationals with increasing frequency since the late 1960s. MacEwan (1982, pp. 9–10) stressed the dual character of these arrangements:

> [It is true that when] multinationals are forced into joint ventures with local capital, they can often turn the relationship to their own advantage, using local partners as instruments to gain a more thorough foothold in the local economy. Nonetheless, the resistance of the multinationals to these changes should not be discounted. Regardless of the degree to which they are able to make the best of a changing situation, the foundations of their long run control are seriously threatened by the changes that are being imposed upon them.[18]

While there may have been some attenuation of these trends during the 1980s as a result of cutbacks in government financing in countries like Singapore and Taiwan and austerity programs imposed on debtor countries by international financial authorities, it is not obvious that the TNCs have themselves increased their leverage during this period. Inter-multinational competition and the volatility of the international environment, if anything, have intensified with continued international stagnation and the wide swings of the dollar since 1979.

It is perhaps most useful, at a more abstract level, to view the relationship between multinationals and governments as both cooperative and competing, both supportive and conflictual. They operate in a fully dialectical relationship, locked into unified but contradictory roles and positions, neither the one nor the other partner clearly or completely able to dominate. Susan Strange (1986, p. 302) echoes this conclusion: "there is a symbiosis between state and transnational corporation from which both benefit ... they are allies as well as competitors or opponents."

(5) *Capital mobility.* Many conventional renditions of the NIDL/GOP hypotheses suggest a more competitive and open global economy since the early 1970s. My own account suggests the opposite. One possible criterion for evaluating this

difference in expectations has to do with capital mobility. The NIDL/GDP perspectives would suggest intensifying competition and an increasingly unrestrained and rapid mobility of capital since the early to mid-1970s, a pace of circulation which Bluestone and Harrison (1982) call the "hypermobility of capital." The analysis sketched above would appear to suggest a diminishing importance of labor costs and dampened mobility of capital since the mid-1970s – as corporations have placed increasing emphasis on investment and production in havens from the swirling trade winds. In order to assess these expectations, we can look at the degree of variability in profit rates among countries. Other things being equal, increasing capital mobility and its associated international competition should result in a reduction in the variance of profit rates among national economies – the classic tendency toward an equalization of profit rates. By contrast, again holding other factors constant, decreased capital mobility should result in a modulated tendency toward equalization of profit rates and even, perhaps, in a widening variability of profitability among countries.

Evidence is difficult to obtain for these purposes and I have not conducted separate primary research on profit rate variations. There are nonetheless some basic data, constructed in consistent fashion, for net rates of return in manufacturing from 1952 through 1983 for the seven leading advanced countries.[19] I have calculated the coefficient of variation in manufacturing profitability among these seven countries and plotted the resulting index in Figure 15.1.

What do the numbers tell us? We would expect a rising coefficient of variation during the period of movement toward the peak of the postwar long swing, particularly as US economic power helped provide some rents accruing to US corporate advantage and as relatively protectionist policies bore economic fruit in Japan. We would then expect a diminishing coefficient of variation from the mid-1960s to the early 1970s as increasing international competition began to threaten US corporate profits and pull it toward the mean of the other advanced countries.

The index plotted in Figure 15.1 confirms these expectations. But what about the subsequent period? If the NIDL/GOP hypotheses are correct, we should expect a continuing narrowing of profit rates, as a result of increasing international competition, through the early 1980s. But we find, in fact, the opposite, with a sharp increase in the coefficient of variation of manufacturing profit rates from 1977 through 1982.[20] This trend would appear to be more consistent with the SSA-decay perspective.[21]

Conclusions

The analysis of the previous section, however schematic, helps clarify some important differences from prevailing views on recent changes in the global economy. Two major differences of analytic emphasis seem most important. First, I would argue that we have *not* witnessed movement toward an increasingly "open" international economy, with productive capital buzzing around the globe, but that

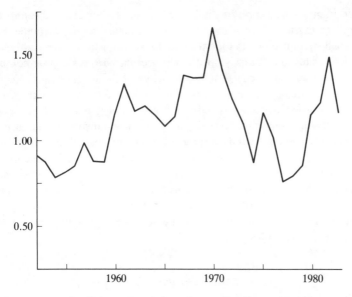

Fig. 15.1. Coefficient of variation of manufacturing profitability among seven advanced countries. (*Source*: Calculated from data in Armstrong and Glyn [1986, table 15].)

we have moved rapidly toward an increasingly "closed" economy for productive investment, with production and investment decisions increasingly dependent upon a range of institutional policies and activities and a pattern of differentiation and specialization among the LDCs. The international economy, by the standards of traditional neoclassical and Marxian models of competition, has witnessed *declining* rather than *increasing* mobility of productive capital. Production and investment decisions are less, not more, influenced by pure market signals about short-term cost and price fluctuations. Second, and correspondingly, the role of the state has grown substantially since the early 1970s; state policies have become increasingly decisive on the international front, not more futile. Governments have become more and more involved in active management of monetary policy and interest rates in order to condition exchange rate fluctuations and short-term capital flows. They have become potentially and actually decisive in bargaining over production and investment agreements. And, small consolation though it may be, in an era of spreading monetarist conservatism, everyone including transnational corporations has become increasingly dependent upon coordinated state intervention for restructuring and resolution of the underlying dynamics of crisis.[22]

But why the fuss? Some who have seen or heard early versions of this analysis have wondered if I was splitting hairs, emphasizing differences beyond any reasonable proportions. (One friend remarked that he had never known me "to hang so closely on a second derivative.") I think that these differences in expectations matter, in the end, for political reasons. The NIDL/GOP perspectives have helped foster, in my view, a spreading political fatalism in the advanced countries. If we struggle to extend the frontiers of subsistence and security at home, one gathers, we shall stare balefully at capital's behind, strutting across the continents and seas, leaving us to amuse ourselves with our unrealized dreams of progress, and the reality of our diminishing comparative advantage.

I disagree with these political inferences. The breakdown in the postwar system has reflected an erosion of socially determined institutional relationships. TNC responses since the early 1970s reflect their own political and institutional efforts to erect some shelters against the winds of spreading economic instability. The TNCs are neither all-powerful nor fully equipped to shape a new world economy by themselves. They require workers and they require consumers. Workers and consumers helped shape the structure of the postwar system, and we are once again in a position to bargain over institutional transformation. The global economy is up for grabs, not locked into some new and immutable order. The opportunity for enhanced popular power remains ripe.

Acknowledgments

This chapter is drawn from a much longer and more detailed analysis in Gordon (1988). It has not been updated to reflect developments since the mid-1980s. I am grateful to Lyuba Zarsky for excellent research assistance. I would also like to thank Perry Anderson, Samuel Bowles, Mike Davis, Bennett Harrison, Timothy Koechlin, Arthur MacEwan, Alain Lipietz, Hugo Radice, and Bill Tabb for helpful reactions to earlier formulations of some of these arguments.

Notes

1 The NIDL hypothesis is probably best represented by Fröbel *et al.* (1980).

2 Although the literature does not stress this distinction between the NIDL and the GOP perspectives, the latter is probably best represented by Ernst (1981), Bluestone and Harrison (1982), United Nations Centre on Transnational Corporations (1983), Piore and Sabel (1984), and Harrison (1987). See also, for a somewhat different kind of account, Beaud (1987). I am grateful to Bennett Harrison for help in clarifying the difference between these emphases in the GOP perspective and the sharper North/South focus of the NIDL orientation.

3 For a general review of the methodological and analytic foundations of this approach, with references to earlier work, see Gordon *et al.* (1988) as well as other chapters in this volume.

4 While our own work has focused almost exclusively on the United States, there is a parallel institutional, historical account dealing with all the major advanced countries which outlines a similar kind of dynamic. See Armstrong *et al.* (1989) See also Lipietz (1986) for a summary of a parallel interpretation of the case of France.

5 The analysis in this section is very close to and relies heavily on recent discussions by Arthur MacEwan (1982, 1984, 1985, 1986), for whose insights and continuing attention to the global dimensions of the current crisis I am especially indebted. The arguments here also depend heavily on Bowles *et al.* (1990) although the three of us would all admit that the international dimensions of our analysis have not yet been sufficiently developed.

6 See MacEwan (1984).

7 MacEwan (1982) provides an excellent review of many of the sources and effects of these short-term financial flows. See also Hawley (1979).

8 I have been limited primarily to an investigation of US-based firms.

9 See Andreff (1984) for further discussion on this point.

10 United Nations Centre on Transnational Corporations (1985, table 1.2).

11 Ibid.; and MacEwan (1982).

12 All of the comparisons below are based on data in United Nations (1984).

13 For these purposes, "trans-Atlantic trade" is defined as exports in both directions between the European DMEs and the US, Canada, and Latin America. "Pacific Basin trade" is defined as trade between Japan and Asian developing countries and trade between those two Asian groupings and the Americas grouping of the US, Canada, and Latin America.

14 The comparisons of the relative influence of different variables are based on the values for their standardized regression coefficients averaged for the three regressions reported for 1976, 1979, and 1980.

15 These specific results were kindly provided by the author.

16 It is further important to note, as MacEwan emphasizes, that sales by Canadian subsidiaries to the US market account for two-thirds to three-quarters of all subsidiaries' sales to the US market – of which Canadian subsidiaries' sales of transport equipment comprise a substantial proportion. "This relatively strong connection of Canadian subsidiaries to the US market," MacEwan (1982, p. 50) writes, "hardly fits with the cheap labour model of foreign investment."

17 US Department of Commerce (1986, p. 33); US Executive Office of the President (1986), table B-100).

18 MacEwan (1982, p. 60) points out that there have been some significant differences between US TNCs and those with roots in other advanced countries in their resistance to such impositions: "While US firms have strongly maintained their aversion to joint ownership arrangements, firms from the other advanced capitalist nations are generally more flexible ... The Japanese, on [one] extreme, are caricatured by a position that says: take any arrangement necessary to get established in a country and make the most of it."

19 The data on profitability are expressed as the net before tax rate of profit on the net fixed capital stock for manufacturing and are from Armstrong and Glyn (1986, table 15).

20 I have not been able to update these data beyond 1983, so I cannot speculate about whether the downturn from 1982 to 1983 reflects the beginning of a more sustained reversal of the 1977–82 trend.

21 Herbert Gintis (1986) makes a similar kind of point in reviewing the vast literature on investment determinants within traditional economic analysis, suggesting on balance that "capital mobility does not appear to sever the link between domestic investment and domestic saving (p. 45)." I have paid scant attention here to that literature primarily because it does not explicitly discuss *changes over time* in the degree of openness and capital mobility in and among the advanced economies.

22 Bennett Harrison has suggested to me that there may be an asymmetry in state capacity between situations in which the state directly intervenes to promote accumulation, e.g. South Korea, and those in which it intervenes directly to promote working-class interests, e.g. France in 1981–83. This is an important point which warrants much further discussion. At first glance, I think it depends critically on the sorts of policies which the state pursues in either case. I look forward to further exploration of these issues.

References

Andreff, Vladimir, 1984. "The Internationalization of Capital and Re-ordering of World Capitalism," *Capital and Class*, no. 22: 59–80.

Armstrong, Philip, and Andrew Glyn, 1986. "Accumulation, Profits, State Spending: Data for Advanced Capitalist Countries, 1952–1983," unpublished tables, Oxford Institute of Economics and Statistics (August).

Armstrong, Philip, Andrew Glyn, and John Harrison, 1991. *Capitalism since 1945*. Oxford: Blackwell.

Beaud, Michel, 1987. *Le Système national-mondial hiérarchisé: une nouvelle lecture du capitalisme mondial*. Paris: Editions la Découverte.

Bluestone, Barry, and Bennett Harrison, 1982. *The Deindustrialization of America: Plant Closings, Community Abandonment, and the Dismantling of Basic Industry*. New York: Basic Books.

Bowles, Samuel, David M. Gordon, and Thomas E. Weisskopf, 1990. *After the Waste Land: A Democratic Economics for the Year 2000*. Armonk, N.Y.: M. E. Sharpe.

Ernst, Dieter, 1981. *Restructuring World Industry in a Period of Crisis – The Role of Innovation: An Analysis of Recent Developments in the Semi-conductor Industry*. Vienna: UNIDO.

Fröbel, Folker, Jurgen Heinrichs, and Otto Kreye, 1980. *The New International Division of Labour*. Cambridge University Press.

Gintis, Herbert, 1986. "International Capital Markets and the Validity of National Macro-economic Models," unpublished paper, University of Massachusetts at Amherst (June).

Gordon, David M., 1988. "The Global Economy: New Edifice or Crumbling Foundations?". *New Left Review*, no. 168: 24–64.

Gordon, David M., Thomas M. Weisskopf, and Samuel Bowles, 1988. "Progress, Accumulation, and Crisis: The Rise and Demise of the Postwar Social Structure of Accumulation," in *The Imperiled Economy*, ed. R. Cherry *et al.*, vol. I, pp. 43–57. New York: Union for Radical Political Economics.

Harrison, Bennett, 1987. "Cold Bath or Restructuring?" *Science and Society*, 51(1): 72–81.

Hawley, James, 1979. "The Internationalization of Capital: Banks, Eurocurrency and the Instability of the World Monetary System," *Review of Radical Political Economics*, 11: 78–90.

Koechlin, Timothy, 1989. "The Location of US Direct Foreign Investments: A Study of the Effects of Market Size, Labour Costs, and Social Institutions," unpublished Ph.D. dissertation, University of Massachusetts.

Lipietz, Alain, 1986. "Behind the Crisis: The Exhaustion of a Regime of Accumulation. A 'Regulation School' Perspective on Some French Empirical Works," *Review of Radical Political Economics*, 18 (Spring/Summer): 13–32.

Lipsey, Robert E., 1982. "Recent Trends in US Trade and Investment." Working Paper no. 1009 (October), National Bureau of Economic Research, Cambridge, Mass.

Lipsey, Robert E., and Merle Yahr Weiss, 1981. "Foreign Production and Exports in Manufacturing Industries," *Review of Economics and Statistics*, 63: 488–94.

MacEwan, Arthur, 1982. "Slackers, Bankers, Marketers: Multinational Firms and the Pattern of US Direct Foreign Investment," unpublished paper, University of Massachusetts.

1984. "Independence and Instability: Do the Levels of Output in the Advanced Capitalist Countries Increasingly Move Up and Down Together?" *Review of Radical Political Economics*, 16: 57–80.

1985. "Unstable Empire: US Business in the International Economy," *IDS Bulletin*, 16: 40–6.

1986. "International Debt and Banking: Rising Instability within the General Crisis," *Science & Society*, 50: 177–209.

Piore, Michael J., and Charles F. Sabel, 1984. *The Second Industrial Divide: Possibilities for Prosperity*. New York: Basic Books.

Schneider, Friedrich, and Bruno S. Frey, 1985. "Economic and Political Determinants of Foreign Direct Investment," *World Development*, 13(2): 167–75.

Strange, Susan, 1986. "Supranationals and the State," in *States in History*, ed. John A. Hall, pp. 289–305. London: Blackwell.

United Nations, 1984. *Yearbook of International Trade Statistics*. New York.

1985. *Supplement to World Economy Survey*. New York.

United Nations Centre on Transnational Corporations, 1983. *Survey on Transnational Corporations*. New York.

1985. *Transnational Corporations and International Trade*. New York.

United States Department of Commerce, 1986. *Survey of Current Business*, 66(4).

United States Executive Office of the President, 1986. *Economic Report of the President*. Washington, D.C.: Government Printing Office.

Afterword: New international institutions and renewed world economic expansion

DAVID M. KOTZ, TERRENCE MCDONOUGH, AND MICHAEL REICH

Introduction

From its inception capitalism has been both an international system and a system based on individual nation-states. This presents a challenge for the social structure of accumulation approach, which has tended to emphasize the relation between institutions and accumulation in particular countries. To take account of the international dimension of capitalism, the social structure of accumulation of a given country should be seen as composed of the particular domestic institutions which condition capital accumulation, which may differ from the accumulation-promoting institutions of other countries, together with the international institutions that bear upon accumulation. The latter are, of course, common to all countries in a given period.[1]

Each of the three periods of rapid capitalist expansion identified in the social structure of accumulation literature – 1840s–70s, 1890s–World War I (or 1929), and 1940s–60s (or 1973) – has been associated with a particular set of international institutions that promoted accumulation. Each such set of international institutions has supported domestic components of various national social structures of accumulation in the major capitalist countries. The international part of a social structure of accumulation promotes accumulation by contributing to stability and predictability in key international economic and political relations. By so doing, the international institutions of a social structure of accumulation help solve the problems of obtaining inputs at stable, predictable, and reasonably low prices; of making the operation of the production process predictable and effective; and of assuring predictable and profitable markets for products.[2] The international institutions most important for accumulation can be grouped under three headings, (1) the international monetary and credit system, (2) the system of international trade and investment, (3) the world political/military system.

Most followers of the social structure of accumulation approach view the current condition of world capitalism as a continuation of the stagnation that began in the late 1960s or early 1970s. The long duration of this period of stagnation results from the failure so far to create a new, viable social structure of accumulation. A new period of vigorous expansion would require a new set of effective international institutions, as well as effective domestic institutions in the major capitalist countries. The new international institutions would have to be compatible with the domestic institutions that developed in the major capitalist countries (and vice versa). What are the possibilities for the development of new and effective international growth-promoting institutions in the near future? As background for looking into this question, we will consider how the postwar international order promoted capital accumulation.

The postwar system

The international monetary system of the immediate postwar period was known as the Bretton Woods system.[3] It was a system of fixed exchange rates, with the gold-backed US dollar serving as the capitalist world's reserve currency. Fixed exchange rates reduced the risk and increased the predictability of international exchanges, which promoted investment in all projects having any international exchange components, such as use of imported inputs, the foreign sale of output, or production that competed with foreign-produced goods. The International Monetary Fund ran the Bretton Woods system and, along with large private banks, provided the short-term credit needed to smooth adjustments to the balance-of-payments pressures that inevitably arise in a system of fixed exchange rates.

The international trade and investment system of the postwar social structure of accumulation was based on the principles of relatively open economies and multilateralism. The major capitalist countries agreed in theory that both trade and investment should be relatively free, at least for manufactures. This represented a break from the prewar system of colonies and spheres of influence, and the establishment of the new open system had to overcome resistance from the advocates and beneficiaries of the old colonial system (Block, 1977)

While completely barrier-free trade and investment was not achieved, it was sufficiently free in the major capitalist countries to encourage rapid growth in world trade and investment. It also permitted the United States, which emerged from World War II with the strongest economy, to gain a large share of world trade and investment. This system enabled, and even encouraged, the major corporations of advanced capitalism to expand their investments across national boundaries.[4] While so-called multinational corporations (in sphere of operations, if not ownership) predated World War II, the vast postwar growth of foreign direct investment made the multinational corporation a central international institution of the postwar social structure of accumulation.

Production and trade in primary products did not partake of this system of relative openness. A key institution of the postwar social structure of accumulation was control of natural resources, and production from them, in the Third World by large corporations based in the US and Europe. For example, development, production, and sale of petroleum from the Middle East and Latin America was tightly controlled by the Seven Sisters oil companies, with backing by Western governments when needed.[5] This arrangement kept crude oil prices relatively stable for several decades, at a level that assured both large profits for producing companies and a growing market for petroleum. It was a very favorable system for world capitalist growth. Other Third World primary products, such as sugar, were sold at negotiated prices under agreements between producing and consuming countries.

The above international institutions – the Bretton Woods monetary system, relatively free trade and investment, the multinational corporation, and Western corporate control of Third World resources – were supported by the system of political and military power that emerged from World War II. The political and military dominance of one country, the United States, over the entire capitalist world was the centerpiece of this power system. US power was a major factor in creating the above institutions and in safeguarding them over time. The US was able to squelch initial opposition to the Bretton Woods monetary system and free trade and investment. This was done through hard bargaining, by using the promise of economic aid, and by covert financial support of friendly political parties in major Western countries. The US also established friendly governments throughout the Third World to assure Western corporate control of resources, and it used covert or overt intervention to maintain such friendly governments in power.

One reason the US was able to exert so much power was that the Cold War promoted unity among the major capitalist powers, under US leadership. While frictions existed and conflicts broke out from time to time – the conflict between the US and France under President Charles de Gaulle being the most publicized example – Europe followed the US lead on matters of central importance. This was a different situation from the previous period of single-country domination, in the mid-nineteenth century, when Britain was the dominant power. Britain had had to face continual rivalry, and little cooperation, from the other colonial powers. In the postwar period, the Cold War unified the capitalist powers and relegated their differences to a secondary position.[6]

The above set of international institutions created a high degree of stability and predictability in international economic relations. It promoted rapid growth of world trade. The volume of world trade grew at an annual rate of 6.6 percent during 1948–66, substantially higher than during earlier long-swing expansions. World industrial production grew at 9.0 percent annually during that period, much faster than in earlier long-swing expansions (Gordon, 1988, p. 43).

This set of international institutions was compatible with several different configurations of domestic institutions in the industrialized capitalist countries. It fit in well with the conservative Keynesian institutions which characterized the US in this period. It was compatible with the social democratic institutions of West Germany, Scandinavia, and other European countries. And it fit in with the corporatist configuration of institutions in Japan.

The collapse of the international institutions of the postwar social structure of accumulation during 1967–73, along with the collapse of domestic institutions in many capitalist countries, brought stagnation to the world economy for several decades.[7] The possibilities for new international institutions are constrained by the realities of world power relations. Two such realities are important and unlikely to change soon. The first is the absence of a truly dominant country in the world. By the early 1970s the US, having lost its dominant economic position, and having been successfully challenged militarily in Vietnam, had lost the power to impose its will in the world. A decade of rearmament, together with the collapse of the Soviet Union, has made the US the strongest military power by far. But the US has continued its relative economic decline. Japan's per capita gross national product has surpassed that of the US, and Germany's exports exceed those of the US.[8] The lack of economic strength seriously erodes the political power that flows from US military strength.

The second reality is the dissolution of the Soviet Union, and the rush of its successor states and former allies toward capitalism. This leaves the major capitalist powers without a common enemy and will make it more difficult for the strongest capitalist power, the US, to create the kind of unity behind its leadership that prevailed in the immediate postwar decades. Ironically, while the immediate effect of the collapse of the Soviet bloc was to strengthen US military standing in the world, over the long run it may well reduce the ability of the US to exercise power in the world.

Under these conditions, two possible constellations of new international institutions seem possible. One is a set of free-market institutions, and the other is a new world bloc system. Each will be considered in turn.

Free-market international institutions

One possible set of new international institutions would be based on the free-market approach to economic policy-making. The United States and Britain sought to create such a new set of institutions during the 1980s, and it is possible there will be a revived attempt to do so in the future. This approach would replace the fixed exchange rates of the Bretton Woods system with fully flexible exchange rates, letting market forces set exchange rates based on the supply and demand for national currencies. International Monetary Fund loans to help deficit countries would be unnecessary, in theory. Advocates argue that this approach would free countries from balance-of-payments constraints and gain the efficiency advantages of allowing the free play of market forces, with exchange rates that reflect the "true" value of each currency.

All national barriers to free trade and investment would be eliminated under this approach. Even primary products, including agricultural products, would become free of tariffs and quotas. Advocates claim this would bring the full benefits of comparative advantage to the world economy, with all countries gaining. A sidelight of this approach is that, with unrestricted foreign investment, and with all resources open to private development, Third World resources would presumably come under the control of the most powerful Western corporations.

Fifteen years ago the US advocates of this approach began pressing for a big military build-up as a major part of their program, including both forces then arrayed against the USSR and forces designed for rapid intervention in the Third World. The aim seemed to be, first, to reassert US political and military dominance within the capitalist world, and second, to reclaim the position of US superiority over the USSR that existed in the early postwar period. Evidently it was felt that the free market must be spread and secured by the sword.

The attempt to create such a new institutional framework has produced some successes, from the viewpoint of the advocates of this approach. Renewed US economic and military pressure may have played a role in the collapse of the Soviet bloc. The Gulf War was a triumph in the US campaign to reassert hegemony over both its allies and the Third World. Western control over Third World resources has been strengthened in some cases – for example, many OPEC governments have grown increasingly dependent on the US, making the US virtually a member of OPEC. In the US, free-market domestic economic policies, together with the effects of relatively free trade in manufactured goods, have succeeded in weakening the power of labor, driving real wages down and increasing the rate of profit.

But the effort to create a free-market international system has failed, in two senses. First, the new international institutions created since the collapse of the postwar social structure of accumulation are not what the free-market program called for. The Bretton Woods fixed exchange rate system was replaced, not by freely fluctuating exchange rates, but by a managed floating rate system, in which central banks regularly intervene to achieve desired target exchange rates. International trade negotiations have not been able to significantly reduce, much less eliminate, trade barriers. The GATT negotiations in recent years have failed to bring any significant progress in that direction. Each major country seeks to batter down foreign barriers that obstruct its exports, while preserving those of its own protections most dear to powerful domestic interest groups.

There are good reasons why real free-market international institutions have not been created. The experience with flexible exchange rates after 1973 demonstrated the enormous costs of swings in exchange rates. This experience convinced the major capitalist governments, including that of the US, that rates have to be managed. Likewise, genuinely free trade is an impossible goal, because it threatens too many powerful interests and, like flexible exchange rates, would bring rapid and costly swings in production specialization patterns that nation-states will not tolerate. Furthermore, the effort to reassert dominance by the US, along the lines of the 1950s, is unlikely to succeed given the relative economic weakness of the US. In the capitalist era no nation can maintain political and military dominance if it cannot maintain economic dominance.

The second way in which the effort to build a free-market international system has failed is that that effort has not brought a return of rapid long-run economic growth to the industrialized capitalist countries. In the 1980s, growth rates in the US, the European Community, and Japan failed to attain even the lackluster levels of the 1970s, much less those of the 1960s.[9]

Another problem with the free-market approach is that it does not fit in well with the domestic institutions in either corporatist Japan or the social democratic countries of Europe. Both of those domestic constellations require significant state management of the economy. While there have been moves to create domestic institutions in the US and Britain that fit the free-market prescription, the relatively poor economic performance of those two countries in recent years does not make an attractive model. Despite occasional rhetorical accommodations to the US, Japan and the European social democracies are not adopting the free-market approach. There has even been a move away from the free-market domestic approach in the US since the mid-1980s, and in Britain since John Major replaced Margaret Thatcher as Prime Minister.

The underlying problem with the free-market international program is that it does not lead to the stability and predictability necessary for another long period of rapid growth. Hence, it cannot form the basis of a new, viable social structure of accumulation. Whatever the validity of the efficiency claims of the free-market approach, it is clear that unregulated world markets in currencies, goods, and capital do not bring the kind of stability that is required for a long-swing expansion.

A bloc system of international institutions

A second possible set of new international institutions would be based on a system of three political-economic blocs. The outlines of such a system may be forming today, as the European Community presses toward economic integration and the three countries of North America do likewise through the North American Free Trade Agreement. Japan, left out of both arrangements, may be forced to integrate more closely with such East Asian neighbors as South Korea and Taiwan.

This hypothetical bloc system would have, within each bloc, fixed exchange rates, with a common monetary policy and evolution toward a single bloc currency and central bank. This would provide a stable environment for trade and invest-ment within the bloc. Exchange rates between the three blocs might be regulated by a managed flexible rate system, run by the central banks of the blocs. Trade and investment would be subject to few barriers within each bloc, while between blocs barriers would remain and trade would be "managed." Each bloc would have a hinterland of less developed countries which it dominated and with which it maintained close trade and investment relations. The hinterland for the North American bloc would be Central and South America. For Western Europe the hinterland would be the newly open countries of Eastern Europe. For the East Asian bloc the hinterland would be the less developed areas of East Asia including Indochina, Indonesia, the Philippines, and possibly Siberia. The three blocs would contend for markets and influence in the other parts of the Third World, including the Middle East, Africa, South Asia, and China.[10]

A bloc system would permit the further development of the latest form of the centralization of capital, the joint venture. A form that originated in petroleum exploration and other particular costly, risky activities, joint ventures involving corporations with different national bases have recently spread to many manufacturing industries, from automobiles to computers. Joint ventures could take advantage of newly enlarged free markets within a bloc, including its hinterland. And joint ventures could become important in the contest over markets and raw materials outside the blocs.

A bloc system is a concession to the economic and political reality of the absence of a dominant capitalist state and the absence of any noncapitalist bloc to unify the capitalist states. It is an international system that is built on this polycentric situation. Such a system may emerge out of the efforts by political leaders of the major capitalist countries to construct unified market regions that are as large as political realities permit.

There are two main potential strengths of such a bloc system as an international basis for a new social structure of accumulation. First, it would provide large multinational regions within which a reasonable degree of stability would prevail, encouraging economic growth. While this is not as favorable for economic growth as a single worldwide monetary and trading system, it may be the best one possible under currently foreseeable conditions. If relations between blocs could be managed effectively, a still larger region of stability would be created.

Secondly, a bloc system would allow for the different constellations of domestic institutions in Japan, Western Europe, and the US. Each bloc could develop bloc-level institutions suited to the domestic institutions of the major countries in that bloc. For example, the European Community has adopted a social pact embodying social rights and benefits won by workers and the general public under labor and social democratic leadership. Such a pact could prevent individual bloc countries from exerting competitive pressure that would tend to undermine such rights and benefits; and trade with outside countries could be managed to control such competitive pressure emanating from outside. Thus, it may be possible for social democratic domestic social structures of accumulation to exist in countries of that bloc, while the other blocs might develop different kinds of domestic institutions.

Such a bloc system would also have problems. It would be difficult to contain capital within blocs, as trade, foreign investment, and joint venture formation would have a tendency to cross bloc lines, undermining each bloc's unity and stability. For example, in the North American automobile industry, Japanese imports, transplant production and joint ventures account for a large fraction of domestic sales. Many large US and European companies also maintain extensive cross-bloc formations. Blocs are likely to be more open and ill-defined than a simplistic model might suggest.

Managing relations between the blocs would be difficult. Such a polycentric system, facing the rivalry and pressures generated by capitalist accumulation and competition, would have the danger of producing serious political and economic conflicts, and in the extreme case, major wars. Of the three social structures of accumulation to date, the one that lacked a single dominant power, the early twentieth-century social structure of accumulation, produced both the slowest economic expansion and the greatest armed conflict. One should not expect history to repeat itself in any simple fashion, especially given the economic overlap and interpenetration among the blocs, but past experience should serve as a warning of the dangers of a bloc system.

Despite the problems and dangers in a world system of three political-economic blocs, this appears at present to be the most likely international framework for a new social structure of accumulation and a new long swing of economic expansion.

Notes

1 Although a single set of international institutions exists in a given period, the effects of this set of institutions on individual countries can vary from one country to another. For example, the Bretton Woods monetary system, resting on the US dollar as the world's reserve currency, affected the US economy differently from that of other countries.

2 This description of the relation between capital accumulation and social structures of accumulation should not be taken to imply that either a social structure of accumulation, or the accumulation process which it supports, is free from contradictions. See Kotz (this volume, ch. 3) for elaboration on this point.

3 The term "Bretton Woods system" is sometimes used more broadly to include the international trade and investment system of the postwar period, along with the international monetary system of that period. We use the term here in its narrower meaning of the monetary system only.

4 The fact that some barriers to imports were allowed to remain gave impetus to direct foreign investment, as large manufacturing firms sought to avoid the trade barriers.

5 In 1949 the Seven Sisters controlled 69 percent of the non-Communist world's oil reserves (Tanzer, 1974, p. 17).

6 Another reason the US was able to exercise so much power during this period was that, at the start of the postwar period, the US had an enormous advantage over the other capitalist powers in both economic and military strength. The others needed US economic aid, and none was in a position to challenge the US position as military leader.

7 In the US, productivity growth slowed significantly after 1966, and it slowed in Germany and Japan in the early 1970s (Glyn et al., 1990, p. 74). A sharp slowdown in long-run economic growth began in both the US and the European Community after 1973. Japanese growth also slowed in the 1970s, from its previous double-digit rates to the 4–5 percent range. However, in much of the Third World, growth remained strong until the 1980s, when stagnation took hold in almost all parts of the capitalist world.

8 In 1990 Japan's GNP per capita was $25,430 while the US figure was $21,790. That same year West Germany's merchandise exports were valued at $398 billion, compared to US exports of $371 billion, despite the fact that the US population was four times that of West Germany (World Bank, 1992, pp. 219, 245).

9 Economic Report of the President (1992, p. 421; 1988, p. 374). Of course, economic growth is affected by many factors other than the international institutions under consideration here.

10 The Third World is not simply a passive subject for domination by more powerful countries. Events in the Third World can have major effects in Europe, North America, and Japan. For example, the rise of OPEC and the US defeat in Vietnam played major roles in the collapse of the postwar social structure of accumulation and the onset of stagnation in the industrialized capitalist countries.

References

Block, Fred, 1977. *The Origins of International Economic Disorder*. Berkeley: University of California Press.

Bowles, S., D. Gordon, and T. Weisskopf, 1983. *Beyond the Wasteland: A Democratic Alternative to Economic Decline*. Garden City N.J.: Anchor Press/Doubleday.

Economic Report of the President, 1988 and 1992. Washington, D.C.: US Government Printing Office.

Glyn, Andrew, Alan Hughes, Alain Lipietz, and Ajit Singh, 1990. "The Rise and Fall of the Golden Age," in *The Golden Age of Capitalism: Reinterpreting the Postwar Experience*, ed. Stephen Marglin and Juliet Schor, pp. 39–125. Oxford University Press.

Gordon, David M., 1988. "The Global Economy: New Edifice or Crumbling Foundations?" *New Left Review*, no. 168 (March–April): 24–66.

Tanzer, Michael, 1974. *The Energy Crisis: World Struggle for Power and Wealth*. New York: Monthly Review Press.

World Bank, 1992. *World Development Report 1992*. Oxford University Press.

Comprehensive bibliography on the
SSA approach

Albelda, Randy, 1985. "'Nice Work If You Can Get It': Segmentation of White and Black Women in the Post-War Period," *Review of Radical Political Economics*, 17(3): 72–85.

Armstrong, Philip, Andrew Glyn, and John Harrison, 1991. *Capitalism since 1945*. Oxford: Basil Blackwell.

Arsen, David, 1991. "International and Domestic Forces in the Postwar Golden Age," *Review of Radical Political Economics*, 23(1/2): 1–11.

Birecree, Adrienne, and Stephen C. Stamos, 1984. "The Search for Alternative Economic Policies," *Review of Radical Political Economics*, 16(4): 165–76.

Blecker, Robert A., 1989. "International Competition, Income Distribution and Economic Growth," *Cambridge Journal of Economics*, 13(3): 395–412.

Boswell, Terry, 1987. "Accumulation Innovations in the American Economy: The Affinity for Japanese Solutions to the Current Crisis," in *America's Changing Role in the World System*, ed. Terry Boswell and Albert Bergesen, pp. 95–126. New York: Westport.

Bowles, Samuel, 1982."The Post-Keynesian Capital–Labor Stalemate," *Socialist Review*, no. 65: 44–72.

1989. "Social Institutions and Technical Change," in *Technological and Social Factors in Long Term Fluctuations*, ed. Massimo DiMatteo, Richard M. Goodwin, and Alessandro Vercelli, pp. 67–88. New York: Springer-Verlag.

Bowles, Samuel, and Robert Boyer, 1990a. "A Wage-led Employment Regime: Income Distribution, Labor Discipline and Aggregate Demand in Welfare Capitalism," in *The Golden Age of Capitalism: Reinterpreting the Postwar Experience*, ed. Stephen A. Marglin and Juliet B. Schor, pp. 187–217. Oxford University Press.

1990b. "Labour Market Flexibility and Decentralization as Barriers to High Employment? Notes on Employer Collusion, Centralized Wage Bargaining and Aggregate Employment," in *Labour Relations and Economic Performance*, ed. Renato Brunetta and Carlo Dell'Aringa, pp. 325–52. New York University Press.

Bowles, Samuel, and Richard Edwards, 1985. *Understanding Capitalism*. New York: Harper and Row.

Bowles, Samuel, David M. Gordon, and Thomas E. Weisskopf, 1983. *Beyond the Wasteland: A Democratic Alternative to Economic Decline*. Garden City, N.J.: Anchor Press/Doubleday.

1986. "Power and Profits: The Social Structure of Accumulation and the Profitability of the Postwar U.S. Economy," *Review of Radical Political Economics*, 18(1/2): 132–67.

1988. "Social Institutions, Interests, and the Empirical Analysis of Accumulation: A Reply to Bruce Norton," *Rethinking Marxism*, 1(4): 44–58.

1989. "Business Ascendancy and Economic Impasse: A Structural Retrospective on Conservative Economics, 1979–1987," *Journal of Economic Perspectives*, 3(1): 107–34.

1990. *After the Wasteland: A Democratic Economics for the Year 2000.* Armonk, N.Y.: M. E. Sharpe.

Boyer, Robert, 1991. "The Transformations of the Capital–Labor Relation and Wage Formation in Eight OECD Countries during the Eighties," in *Making Economies More Efficient and More Equitable: Factors Determining Income Distribution*, ed. T. Mizoguchi, pp. 297–340. Oxford University Press.

Brody, David, 1984. "Review of 'Segmented Work, Divided Workers'," *Journal of Interdisciplinary History*, 14 (Winter): 701–5.

Cherry, Robert, 1991. "Race and Gender Aspects of Marxian Macromodels: The Case of the Social Structure of Accumulation School, 1948–68," *Science and Society*, 55(1): 60–78.

Coriat, Benjamin, 1989. "Structure sociale d'accumulation vs. theorie de la régulation: une étude comparative et ses enseignements," unpublished paper, CEPREMAP, Paris.

Devine, James N., 1983. "Underconsumption, Over-Investment, and the Origins of the Great Depression," *Review of Radical Political Economics*, 15(2): 1–29.

1984. "Review of 'Beyond the Wasteland: A Democratic Alternative to Economic Decline'," *Science and Society*, 48(2): 224–9.

Dymski, Gary A., 1991. "From Schumpeterian Credit Flows to Minskyian Fragility: The Transformation of the U.S. Banking System, 1927–1990," unpublished paper, University of Southern California.

Ebizuka, A., and A. Isogai, 1991. "Analytical Perspectives on the Current Economic Crisis: SSA Approach vs. Regulation Approach," 2 parts, *Keizaigaku-zasshi*, 91(5/6), 92(1).

Edwards, Richard, 1979. *Contested Terrain: The Transformation of the Workplace in the Twentieth Century.* New York: Basic Books.

Edwards, Richard, and Michael Podgursky, 1986. "The Unraveling Accord: American Unions in Crisis," in *Unions in Crisis and Beyond: Perspectives from Six Countries*, ed. Richard Edwards, Paolo Garonna and Franz Tödtling, pp. 14–60. Dover, Mass.: Auburn House.

Epstein, Gerald A., and Juliet B. Schor, 1990. "Macropolicy in the Rise and Fall of the Golden Age," in *The Golden Age of Capitalism: Reinterpreting the Postwar Experience*, ed. Stephen A. Marglin and Juliet B. Schor, pp. 126–52. Oxford University Press.

Fairris, David, 1990. "Appearance and Reality in Postwar Shopfloor Relations," *Review of Radical Political Economics*, 22(4): 17–43.

1991. "The Crisis in U.S. Shopfloor Relations," *International Contributions to Labour Studies*, No. 1: 133–56.

Glyn, Andrew, Alan Hughes, Alain Lipietz, and Ajit Singh, 1990. "The Rise and Fall of the Golden Age," in *The Golden Age of Capitalism: Reinterpreting the Postwar Experience*, ed. Stephen A. Marglin and Juliet B. Schor, pp. 39–125. Oxford University Press.

Gordon, Avery, Andrew Herman, and Paul G. Schervish, 1987. "Corporatist Structure and Workplace Politics," *Research in Social Problems and Public Policy*, 4: 73–97.

Gordon, David M., 1978, "Up and Down the Long Roller Coaster," in *U.S. Capitalism in Crisis* ed., Union for Radical Political Economics, pp. 212–35. New York: Union for Radical Political Economics.

1980. "Stages of Accumulation and Long Economic Cycles," in *Processes of the World System*, ed. Terence Hopkins and Immanuel Wallerstein, pp. 9–45. Beverly Hills, Calif.: Sage Publications.

1989. "What Makes Epochs? A Comparative Analysis of Technological and Social Explanations of Long Economic Swings," in *Technological and Social Factors in Long Term Fluctuations*, ed. Massimo DiMatteo, Richard M. Goodwin, and Allessandro Vercelli, pp. 267–304. New York: Springer-Verlag.

1991. "Inside and Outside the Long Swing: The Endogeneity/Exogeneity Debate and the Social Structures of Accumulation Approach," *Review*, 14(2): 263–312.

1992. "Kaldor's Macro System: Too Much Cumulation, Too Few Contradictions," in *Nicholas Kaldor and Mainstream Economics: Confrontation or Convergence?*, ed. Edward J. Nell and Willi Semmler, pp. 518–48. London: Macmillan.

1993. "From the Drive System to the 'Capital–Labor Accord' in the United States: Econometric Tests for the Transition between Productivity Regimes," Working Paper no. 29, Department of Economics, New School for Social Research, New York.

1994a. "Growth Distribution and the Rules of the Game: Social Structuralist Macro Foundations for a Democratic Economic Policy," in *Investment, Saving, and Finance: A Progressive Strategy for Renewed Economic Growth*, ed. Gerald Epstein and Herbert Gintis. Cambridge University Press.

1994b. "Putting Heterodox Macro to the Test: Comparing Post-Keynesian, Marxian and Social Structuralist Macroeconometric Models of the Postwar U.S. Economy," in *Competition, Technology, and Money: Comparing Classical and Post-Keynesian Views*, ed. Mark Glick and E. K. Hunt. Aldershot: Edward Elgar.

Gordon, David M., Richard Edwards, and Michael Reich, 1982. *Segmented Work, Divided Workers: The Historical Transformation of Labor in the United States*. Cambridge University Press.

Gordon, David M., Thomas E. Weisskopf, and Samuel Bowles, 1983. "Long Swings and the Nonreproductive Cycle," *American Economic Review*, 73 (May): 152–7.

1984. "Long-term Growth and the Cyclical Restoration of Profitability," in *Nonlinear Models of Fluctuating Growth*, ed. R. M. Goodwin, M. Kruger, and A. Vercelli, pp. 86–102. New York: Springer-Verlag.

1988. "Power, Accumulation and Crisis: The Rise and Demise of the Postwar Social Structure of Accumulation," in *The Imperilled Economy*, ed. R. Cherry *et al.*, pp. 43–57. New York: Union for Radical Political Economics.

1993. "Power, Profits, and Investment: The Postwar Social Structure of Accumulation and the Stagnation of U.S. Net Investment since the Mid-1960s," Working Paper no. 12, Department of Economics, New School for Social Research, New York.

Gülalp, Haldun, 1989. "The Stages and Long-Cycles of Capitalist Development," *Review of Radical Political Economics*, 21(4): 83–92.

Hamilton, Rosalea, 1990, "The Nexus of Real Wages, Prices and Productivity and the Effects of State Intervention in Caribbean-type Economies: the Case of Jamaica," unpublished Ph.D. dissertation, New School for Social Research, New York.

Harrison, Bennett, 1987. "Cold Bath or Restructuring? An Expansion of the Weisskopf–Bowles–Gordon Framework," *Science and Society*, 51(1): 72–81.

Heilbroner, Robert L., 1985. *The Nature and Logic of Capitalism*. New York: W. W. Norton.

Hillard, Michael, and Richard McIntyre, 1991. "A Kinder, Gentler Capitalism? Resurgent Corporate Liberalism in the Age of Bush," *Rethinking Marxism*, 4(1): 104–14.

Hinojosa-Ojeda, Raul, 1990. "International Accumulation Regimes and Class Relations: Formal and Historical Perspectives on the North–South Crisis," unpublished paper, University of California, Los Angeles.

Houston, David, 1992. "Is There a New Social Structure of Accumulation?" unpublished paper, University of Pittsburgh. Presented at ASSA meeting, New Orleans (January 3).

Jessop, Bob, 1990. "Regulation Theories in Retrospect and Prospect," *Economy and Society*, 19 (May): 153–216.

Jones, Evan, 1983. "Industrial Structure and Labor Force Segmentation," *Review of Radical Political Economics*, 15(4): 24–44.

Kotz, David, 1987. "Long Waves and Social Structures of Accumulation," *Review of Radical Political Economics*, 19(4): 16–38.

1990. "A Comparative Analysis of the Theory of Regulation and the Social Structure of Accumulation Theory," *Science and Society*, 54(1): 5–28.

Lembcke, Jerry, 1991. "Working-Class Formation and Long Cycles," *Science and Society*, 55(4): 417–45.

McDonough, Terrence, 1988. "The Marxist Long Wave: A Theoretical Assessment," *Research and Society*, 1(1).

1989. "The Construction of Social Structures of Accumulation: The Resolution of Crises in American History," unpublished Ph.D. dissertation, University of Massachusetts at Amherst.

1990. "The Resolution of Crises in American Economic History: Social Structures of Accumulation and Stages of Capitalism," *Research in Political Economy*, 13: 129–83.

McDonough, Terrence, and Robert Drago, 1984. "Capitalist Shopfloor Initiatives, Restructuring and Organizing in the 80s," *Review of Radical Political Economics*, 16(4): 52–71.

1989. "Crises of Capitalism and the First Crisis of Marxism: A Theoretical Note on the Bernstein–Kautsky Debate," *Review of Radical Political Economics*, 21(3): 27–32.

Marglin, Stephen A., 1990. "Lessons of the Golden Age: An Overview," in *The Golden Age of Capitalism: Reinterpreting the Postwar Experience*, ed. Stephen A. Marglin and Juliet B. Schor, pp. 1–38. Oxford University Press.

Marglin, Stephen A., and Juliet B. Schor (eds.), 1990. *The Golden Age of Capitalism: Reinterpreting the Postwar Experience*. Oxford University Press.

Martin, Cathie J., 1991. *Shifting the Burden: The Struggle over Growth and Corporate Taxation*. University of Chicago Press.

Mihail, Dimitrios M., 1989. "Power, Profits and Industrial Capital Accumulation in Postwar Greece," unpublished Ph.D. dissertation, New School for Social Research, New York.

Miller, John A., 1989. "Social Wage or Social Profit? The Net Social Wage and the Welfare State," *Review of Radical Political Economics*, 21(3): 82–90.

Montgomery, David, 1987. *The Fall of the House of Labor: The Workplace, the State and American Labor Activism, 1865–1925*. Cambridge University Press.

Moseley, Fred, 1986. "The Intensity of Labor and the Productivity Slowdown," *Science and Society*, 50(2): 210–18.

Naples, Michele I., 1981. "Industrial Conflict and Its Implications for Productivity Growth," *American Economic Review*, 71(2): 36–41.

1982. "Erosion of the Postwar Truce: Worker Militance and Labor Productivity," unpublished Ph.D. dissertation, University of Massachusetts, Amherst.

1986. "The Unraveling of the Union–Capital Truce and the U.S. Industrial Productivity Crisis," *Review of Radical Political Economics*, 18(1/2): 110–31.

Nissen, Bruce, 1990. "A Post-World War II 'Social Accord'?" in *U.S. Labor Relations, 1945–1989: Accommodation and Conflict*, ed. Bruce Nissen, pp. 173–208. New York: Garland Publishing.

Nolan, Peter, and P. K. Edwards, 1984. "Homogenize, Divide and Rule: An Essay on 'Segmented Work, Divided Workers,'" *Cambridge Journal of Economics*, 8(2): 197–215.

Norton, Bruce, 1988a. "The Power Axis: Bowles, Gordon, and Weisskopf's Theory of Postwar U.S. Accumulation," *Rethinking Marxism*, 1(3): 6–43.

1988b. "Epochs and Essences: A Review of Marxist Long-Wave and Stagnation Theories," *Cambridge Journal of Economics*, 12(2): 203–24.

Oden, Michael Dee, 1992. "Military Spending, Military Power, and U.S. Postwar Macro-economic Performance," unpublished Ph.D. dissertation, New School for Social Research, New York.

Rebitzer, James B., 1987. "Unemployment, Long-term Employment Relations, and Unit Labor Costs," *Review of Economics and Statistics*, 69(3): 627–35.

Reich, Michael, 1984. "Segmented Labor: Time Series Hypotheses and Evidence," *Cambridge Journal of Economics*, 8 (March): 63–82.

1989. "Capitalist Development, Class Relations, and Labor History," in *Perspectives on American Labor History*, ed. C. Moody and A. Kessler-Harris, pp. 30–54. Dekalb, Ill.: Northern Illinois University Press.

Riddell, Tom, 1986. "Military Power, Military Spending and the Profit Rate," unpublished paper, Smith College, Northampton, Mass.

1988. "U.S. Military Power, the Terms of Trade, and the Profit Rate," *American Economic Review*, 78(2): 60–5.

Rosen, Marvin E., 1983. "'Segmented Work and Divided Workers': A Review Article," *Journal of Economic Issues*, 17(1): 215–24.

Rosenberg, Samuel, and Thomas Weisskopf, 1981. "A Conflict Theory Approach to Inflation in the Postwar U.S. Economy," *American Economic Review*, 71(2): 42–7.

Schor, Juliet B., and Samuel Bowles, 1987. "Employment Rents and the Incidence of Strikes," *Review of Economics and Statistics*, 62(4): 452–68.

Segal, Sven William, 1987. "Economic Dualism and Collective Bargaining Structure in Food Manufacturing Industries," unpublished Ph.D. dissertation, University of California, Berkeley.

Sherman, Howard J., 1989. "Theories of Economic Crisis: Demand Side, Supply Side, and Profit Squeeze," *Science and Society*, 53(1): 62–71.

Song, Ho K., 1989. "State and the Working-Class Labor Market in South Korea, 1961–1987," unpublished Ph.D. dissertation, Harvard University.

Szymanski, Al, 1984. "Productivity Growth and Capitalist Stagnation," *Science and Society*, 48(3): 295–322.

Tsuru, Tsuyoshi, 1991. "The Reserve Army Effect, Unions, and Nominal Wage Growth," *Industrial Relations*, 30(2): 251–70.

Uemura, Hiroyasu, 1991a. "The Analytics of Macroeconomic Dynamics of *Regulation*/SSA Theories," *Bulletin of Political Economy*, Aoki-shoten.

1991b. "Growth and Distribution in the Post-War Regime of Accumulation: A Theory and Realities in the Japanese Economy," unpublished paper, Ibaraki University.

Weisskopf, Thomas E., 1981. "The Current Economic Crisis in Historical Perspective," *Socialist Review*, 57: 9–53.

1987. "The Effect of Unemployment on Labour Productivity: An International Comparative Analysis," *International Review of Applied Economics*, 1(2): 127–51.

1988. "The Analytics of Neo-Marxian Crisis Theory: An Illustrative Model," *Keizai Kenkyu* (*The Economic Review*, Hitotsubashi University, Tokyo, Japan), 39(3): 193–208.

1992. "A Comparative Analysis of Profitability Trends in the Advanced Capitalist Societies," in *International Perspectives on Profitability and Accumulation*, ed. Fred Moseley and Edward N. Wolff, pp. 13–41. Aldershot: Edward Elgar.

Weisskopf, Thomas E., Samuel Bowles, and David M. Gordon, 1985. "Two Views of Capitalist Stagnation: Underconsumption and Challenges to Capitalist Control," *Science and Society*, 49(3): 259–86.

Weisskopf, Thomas E., David M. Gordon, and Samuel Bowles, 1983. "Hearts and Minds: A Social Model of U.S. Productivity Growth," *Brookings Papers on Economic Activity*, 2: 381–450.

Willoughby, John, 1983. "Internationalism and the Development of An Alternative Economic Strategy in the United States: A Review Essay on 'The Deindustrialization of America' and 'Beyond the Wasteland,'" *Capital and Class*, 21: 123–33.

1989. "Is Global Capitalism in Crisis? A Critique of Postwar Crisis Theories," *Rethinking Marxism*, 2(2): 83–102.

Index